D0151543

CALIFORNIA CRUCIBLE

POLITICS AND CULTURE
IN MODERN AMERICA

Series Editors:
Margot Canaday, Glenda Gilmore, Michael Kazin, and
Thomas J. Sugrue

Volumes in the series narrate and analyze political and social change in the broadest dimensions from 1865 to the present, including ideas about the ways people have sought and wielded power in the public sphere and the language and institutions of politics at all levels—local, national, and transnational. The series is motivated by a desire to reverse the fragmentation of modern U.S. history and to encourage synthetic perspectives on social movements and the state, on gender, race, and labor, and on intellectual history and popular culture.

CALIFORNIA CRUCIBLE

The Forging of Modern American Liberalism

JONATHAN BELL

PENN

UNIVERSITY OF PENNSYLVANIA PRESS

PHILADELPHIA

Published by
University of Pennsylvania Press
Philadelphia, Pennsylvania 19104-4112
www.upenn.edu/pennpress

Printed in the United States of America on acid-free paper
10 9 8 7 6 5 4 3 2 1

Library of Congress Cataloging-in-Publication Data

Bell, Jonathan, 1976–
California crucible : the forging of modern American liberalism / Jonathan Bell.
p. cm. — (Politics and culture in modern America)
Includes bibliographical references and index,
ISBN 978-0-8122-4387-1 (hardcover : alk. paper)
1. Liberalism—California—History—20th century.
2. Liberalism—United States—History—20th century.
3. California—Politics and government—20th century. I Title.
II. Series: Politics and culture in modern America.
JS451.C25B34 2012
320.51'309794—dc23 2011032476

For Julia and Ray

CONTENTS

INTRODUCTION

Placing California in Post-World War II American Politics

In April 1959, Cricket Levering, legislative chairwoman of Democratic clubs in the suburb of Claremont and the surrounding neighborhoods of the Forty-Ninth Assembly District in the northeastern corner of Los Angeles County, wrote a memo to fellow club organizers. Giddy from the landslide victories of gubernatorial candidate Pat Brown and other Democratic legislative candidates in the 1958 elections, Levering wanted to maintain the momentum that had helped bring about those victories through tireless precinct walking, leaflet distribution, rally organizing, and voter registration drives. Those who met in living rooms and poolside backyards in the Forty-Ninth District Democratic clubs discussed issues like the legitimacy of capital punishment, wider access to health care, the Cuban Revolution, and the civil rights movement, often taking stances far to the left of many of their fellow citizens in Southern California.

Across the state, Democratic clubs like those in the Claremont area used meetings to provide a social focus for their rapidly growing communities, to take stands on major issues of the day, and to lobby their elected representatives to reflect their political concerns in legislative debates. "Let us not lose sight of the importance of this task," Levering wrote. "We have helped to elect a Governor who is putting the weight of his office behind a legislative program that is unprecedented in California. We who are the working Democrats now have an obligation and responsibility to keep ourselves informed on the issues, and to support that program."[1]

This intersection of grassroots organizing, left-of-center ideology, and organizational politics in the reshaping of California's political terrain between World War II and the end of the 1970s is the subject of this book. In this period, California was not only the fastest growing state in the Union and one of the world's largest economies in these decades, but was also the site of significant political change in the 1950s and 1960s that illustrates a broader national process of ideological affiliation based on notions of economic and civil equality in an age of growing prosperity. Liberal activists in California built a new political base in the 1950s that used grass-roots engagement to mobilize a cross-class coalition of voters behind a legislative program that would transform the political landscape of the state and the nation. This new generation of liberal politicians interpreted the human rights of Americans broadly to include the right to a subsistence income regardless of economic status, together with the right to racial and sexual equality.

Debates in California about the expansion of the welfare state and economic growth gave these new Democrats the political language with which to interpret broader questions of civil and sexual rights, in many cases before the explosion of rights discourses on the national stage in the 1970s. The increasing political power of liberal politicians on the West Coast provoked sustained and increasingly bitter hostility from their conservative counterparts. Indeed, in many ways, the rhetorical power of the right in California must be seen through the lens of liberal successes in reframing the terms of state-level political debate in the postwar era. Though California began the postwar period as a political outlier with its own peculiar culture and traditions, it ended the 1970s as a harbinger of trends in interest group strategies, media-driven performative politics, and debates over economic power and individual rights that would come to define American politics writ large.

In this book I try neither to particularize nor to overly generalize the California experience, but rather to place the nation's most populous state and one of the world's largest economies into a wider context of significant political upheaval over questions of economic citizenship, public infrastructure, civil rights, and individual freedoms that transformed the relationship between government and society in the postwar decades. Left-leaning intellectuals on both sides of the Atlantic in the 1950s viewed the United States as the archetype of advanced capitalist democracy, in which rapid technological advances and economic dynamism could provide wealth and security for all if harnessed to a social safety net designed to smooth the rough edges of the market.[2] Fast becoming the premiere economic engine for the United States in the years after World War II, California early on demonstrated problems of racial and social inequality that came to characterize advanced capitalism in the U.S. context. The Golden State was also an important example of the emergence of a cross-class coalition of liberal Americans who transcended the New Deal politics of the 1930s, as the nation's economy became ever more dominated by the service sector, and as the middle class became employees bound tightly to the increasingly sophisticated corporate welfare system of insurance, retirement pensions, and other benefits.[3] The growth of Democratic-inclined professional voters sympathetic to civil rights and social justice affected other states in these years, but California was the largest and most politically significant: repeated congressional reapportionment gave it the legislative seats through which to cultivate many of the most important liberals to lead the Democratic Party in the last decades of the twentieth century and the first decade of the twenty-first, including Phil Burton, Henry Waxman, Barbara Boxer, and Nancy Pelosi.[4]

California had by the 1970s become a trailblazer for national debates over taxation, sexual and gender rights, racial discrimination, and the welfare state, and also reflected international political trends as countries grappled first with establishing a new social democratic order in an era of prosperity and then struggled to maintain it as a global economic crisis unfolded by the end of the seventies. As a new generation of liberal activists fought to invigorate the moribund system of party politics in California in the 1950s, and as they made common cause with organized labor in an effort to halt forces trying to roll back labor rights on the West Coast, they were forced to engage with questions of ideology and political affiliation that placed them in a broader social democratic political shift anchored not in Depression-era crisis but in the 1950s culture of affluence.[5] Though a great deal of state-building occurred in California during the New Deal and World War II, under mainly Republican administrations, legislators' commitment in this period to an overarching reform program that included welfare and civil rights as well as infrastructure projects remained tentative and unfulfilled. It took a dramatic shift in the nature of the state's electoral politics in the 1950s to spur a massive transformation in the terms of political debate. This shift established a left-right dichotomy in California party politics that later came to define the American political spectrum in a wider sense.

California's postwar social democratic politics—which envisaged government maintenance of economic and social rights through a more ambitious social welfare safety net, strong labor unions, and antidiscrimination legislation, in addition to major public infrastructure projects—needed people—voters—to believe in it for it to take root. California's status as a media-rich state—home to the nation's movie industry and a significant share of the booming television industry—gave the new generation of state Democrats (as well as Republicans) an ideal opportunity to take advantage of a new style of campaigning, one that involved carefully staged and scripted performances relayed to thousands of voters, which broadened the appeal of liberal politics beyond the cadre of true believers in Democratic clubs and in the legislature. The fact that the dominant Republican Party in the 1950s enjoyed electoral hegemony without a clear, unifying message underpinning it offered liberal activists an opportunity to use mass rallies, TV spots, and press campaigns to sell a policy agenda to the electorate. By the early 1960s election campaigns based on clearly defined ideological fissures between left and right were the norm in California, setting the scene for a more adversarial, media-driven politics that would come to characterize American politics more generally in later decades. The fact that Democrats needed to legitimize themselves anew in the 1950s and 1960s, and could not simply present themselves as standard bearers of the New Deal, forced Californian liberals to engage with big debates over social democracy and economic rights in campaigns in ways that linked west coast politics to wider international discussions on the left even if the carefully crafted electoral appeals often eschewed the emotive language of class.

Another crucial aspect of the construction of a new liberal politics in California was the need to legitimize social forces outside the political mainstream. Unlike their new right counterparts, who drew upon volunteers and sources of patronage very much part of dominant social forces even if they liked to portray themselves as insurgents, California liberals depended upon coalitions of the marginalized as well as sympathetic bankrollers in order to establish themselves as viable contenders for legislative power. An analysis of the language liberals used to establish their ideas in political debate in the 1950s and 1960s helps us to contextualize how and why interest groups gained traction within mainstream political discourse. The reasons why there was such a major change in political definitions of what constituted normative behavior in questions of sexuality and lifestyle choice in the 1960s remain only partly understood. This study argues that the goal of California liberal politicians to sell their program through a commitment to social equality provided the language through which marginalized groups, including gay rights and civil rights organizations, could tie their agendas to the broader agenda of postwar liberalism. There is a voluminous literature on the development of various rights movements in this period, but this work exposes the gendered, racialized, and economic discourses cultivated by those in legislative power that in part drove the success and failure of these movements to alter the political landscape. To put it another way, only by addressing the questions of economic and social rights together, linked by the rise of liberal electoral politics in California, can we understand how mainstream politicians came to widen their understanding of who would be included under their protective umbrella in these years.[6]

As much as California Democrats relied on energizing people formerly outside mainstream politics and reaching voters through a new style of campaigning, they also drew on a more traditional constituency—labor. By the 1940s, the Republican Party of progressive governors Hiram Johnson and Earl Warren was the established machine of power and patronage in California. Its sudden and unprecedented break with labor in the late 1950s served to strengthen the position of unions in California politics and provided liberals with significant electoral and organizational muscle that allowed California to take the lead in responding to the significant expansion in federal funding opportunities in the Kennedy and LBJ years. This development had an additional effect in encouraging Californians—of wide-ranging political beliefs—to raise their expectations of what government could do for them. In the process, a politics predicated on quality of life issues encouraged many suburban communities to embrace Democratic (and maverick liberal Republican) candidates for office, thus complicating the commonly held notion that the California suburbs were little more than a fulcrum for right-wing politics by the 1970s. Bitter contests over fair housing and property taxes certainly contributed to a right turn in much of California's Republican Party, and helped to undermine the governorships of liberal Democrat Pat Brown in the 1960s and his son Jerry in the late 1970s. But California ended the 1970s as the spiritual home of the liberal wing of the Democratic Party as much as that of John Birch sympathizers, complicating our understanding of how ideological trends and grassroots activism intersected in these decades.

Indeed, a study of California politics helps to shed light on how we define "liberalism" in the postwar period, with important ramifications for our understanding of American politics more generally. If the California experience proved anything, it was that the notion of state-sponsored economic citizenship encouraged in post-New Deal America led inevitably to identity politics, as more and more heretofore marginalized social groups began to clamor for inclusion in the political process. In opening up this process to a greater number of interests, liberal politicians oversaw a dramatic widening of the parameters of their worldview that helped make California the archetype of socially engaged left politics, which prized individual and civil rights as a necessary corollary of economic liberalism. The development of an expanded welfare state, for instance, required policymakers to engage with questions of social inclusion that furnished them with a language of rights that expanded their understanding of what constituted normative behavior. The complex interactions of race and economic rights discourses in California allowed a social democratic ideology to develop that built upon a strong popular front heritage on the West Coast, and pulled together interests ranging from Latino farm workers to wealthy suburban homemakers into a shared political project. This process of adapting the New Deal to a diverse population caused antagonistic and self-defeating disputes, which served to embed factional animosities in the Democratic Party and alienate many liberal Republicans, problems that have continued to afflict liberal politics in the United States in the recent past. By the 1970s, this factionalism, and an inability to unify interest groups behind a larger message, prevented legislative Democrats from addressing the thorny question of tax relief. Moreover, issues such as the right of farm laborers to bargain for better working conditions tested the capacity of Democratic Party politics to challenge the entrenched inequality of market capitalism. At times liberals lacked the linguistic confidence of their conservative rivals to tie their ideological precepts to homegrown American values. Yet by the late twentieth century a politics of big government, social welfare, public funding for education and health, and strict protections of civil and human rights was a powerful influence on public life both in California and in a national Democratic Party. This book goes some way toward explaining the processes through which such a politics came of age between World War II and recent times.

It is instructive to note that studies that have explicitly linked grassroots activism to wider themes of political party history have tended to be histories of the right, viewing conservative activism, most notably in Orange County, California, as exemplifying an inexorable shift in the zeitgeist of American politics rightward in the 1960s and 1970s. Historians of the right have been much more confident in nationalizing their story than historians of political struggles that encompass a much wider range of forces.[7] Yet even if we restrict our angle of vision to the politics of suburban communities that have done so much to enhance our understanding of the tax revolts, school district controversies, and zoning laws that shaped American political trends by the 1970s, it is by no means clear that these histories are purely narratives of conservatism. Orange County may have been "at the leading edge of economic and social changes that have propelled a deep-rooted and ever more powerful conservative political culture in significant areas of the Sunbelt and West," but other California counties, including Santa Barbara, Marin, and San Mateo, manifested concern over taxes and schools alongside a strong attachment to environmentalism, individual rights, and high public spending.[8] Suburbs and wealthy neighborhoods of cities like Los Angeles were also home to a vibrant popular front during the 1940s that endured and prospered in the repackaged Democratic club movement of the 1950s. And many of the Democratic bastions of the early twenty-first century can be found in high-income communities around the cities of the Golden State. The California experience of the decades following 1945 forces us to resist easy generalizations about suburban selfishness, racism, and Cold War anticommunism, and to place the politics of postwar market capitalism—with all its attendant class, racial, and ideological contradictions—back into a study of party politics at a time of massive shifts in party affiliation and strategy at a crucial time in the state-building process in the United States and elsewhere.

The development of a revitalized antistatist private business community on the West Coast does not support the narrative of the breakdown of the New Deal order. For one thing, the chronological trajectory of the growth of militant business and GOP anti-unionism in California differed from that of Sunbelt and Southern states, regions that have received much recent scholarly attention.[9] The Republican Party was the established party of government in California at the height of the New Deal, and had come to a basic understanding with labor unions about maintaining good labor-management relations. California was heavily unionized, and when the Republican leadership decided to push anti-union legislation in 1958, they helped legitimize Democratic liberalism as the natural party for union members and bolstered labor organizing at precisely the time insurgent Republicans and business elites in sunbelt states were beginning to mount an assault on the citadels of power. As a New Deal order was collapsing in Arizona and elsewhere, it was only just coming together in California, forcing us to particularize the experience of different states of the United States when fitting the American case into the broader history of the rise of free market ideology and modern corporate capitalism in the later twentieth century.

A study of California politics after World War II also encourages us to rethink the widely held thesis that civil rights liberalism became divorced from economic rights in this period, as advocates of racial equality became increasingly involved in school desegregation and legal rights and less committed to workplace equality and economic justice.[10] Such an argument sees struggles for mass unionism and fairer working conditions during the New Deal and World War II as the crucial window of opportunity in which to link economic security to racial equality, a window that closed when the Cold War and a national turn away from New Deal class politics in the 1950s made courtroom battles to eliminate Jim Crow laws more feasible as a civil rights strategy than a direct assault on the economic structures of the nation. Given that California does not fit into the chronology of a New Deal order betrayed by the political upheavals of the postwar period, this thesis does not stand up to scrutiny. Liberals committed to civil rights legislation in the 1950s, and who enacted the Fair Employment Practices Commission (FEPC) and fair housing legislation in the 1959–1963 period, encountered bitter opposition from business and civic leaders convinced that civil equality interfered with private sector prerogatives. Conservatives also noticed that the coalition of civil rights activists, labor unions, and Democratic club members that ended decades of Republican dominance in state politics were able to expand enormously the scope and generosity of the state's welfare system in ways that would dramatically alter the economic status of hundreds of thousands of Californians of all races. Furthermore, civil rights was not a biracial issue, given the vital significance of Latino, often immigrant, agricultural labor to the state economy: questions of how the economy worked, and how the state could intervene in private economic relationships to head off major labor disputes, lay at the heart of the Democratic project in California in the postwar decades, leading to the integration of farm labor into the National Labor Relations Act in California in 1975. The Golden State was not an outlier in this regard, but a stark reminder of the fact that questions of economic and social equality remained thoroughly entwined throughout the Cold War.

This book also challenges the notion that identity politics unpicked a grand New Deal coalition in the 1960s and 1970s and set the United States on a more conservative path. To historian Donald T. Critchlow, liberalism had by the 1970s become "little more than a boiling cauldron of identity politics that pandered to the jealousies of ethnic and minority groups. Liberal candidates were elected to local and state office, but by the late 1960s liberalism as an intellectual force was placed on the defensive and appeared to have run out of fresh ideas, living on by wrapping itself in the legacy of the New Deal of the 1930s."[11] Until the political revolution in 1958 in California, the only way for interest groups like labor unions to buy into the political compact of the New Deal was by appealing unilaterally to a disorganized and amorphous political leadership in Sacramento. After the late 1950s liberal legislators were able to stitch together a variety of interest groups into a more unified, powerful coalition that often traded on the same ideological premises to advance an agenda that brought together questions of poverty, welfare, gay rights, and labor rights into one package. The 1960s did not cause the New Deal coalition to unravel, at least not at the state level: that decade instead witnessed the extension of a New Deal politics of social democracy to groups who had never seen its fruits in earlier decades, a fact that has relevance to the history of American liberalism.

CHAPTER 1

Politics and Party in California at Mid-Century

The social and economic changes of the Depression and World War II had affected California at least as manifestly as anywhere else in the Union. Whether we think of the mass of displaced Okies in the 1930s or the millions who descended on the Golden State to seek employment in war industries in the 1940s, there was no question that California was undergoing rapid and significant social changes that required collective solutions. The state population had swollen in the 1940s alone from a little under seven million to 10,586,223. The African American population had rocketed from 124,000 in 1940 to over 462,000 ten years later.[1] Between 1941 and 1944 California's manufacturing employment rose an extraordinary 201 percent, compared to the national average of 51 percent. The state government had become responsible for coordinating one of the nation's largest war economies, a network of plants and factories that had sprung up almost overnight and required new roads, water supplies, and public power.[2] Undergirding this picture of change was a history of political progressivism and radicalism that had found expression with the gubernatorial campaign of Upton Sinclair in 1934 and the pension campaigns of Francis Townsend and George McLain through the 1930s, together with the rise of a powerful Communist movement in the state that was among the largest in the nation. The party had by the outbreak of war infiltrated the left wing of the Democratic Party and most of the CIO unions on the West Coast, and was involved in any number of civil rights and civil liberties organizations that formed the lynchpin of mass political engagement in these years.[3] California was the home of the progressive wing of the Republican Party, symbolized by senator

Hiram Johnson and congressman Richard Welch of San Francisco, and also home of stalwart supporters of the New Deal such as Democratic congressmen Jerry Voorhis of LA and George Outland of Santa Barbara. Though the state's citizens had only elected a Democrat to the governorship once since 1888—Culbert Olson in 1938—they were comfortable with Republicans like Earl Warren who, having defeated Olson's chaotic administration after just one term, would oversee the largest expansion in state government capacities in California's history up to that time. A casual observer could be forgiven for thinking that the postwar settlement would involve a progressive pact between government, social movements, and private enterprise that would invigorate the liberal spirit of the New Deal age.[4]

In fact, California politics at the midpoint of the twentieth century was a world unusually unsuited to the demands of a modern industrialized state. The reforms of Hiram Johnson's administration in the 1910s that had been designed to break the power of organized factions and lobbyists over the state's political system had by the 1930s had the opposite effect, and had calcified political activity into an organized chaos of individual candidacies, one-party dominance over the legislature and local government, and a lack of serious mainstream public debate about the ideological direction of the state and the country.[5] Yet it is important to lay out the dynamics of late 1940s California politics to show what was missing from public discourse and political organizing in these years, and how that lack of a serious engagement with programmatic ideas in postwar party politics would shape the formation of a new age of political activism in later years.

Political Culture in California at Mid-Century

Recent studies of political movements associated with the left in California have inevitably focused on local studies of neighborhoods, local civil rights efforts, and nonparty campaigns for civil and economic rights centered in specific communities, whether they be the bohemian enclave of Edendale in Los Angeles or African American sections of West Oakland.[6] Yet these localized examples of political pressure usually met with successful statewide opposition, as in the case of the repeal of a welfare rights proposition by powerful antiwelfare interests in 1949.[7] The Republican Party's control of the legislature and most local governments, due in part to a tradition of Republicanism in the state and in part to the effects of California's peculiar cross-filing law, severely restricted the political options open to Californians between the 1920s and 1950s, and helped to reinforce a strong rightward turn in the state's politics in these years.

The practice of cross-filing in California virtually eliminated the party political impact of the New Deal in the state. Brought in as part of Johnson's reform package to rid the state of political corruption, the law allowed candidates for state and federal office to enter the primary of parties other than their own. Often during the 1930s and 1940s Republicans won Democratic primaries and vice versa, thus eliminating meaningful competition at the general election. It had been hoped that this free-for-all between candidates of different parties for the nomination would assert the primacy of the individual candidate and his or her suitability for the post, and eliminate the supposedly corrupt picking of candidates by political bosses behind closed doors. Indeed, party organizations were forbidden by law from endorsing any candidate for office, which meant in practice at least half a dozen candidates from each party would enter each primary. The last man standing with a large enough war chest and the loudest message tended to emerge victorious. The need for money and airtime inevitably increased the reliance of politicians on lobbyists and business elites rather than the reverse, and the superior discipline and organization of the Republican Party ensured that they would win the majority of contests regardless of the national political picture. Despite having a three to two advantage in political registration by the late 1930s, the Democrats had half as many seats in the State Senate and far fewer seats in the Assembly throughout the New Deal era and well into the 1950s.[8] Even when the state elected a left-wing Democratic governor in 1938, the GOP-controlled legislature ensured his administration left little by way of a positive legacy, and rendered many of the local campaigns for welfare and civil rights bereft of the political power needed to pass the kind of social legislation—a Fair Employment Practices law, for instance—being pioneered elsewhere.[9]

In cities like New York, Chicago, and Detroit, Democrats had built a new political order based on a coalition of organized labor, urban liberal activists, and Democratic Party regulars. In Los Angeles, by contrast, an antistatist Republican in 1950 could win both Republican and Democratic primaries in congressional districts like the Fifteenth, extending west though Hollywood and including coteries of liberals in the movie industry and far-left activist networks near Silver Lake reservoir. The main Democratic candidate complained bitterly that Republican Congressman Gordon

McDonough was conservative in a district in which Democrats were the majority of registered voters, yet he had triumphed nonetheless. "Presenting that picture to the voters was difficult and expensive," he wrote. "The population of the Fifteenth is almost as much as the city of St. Louis. There is no party organization, and no time to form one during a campaign. Precinct work is unknown." A single mailshot to registered Democrats in the district cost $1,600, a large amount of money for a party with little centralized organization. Some candidates did establish robust campaigns, with fund-raising drives, local party workers, and enthusiastic supporters, such as Esther Murray in the neighboring Sixteenth District that same year, but even then she only managed to win her primary in her West Los Angeles-Beverly Hills district, not the general election.[10]

Democrats not already ensconced in congressional or Assembly seats faced another major hurdle in their quest for election: the Republican legislature controlled the redistricting process that redrew the district boundaries every ten years. In 1951, slightly rattled by Esther Murray's vigorous campaign to unseat arch-conservative Donald Jackson in West Los Angeles, and required by the census to give new congressional seats to the rapidly growing Los Angeles region, the GOP-controlled reapportionment committee decided to create a new seat that gathered together all the scraps of the city of Los Angeles that had large majorities of Democratic registrants, leaving the rest of the city with safe Republican districts. The new seat, the Twenty-Sixth District, took in the heavily African American Sixty-Second and Sixty-Sixth Assembly Districts that made up the existing Fourteenth Congressional District and tied them by a thin strip of land to the Sixty-First Assembly District in Jackson's old Sixteenth District, a seat taking in the heavily liberal and Jewish portions of Fairfax and Beverly Hills as well as Venice and Culver City. "It is the most heavily gerrymandered district in the history of California," decried a 1954 flyer for the new Twenty-Sixth candidate, James Roosevelt. "It is not a geographical unit; it has widely varied interests; and it is large enough to make TWO congressional districts instead of the one we now have. The districting is so outrageous that even Governor Warren, back in 1951, asked his Republican-dominated reapportionment committee how they could justify what they had done. He was told: 'Those are the leftovers. When we had the other districts laid out the way we wanted them, those pieces were left. Nobody wanted them. So we threw them together and made a district.'"[11] Later in the twentieth century, when California became an electorally competitive state, the Democrats were able to adopt this practice themselves, just as the two parties did in every state in the country. Until the 1960s, however, the Republicans in California had a monopoly on reapportionment prerogatives. This, together with the fact that allocation of State Senate seats by county dramatically skewed allocation in favor of rural areas (Los Angeles had one Senate seat until the 1960s, as did a few tiny counties in the Sierra mountains), left urban, liberal voters and politicians with little influence over policymaking.

The clear disjuncture between the diverse and rapidly changing social make-up of California and the limited range of political choices open to voters was reinforced by the role of the media in state politics. Most of the state's newspapers were run by Republican-supporting owners and editors, including Norman Chandler of the *Los Angeles Times* and Joseph Knowland of the *Oakland Tribune*, whose son was a California senator and who was also a major contributor to the campaigns of Governor Warren. Of the major dailies only one, the *Sacramento Bee*, had any sympathy for Democratic candidates. In the late 1950s all but 9 of some 120 state newspapers supported Republican candidates for senator.[12] More important, the editorial policy of almost all the California press was to impose an unashamedly anti-Democrat, antistatist spin on all copy, news stories as well as editorials. "We will not be able to carry on in defeat like the Republicans," warned Democratic candidate Patrick McDonough after the party's horrendous 1946 electoral drubbing. "We do not have the newspapers, radio, nor do we have the money to battle adversity."[13] Jimmy Roosevelt informed the Greater LA Press Club during his 1950 gubernatorial campaign that in his view "news stories and headlines reflect the economic, social, and political views of the publisher far more than they do an actual and truthful situation, event or issue."[14]

A cursory glance at any California newspaper from the mid-twentieth century reveals not just a lack of real engagement with the diversity of political opinion in the world, but a reluctance even to mention political opponents of preferred candidates. Often candidates for office who failed to win the endorsement of the major dailies had to buy advertising space to gain any coverage at all. Senatorial candidate Helen Douglas resorted to this tactic in 1950, placing an advertisement in several newspapers in which she argued that she had uncovered during the course of her canvassing "growing resentment that there is no news of my campaign being carried in the Los Angeles newspapers. . . . My campaign has bought this space in order that I might bring light to the blackout and let my supporters know how the campaign is progressing."[15] Senate candidate Sam Yorty did the same in 1954 to rebut claims by Democratic supporters of his Republican opponent that he had a past as a far-left radical, claims reported prominently in the *LA Times*.[16] When Adlai Stevenson swung though San Diego during his 1952 campaign for the presidency, a local campaign supporter reported that his keynote speech "was given little coverage in the local newspaper, either before or after it was delivered." The only Democratic newspaper had been bought out by the Republican paper "and the coverage that was given came out in a thoroughly garbled report, with the quotations, as usual, torn out of context, and the effectiveness rendered nil."[17] Republicans, on the other hand, gained high-profile coverage in outlets like the *Times*, often finding their political stances discussed approvingly in items that were supposedly news stories, not editorials. In one such story, a right-wing Republican assemblyman was praised for fighting "the increased unemployment insurance benefits . . . because he wanted the fund protected better from mooching and chiseling." His Democratic opponent was briefly dismissed as "an amateur" who dared to oppose an incumbent whose work had been "outstanding on the side of reasonableness in government and to protect the interest of the people from dreamers and those whose plans would load the taxpayers with unreasonable burdens."[18]

Floating above this apparent vipers' nest of poisonous antiliberal invective and political chicanery in the 1940s and early 1950s was the benign, avuncular figure of Governor Earl Warren. His years on the U.S. Supreme Court, not least his landmark ruling in *Brown*, have added to an impression of judicial fairness, strength of character, and political moderation that had already been assiduously developed during his years as California attorney general and as governor. The editors of his memoirs, published posthumously, wrote in a prologue that "he believed in dealing directly, openly, and in a nonpartisan way with any problem," and that he "steadfastly refused to be obligated to any special interest."[19] State legislative analyst A. Alan Post, a key figure in a rapidly growing state regulatory and legislative apparatus in the postwar years, recalled that government officials referred to him as "the Earl of Warren" because "he had a kind of regal bearing, and he was stiff but a real glad-hander. . . . He had close affiliations with labor and took care of them and was an affable and well-meaning, thoughtful, cautious sort of person."[20] Born in Los Angeles, Warren moved to northern California as a boy, attending law school at Berkeley and soon getting a job in the Alameda County district attorney's office in Oakland. An astute, careful operator, Warren came of age politically at a time when the progressive Republican challenge to the corporate interests of the Southern Pacific Railroad had reached its high point, and the fact that his father had worked for Southern Pacific for little pay convinced the young Warren that his own political inclinations were on the side of Hiram Johnson and the progressive forces. As he later wrote, the "things I learned about monopolistic power, political dominance, corruption in government, and their effect on the people of a community were valuable lessons that would tend to shape my career throughout life."[21] He became Alameda district attorney in 1925, and gained a reputation as a principled law enforcer and an opponent of partisan affiliation: he refused campaign contributions for his campaign for district attorney in 1926, and believed fervently in California's cross-filing rule, allowing him to court support on the basis of his achievements and manifesto promises rather than party favors. He won election as California's attorney general in 1938, and ended four difficult years of popular front and Democratic rule in 1942 with his elevation to the governorship.[22]

Under his administration a massive industrial war economy came into existence, regulated by a vastly enlarged governmental apparatus.[23] His tenure saw the creation of a Postwar Reconstruction and Reemployment Commission, a program of public works, and vast investment in state-funded higher education, which helped fund a 156 percent increase in enrollment between 1944 and 1950.[24] Warren's presence as Republican figurehead, supported by a significant group of labor-backed Republican progressive legislators, surely suggested that the political system could cope with the demands of a rapidly diversifying and growing population.

In many respects, however, Warren's occupation of the governor's mansion in Sacramento marked the peak of progressive ascendancy in the state's Republican Party. For one thing, the limited ideological reach of political discourse among state Republicans meant their solutions to social problems could never keep pace with demand. Warren himself was dependent on the support of important conservative interests like Joe Knowland's *Oakland Tribune*, and responsible for placing future darling of the American right Bill Knowland in the Senate in 1945. For another, pro-business, bitterly antigovernment interests in the party were after 1945 making a serious challenge to the broker state being delicately established under Warren, determined to sweep aside any political consensus in a bid to establish private sector control over the economy. Warren's short-lived attempt to establish some kind of state health insurance system was a major casualty of the growing political clout of antistatist Republican legislators and their powerful financial backers in the California Medical Association (CMA) and Chamber of Commerce. Days after Warren's announcement of his social security-based insurance scheme in January 1945, the CMA met in Los Angeles and, in Warren's words, "all but declared the plan to be the work of the Devil." In a propaganda campaign that formed part of a wider 1940s national campaign against government-administered health care, the CMA "stormed the legislature with their invective," and Warren's bill "was not even accorded a decent burial."[25] The *New Republic* verdict that when Warren "discovered the hornet's nest that he had uncovered, he began to run for cover and had it conveniently killed in committee" is perhaps unfair, but its broader accusation that the vigorous actions of conservative interests in rolling back social welfare entitlements in the years after the war demonstrated the limits of progressive political activity in Sacramento in these years is hard to refute.[26] As the forces of capital began to gear up for a full-on assault on the post-New Deal regulatory state, an attack that would culminate in an attempt to reintroduce open shop labor contracts in the late 1950s, it was not at all clear that progressive Republicanism had the political strength or ideological conviction to stem the antistatist tide.

A lack of political muscle or ideological clarity were not weaknesses of the forces of the private enterprise lobby in California. Figures such as Lemuel Boulware of the public relations wing of General Electric had become increasingly aware in the immediate postwar years of the potential of ideologically driven PR campaigns against the regulatory state, and of the need to fund politicians who would drive their free market, antilabor agenda in the halls of power. In a 1945 memo Boulware set out the terms of his forthright campaign to rein in union power and establish senior management as the sole arbiters of company policy: "Management is in a *sales* campaign to determine *who* will run business and the country,—and to determine if business and the country will be run *right*" (emphasis original).[27] A test case of this battle in California came when the city of Los Angeles attempted to establish a public housing program after the passage of the Housing Act of 1949. Congresswoman Helen Douglas had in 1947 bitterly attacked Congress for not passing legislation to ease the chronic housing crisis in America after the war: "When certain parts of my congressional district in Los Angeles . . . are full of slums that would put Port Said to shame, that, in my view, is a political matter. When rents are raised beyond the ability of the average working man and woman to pay. . . .And when newly-married veterans of World War Two are forced to start their families under the handicap of a hopeless debt because they have to pay $13,000 for a huddle of Number Three white pine with naked wiring running through the knot-holes, that, in my humble opinion, is a political matter too."[28] The scale of the housing shortage in the late 1940s had prompted Congress to take action, and Republican mayor of Los Angeles Fletcher Bowron was keen to take advantage of the federal funding for his city. Private real estate interests quickly moved to call in favors from city councilmen, and the council blocked the proposals. The *Reporter* noted that the "Los Angeles uprising is part of a test case instituted by national and local real-estate groups to determine whether the nation shall have federally subsidized slum-clearance and low-rent housing programs in the future."[29] In 1952 Bowron visited President Harry Truman to discuss the difficulties inherent in any attempt by government to compete with private enterprise or to regulate its affairs. As a White House official described it, Bowron had "broken with the local GOP leadership and the powerful *LA Times* on the public housing issue and the 'interests' have ganged up on him and forbidden him radio time. He says the Republicans have given the Democrats a ready-made issue they can win on in the city."[30] As in the case of later campaigns against racial discrimination in housing and employment, the issues were there to create a political groundswell against the status quo, but the organizational infrastructure had yet to be established, a significant weakness given the influence of private business interests in the corridors of power on the West Coast.

Professional public relations gurus had long bridged the divide between private enterprise and Republican party politics. Murray Chotiner, Richard Nixon's right-hand man in his campaigns for office, had in the 1930s been a leading figure behind the formation of the Republican Assembly, an extra-party organization established to give the nod to favored Republican primary candidates, a useful way of getting the "right" candidates elected to office in a state where official party endorsement was banned. By 1946 those opposed to enlargement of the regulatory state and in favor of the rollback of the New Deal and elimination of wartime controls had gained control of the Republican Party National Committee, and thus the party's midterm platform, and were quietly using their power in California circles to gain leverage over the party apparatus there. Southern Californian business interests carefully vetted a young Richard Nixon, including asking him to two interviews with right-wing California congressmen Carl Hinshaw and John Phillips, before giving him their full backing in the GOP primary for the

Twelfth District, a key race to unseat prominent New Deal Democrat Jerry Voorhis.[31]

The Republican right also zeroed in on pro-New Deal congressmen like George Outland of Santa Barbara, key player in the fight to get the Full Employment Act through Congress in 1946, and Ned Healy of the Thirteenth District in Los Angeles. They financed pro-business Donald Jackson in the Sixteenth District of left-wing popular frontist Ellis Patterson, and fashioned the antistatist lexicon that would form the common campaign strategy of the vast majority of Republican candidates in 1946. According to a Nixon campaign leaflet, "basically, the issue to be settled in this election is conflict between political philosophies. The present congressman from this district [Voorhis] has consistently supported the socialization of free American institutions."[32] A campaign letter to professional groups in the Twelfth District, an area centered on wealthy South Pasadena and similar communities east of LA, argued that voters' "liberty and freedom are being threatened by Federal encroachment and centralized bureaucracy. Our state and nation need men like Richard Nixon to protect private business and free enterprise."[33] The common thread of campaigns of candidates like Nixon was that Republicanism represented all sections of society equally under the umbrella of private citizenship, as opposed to "those who espouse the regimentation of our people, collectivism or communism in some form [who would act] according to the wishes of minority pressure groups of which the Political Action Committee is an example."[34] The U.S. Chamber of Commerce cleverly stitched together antiregulatory rhetoric with elements from the global situation of the day to provide an anti-New Deal synthesis in its public relations literature. "In the agony and chaos of recent years," stated one such booklet in 1946, "we detect two recurrent themes. The first is the worship of the State. The second, and correlative theme, is the denial of the rights of the individual. As the State takes over, the individual must give way. The absolute State reached its malign perfection under Fascism, Nazism, and Communism."[35]

The emerging Cold War interacted with the increased self-confidence of anti-New Deal interests to place anticommunism at the center of the campaign to establish a pro-business, antiregulatory consensus in American politics. At the national level this was manifested by the use of antitotalitarian arguments in the fight to repeal the Office of Price Administration, or to combat President Truman's federal health insurance proposals.[36] In California the state legislature had established its own "Little Dies" committee under the leadership of Los Angeles state senator Jack Tenney in order to uncover evidence of political subversion and so-called un-Americanism in state government and the professions.[37] As the drive to oust the remaining liberal Democrats from political office gained pace in the late 1940s, anticommunism became the main weapon in destroying the political careers of Helen Gahagan Douglas in 1950, congressman Franck Havenner of San Francisco in 1952, and Robert Condon of the East Bay in 1954. As early as 1946 Douglas was finding anticommunism a problem in her reelection campaign in Los Angeles, writing prominent New Dealer Harold Ickes that her campaign "gets dirtier and dirtier. . . . They've put out an enormous flyer, asking me how I happened to go to Moscow, what Stalin said to me, what I told Stalin, etc."[38] Los Angeles Democratic Party warhorse and fixer Carmen Warschaw recalled Nixon's campaign against Jerry Voorhis in similar terms: "People used to get phone calls that Jerry Voorhis is a communist. 'We can't give you our name because, you know, you can't say that, but believe me, Voorhis is a communist.' And they used to have young people come in when Jerry Voorhis was speaking and they would boo so that you couldn't hear. Hold signs."[39] Robert Condon had barely arrived in Washington when the allegations that he had been denied security clearance for atomic bomb tests during the war because of his associations with a prominent local communist surfaced in the state media, and even his own party had to abandon him in 1954, prompting one local supporter to despair that national Democrats "did more harm to the Democratic Party in California than all the Republican newspapers with their rapacious party line."[40] The iron grip of antitotalitarian imagery on political discourse in postwar California drastically restricted the capacity for serious debate over the future development of the public sphere without some sort of radical overhaul of the political balance of power in the state.

Why No Democratic Political Order in California?

Democratic Party figures or national activists who arrived in California from the East Coast in the late 1940s or early 1950s would usually comment upon the relative youth of the political world found there. One of Adlai Stevenson's campaign chiefs argued that the lack of an organized precinct structure to the Democratic Party like that common in Illinois or New York was due to the fact that precinct work "takes place in large cities and . . . it takes many years to develop these cohesive groups. There is no large city in California that is even fifty years old and the greatest growth has taken place in the last twenty-five years, so that eastern politicians, professional or otherwise, are inclined to be frustrated and baffled by this lack of organization."[41] One visiting Democrat, musing on the seeming political ineffectiveness of the state's labor movement, noted that "the labor movement here is so much younger, it's still having growing pains and is in an earlier stage of development."[42] If the state's Republicans were becoming ever more organized and coordinated in this period, the Democrats and their natural allies in liberal interest groups and labor represented a plethora of competing clusters, factions, and organizations. In the words of one activist, "California Democrats are overorganized. For a party which has been so conspicuously unsuccessful at the polls this is a curious condition; but the fact is that the political landscape teems with unnecessary committees, councils, coordinating groups, and groups to coordinate the coordinators."[43] The fact that California had missed out on the organizational discipline brought about elsewhere in the country during the New Deal would make life extremely difficult for those on the left in the years after the war, but it would also allow for the development of a new movement of liberals in the 1950s predicated on ideological and organizational premises developed after the war. It is this contradiction that is the subject of the pages that follow.

The Democratic Party was in California a political party in name only. It was in practice a collection of local fiefdoms, county committees, activist groups that often included communists and fellow-travelers, some labor affiliates, all presided over by a state central committee that was split into two to satisfy the longstanding rivalry between the northern and southern California leadership. There were even rival fund-raising outfits in the 1950s to satisfy the power hunger of various warring factions. In some areas a strong personality would establish control over a local area and become the conduit for political patronage, such as Bill Malone in San Francisco, but in most areas individuals launched themselves into political campaigns for office without much in the way of centralized control. "From choice or necessity," reported political scientist Currin Shields in 1954, "most Democratic nominees campaigned as individuals, rather than as Party men; they raised their own funds and recruited their workers on a personal basis, with little organizational help. Some professed leaders of the Party with fair consistency supported Republican candidates, and generally tried to work both sides of the political street."[44] A Democrat in Berkeley informed Americans for Democratic Action (ADA) chairman James Loeb that there was "no cohesion within the party; there is, in fact, no party in the real sense. What the party consists of is a loose business alliance between various clots of opportunists who congeal about local 'strongmen.' And the liberals in the Party prefer to align themselves with these clots rather than seek through collective action to build a liberal force in the state."[45] Democratic State Committeeman Roger Kent, a central figure in party politics in the 1950s, recalled his run for Congress in 1950 in the First District, which ran from Marin all the way up the coast to the Oregon border: "there was absolutely *no* Democratic organization whatsoever in the first district—there were two or three counties that didn't have any county committees at all. There were a couple of committees—Humboldt and Sonoma—that were controlled by actual Communists, and I don't use that word lightly."[46] While the Republican Party could benefit from a long history of dominance of the political system in California and the use since the 1930s of an organization, the Republican Assembly, designed to secure preprimary endorsements of favored candidates, the Democrats had no disciplining force and little organizational zeal in the late 1940s. The fact that the GOP had dominated legislative politics for so long had also allowed Republican legislators to build links with labor organizations as well as with business interests, and had constructed a coalition of the state's different socioeconomic factions within a single party.

The power of the left in California radical politics in the 1930s and 1940s had invigorated some of the CIO and AFL unions in their fight for better conditions, and had created an array of enthused activists in a host of civil rights and political organizations such as the Civil Rights Congress in Los Angeles.[47] But in an increasingly hostile political climate such radicalism could become a political liability. Not only would it open liberal and leftist political actors to the accusation of communist sympathy at a time when such accusations were politically devastating, but it also forced them into a preoccupation with the question of the legacy of the popular front that had implications for their future.

The labor movement, in particular, was in the late 1940s reeling from the twin pressures of bitter internal divisions over the legacy of the popular front and its peculiar relationship with the two main political parties in California. The November 1947 meeting of the state CIO demonstrated the damaging schism appearing within organized labor over the putative third party challenge to President Truman over the question of communism and the nation's relationship with the Soviet Union. Some unions, led by CIO state secretary Bjorne Halling of the ILWU, remained popular front advocates, and in many cases were overtly communist-led. Others rallied to the resolution of the United Steel Workers, led by anticommunist John Despol, that stated that the "so-called Independent Progressive Party is neither independent nor progressive. Instead, it is more accurately described as a 'Trojan Horse' party under the control of the fellow-travelers of the reactionary American agents who, consciously or unconsciously, work for the establishment of a world police state which would deny the individual dignity of man." Though the open challenge to Halling's leadership was defeated at the Santa Cruz meeting, the *San Francisco News* noted that a "growing influence of a rightist faction was apparent at the four-day session."[48] By mid-1948, CIO national chair Philip Murray had initiated a purge of communist-dominated unions from the organization, symbolized in California by Murray's removal of Harry Bridges of the International Longshore and Warehouse Union (ILWU) as northern director of the California CIO.[49]

The difficult political position of labor in California was underscored by an examination of the role of the much larger California Federation of Labor (CFL) in the postwar years.[50] In the crucial election year of 1950, in which James Roosevelt was running for governor on an unashamedly left-of-center platform and Helen Douglas was struggling to help maintain the liberal forces' tenuous hold on the U.S. Senate, a key battleground in the fight to do something about Taft-Hartley, the Federation's League for Political Education held its first formal preprimary endorsing convention. As political parties were forbidden from endorsing primary candidates, and since the Democrats had not yet managed to establish their own equivalent to the Republican Assembly, the role of organized labor in giving guidance to its membership on whom to support could be significant in determining the future direction of state politics. This fact was not lost on the national director of the AFL's political action wing, Joe Keenan, who told the assembled convention in San Francisco in April that the "year of 1950 is all-important for American labor. The labor movements of the whole world are watching us, and we are going into the bitterest campaign in the history of this country." Keenan fiercely attacked Richard Nixon for distorting a debate about the future of the New Deal into one about communism, noting the devastating impact anticommunism had already had on primary elections in Florida and North Carolina, as well as on labor's chances of toppling the author of the notorious Taft-Hartley Act, Senator Robert Taft of Ohio. "We in Washington," he told the California delegates, "hope to get enough information to you so that you can acquaint the people with the laws that the American Federation of Labor is concerned with . . . laws such as social security, minimum wage, aid to education, housing, and, most of all, health insurance."[51] The battles for Fair Deal measures such as federal health insurance and against Taft-Hartley had further welded together the political fortunes of labor and the Democratic Party, and in some respects the San Francisco meeting of the AFL's California membership reflected this development: Helen Douglas and James Roosevelt both gained labor's blessing, and both addressed the assembled throng. "My fight has been your fight," proclaimed Douglas in an impassioned speech, "and I will continue to work for the economic bill of rights that President Roosevelt outlined for us: a decent home for every family; a job at a decent wage; the repeal of the Taft-Hartley Act [loud applause]; the extension of the social security program; the extension of our educational opportunities for young people; the realization of our civil liberties for all the people."[52]

In the topsy-turvy world of California politics, however, the growing realization that organized labor would have to work with the Democratic Party to offset the impact of the revitalization of the private business community gave way to the realities of political patronage on the West Coast. At the same time as Roosevelt and Douglas were giving their fighting speeches in defense of liberal principles and the legacy of the New Deal, the convention was voting to endorse all incumbent assemblymen and state senators—of either party—seen to be "friendly" to organized labor. More controversially, a vocal minority on the convention floor objected to the endorsement of Pat Brown for the office of attorney general. Brown, a prominent San Francisco Democrat and the city's district attorney, seemingly had the best chance of a Democratic victory in that difficult year: his Republican opponent, Fred Howser, had served a term in office beset by scandal, to the extent that Governor Warren was openly encouraging primary challengers. Howser had, however, made decisions deemed by many in the California Federation of Labor as favorable, and in a state in which established Republican patronage, however unreliable, was seen as far more valuable to union members than a commitment to an untested opponent, it was no surprise when the floor voted by 79,961 to 40,296 to override the leadership's recommendation and endorse Howser.[53] It would not be the last time such a controversy would distract the assembled gathering from the realization that gathering crumbs from the Republican Party's table was not helping place labor's concerns at the center of the political agenda in California. In 1950, in any case, the convention's achievements could be summed up by the fact that while labor's champions Douglas and

Roosevelt were suffering ignominious defeats, Howser had lost the Republican primary to Ed Shattuck, who in turn became the only statewide victim of a Democratic victory that year when he lost to rising star, and future champion of organized labor, Pat Brown.[54]

Hope Mendoza Schechter, a leading figure in the garment workers' union and Democratic activist in a predominantly Latino part of southeastern Los Angeles, recalled with frustration the political ambivalence of the AFL in her neighborhood and statewide: "CIO—you could almost bank on Democratic endorsements—but not AFL. That was touch and go and a lot of politicking and a lot of work, in order to swing meaningful endorsements for Democrats." She was determined to build up a liberal Democratic movement in her overwhelmingly working class district, but found her union leadership unwilling to ruffle the feathers of Republican contacts in Sacramento, including Fred Howser: "In the nineteenth congressional district, I maintained a totally Democratic headquarters. . . . I remember going to a Central Labor Council meeting . . . and [ILGWU Director of Public Relations and Education Sigmund Arywitz had] bounced me off . . . because I had worked for Pat Brown. The irony is that Pat Brown later appointed him Commissioner of Labor." Schechter argued that labor's reluctance to be more daring in its efforts to shape state politics frustrated ambitious and hard-working activists like her. The leadership "were being opportunistic. They knew [a Republican] was going to win anyway, and so they might just as well—there was no sense in fighting it. . . . I just took the position that they could have gone for no endorsement and that way, leave those of us who want to retain a few ideals, a little flexibility. This other way . . . your hands were tied."[55] The AFL endorsement process often did refuse to endorse Republicans if they were antilabor or had overwhelmingly conservative records, but in many cases the conventions in the early 1950s were plagued by disputes between delegates over whether or not to endorse both Republican and Democratic candidates in a district where both were friendly to labor, or whether to withhold endorsement in cases where insufficient information about candidates had been made available.[56] California Labor League for Political Education (CLLPE) secretary C. J. Haggerty even confessed in his speech to the 1952 convention to being "almost nauseated" by the choice of endorsements for the State Legislature. Comments from the floor were more categorical: "I have looked through these endorsements," said one delegate, "and I think in very few instances are we going to be at battle with the Chamber of Commerce or the Merchants and Manufacturers. In many instances I think we are going to be in the same corner with them. . . . It seems to me that we have reached not the basic fundamentals of 'rewarding our friends and defeating our enemies,' but a placating of the powers-that-be in the spirit of 'we will be nice to you if you will be nice to us.'" The delegate noted that Earl Warren, praised in the league political newsletter, had signed the reapportionment bill, and that reapportionment along GOP-approved lines "is going to do us more harm than any acts that the Legislature passed during the 1951 session."[57] It was certainly true that absence of a natural alliance between organized labor and a New Deal-dominated political establishment made the prospects of an amicable settlement of industrial relations questions particularly unlikely in California as the 1950s wore on.

Nowhere was this more apparent than in the case of agricultural labor, a thorny political question that perfectly demonstrated the enormous gulf separating the wealthy and well-connected from the poor and politically powerless. Huge landholdings inherited from Spanish and Mexican grants or from awards to railroads made California by the late nineteenth century ahead of its time in the development of massive agribusiness operations as the principal producers of farmed goods. British observer James Bryce in his *American Commonwealth* in the 1880s commented that "the land system in California presents features both peculiar and dangerous, a contrast between great properties, often appearing to conflict with the general weal, and the sometimes hard pressed small farmer, together with a mass of unsettled labor, thrown without work into the towns at certain times of the year."[58] Landowners could depend upon a ready supply of immigrant labor from Asia and Mexico as well as periodic waves of domestic unemployed pushed westward by economic crisis or drought. High capitalization costs for enormous holdings concentrating on single crops necessitated a flexible, mobile labor force that could be rapidly increased at harvest times and then reduced out of season.[59] The economic realities of California agriculture created a system in which a small number of wealthy landowners controlled the economic well-being of hundreds of thousands of rural poor who held little political sway and who in many cases were not even American citizens, thereby condemning them to the status of indentured wage slaves at the mercy of the needs of their employers and their allies in government.

The politics of farm labor conspired with the economic factors to leave rural workers outside the protective umbrella of progressive governance well into the post-World War II era. A riot at the Durst Brothers Hop Ranch in

Wheatland in 1913 brought the plight of rural laborers into the public eye and prompted the recently established California Commission of Immigration and Housing to inspect labor camps "with the object in view of rendering the immigrant that protection to which he is entitled," and the legislature gave the Commission funds and a remit to attempt to force an improvement in camp conditions.[60] An improvement in living arrangements and sanitation in the camps was seen as the solution to the farm labor problem; happier, healthier workers would be less prone to riot or strike, and social peace would be restored. The larger question of the economic status of lowly paid, seasonal workers was never addressed, and there was no direct organizational link between government and the agricultural workforce to match the development of labor unions for industrial workers. Indeed, despite efforts in the 1930s to unionize and politicize farm labor, it quickly became clear that differences of ethnicity, citizenship, and patterns of work in the fields rendered agriculture a far cry from urban industry in its place in the economic structure.[61] Progressive politics in California saw questions of labor relations and economic inequality as individual technical problems to be addressed on a case by case basis. Without a coherent ideological worldview to unite elected politicians and the economically disenfranchised it was difficult to see how the overall position of farm workers could be improved.

In the 1940s the question of the economic and political position of farm workers gained new salience with the passage of the bracero law in 1942 and the decision of the AFL-affiliated National Farm Workers' Union to organize in California in early 1947. The wartime pressure for maximum agricultural production led to leaders of agribusiness to press Congress into allowing the legal importation of Mexican farm labor into the United States, initially on an emergency basis but extended indefinitely in 1951. The bracero program was also supported by a ready supply of illegal immigrant labor that made it virtually impossible for labor organizers to exert upward pressure on wages, as farm owners increasingly turned away from a reliance on domestic labor in order to ensure complete employment flexibility and to keep wages low. Out of some half million people involved in harvesting crops in California in the 1940s, only about 140,000 were local day wage laborers, meaning that imported labor constituted much of the rest. "Vast differences in culture and ethos separated [braceros, domestics, and illegals] despite their common class status as rural proletarians," wrote Ernesto Galarza, farm labor organizer in the NFLU in the late 1940s. "Significant savings in the wage outlay for harvesting became possible by discarding domestics and lowering wage scales to more economical ratios with fertilizer, machinery, fuel, and other non-human inputs."[62] Rivalries between domestics and non-U.S. citizens for jobs undermined efforts to create solidarity over issues of pay and conditions, and the flexibility of the bracero system allowed owners and managers to circumvent unionization efforts by firing striking workers and bringing in extra imported labor.

The first serious effort by the NFLU to make headway in California was the strike at the DiGiorgio ranch in 1947, but the protracted and bitter dispute over union recognition at the largest estate in the Central Valley revealed serious political roadblocks to the union's goal of transforming working conditions in the farming heartland of the state. The problem was not just one of supply and demand—the fact that the availability of cheap and willing labor outweighed the number of workers willing to strike—it was also one of political power. Not only did Robert DiGiorgio benefit from the support of local officials in Kern County, including the sheriff, the Board of Supervisors, and the justice of the peace, but he also drew upon larger reserves of political patronage at the state level, and knew that the weight of legislative and legal machinery could be brought to bear.[63] Membership of the state board of agriculture, for instance, was restricted to leading figures in the Farm Bureau, the Associated Farmers, grower-shipper associations, and business leaders, all hostile to union organizing.[64] Farm owners had almost exclusive access to state and federal officials who implemented and managed the bracero agreements with Mexico, allowing them to write wage agreements and dictate the terms of the program to their advantage. And when in the wake of the unsuccessful DiGiorgio strike the NFLU and AFL organized a boycott to pressurize owners into recognizing the union, DiGiorgio's lawyers filed suit against the boycotters, invoking the ban on secondary boycotts in the recently passed Taft-Hartley Act despite the fact that agricultural labor was excluded from federal collective bargaining legislation. Agricultural labor was thus deprived of the benefits of the National Labor Relations Act but victim of its antistrike provisions, testimony to the major imbalance in New Deal-era industrial relations law between employers and employees.[65]

The very limited success of the farm worker organizing movement in the late 1940s demonstrated the vital need for a shift in the wider political climate in California at mid-century. Without the integration of farm labor into the protective embrace of collective bargaining, minimum wage, and prospective fair employment legislation, the scope for a substantive shift in living conditions on the land in the Golden State remained severely limited, regardless of grassroots organizing activity. Existing power structures in the era of Earl Warren had no incentive to challenge the dominance of grower elites in the Central and Imperial Valleys, and the California Federation of Labor, keen to keep its place at the legislative table in Sacramento and to head off any attempts to roll back its political influence, was by the early 1950s wary of getting too involved in new organizing drives.[66] What was lacking was a language of social inclusion in political discourse at the state level that could embrace farm workers in its legislative and ideological agenda. It would take a new generational of political activists who, on the face of it, had nothing in common with those toiling in the fields to change the landscape of California politics in ways that could open the door at least to a consideration of farm labor as part of a broader question of social citizenship in the 1950s.

CHAPTER 2

Building the Democratic Party in the 1940s

The California Democratic Party needed a message and a program in order to unite all left-of-center interests in the state behind its banner and thus establish a genuine political choice for the public and set up the terms of debate in the postwar years. The difficulties it faced in achieving this task also point up reasons why it would become one of the most radical in reshaping its political perspective during the 1950s and 1960s: liberal political ideology was being thrashed out within the Democratic party hierarchy and in activist organizations against a backdrop of a strong popular front tradition in leftist politics, a powerful antistatist opposition against which to define itself, and a lack of established channels of Democratic patronage of the type that dampened political ambition and radicalism elsewhere. The Democratic political project of the postwar decades that is the subject of this book would unfold anew out of the political circumstances of the very late 1940s and 1950s.

Engaging the Popular Front

When James Roosevelt took over the leadership of the state party in late 1946, he found a party in turmoil, reeling from bitter attacks from business interests and the Republican political establishment, and convulsed by political divisions over the role of communists in the coalition of the left in California. The party's troubles were hardly unique, and in fact California voting patterns in the mid-1940s reflected national trends: the Democrats did relatively well in 1944, carrying the state for the presidential ticket and winning nine of the twenty-three congressional districts and the Senate seat, albeit by narrow margins. In 1946, as elsewhere, the party did appallingly badly, losing five congressional seats, the Senate race, and also failing to win their own primary in the gubernatorial race.[1] But there was more to the party's problems than just national ennui directed at the unpopular Truman administration. For every account of a political house party, public meeting, or Young Democrat group was a story that told a very different tale: a Democratic party in Alameda County, which contained over 200,000 registered Democrats in the late 1940s, that could not get a quorum at its meetings; county committees that never met; bitter infighting among members of the state central committee over some members' links to communists and supporters of the Progressive Citizens of America and other fellow-traveler groups.[2] Fresh from his comprehensive drubbing at the hands of a conservative Republican in the Seventh Congressional District in Oakland in 1946, Democratic candidate and prominent Alameda businessman Patrick McDonough put the blame for the party's electoral disaster squarely on the dissident left-wing elements in the party who had been using it as a popular front vehicle since the 1930s. "The election did not come out as perhaps we all wished," he wrote a business associate, "but as for myself, I do not regret the outcome. The political situation here in California for us Democrats is very much confused. This defeat permits all of us to take a stand and begin inviting those whose views and actions do not harmonize with the best interests of the Democratic Party and our form of government to disassociate themselves from our party, and perhaps the best thing would be to form a party of their own. With this group we are always in danger of losing with their help."[3] Despite the fact that fellow traveler organizations such as the Hollywood branch of the Independent Citizens' Committee of the Arts, Sciences, and Professions (ICCASP) had participated in voter registration drives, get-out-the-vote campaigns, and had authored an FEPC ballot initiative, as well as endorsing favored liberal candidates publicly to their membership, they had not been able to prevent the Republican tide. Nor had they been able to convince enough registered Democrats that their gubernatorial candidate, soon to be Wallaceite Robert Kenny, was a preferable candidate to Earl Warren, nor that Representative Ellis Patterson, a known fellow traveler, should win the party's Senate nomination.[4] After the 1946 political massacre, it was not hard to see why liberal but establishment figures like McDonough saw the popular front hue of the California Democratic party as fatal to the party's political fortunes.

Roosevelt saw things differently. He had been involved in the ICCASP, had seen the power of leftist factions in Los Angeles politics in the late 1930s and during the war when he had worked his way up through the party hierarchy, and had also seen the impact of the dead hand of conservative bosses on the party's fortunes. He saw the year 1947 as a chance to attempt to unite the party's warring factions through a reorganization of the delegate selection system to the national convention to make it more representative of the membership, and the drawing up of a state manifesto that could serve to give energy and direction to the faithful in advance of the 1948 elections. Writing the Chairman of the Democratic National Committee, J. Howard McGrath, in October 1947 about the proposed changes to the delegate selection system, he argued that his aim had been "to secure for President Truman the broadest and most representative backing of the liberals and progressives who joined the Democratic Party from 1932 through 1945. These people joined the Democratic Party because they knew it was not dominated by financial interests or by special interests such as oil, as the Republican Party has always been. . . . A majority of us . . . made a successful beginning to eliminate the influence of this small minority of conservative element and have devoted the intervening months in bringing our party as close as possible to the people." He was careful to underline his opposition to those flocking to the third party candidacy of Henry Wallace that was developing steam in late 1947: "Regardless of how difficult the road may be we shall continue our efforts to make the Democratic Party in California a true home for all liberals and progressives who believe in the basic principles of the New Deal."[5]

This delicate balancing act between placating potential Wallace supporters and the party's established leadership explained Roosevelt's decision to create a policy committee to draw up a manifesto for the party's meeting in Los Angeles at the end of July 1947. The message was clear: California did not need a third party as long as the Democratic Party reaffirmed its commitment to extending and expanding the New Deal. The statement of policy was unashamedly left-of-center, but there were repeated references to the need to achieve economic and social equality through "the American form of democracy," a clear jibe at popular front elements who looked to the Soviet Union in an overly romantic fashion. In an attempt to keep such elements within the broad church of the Democratic Party, however, there was reference to the need to reserve the use of armed force only against a "proven aggressor" and the principles of atomic power sharing, an idea already abandoned in Washington, were restated. The overall message was a wakeup call for those worried that the Democrats were losing their radical edge: "We frankly state that, in our increasingly complex economic and social system, we believe that it will become more and more necessary for us to *plan* as a people. We contend that it is only through intelligent and far-sighted planning on the part of our state and national governments that we can cope with the problems facing us, that we can bring a greater share of prosperity to more people, indeed that in the long term we can survive as a people." There were commitments to a large public housing program "for that section of our population which private enterprise cannot reach," to racial equality in employment, to a state agency "to assist in the providing of work in the event that such individuals are unable to obtain jobs in the private enterprise system," to "a fair and adequate health program in cooperation with the forward-looking members of the medical profession in California." The list of Democratic goals also included a commitment to a minimum income for the elderly of $65 a month, to a rapid transit system in major cities, and concluded with the robust statement that the party would "go forward in its traditional liberal and progressive spirit."[6] Liberals like Roosevelt knew that the party did not have the upper hand in California politics, but argued that an enthusiastic statement of principles would send Democrats into the crucial 1948 elections with enthusiasm and present a united front against the Republicans.

In some respects the strategy seemed to work. Patrick McDonough claimed to be delighted by the July convention, arguing that "the opposition to our President was practically eliminated, particularly the Kenny forces." The statement of policy had been overwhelmingly endorsed by a vote of 179 to 19, and the anti-Truman forces had been brought to heel by a platform that had been impossible to oppose. "I think from now on the true Democratic Party in California knows where it stands and will work harmoniously together."[7] Such optimism was to be short-lived, and McDonough himself had predicted the reasons before the convention when he objected to the idea of a policy statement. In a strongly worded letter to Roosevelt's policy chairman George Outland, a recently defeated representative from Santa Barbara, he argued that nothing could unite the party except the purging of the far left and the establishment of better campaign organization in the run-up to Truman's reelection effort. "There is only one thing of importance to Democrats today," he wrote. "That is the election of President Truman in 1948. With him will go the failure of the Democratic Party for 50 years."[8] McDonough had already asked Roosevelt to concentrate on organizing the party along the lines the Republicans had done with the Republican Assembly, using a proxy group to endorse candidates, purge extremists from the ranks, and energize the party's base. "Such an organization would help us in getting votes, acquiring practical workers, and would bring political brains into our party that are now not able to find a place in the Democratic organization," he wrote in February. "This Democratic Assembly would be in a position to endorse candidates to the end that most of our imbroglio would be eliminated."[9]

Outland and Roosevelt took a different view, arguing that a strong ideological statement of policy would help convince Californians to back the party, and that a debate within party ranks over policy would revitalize a demoralized organization. Outland asserted that voters had "every right to ask that the Democratic leadership in this state develop a clear-cut statement of its stand on the problems that face the state and nation. Unless such a position is taken how can any intelligent person be in a position to align himself in the ranks of any political party?"[10] Underlying Outland's argument was the tacit assertion that it was better to use policy statements to try to maintain harmony in the ranks than to use organizational structures to carry out a putsch of problematic factions.

As it would turn out in the following decade both Outland and McDonough were right: left-of-center politics would emerge out of the shadows due to a new combination of tighter organization and greater ideological unity. A rethinking of the party's political role and its organizational structure in the particular context of the late 1940s and early 1950s would provide the party in California with a unique springboard to political power with a new, postwar political agenda. This was not immediately clear in 1948. Henry Wallace announced his presidential candidacy in the pages of the *New Republic* in January, and the divisions within the Democratic Party over what to do about the deep unpopularity of President Truman in the party and the country affected the California party with particular force because of its internal divisions concerning foreign policy and the popular front.[11] One Berkeley Democrat informed Roosevelt that she was "deeply concerned about the breach in our party ranks over Foreign Policy which appears to be widening each day. . . . Never have we so needed to be united to combat anti-American activities which are threatening to disrupt our party and our real democracy."[12] Patrick McDonough, having initially welcomed the Wallace candidacy because to McDonough his supporters had been "like lye in our drinking water and their leaving has left the water purified," was by March despairing that the Roosevelt leadership were refusing to make a total break from the party's popular front past and support Truman.[13] In March the leadership withdrew the affidavit commitment of the membership to support Truman for renomination at the national convention, acting on the assumption, common in party circles nationwide in the spring, that there would be a popular challenger to the president, the name Eisenhower often cropping up in debate. McDonough, however, saw State Chairman Roosevelt's actions as a futile attempt to keep the Wallace wing of the party loyal, whereas he and some others such as State Vice-Chairman John McEnery "felt that we were dealing with a political rattlesnake and instead of helping him rattle his buttons, we should de-fang him if possible or at least fail in the attempt before he slithered off and did additional harm to the Democratic Party." McDonough formally broke with Roosevelt over the Truman loyalty issue in mid-1948, noting sadly that since early 1947 "no serious attempt has been made to organize the Democratic Party in California, but you have at all times displayed a genius to promote bickering and disunity."[14]

McDonough became the eyes and ears of the Truman campaign back in Washington, corresponding with members of the Democratic National Committee and with Truman's campaign chairman J. Howard McGrath. In part people like McDonough were simply party loyalists, and in part they felt that the Truman administration was as much committed to the legacy of the New Deal as anyone else and should not be unceremoniously dumped. McDonough had as little time for Republicans as he did Wallace supporters, claiming that "the difference between the Republican Party and the Democratic Party is as wide as between the Republican and Communist parties, except that both the Republican and Democratic Party are interested in the United States only and are not seeking to be affiliated with Russia." For chief Wallace supporter in California Bob Kenny he had brutal words about the nature of the Wallace movement: "Your associates are rodents of the sewer variety. They were great CIOers when the CIO served their interests. Few of them are for labor. That phase of their activity is a cloak to cover their sinister objectives. None of them joined a union until 1936. I joined a union when I was 16. They believe in the same type of unions that can be found in Russia."[15] Publicly, at least, the vast majority of California Democrats echoed his sentiments. "The only cheering for the third party," Roosevelt declared in a speech to the Jefferson-Jackson Day dinner of the Democrats of Tacoma, Washington, "comes from the Kremlin. The complete hypocrisy of the third party is proved by its insistence on running candidates in Illinois, Minnesota, and California against men whose records prove beyond any doubt their long-term adherence to liberal and progressive principles."[16]

In the event, the 1948 elections defied all expectations from right and left and produced a convincing victory for President Truman. Though California demonstrated the hybrid character of its leftist politics in providing the second highest tally for Wallace, around a million votes, Truman carried the state by a narrow margin over Republican challenger Thomas Dewey. Party loyalists put this down to Truman's barnstorming appearances as much as to efforts by the local party, McDonough commenting that when "it is considered that we have approximately one million majority of Democrats and the net result is that we came out with a 17,000 vote lead something is putrid with the Democratic leadership."[17] But a Democratic victory against concerted Republican and Progressive Party opposition in California was a remarkable achievement. Though many in the fractious and divided California party did not realize it, their convulsions over the Wallace candidacy, and their drive to build political campaigns without the benefit of a long-established power base in the state, were setting the scene for a reworking of the party's political faith and alliances in the years that followed. An examination of the attempt to build up grassroots liberal organizations in the early Cold War, together with an analysis of the political impact of the campaigns of Jimmy Roosevelt and Helen Douglas for governor and senator in 1950, demonstrates the importance of the travails of the late 1940s in building a political revolution in the 1950s.

Building a Liberal Movement in California, 1945–1950

The fact that the political world of the California left was preoccupied in the 1940s with divisions over communist influence within its ranks meant that activists, intellectuals, political operators, and elected officials were forced to define what exactly being on the left entailed. We have already seen how politicians like Roosevelt and Henry Wallace frequently used terms like "liberal" and "progressive" interchangeably. Yet in the battles for supremacy among the heirs to the New Deal, their political tussles were implicitly pushing them all toward a new definition of liberalism for a postwar age. This was by no means a clearly defined or straightforward process. Some fellow traveler groups, such as the Democratic Club of Burbank, saw their raison d'être as nothing more than to promote the Soviet foreign policy line, as in their March 1946 resolution at the meeting of the Los Angeles branch of the National Citizens' PAC that the United States should "desist from needling, baiting, and antagonizing Russia, a country that has always been a sincere friend to the United States."[18] Others saw the particular demands of the booming postwar California economy and the state's insatiable demand for water, power, and urban growth to fuel that expansion as a green light for a rethinking of what it meant to be a "liberal." A member of the Berkeley Democratic Club claimed to be "working with the Farmer-Labor-Consumer Association on Central Valley Project matters. . . . We are making a drive for the establishment of an Authority which will function along TVA lines."[19] Others, like Jimmy Roosevelt and George Outland, tried to steer an uncertain course between maintaining the broad church of a party that included the far left and the anti-New Deal right and setting out a political stall that saw the Four Freedoms and FDR's 1944 Economic Bill of Rights as clarion calls for a reengagement with the promise of the New Deal. All, however, faced a new political climate after the war without the inherited baggage of at least a decade in the political driving seat, in contrast to Democrats and labor leaders on the East Coast or Chicago.[20]

National leaders of the American liberal movement had during the war established organizations that had the potential to establish a foothold on the West Coast. The Union for Democratic Action (UDA), for example, had been created in 1941 as an organ of left-of-center political action to help act as an aide to New Deal politicians during the war. AFL political director Nelson Cruickshank was one of many who felt that such an organization had even more significance after the war, particularly given the increasingly obvious splits between the UDA and its fellow traveler offshoot, the Progressive Citizens of America, since 1944. "In the belief that there is today more than ever a need for some agency with which those having a liberal point of view on social and economic problems can work unitedly and which at the same time will not fall for the fake liberalism of the 'united front' organizations and become a tool of the Communist Party, a number of us are doing what we can to strengthen the Union for Democratic Action," Cruickshank wrote his California counterpart C. J. Haggerty in July 1946.[21] Many in California welcomed developments back in Washington, particularly in the wake of the local party's bruising internal fight over the 1946 primary nominations, which had exposed the growing chasm within the party over the issue of communism. "Progressive organizations took a tremendous setback in the recent California primaries," wrote a Beverly Hills party member in June. "The most glaring example was the all-out drive to get over Ellis E. Patterson [for senator]. Patterson, a good man in many ways, nevertheless had a bad record of anti-Roosevelt and anti-preparedness activity in the period when Stalin and Hitler were honeymooning. . . . The Communist handful got their comeuppance—but the real wounds were those suffered by the Progressive cause in California." UDA Chairman James Loeb responded positively, noting that he had sent a senior UDA member out to California to help organize the liberal movement there, and that he was "confident that the UDA idea will be well-received," predicting that "it won't take too long before it is the top organization of its kind hereabouts."[22]

Nathalie Panek arrived in San Francisco in July to spend the whole summer meeting local Democrats, labor leaders, and activist groups to see whether the UDA umbrella could unite the center-left in the face of daunting postwar political challenges. "California is different," she mused to a San Francisco newspaperman as she prepared to travel west. "However, in the national office we reason that regardless of how things seem in your sunny state we think there must be *some* good live liberals who are not slavish followers of the policy of the Soviet Union. I think nothing would be so helpful to us in the national office as to have lively chapters in San Francisco and Los Angeles which could talk back to the CP on the home front and give a little courage to the California delegation who would prefer not to follow Uncle Joe at every turn."[23]

It was soon clear, as was the case with left-wing parties across the industrialized world in the 1940s, that noncommunist leftists had to travel a precarious path between the popular front and capitalism. UC Santa Barbara professor Harry Girvetz, a key intellectual figure in the building up of the UDA and its successor, Americans for Democratic Action, on the West Coast, noted in September 1946 that the UDA was coming under attack from left-wing sources for being "too engrossed in battling the CP to the detriment of its positive program. This is a real danger which an organization which excludes Communists always courts."[24] Still, the January 1947 meeting in Washington that established Americans for Democratic Action as a new national organization of liberals represented at least an effort to come to terms with the collapse of the popular front and a determination among New Dealers to redefine their political agenda. The launch of the new organization, attended by some of the liberal movement's leading lights and up-and-coming stars, including Arthur Schlesinger Jr., Chester Bowles, Philip Murray, and Hubert Humphrey, provided a new focus for followers of the New Deal in an uncertain political climate.[25] Its statement of principles underscored the perceived need to re-brand New Deal politics for the postwar period: "We hold that private enterprise must be controlled only to the extent necessary for fulfilling two basic requirements: the realization of our full productive potentialities, with provision for adequate leisure; the withdrawal from private individuals of economic power so great that it enables them to dominate government and thereby to subvert democracy."[26] This commitment to a form of Keynesian economic management and to standard New and Fair Deal policies such as social security, federal health insurance, the minimum wage, and public housing was coupled with a new and robust commitment to civil rights and to anticommunism.

Initially it seemed as though the ADA would provide an important rallying point for the demoralized left in California. Many major figures in state politics, including labor leader John Despol and Representative Chet Holifield, became members, and a concerted effort was made to set up local chapters across the state to sign up members, hold meetings, and maintain interest in New Deal-type issues. In Los Angeles four chapters sprang up in early 1947, and in July Jeri Despol, wife of CIO leader John, wrote Panek that they had established an office on West Seventh Street downtown. "We have a small foyer and one small room and a telephone," she reported, "but we are gradually getting organized." Despol was optimistic about the new organization's prospects: "we must have a chapter organized in each Congressional district, with at least 50 new members in each one by the 15th of September."[27] The Los Angeles chapters were soon forced to amalgamate into one, but the local ADA played host to prominent British Labor Party politician Jennie Lee in late fall 1947, and to Hubert Humphrey, then the pioneering liberal mayor of Minneapolis and ADA leading light, in October, attended by over 700 people and raising $224 for the LA chapter.[28] Local socialites such as Melvyn and Helen Douglas and Democratic political fixer Paul Ziffren held cocktail parties and pool parties at their homes and invited ADA members to attend and help swell the group's financial coffers, as well as providing a taste of political activism for actors and screenwriters such as Ronald Reagan and Myrna Loy.[29]

Harry Girvetz, head of a thriving chapter in Santa Barbara centered on the university, reported to Washington regularly on local events, informing national director James Loeb in late 1947 that Jennie Lee's visit had been "an overwhelming success. It has definitely established us as a powerful force in the community. More than 600 people turned out to hear her at the famous Lobrero Theatre, despite a football game. Had it not been for the latter we'd have had to turn them away. . . . The Santa Barbara chapter is thriving and more vigorous than ever. We're trying at this time to organize another chapter in our sister city of Ventura." The Santa Barbara chapter soon became a model of ADA organization, raising funds regularly through the invitation of guest speakers and the holding of events such as rummage sales and drinks parties and thereby paying its way without the need for heavy subsidies from Washington.[30] Santa Barbara's experience suggested that even if the official Democratic Party and the state's labor unions remained in disarray in this period, activist organizations such as ADA chapters had the potential to provide new energy and life to left-of-center politics in California in the postwar years.

Faced with the challenge of a Republican Party and pro-business establishment that dominated California politics, the other side of the political spectrum needed more than speaker meetings and garage sales to make a serious impact on the political landscape. Though James Q. Wilson's contemporary analysis of grassroots "amateur" politics applied to Democratic clubs in a slightly later period, it could just as well have described the problems faced by ADA affiliates and even local chapters of the ACLU in the late 1940s: "The amateur club movement is, with few exceptions, a middle class phenomenon. In the long run this, more than its factionalism, will probably prove to be its single greatest weakness."[31] ADA chapters were effectively talking shops for those already committed to New Deal politics, and rarely were they able to coordinate their activities with local welfare rights protests in cities like Oakland, or grapple with the reasons why figures like *California Eagle* publisher and prominent African American Charlotta Bass ran for vice president on the Progressive ticket in 1952.[32] In any case, few ADA groups were as successful as the Santa Barbara chapter. An ADA national board member complained in 1950 that the organization had "probably put as much into the state as we have in any other state outside of New York and with embarrassing results."[33] The San Francisco chapter collapsed in 1951 after it became apparent that its leader was using the group as a powerbase for a personal rivalry with local Democratic Party chieftain Bill Malone, going so far as to endorse a Republican for city supervisor without consulting the local membership and appointing a notorious red-baiting ex-communist to the committee.[34] Girvetz reported in 1951 that he was struggling to help reestablish the Los Angeles chapter after finding it "in a state of complete collapse. . . . The executive committee had many vacancies, met rarely, and meetings were badly attended. . . . ADA had become synonymous with failure in the area and a kind of laughing stock." Furthermore, the chapter's principal financial patron, Gifford Phillips, editor of *Frontier*, was widely distrusted by the national leadership and local anticommunists as a fellow traveler. Los Angeles chapter member Abraham Held referred to the Phillips group, including chapter president Kenneth Brown, as having "played footsie with the Communist fellow-travelers on the County Central Committee."[35] In a state experiencing a massive wave of in-migration and in which few settled in one home for long, ADA chapters could serve as a useful social club or a jumping off point into local politics. They could not, however, function as a political party surrogate that could reach beyond the middle class and high society salons of Beverly Hills and Santa Barbara and provide concrete legislative solutions to California's major political problems.

A forum like ADA was nevertheless a useful conduit for the sharing of ideas and the development of a new sense of purpose for those worried about the resurgence of anti-New Deal Republicanism after the war. Evidence for the tentative emergence of a broad political agenda for postwar liberalism in California came from Harry Girvetz in his scholarship as a professor of philosophy and sociology. Although hardly as well known in later years as David Riesman, C. Wright Mills, John Kenneth Galbraith, or Talcott Parsons, his role as leader of the more successful branches of Americans for Democratic Action in the state and his involvement in Democratic politics made him a good example of an intellectual who also used his ideas in the political arena. He would later advise the Pat Brown administration on welfare policy, and so provides the sort of link between intellectual developments and practical politics that is of concern here. Girvetz articulated a political vision that was expansive enough to adapt to changing social attitudes over the next half century, and this vision would increasingly mould the character of the Democratic Party as it struggled to come to terms with a new political landscape in the postwar years.

Girvetz published his major work on political philosophy: *From Wealth to Welfare: The Evolution of Liberalism* in 1950, the same year in which British professor of social policy Richard Titmuss published his groundbreaking study of the dynamics of social policy in wartime Britain, *Problems of Social Policy*. Both Girvetz and Titmuss would feature as intellectual policy experts cited in deliberations of policy formulators in California after the election of a Democratic administration in 1958, and so a consideration of the intellectual revolution on the left in the early 1950s at a time when the political fortunes of Democratic liberals and Fair Dealers were looking rather desperate is necessary for understanding later developments.[36] Girvetz's study was divided into two parts. The first outlined the principal tenets of "classical liberalism" as an Enlightenment mode of thought that reordered the world around a new, proto-capitalist understanding of human nature. The second he termed "contemporary liberalism," which dismissed the classical liberal notion of human nature as egoistic and individualistic, preferring to emphasize the creative and social instinct in human nature that saw productive endeavor as a collective enterprise. Girvetz traced this intellectual current back into the late nineteenth century, but saw as its high priest in the United States the philosopher John Dewey. Dewey saw human activity as altruistic rather than inherently selfish, and claimed that clashes that occurred within societies over work and the sharing out of the spoils of production "do not lie in an original aversion of human nature to serviceable action, but in the historic conditions which have differentiated the work of the laborer for wage from that of the artist, adventurer, sportsman, soldier, administrator, and speculator."[37] Girvetz wanted to construct a serviceable definition of modern liberalism for a postwar world that was not just concerned with Depression era issues but could be used as a mobilizing ideology for Americans opposed to the growing influence of free-market individualism in American politics. In this effort he was not alone, as the work of Crosland in Great Britain and Francois Mitterrand and Charles Hernu in France in the 1950s and 1960s demonstrates.[38] An understanding of these intellectual currents does provide us with the framework within which to understand the growing political confidence of the Democratic Party in the 1950s, and the sowing of policy seedlings that would presage a reconfiguration of the relationship between mainstream politics and society.

As an ADA organizer, Girvetz was interested in building up left-of-center political activity on the West Coast. As leader of a relatively successful ADA chapter in a state where that organization was having enormous difficulty establishing a foothold in the late 1940s and early 1950s, he was called upon to provide speech material for national politicians such as Hubert Humphrey. One such draft expanded upon the philosophical foundations laid out in his scholarly work and applied it to the United States in the 1950s: "Cognizant of the real achievements of the profit system, present-day liberalism does not seek its abolition, only its regulation and control, that is to say, its modification to meet the requirements of a changing world. . . . Accordingly, liberals have evolved a program of government action which, by a striking consensus of both critics and adherents, has come to be known as the Welfare State."[39] Girvetz defined welfare not simply as the transfer of economic resources or the establishment of personal insurance systems, but as a philosophically self-contained but practically elastic doctrine that could change in emphasis and target over time and in response to changing need. "The approach," he claimed, "is experimental, the solution tentative, the test pragmatic."[40] This welfare state would, he argued, include a response to families in economic need, but also to racial discrimination, and, by implication of the pragmatic test, to other areas of discrimination that might emerge into public discourse in the future.

The campaigns of Democrats for statewide and national office in 1950 suggested that social democratic political ideas were taking roots in California, but that the party had not yet found the political muscle or the favorably social context to make them dominant. Jimmie Roosevelt's fight to defeat the popular Warren and Helen Douglas's drive to sweep aside conservative Democratic Party interests and win her party's Senate race represented clear attempts to push the political center of gravity leftward. Both campaigns sowed the seeds for the development of a vibrant social democratic strain in California politics later in the decade. And both demonstrated vividly the very real political and structural obstacles built into the political economy of California and the nation that still had to be overcome if the class, racial, and ideological kaleidoscope of Californian society was to be fully represented in the state's mainstream political discourse. The Filipino-American author Carlos Bulosan was not just a victim of hyperbole when he argued that Roosevelt's campaign was "the most significant in the history of California politics since 1910," and that "we are back in 1910, but on a higher level, in that our individual freedom and security are challenged by a group more monstrous and corrupted than in former years."[41] The 1950 campaigns, like the battles of the early twentieth century, represented a titanic clash between the forces of capital and those of the New Deal that set up the terms of political debate for the rest of the century.

Few were surprised when James Roosevelt announced his candidacy on 15 November 1949: he had been the titular head of the party through trying times in the mid–1940s and had managed to steer his rag-tag army through a devastating internal storm over whom to support in the 1948 presidential election. More interesting was the fact that Roosevelt's campaign, unlike most Democratic fights elsewhere in the country that year, did not run screaming from an engagement with social democratic issues but made its central strategy against Warren one of openly embracing such issues.[42] His opening gambit deliberately linked together statist economic management and individual rights in a way that would become common in California liberal politics later in the decade. In an open rebuke to Warren's stately nonpartisanship Roosevelt pledged to show voters "on which side of the fence I stand," arguing that all citizens had the "*right* to find a job at a fair wage and under desirable working conditions. We must achieve here in California the goal of *full* employment. . . . Jobs must be free from discrimination because of race, creed, or color. Collective bargaining in an atmosphere of mutual trust and respect between labor and management must have the *active* support of state officials" (emphasis original) He argued that the key issues of public power, economic development, and individual civil rights were interconnected, linked by the central nexus of the state. His statement was not a restatement of the underlying principles of the New Deal, as California had missed out on the political upheavals of the 1930s. It was more a new statement of purpose for the forces of the left in postwar California: "Party responsibility must be restored in California. . . . Non-partisanship . . . has come more and more to mean non-activity, non-responsibility, and non-leadership. . . . The rapid and continuing growth of our State means that our pressing problems can wait no longer for solution. Only leadership not tied down by the ever clinging ties of reactionary and special privilege forces can get the job done."[43]

The clear left turn in California Democratic politics signaled by Roosevelt's announcement was reinforced when he gave a series of campaign speeches to different audiences on the subject of the welfare state. In terms similar to those employed by Girvetz in his extension of the ideas of John Dewey, or Richard Titmuss or Tony Crosland in their reinterpretation of socialism in Britain in the 1950s, Roosevelt attempted to associate individual rights with collective action. Those who shared these values believed that the individual possessed intrinsic value that meant no individual could be neglected: the state "should foster those economic and social conditions in which the individual can be really free. Its aim, in a word, is justice—not justice in a narrow, legalistic sense, but real, substantive justice." Roosevelt used the example of a dynamic, growing state like California to argue for a vibrant public sector through which to manage the state's economic growth: "Perhaps the problems of a small and simple pastoral society or a frontier community can be dealt with through the individual exercise of uprightness and charity. But amid the incredible complexity of our highly industrialized state this cannot be sufficient." At points his increasingly righteous tone became reminiscent of his father in his 1936 election campaign, as he proclaimed himself "weary of the pious cant of those reactionaries who have arrogated to themselves the custody of all the traditional virtues (except charity perhaps) and who somehow confuse freedom with the practices of the more predatory industrialists." But the underlying philosophical current at work was more reminiscent of FDR's 1944 Economic Bill of Rights message that set the tone for California liberals far more than the less specific relief, recovery, and reform message of the 1930s.[44] In a telling attempt to pull his listeners' attention away from past battles and onto the present he argued that the "real issue before us is not whether in fact we shall have the welfare state. The American people have already decided that. They want more than freedom in the abstract. They have already decided that a society as fabulously wealthy and productive as our own can and must make provision for *all* of its members. . . . The achievement of a genuine welfare society, whose government chosen by the people acts in the interest of *all* of them, may be delayed and hindered. But it cannot be averted." This "welfare society" included a shared commitment to civil rights, nondiscrimination, and universal access to health care, issues that framed political debate in California for the 1950s.[45]

Given the unfavorable national political climate and the overwhelming advantage incumbent Governor Warren enjoyed, Roosevelt's campaign seemed an unlikely prospect from the start. Warren barely mentioned Roosevelt in his own reelection campaign, and Roosevelt's increasingly desperate attempts in his speeches and broadcasts to cast Warren as a far right-wing Republican in sheep's clothing and to create as much political space between the two candidates as possible in part represented an attempt simply to get noticed and create some relevancy and purpose for his faltering campaign.[46] The strongly left-of-center tenor of Roosevelt's campaign also represented a calculated strategy based on the findings of polls taken before and during the 1950 race. In the summer of 1949 Jimmy hired a polling firm to establish whether a run for office would be feasible, and the results bear close investigation. The question that mattered—would Roosevelt win—did not look promising: 52 percent of those polled said that if an election were held tomorrow they would vote for Warren, as opposed to 23 percent who preferred Roosevelt. But the election was still eighteen months away. Roosevelt was swayed by the polling data dealing with the depth of feeling of those surveyed: 96 percent of Roosevelt supporters supported his politics and candidacy strongly, compared to 72 percent of Warren supporters; 24 percent of Warren supporters were classed as "weak" in their commitment to Warren. In addition, 15 percent of those asked how they would vote if an election were held tomorrow were undecided. The polling suggested that Roosevelt had to campaign on themes that differentiated himself from Warren: "Those voting for a candidate other than Warren or who are undecided have for the most part a well-formulated negative attitude toward Warren," the poll revealed. "On the other hand, those voting for a candidate other than Roosevelt or who are undecided display merely a lack of knowledge about Roosevelt." A full third of those polled thought that Warren was a Democrat, or a candidate of both parties, helped by the cross-filing system in California elections and overwhelming media coverage of his governorship; 43 percent of registered Democrats planned to vote for Warren in the Democratic primary, as opposed to just 5 percent of Republicans who thought they would cast their Republican primary ballot for Roosevelt.[47] The only hope for Roosevelt's campaign was to convince voters that Warren was an enemy of the Democratic Party and Roosevelt an heir to his father's legacy in a state where registered Democrats still outnumbered Republicans by a near two to one margin.

This fact was reinforced in the wake of the primary elections in July 1950. Warren was the overwhelming winner of his own primary and had gained an alarming number of votes in the Democratic primary, but a deeper probing of voting attitudes among the 2,241 adults surveyed across the state revealed a potentially significant weakness in people's commitment to the Republicans. For one thing, the overwhelming registration bias to the Democrats—53 percent Democratic to 26 percent Republican, and 21 percent unaffiliated—at least suggested a serious disjuncture between the political complexion of California and election results. More significantly, 48 percent of respondents said that the Democrats were doing the most good for the country compared to 30 percent who answered Republican, but many did not know Warren was a Republican. "The survey shows that the majority of the voters are registered or will register as Democrats because they believe that party has done more for them. The majority of those who consider themselves Independent voters are either 'weak' Warren votes or 'Don't know' Senatorial votes at this time, despite the fact that in the main they lean toward Democratic party thinking. A strong united front of the Democratic candidates would be a psychological factor towards crystallizing their Democratic voting behavior." Though the poll warned that ideology was a difficult concept that could send mixed messages in the rough and tumble of a campaign, and terms such as "Fair Dealer," "Reactionary," "Liberal," and "Radical" had multiple meanings and were "newspaper terms and not part of the average person's vocabulary," there was a clear message that some sort of left-wing platform was the only way of creating a serious challenge to bipartisan Warren. "There should be a clear understanding in the voter's mind that James Roosevelt has developed and stands on his own platform—a platform that has meaning for the problems of the State of California. Roosevelt should be identified as a Progressive Democrat. . . . The lower middle and lower economic groups, pro-Roosevelt, did not vote in their true number as did the pro-Warren economic groups, particularly the upper income group. The need for planning and organizing the 'get out the vote' committee is obvious. It should be one vast correlated organization under the *Democratic Party*, with all the various pro-Roosevelt units working together."[48]

The polling companies could not factor in the bitterly factionalized nature of the California Democrats that made such a coordinated campaign impossible, nor could they rationalize the highly personalized nature of California politics that made party-line voting difficult to organize. Even the Roosevelt and Douglas campaigns, both running for statewide office and both sharing the same political principles as well as the same party label, were wary of working together. Indeed, Earl Warren was genuinely angry when Helen Douglas came out and asked her supporters to vote for Roosevelt as well, as Warren had never openly backed Richard Nixon, Douglas's opponent, and such open party loyalty was often seen as unsavory in California.[49] The Roosevelt campaign did, however, expose the fact that there existed in California, underneath the ongoing imbroglio about communism and the popular front, a strong undercurrent of left-of-center politics that had the potential to explode into life under different political circumstances.

Helen Gahagan Douglas's Senate campaign further demonstrated both the limits of leftist influence in California and the potential for its growth. Douglas represented one of the great California Democratic Party success stories of the 1940s, as well as one of its greatest defeats. Born to a socially prominent Scotch-Irish family in Brooklyn in 1900, a young Helen Gahagan dropped out of Barnard College to pursue a career in theater. She was a Broadway star at twenty-two, a leading lady on the New York stage throughout the 1920s and, in George Abbott's words, "a strange classic beauty." She toured Europe as an opera singer before returning to the United States and her theater work, appearing in the David Belasco production *Tonight or Never* in 1930 with leading man Melvyn Douglas, who soon matched his stage romance with Helen with a real-life love affair and marriage. The couple relocated to Los Angeles, where his film career blossomed as her work life stagnated, though she made a comeback in the big budget science-fiction film *She* in 1935. She found a new interest alongside her husband in local Democratic Party politics, campaigning for Sheridan Downey in his successful 1938 Senate race and soon becoming the leading Democratic female activist in the state as a Democratic National Committeewoman during the Culbert Olson governorship. She entered Congress in 1944 from the predominantly African American and inner-city Fourteenth Congressional District in Los Angeles, and rapidly became a vocal champion of the New Deal wing of the Democratic

Party. She managed to ride out the stormy and debilitating battles within the state party during 1947 and 1948 by tending to her duties in Washington and by steering clear of the Wallace party overtures, but her political convictions remained on the left, and her strong personality ensured that she paid little attention to the social niceties of freshman life in the House of Representatives. She preferred delivering dramatic speeches on the floor of the House to courting lobbyists and her congressional colleagues, at one point striding purposefully onto the floor of the chamber with a basket of groceries to demonstrate the difficulties faced by ordinary families in the wake of the end of price controls in 1946. Her growing frustration at the rightward drift of Senator Downey in the 1940s on questions of corporate power, particularly in terms of big farm interests, prompted her to declare her candidacy for his seat in the fall of 1949.[50]

Acting as the launch pad for Richard Nixon's inexorable rise into national politics and as a prime example of a titanic clash between huge personalities in a crucial postwar political battle over the future direction of American politics, the Nixon-Douglas race has received wide attention.[51] Most accounts of this battle royal take a well-known path. Douglas was a well-meaning, principled liberal who had famously taken that basket of groceries into Congress in 1947 to demonstrate the impact of inflation on the average American's shopping bill. She had decided to take on conservative interests backing incumbent senator Sheridan Downey and run for the Senate, but soon found she was running a hopelessly underfunded, poorly timed campaign against the slick, well-funded champion of anticommunism and antistatism in Congress at a time when Cold War antitotalitarianism was the main issue in America. Nixon's campaign followed closely the strategy of the Republican National Committee in 1950, one of associating the Democrats with socialism and, by implication, communism. Referring to the forthcoming elections as "the most important in our nation's history," Nixon in a recorded speech to an audience in Modesto in March 1950 argued that President Truman had gone "right down the line for his socialistic program which he first presented to the special session of the 80th Congress in the summer of 1948 and which he made the basis of his campaign for reelection." In another speech he assailed "the president's program for socializing the nation's industry and agriculture and schools and medicine." Nixon's campaign was able to tie this in with a foreign policy that had seemingly failed to halt the expansion of communism in Asia, and with a candidate, Douglas, who was committed to expending the nation's wealth on leftist schemes rather than on combating Soviet expansionism.[52] Faced with a vast Chinese Red Army sweeping down the Korean peninsula, and a relentless Republican onslaught against statist planners in Washington and their supposed communist friends in government like Alger Hiss, Helen Douglas had little chance against the man credited with exposing Hiss and standing against the Fair Deal.

It is certainly true that Douglas's campaign faced numerous debilitating handicaps that have lent an air of resigned inevitability to historical treatments of the events of that tumultuous year. Some of the problems she faced have been sketched out in the preceding pages. Just to get the nomination she had needed to take on powerful elements within her own fractious party, people who had first of all remained steadfastly loyal to Senator Downey before shifting their allegiance to anyone but Douglas after Downey announced his retirement in the spring. The eventual challenger to Douglas, Manchester Boddy, a Los Angeles newspaperman, conducted his own bitterly anticommunist, anti-Fair Deal campaign against her, which left Douglas's campaign broke and exhausted before the main Republican onslaught had even gathered pace. Conducting a major statewide campaign in a huge, media-dominated state like California was a vastly expensive task, and Douglas had even hired a helicopter, "the flying egg-beater," to take her from city to city quickly and efficiently and to gain media coverage in a media market resolutely hostile to her campaign.[53] Nixon, by contrast, had the unequivocal support of almost all the major newspapers, and almost limitless cash from an array of financial backers, prompting the *New Republic* to comment on the 1,400 Nixon billboards that stretched as far as Tijuana in Mexico to attract the attention of the tourists and day-trippers, and the planes flying overhead spelling out pro-Nixon messages in the sky at $50 an hour.[54]

Even so, Nixon's campaign later admitted to being afraid of the potential for left-of-center politics to attract support, which is why they attacked Douglas so mercilessly. Murray Chotiner, Nixon's campaign organizer and right-hand man throughout his political career, emphasized his concern about the potential strength of the opposition in a campaign manual he wrote in the mid–1950s for prospective Republican candidates. He pointed out the need for a candidate to have a strong political message, echoing the advice Jimmy Roosevelt's pollsters had given him. For Nixon in 1950 this had been "A strong America" and was based on the idea that "as long as our boys were fighting communism overseas, the least we could do was to see to it that the communists did not get a foothold here." The flip side of this point, Chotiner continued, was the "very fundamental point that we must keep in mind, and that is never attack the strength of the opposition. I remember, as an illustration, that there were some issues that came up where frankly we were a little weak, and the other side was a little stronger than we were. . . . You are not going to be able to tear down the strength. You can attack the weakness of the opposition and just keep hammering and hammering those weak points until your opponent can no longer exist in the election drive." Chotiner's argument that Republicans could not "outbid the administration . . . because the Republican Party did not stand for the same thing that Mrs. Douglas was espousing" explained the need to make communism the central theme: "Nobody could ever hope to outpromise a New Dealer." He also noted that his team in 1950 had not bothered organizing a labor committee as they could "not compete against the opposition with top-name individuals. Never show your weakness at any time." This confession demonstrated clearly that the bipartisan politics practiced by men like Earl Warren was on the way out by 1950, with antistatist business interests determined to attack the remaining citadels of the New Deal order lest any further advances in the corporate alliance between business, labor, and the state be sanctioned. Douglas's mistake, Chotiner argued, was to attack Nixon's strength and, by implication, to neglect her own: that of potentially benefiting from the more clearly demarcated lines of debate on the subject of the Fair Deal and political rights for the disadvantaged. "She made the fatal mistake of attacking our strength instead of sticking to attacking our weakness."[55]

Certainly, Douglas's desperate attempt to retaliate against the Nixon team's allegations that she and the administration had inadequately opposed Soviet expansionism was ill-judged. It was unconvincing enough to argue that had it "not been for this aggressive, far-sighted policy . . . proposed by a Democratic administration, which I supported and helped write into law, America would today be standing alone and isolated in a sea of communism or chaos." She had opposed the Truman Doctrine and other early containment measures, and in any case her grim portrayal of the Soviets as terrifying megalomaniacs just did not ring true given the care she had taken not to be caught up in the increasingly febrile rhetorical game that was paralyzing political debate in Washington. But her attempt to argue, in response to Nixon's infamous pink sheet claiming she had voted with the extreme leftist Representative Vito Marcantonio 354 times, that Nixon had in fact voted with Marcantonio against overseas aid and economic assistance to Korea was sheer madness.[56] Clearly it was a reaction to the deeply unpleasant tactics employed against her by Chotiner and his sinister band of campaign coordinators: the pink sheet associating her directly with communism; the whispered phone calls reminiscent of those employed against Jerry Voorhis in 1946; the use of researcher Edna Lonigan to dredge up supposed links between Douglas and communist front organizations.[57] Her bid to challenge the GOP on foreign policy was not unusual in the fall of 1950, as many Democrats in races across the country were being worn down by the constant jibes of socialism and wanted to establish their own antitotalitarian credentials against a party only just coming to terms with its isolationist past.[58]

Her positive political message was, nonetheless, very real, and the bitter campaign against her was part of a broader national strategy, funded by organizations such as the National Association of Manufacturers and American Medical Association, to cast the demon of federal regulation out of the private business economy once and for all. In the lexicon of the increasingly dominant antiregulatory right the issue of the 1950 elections was, in Nixon's words, "the type of slavery in which an all-powerful state seeks complete domination and control over the lives and liberties of the people. The Soviet Union is an example of the slave state in its ultimate development; Great Britain is half-way down the same road; powerful political interests are striving to impose the British socialist system upon the people of the United States. The Republican Party must meet this issue squarely if it is to survive."[59] Douglas strenuously denied the assumed link between social democracy and communism or totalitarianism, decrying the Republican attempt to "associate every Democratic proposal in your minds with something alien, terrible, and hateful." In so doing, she was encouraged to articulate ever more defiantly what exactly it was that she stood for. In some respects she, like many Americans adjusting to life after FDR's death, remained unsure where to go from the New and Fair Deals: in her speech defending Democrats against the charge of communism she stressed that she epitomized "the struggle to win legislative recognition of America's needs through the enactment of the Democratic platform. . . . I am an advocate of the reforms begun by FDR and carried forward by Harry S Truman."[60] Yet her articulation of a statist political vision was more clearly delineated than ever as she headed for electoral disaster in 1950. "I believe that government should be ever alert to the needs of the people, should seek to better their health, to extend their opportunities for education, should concern itself with the problems of old age and insecurity, should act to maintain a steadily advancing economy without valleys of depression or mountains of inflation," she stated in a radio broadcast during her campaign. "I believe that government should be ready and able and willing to assist in replacing slums with decent homes for families with incomes too low to afford such homes without help. I believe that government should protect us from want in periods of unemployment."[61]

Her doomed campaign represented the beginning of a closer affiliation in California between an increasingly dominant liberal wing of the Democratic Party and a range of grass-roots reform movements pressing for political recognition. Phil Burton, then a law student at USC and a rising star in the Young Democrats of California, and Willie Brown, a young African American law student in San Francisco, became politically active in her campaign, and would later lead the way in reshaping the landscape of California politics. Brown later recalled how student politics came alive over her candidacy, paving the way for the landmark Adlai Stevenson movement in 1952: "As a matter of fact," he said, "it was a little more left than that. It was really the left wing of the Democratic party that was trying to organize on campus." Young Democrats were stung by the internal opposition to her campaign within the party, prompting many to sign up for active political duty. Bill Malone and most of the San Francisco Central Committee "were just too conservative," Brown recalled, "and were holding on to everything. They showed zero interest in the problems of old people, zero interest in the problems of racial minorities and clearly were indifferent to students."[62] The 1950 campaigns coincided with the picking up of the pace of fair employment and Young Democrat movements that would play important roles in the political world of California in the 1950s.

It was hard for Douglas's wide-eyed, idealistic supporters like Phil Burton to see much in the way of a silver lining in the final results in November. Roosevelt lost to Warren by a landslide of over a million votes. Democratic strategists tried to put some gloss on the catastrophic defeat by arguing that his campaign had been "extremely vigorous, well-organized, although not too well-financed," and claimed the consistency and power of Roosevelt's hard-hitting attacks on the Republicans had helped Democrats hold all but one House seat. The post mortem also blamed the press for the scale of the defeat, claiming the "big factor" was the "vicious personal attacks upon Roosevelt by the press (about 100 percent)." Douglas fared better, losing by 600,000, itself a terrible result given her only win in a county of any size was in Contra Costa, but it looked good when put next to Roosevelt's catastrophic defeat. To the Democratic high command, "the false charge of Communism was the major contributing factor to her defeat." The Democratic state chairman's report noted that Douglas's hard work in her congressional district in South Central

Los Angeles over the previous six years had helped her Democratic successor Sam Yorty win by a respectable margin with "solid support from all segments in the district, labor, minority groups, and so forth."[63] The Democratic tide among African Americans was particularly evident given the fact that the *Los Angeles Sentinel* had backed Nixon in the closing stages of the campaign, citing his anticommunism, but had not been able to sway many in the African American districts of southern California.[64] There was little doubt, however, that the Republican machine had crushed the hopeful band of Democratic insurgents, helped along by elements in the Democratic Party hierarchy who feared the consequences of a political revolution for their own sinecures. It was hard for Roosevelt and Douglas to appear credible when figures in their own party were arguing that their vision for America would "turn the country over to the Communists or reduce it to bankruptcy."[65]

Yet opponents of Helen Douglas were right to fear what she represented, and what her campaign suggested was happening to California politics. The bitter attacks on her suggested that the cozy harmony between moderate and far right elements in the ruling Republican coalition was coming unstuck. The right had embarked upon an all-out drive to crush the New Deal order that risked putting the old internal division on the left over the popular front to bed in favor of a united front against the antistatist onslaught. Douglas and Roosevelt's rethinking of a left-of-center vision, however tentative, would begin to tie together grassroots racial, gender, and sexual political movements to a Democratic renaissance in the 1950s and 1960s. Some of the defeated Democratic duo's most unpleasant opponents among the general public hoped that 1950 signified the end of the politics of welfare and civil rights in California. One claimed to speak for the whole state in suggesting "that Mrs. Douglas gather up the market basket with its chuck roast and other groceries she loved to use in her act together with other Fair Deal clap-trap and get out. Gullible people who fell for her act are no longer in these parts."[66] Douglas took the advice and moved to New York after her defeat, but events were soon to show that her friendly correspondent was wrong to think the debate had been won.

CHAPTER 3

The Stevenson Effect

When Helen Myers, delegate to the Democratic convention in Chicago in 1952, landed back home in Los Angeles after watching the nomination of Adlai Stevenson, she found that events had not gone unnoticed in California. "As soon as I got back," she recalled, "there was a stack of phone calls on my desk—people calling in wanting to know if they could work for Adlai Stevenson." This sudden enthusiasm for national Democratic politics in Los Angeles came at just the right time for activists like Myers. "The Stevenson people came into politics just at the time we were trying to create a new structure in the county," she remembered. "I collected all the names, found out what assembly district they lived in, and sent them out to the campaign manager in that district."[1] Stewart Udall, influential Democratic congressman from Arizona who later became JFK's secretary of the interior, claimed in a 1958 article that "Stevenson acted as a fulcrum for the upsurge of his party in several of the states. It was hardly accidental that many of the Stevenson strongholds of 1956—California, Oregon and Pennsylvania, to name a few—were the states where Stevenson's 1952 campaign set in motion new forces and personalities. In many instances it was this fresh corps of amateurs and egghead recruits who provided the extra drive that revitalized weak party organizations."[2] The Stevenson presidential bid energized left-of-center activism in California, and provided a new lease on life for the Democratic Party, and in particular the more radical elements within the liberal coalition. But why Stevenson, and why 1952? Californians had voted happily for FDR or Truman without at the same time seeming particularly interested in Democratic Party politics more generally. The Stevenson campaign helped to unify a range of grassroots movements just coming together in California behind a search for meaning for the left in affluent 1950s America. The campaign provided the organizational impetus for the formation of a new Democratic Party infrastructure in the mid-1950s, and also provided the kind of ideological soul-searching needed to propel the party to power later in the decade.

Americanism Versus Foreignism

The parallel story to this rejuvenation of political debate among Democrats is the remorseless rise of the Republican right in 1952, marshaling its forces and planning another clearly delineated left versus right battle that had worked so effectively for them in 1950. Republicans held most of the political advantages: they were well-financed; their political message was simple and easy to articulate; their campaign team was in place early; incumbent senator William Knowland was a major political player on the national stage whom no Democrat wanted to take on and who could act as a central figure around whom the other campaigns could revolve. Knowland, a darling of the right because of his hard-line stance on opposing communism in the Far East and his staunchly anti-Fair Deal voting record, also served as an antidote to the moderate Republicans who were largely blamed for the 1948 defeat: Earl Warren had been the vice presidential candidate and was increasingly seen as useful only for his own election. "Has [Warren] forgotten," wrote one angry Southern Californian to Knowland in November 1951, "that his name was not magic in 1948. . . . He has too many socialistic ideas to please any real American." Another correspondent to Knowland and Richard Nixon begged them not to nominate "another 'Me-tooer' for president. Dulles, Eisenhower, Stassen, Truman, Warren and Willkie, birds of a feather. 'FOREIGNISTS' all. The 1952 campaign will be a clear issue of Americanism vs. Foreignism."[3]

Knowland was perfectly placed to represent the forces of the California right in a campaign of this kind. He was a vocal champion of conservative causes, foreign and domestic, in the U.S. Senate, and the family name had considerable political clout in Oakland and the East Bay. His grandfather, Joseph Knowland, had arrived in California in the 1850s and had made a huge fortune in lumber, mining, shipping, and banking in the Bay Area, and Bill's father, J. R. Knowland, had combined an equally successful business career as owner-editor of the *Oakland Tribune* with his role as a prominent advocate of conservative and Republican Party political causes. Before buying the *Tribune* in 1915 he had been a Republican member of the California State Assembly and then a U.S. congressman, but his failure to win a Senate seat in 1914 because of the break with the Bull Moose forces in the party prompted him to wield his considerable political influence from his offices in the Tribune

Tower for the rest of his life. One of the beneficiaries of J. R.'s editorial patronage was a young Alameda district attorney named Earl Warren, and it was ironic that by 1952 Bill Knowland's campaign backers were so aroused against Warren given the fact that Warren had shown his gratitude for the Knowland family's careful nurturing of his legal and political career by appointing Bill to the Senate in 1945 after progressive warhorse Hiram Johnson's death. In the Senate Knowland became renowned for the grim intensity of his conservative convictions. He supported abortive legislation in 1946 to force the federal government to balance its budget, and was a relentless advocate of low taxation and an end to New Deal programs. He was an enthusiastic supporter of the Taft-Hartley Act and a staunch critic of organized labor and of government mediation between management and unions, having acted as a fearsome opponent of union power during the Oakland General Strike of 1946. A reluctant convert to the Truman administration's foreign policy, like many former isolationists and antispending critics of American Cold War foreign policy, Knowland saw Asia rather than Europe as the primary arena of U.S. foreign policy interests and became a passionate supporter of the Chinese Nationalists after their defeat by Mao's Communist forces on the mainland in 1949, a cause that soon earned him the title "the Senator from Formosa."[4]

Knowland's Senate campaign gave the Republican right in California a clearly defined route into political action in 1952. Murray Chotiner, fresh from his successful effort to elect Nixon two years earlier, was chosen as Knowland's campaign manager, and immediately set out to create a mass coalition for Knowland that would, he felt, have a knock-on effect on other Republican candidates, including presidential candidate Dwight Eisenhower. Chotiner's strategy involved making an association between the Republicans and American values, attracting registered Democrats on the basis that Democratic candidates were out of step with the national ethos. "We *must* appeal to Democrats to vote for Bill Knowland," Chotiner's campaign manual argued. "Therefore, do not make a blanket attack on Democrats. Refer to the opposition as a supporter of the Truman spend-spend-tax-tax program. As pointed out on our campaign strategy sheet, do not mention the opposition unless you are asked about him." Knowland was painted as "sincere, hard working" and as "an outstanding authority on international affairs." His opponent, Democratic representative Clinton McKinnon of San Diego, had "a 96% record of voting along with the Truman, Fair Deal, spend-spend program during 1951."[5] The campaign gained valuable endorsements from conservative Democrats, and made carefully worded references to both parties in speeches and broadcasts as Knowland successfully associated his own candidacy with the Cold War fight against totalitarianism and foreign political values.[6]

The Democrats, reeling from the disaster of 1950, simply did not have the resources to challenge the Knowland juggernaut, backed as it was by the state's media and a national tide that was heading the Republicans' way. Knowland won both party primaries in a landslide, capturing nearly a million votes in the Democratic primary alone to McKinnon's 633,556. He garnered ten times as many votes as McKinnon in the Republican primary, and swept every county in the state except for McKinnon's home city of San Diego, which he carried in his own primary but not in that of the Democrats. Thus Knowland had effectively clinched victory on June 3, five months before the November general election, facing only a selection of minor candidates headed by Progressive Party candidate Reuben Borough. Borough had received 5,258 votes in his own primary; Knowland, by contrast, had in two primaries gained the votes of 2,308,051 Californians in a state in which Democrats in theory had a registration advantage.[7] The natural political advantage the Republicans enjoyed in California combined with the electoral climate of 1952 to produce an almost impossible situation for Democratic candidates searching for a message after their 1950 drubbing.

The seemingly impregnable Republican fortress contained, nonetheless, some almost imperceptible weaknesses that would not impact upon election results in 1952 but which would become significant during the 1950s. For one thing, the GOP's bipartisan strategy was no longer based upon Earl Warren's brand of centrist Republicanism, but upon a staunch antitotalitarian message that suggested a strong swing to the right. This seemed appropriate in the political world of 1952, with the war in Korea and Joseph McCarthy's charges about communists in government on all the front pages. But in the long term the strategy pushed the Republican Party increasingly into the hands of the far right in California, and away from the broader political base, which in the 1940s had included organized labor, that had guaranteed its position of power in state politics. The Republican strategy in 1952 created in a sense a political gap into which a new opposition movement, energized by the influx of personnel and the circulation of new ideas, could move.

In California the rise of a brand of far-right politics was symbolized by the activities of State senator Jack Tenney of Los Angeles and congressman Thomas Werdel of Bakersfield, who represented a growing force in state Republican politics. They also worried state Republican leaders, with good reason since their respective stars shone briefly before plunging into oblivion: Tenney thanks to a primary challenge in 1954 as McCarthyism was on the wane; Werdel in the general election in 1952. Their political strategies revealed the contradiction inherent in right-wing politics in California in the 1950s: the brand of bitterly anticommunist, anti-left rhetoric they espoused was becoming more mainstream in the state party just as it was becoming less appealing to society at large. Tenney's indiscriminate hounding of those suspected of communist leanings from his position on the state un-American activities committee was helping to mobilize thousands of Angelenos to defeat him. Werdel was even more extreme: affiliated to extremist organizations such as Merwin K. Hart's National Economic Council, which had an office on Wilshire Boulevard in Los Angeles, he was one of the not insignificant band of Taftites who went beyond Taft. Werdel remained isolationist because he felt foreign policy spending helped push the United States down the road to big government.[8] In some senses, Werdel was a maverick, unrepresentative of the forces that controlled state politics. In part he represented part of a broader Republican strategy of playing to a right-wing faithful in advance of the first election the GOP seemed clearly on course to win since the 1920s, married to a concurrent strategy of mobilizing the private business community in a coalition to roll back the New Deal. One antiregulatory group sent Bill Knowland a campaign pamphlet entitled "So, the Fair Deal Lost," described as "part of a series of pamphlets and graphic charts, designed to educate the rank and file on the benefits of the Free Enterprise System. This series is sold to the boss man for distribution to his employees. . . . While this one particular brochure has a strong political slant, the reception from both the employer and employee, on this particular piece, is most enthusiastic."[9] The Republican Party, in California as elsewhere, was becoming more obviously a vehicle for the establishment of an antigovernment ideology that saw the unfettered private accumulation of capital as the sole economic goal for the postwar age.

Despite William Knowland's massive victory in the Senate race, the election results for the state as a whole sent a shot across the bows of the Republican political leviathan. The party had redistricted the state, benefiting not only from favorable district boundaries but also from the increase in the number of seats in Congress from 23 to 30 to reflect California's rapid and significant population increase since 1941. Yet although the Republicans finally managed to oust Democrat Franck Havenner from his San Francisco seat after several close races and plenty of mud slinging over alleged communist ties, they lost two races they should have won: in the Third District, based on Sacramento and its rural hinterland, and in the Sixth, in Contra Costa. The Democrats also disposed of Thomas Werdel in the new Fourteenth District, and came very close to regaining the Santa Barbara/Ventura Thirteenth District they had lost in 1946. The GOP ended up with a 19–11 majority in the House delegation, a crucial margin given their wafer-thin victory over the Democrats in total number of House seats, but hardly reflective of a landslide in a state in which almost every elected office was held by a Republican. Only eight Republican House candidates had both party nominations, and six Democrats also won the Republican primary. Crucially, a proposition to put the party affiliation next to each person's name on the primary ballot so that voters could not be deceived into thinking conservative Republicans were actually Democrats passed the popular vote in November. The 1952 election would be the last in which party labels could be immaterial.[10]

Stirrings on the Left: Intellectual and Political Currents

The gradual weakening of the Republican Party's grip on political power and, just as importantly, the decline of its dominance over political debate, became both more obvious and more significant when compared to the intellectual and practical upheavals occurring on the other side of the political divide. Whoever was to become the Democratic Party standard-bearer in the 1952 presidential election would benefit from three interrelated trends in California politics that would have repercussions beyond the election itself. First, there existed a growing realization within the California labor movement and civil rights organizations that the right turn in the state GOP meant they needed to build up the kind of left-labor coalition that they had failed to establish in the 1930s. Second, left-of-center political activists were finding new energy in an intellectual debate emerging on the left in various industrial democracies over the future of social democracy in an age of prosperity. Third, the obvious excesses of the domestic Cold War enabled a backlash against right-wing demagoguery to crystallize to a far greater degree than in the previous few years. The campaign of Adlai Stevenson for president in 1952 served as a focal point for the coming together of these phenomena, but his campaign was just the beginning of a massive reshaping of the relationship between Democratic politics and California society that would gather pace later in the decade.

The rhetorical strategy of state Republicans finally encouraged the development of an explicitly social democratic antithesis in a labor movement previously hamstrung by the peculiar dynamics of California party politics.

Although the State Federation of Labor remained, as we have seen, unable fully to divorce itself from an endorsement strategy that rewarded the GOP as much as Democrats, the executive committee of the CLLPE had become concerned enough about the prospects for an emerging left-right divide to draw up a statement to be presented to the pre-general election convention in Santa Barbara at the end of August. Though careful to deny that the League was changing its practice of supporting politicians of any party that supported labor's economic and political aims, the committee made it clear that it had been forced to take sides, at least in terms of basic party political philosophy. The statement drew attention to the continued GOP support for Taft-Hartley; to the party's increasingly shrill antilabor rhetoric in which it referred to labor leaders as "bosses" and "dictators"; and, in pointed reference to the California situation, to "the punishment of candidates within their own party who have supported the program of social and economic reform . . . and by the further punishment of those who refuse to enter into their schemes to destroy labor." The statement of intent alleged that the Republican Party was acting increasingly as a vehicle for private enterprise "to manipulate the institutions of government to defeat every effort to spread the benefits of our political and economic system fairly among those who create the nation's wealth." The Democratic Party, by contrast, had "adopted a platform that recognizes the rights of labor and the common people throughout the world."[11]

The statement, which endorsed the Stevenson-Sparkman ticket for president and declared a formal break with bipartisan politics, was unanimously accepted at the convention. The party's post-primary endorsements were a stark contrast to the muddle and fudge of the preprimary convention, throwing support to Democrats for Congress and State Assembly with very few nods of support for a handful of pro-labor Republicans. William J. McSorley Jr., Assistant Director of the National League for Political Education, worked the delegates into a frenzy with his bitter attack on antistatist politics. "This year of 1952 is indeed the most crucial year in the history of the American labor movement," he claimed. "We can become active politically; we can work politically to destroy reaction; to retire the peddlers of reaction from the halls of the United States Congress and the State legislatures. . . . It was our failure to take part in the election in 1946 that has put us in the position we are in today."[12] For those in the ranks of labor already committed to Democratic politics, such as Hope Schechter in East Los Angeles, the links being forged between labor activism and party political mobilization changed her political world. She had found the opportunistic marriages between labor and some state Republicans depressing, and was pleased to be able to go into her Latino communities as a proud Democrat, making calls on voters in the early evening before attending a labor or political committee meeting.[13]

It was not just labor's clarion call to political action that mobilized grassroots party workers in 1952. The campaign of Adlai Stevenson for president also set the scene for the development of a left-right political spectrum in California in the 1950s. "There was no Democratic Party," recalled Roger Kent about the political situation in 1952, until "the Stevenson campaign of '52 brought in this large number of idealistic people who were just crazy about Stevenson. . . . Then they had to go out and create [the party] themselves, which they did, and started the Stevenson clubs and everything else."[14] There was no doubt that the "surge" for Stevenson's nomination was national in scope and born in part of a large amount of favorable coverage in the national print media, including *Time* and the *Atlantic Monthly*. To prominent ADA supporter Arthur Schlesinger, the Stevenson movement "indicates the extent to which the Stevenson candidacy is filling a political vacuum. The vacuum exists for professional politicians and liberals alike; and Stevenson combines geographical desirability, political strength and moral courage in a package which appeals equally to northern city bosses and to members of Americans for Democratic Action."[15] Stevenson had impressed the machine politicians and liberal intellectuals alike with his massive win in the 1948 governor's race in Illinois against a corrupt, reactionary incumbent Republican, and his record in the governor's mansion had been at least in the tradition of the New Deal, if not exactly radical. His campaign's eighteen-page report detailing his accomplishments in Springfield pointed to his support for increased public assistance grants, together with the fact that his "four-year public aid program has made available $128 million more for old age pensions, blind pensions, and aid to dependent children than was spent in the previous four years, but it is also a program of getting rid of the 'cheaters' and of conserving public funds for those legitimately in need."[16] He had gained national attention for his controversial and widely admired veto of a hysterical loyalty oath bill passed in the Illinois State Legislature, memorably stating that in attempting to protect the nation against communist subversion Americans "must not burn down the house to kill the rats."[17] He cast himself as a morally upright crusader for standards in public life and as an arbiter of fairness in his oversight of public affairs. He supported a fair employment practices law for Illinois. He possessed a gift for rhetorical flamboyance that served him well in his political career. At a time when McCarthyism and the horrors of the day filled political headlines, he seemed the perfect antidote for American liberals: calmly rational, articulate in his defense of democracy and freedom in American life.

Yet it is difficult to understand at first his massive appeal to the liberal movement in California. As his roll call of achievements, claiming a purge of "chiselers" from the relief rolls among them, demonstrated, Stevenson was hardly a typical standard bearer of the leftist tradition in American politics. He gathered round him during the campaign a distinguished group of political and intellectual advisers, among them economist John K. Galbraith, law professor Willard Wirtz, *Harper's* editor Jack Fischer, and David E. Bell, who would subsequently serve, as would Wirtz, in the Kennedy administration and philanthropic organizations such as the Ford Foundation. Yet he remained distrustful of the political left, worrying, as Galbraith recalled, "lest he had been taken over by radicals. We felt that he was insufficiently committed to the constituency and the policies that had brought the magnificent string of Democratic victories all the way from 1932 to 1948. . . . Stevenson's fear . . . was that he would be thought automatic in his political responses, a predictable voice for the liberal clichés of the New Deal and Fair Deal years." Galbraith also noted Stevenson's social background and his affluent Chicago friends and neighbors. "They were not enamored of the Roosevelt or especially the Truman oratory, and they didn't wish to see their friend seduced. . . . Stevenson never fully escaped their hand."[18]

More seriously, his campaign's desire to hold the Democratic Party together nationwide, leading to his choosing Alabama senator John Sparkman as his running mate, suggested that the thorny question of race would loom large in 1950s Democratic politics. Stevenson would find that this fact would cause problems in California, where a civil rights movement was rapidly gathering steam in the early 1950s. New York representative Adam Clayton Powell was forthright in his attack on both main parties for retreating from their 1948 civil rights planks, noting that the Republicans had mentioned FEPC by name in their 1948 platform but had not in 1952, while the Democrats had also toned down their support for the civil rights of all. "I think the best description of it is the one that Clifton Utley, of NBC, gave me," said Powell in an interview in the summer of 1952. "'Well,' he said, 'this is a little bit to the left of the Republicans and a little bit to the right of the 1948 Democrats.' . . . In this changing world, unless we keep pace, ethically with our material progress, all is lost. 1952 demands stronger planks than 1948."[19] Prominent Los Angeles African American newspaperwoman Charlotta Bass publicly abandoned mainstream party politics to embrace the by now moribund Progressive Party as their vice presidential candidate over the question of civil rights and her opposition to the shrill, politically debilitating rhetoric of the Cold War that dominated political debate. It was, she claimed, "my government that supports the segregation by violence practiced by a Malan in South Africa, sends guns to maintain a bloody French rule in Indo-China, gives money to help the Dutch repress Indonesia, props up Churchill's rule in the Middle East and over the colored people of Africa and Malaya. . . . I have fought and will continue to fight unceasingly for the rights and privileges of all people who are oppressed and who are denied their just share of the world's goods their labor produces."[20] To Bass, like many African Americans a Republican until the New Deal shook the political certainties of the progressive era in California from their moorings, mainstream party politics had a long way to go on the civil rights question globally if Eisenhower and Stevenson represented the best choice available to people of color.[21]

Stevenson may not have been the perfect standard-bearer for a revitalized left in places like California, but he benefited there from the state's intensely media-driven, celebrity politics that thrived on candidates, like Stevenson, who were able effortlessly to court the support of the national liberal press and to establish a media personality for themselves. As Thurman Arnold observed, California had grown so rapidly and was so vast that candidates who wanted the statewide vote had to rely on "personal campaigning, radio, and advertising," all of which the Stevenson movement used with skill and ease.[22] The boosting of Stevenson in publications such as the *New Republic* as the great hope for those disgusted by the erosion of civil liberties and the Republican Party's anti-New Deal cries of socialism and communism was attractive to the demoralized and poorly organized political left in California. In February the *New Republic* described his record as Governor of Illinois as "outstanding in reorganizing state government, increasing aid to schools, overhauling roads and road financing, improving welfare services, attacking gambling and corruption, working deftly to get the most from a Republican legislature."[23] This media portrayal of Stevenson as a crusader for fairness and civil liberties chimed with the political zeitgeist for a political left reeling from the defeats of the previous few years.

The use of California's media-driven, style-obsessed political world to create a groundswell of popular support for Stevenson was carefully orchestrated. The strategy of promoting a spectacle of massive crowds and enthusiastic volunteers provided much needed excitement for a demoralized liberal movement. Stevenson's publicity director carefully groomed the mushrooming Volunteer for Stevenson groups, ordering them to "augment in every possible way work being done by regular party organizations to create crowds along motorcade route and at speaking places. Use sound trucks, newspaper ads, radio and TV spots to the absolute limit of your budget. Handbills announcing [the] Governor's schedule should be printed and distributed on strategic street corners. Banners should be strung at every intersection along route. Placards and signs should be placed in store windows and telephone poles and lamp posts along the route of the motorcade."[24] An officer of the "Hollywood for Stevenson-Sparkman Committee" told members they must attend "all political rallies and speeches in person. Remember that most major political meetings are televised and nationwide. *Be in the audience.* Recruit as many more people as you can. . . . Wear your button and display your Stevenson stickers."[25] Stevenson's public appearances were carefully choreographed for television as well as live audiences, including a press meeting in San Francisco at which Stevenson was flanked by several actors, including Lauren Bacall and Humphrey Bogart. As the flash bulbs lit up the room local Stevenson club president Allen Rivkin was on hand "to see that the press doesn't murder our actors by throwing framed questions at them."[26] If a radio broadcast was particularly well-received, it was rebroadcast with a new introduction underlining just how popular it had been.[27] The content mattered less than the spin that was placed on it, encouraging grassroots support for the Stevenson movement on the basis that he was a dynamic political force who inspired personal devotion in members of the public.

The fact that the Republican turn to the right in California was pushing the Stevenson movement leftward was made explicit when Stevenson's strategists explored issues pertaining to the Golden State. California's economic development and rapid population growth, making it a prime symbol of modernity in the eyes of many observers, created challenges that required the guiding hand of government. This argument dominated reports to the Stevenson campaign compiled with the help of local Democratic politicians and activists across the state in the fall of 1952. Rapid economic development had exposed the inadequacies of housing and public facilities; had shown up in sharp relief the reality of racial segregation in California's cities; had placed increasing strain on the state's social welfare resources as many of the previous waves of migrants grew old. In Oakland the key issue was a crisis in housing: "Oakland, like Los Angeles, has had a long running fight over public housing. . . . Housing conditions for minorities—Negroes, Mexicans,

Asiatics—are very bad," reported Stevenson's Bay Area sources, including San Francisco State Chair George Bradley and Mr. and Mrs. R. A. Gordon of the Berkeley chapter of ADA. They noted the NAACP's recent court challenge to segregated housing in San Francisco, and the need for Stevenson's campaign to embrace civil rights. In Los Angeles local congressmen Cecil King and Clyde Doyle reported that "Los Angeles has more persons over 65 than any other county in the country—378,000 or more than 12% of the voting population." A "liberal view on old age and disability allotments" would be a "helpful" way of framing Stevenson's campaign in LA. The increasingly unacceptable term "socialism" had to be tackled head-on in a city in which the genuine left and hard right coexisted in large numbers. Socialism was, the report stated, a "large issue in Southern California. Think it should be pointed out that the Government put out large sums to subsidize airlines, ships, railroads, farm prices, plants for such outfits as U.S. Steel. Stockholders think those expenditures are fine, but they object to Democratic programs for the little people—such as [Home Owners Loan Corporation] which has saved millions of homes. A good example of a 'socialistic' experiment is the Los Angeles Bureau of Power and Light. It was founded in 1900, the year of Stevenson's birth in Los Angeles, and is the greatest municipally owned power enterprise in the world. Is this socialistic?" In Richmond, a city in which the party's candidate for Congress was successful in 1952, rapid growth had set the agenda: "Population rose from 24,000 in 1940 to 100,000 in 1950, about equal to the wartime peak. . . . Economic distress after the war was the most serious in California because of the closure of the shipyards. . . . Major issues are reactivation of the shipyards, need for industrial water, Taft-Hartley, FEPC, Social Security, other progressive measures."[28] The particular demands of a modern, industrialized world placed pressure on resources, planning policy, and social cohesion in a way that made a new articulation of the place of the state in 1950s California necessary, at least in the view of those surveyed by Stevenson campaign managers.

The debate within California over the future of liberalism took on added significance at the time of Stevenson's first run for the White House because it coincided with a wider intellectual debate on the left internationally about these very same themes.[29] In January 1952 a *New Republic* article tried to capture the flavor and tone of this emerging ideological agenda when the author, J. R. Feyrel, noted the way opponents, as well as supporters, of the New Deal state argued even more bitterly about welfare in the 1950s than twenty years earlier. "The main issue of today," he wrote, "is surely the struggle for or against the Welfare State, or perhaps one can already say over the shape, development and control of the Welfare State. We live today in a collectivist society, in the broad sense of the word, and the pace of collectivism is likely to increase, for better or worse. . . . And if such a society is to function efficiently, it seems already clear that it must be governed by Welfare State concepts, in one form or another." The momentum of change had been picking up pace since the industrialization of the late nineteenth century, Feyrel argued, with the legitimization of labor unions and the end of the open shop forming one major milestone, and the reduction of economic inequality by means of social legislation and redistributive taxation signifying another. "In such measures as the TVA," he wrote, "one can see at least the wedge of the mixed economy, in the recent legislation in, say, California on the various trade-union and other 'private' insurance schemes at least the first sign of the Welfare State." The 1950s would, he argued, throw up new problems and challenges that would conceivably herald a major step toward social democracy configured for a prosperous world. A crucial question, and one that frames much of the present study, was "the cultural one. 'After the leveling, after the British National Health Service or the American owner-occupied home, what next?' "[30]

It is not difficult to point to a wealth of recent historiography on the American political economy of the postwar era that throws plenty of cold water on the implied optimism of Feyrel's assessment. As it turned out, the accord between labor and management over access to a private welfare state did not prove durable when the economic weather turned inclement, nor did it lead to an automatic federal expansion of entitlements for the laboring man and woman and their dependents. The term "welfare state" was in any case hardly appropriate for the patchwork of work-based welfare schemes, private pension agreements, and healthcare plans that reached only some of the workforce and very few of the laboring and out of work or retired poor.[31] Still, several interesting trends could be discerned when thinking about Feyrel's analysis and its implications for California. Certainly the state did witness the capture of the Democratic Party by partisans committed to constructing the sort of economic and social policies that would contribute toward greater social equality later in the century. And evidently the campaign of 1952 did point toward a clearer articulation of a social democratic message for the 1950s: economic growth and social diversity together required the regulatory hand of government to encourage a collectivist conception of social citizenship. The dynamic shifts in California society in the postwar era made the

Golden State a stark case study of left-of-center political development in this period.

The fact that California fascinated left-wing visitors from overseas desperate to find a new message for their own discredited parties in the 1950s strongly supports this argument. When British Labor politician and theorist Anthony Crosland landed on the West Coast, remarking in his diary on the "spectacular harbour, hills, much older houses, European, or rather cosmopolitan, atmosphere" of San Francisco, Dwight Eisenhower had defeated Adlai Stevenson and was already settled into the White House.[32] His mission, however, was of great relevance to the Democratic left in California throughout the 1950s. His own party had enjoyed six years in power after World War II, during which time they had established a National Health Service, nationalized major industries, expanded the welfare state on universalist principles, and changed the economic and social landscape of postwar Britain. In 1951, they had been unceremoniously ejected from power by the British electorate, despite gaining the highest number of votes cast for any party in British electoral history up to that point. Labor and Socialist parties in Australia, New Zealand, and continental Europe had also lost power at the end of the 1940s or were struggling to find a role in an international political system dominated by the United States and its powerful brand of anticommunist politics.[33] Crosland was conducting research in the United States for his book *The Future of Socialism*, intended as a road map for a left that he felt needed a fresh message if it was to adapt to the political demands of an age of consumption and technological change. In essence, he was trying to find answers to the question Feyrel had posed in early 1952: what next?[34]

Crosland's travels around California and some other parts of the United States led him to agree with Feyrel that the economic development of the nation since the regulatory and statist reforms of the New Deal did show the extent to which the politics of the broker state between government, management, and labor had changed the ideological landscape. He studied a California bakers' union and noted its "very detailed statewide trade union agreement, giving the trade union considerable power over firms' decisions in labor policy, including in discretion of restrictive or inflexible practices." American trade unions, he felt, were "probably more militant than in the UK" with "more emphasis on strikes, less on arbitration. . . . Indeed, they've become a powerful entrenched empire, equal in strength to big business, farmers, etc."[35] He found little enthusiasm for a dramatic change in the party system, but did note widespread criticism among Democrats of the Republicans' regressive tax policies and its abandonment of public works and large-scale public spending as an instrument of economic growth. He even found a corporate executive, Ernest T. Weir of National Steel, who was "convinced government has [a] clear responsibility for keeping economy in balance: admits this is a big change in business thinking from 1930s."[36] Crosland did observe the need for greater state control over the economic development of places like California: he reflected sadly on the lax zoning laws in many cities that led to "hideous urban sprawl, appalling traffic problems created, no open spaces." Suburbs of California cities were "sprawling, ugly, very industrial—quite different from suburbs of smaller, less industrialized towns." Los Angeles was "hideous except for lovely Italian surrounding hills."[37] Crosland's trip left him in no doubt that the United States had witnessed dramatic political changes since the 1930s as well as vast economic growth that gave him ammunition for arguing that social citizenship and a dynamic private economy were potentially compatible. He also saw the limits of Americans' acceptance of a statist solution of economic problems, noting that unions still had legislative battles ahead to resist right-to-work laws and maintain high-wage settlements. The next problem remained how to reconcile economic growth with social equality.

When left-wing colleagues and friends back in London read drafts of *The Future of Socialism*, they were somewhat taken aback by the influence his American trip had evidently cast over the thesis of the book. One friend wrote that "I feel that perhaps you are rather carried away by America," and Richard Crossman, Labour Party heavyweight, disagreed with Crosland's arguments about American politics and society in a spirited correspondence. "If I understand you aright," he wrote, "you believe that Socialism is now about equality, not about public ownership, and that we should accept much of the American attitude to social equality and equality of opportunity and add to these concepts of radical democracy a specifically Socialist content, the move towards equalization in the distribution of property, purchasing power and responsibility in industry." Indeed, Crosland did see the implicit connection between equality of opportunity in economic terms and social equality in terms of equal access for all to a common citizenship, an idea being worked out in America through pressure from civil rights activists for racial equality, though it had broader implications than that. Crossman was, however, unconvinced. "Social equality à l'Americaine not only assumes inequality in property distribution etc but glories in it. It is only in a society where there are millionaires as well as newspaper boys, and vastly more of the latter than the former, that everyone has an equal opportunity to rise from one status to the other. It is no good, therefore, suggesting . . . that American ideology comes much closer to the egalitarian ideas of the British Left than to those of the British Right. . . . As for equality as you define it, they would regard it as completely fatal to their free enterprise system."[38] It was difficult to deny the fact that the ongoing struggle for supremacy between management and labor for control over the industrial relations process in the United States rendered Crosland's notion of social equality through progressive taxation and a large public sector rather too radical for the American political scene. But it was also true that Crossman's failure to distinguish between all the different shades of political opinion led him to miss the perceptible changes in American political life, evident especially in California, that were taking place in the wake of Stevenson's campaign.

Even if the Stevenson campaign itself was unsuccessful, and the ideological direction of the candidate uncertain, the personalities and men of ideas around him in California and nationally contributed toward a vibrant debate over the future of left-of-center politics in the United States. The impact of thinkers such as Galbraith, Schlesinger, and Leon Keyserling at a national level over the possibilities for economic equality of opportunity in prosperous times has been well documented by historians.[39] The debate was in full flow during the 1952 campaign, prompting an interesting take on the international dimension to leftist political thought in a *New Republic* editorial in August. The possibilities of the nation's vast economic output for the promotion of social cohesion and abundance for all were viewed as central to Stevenson's message to the country. "This theme," the editors argued, promoted "an intelligent and helpful treatment of the Republican epithet: Socialism." Whereas in Europe, they suggested, socialism had arisen out of economies of scarcity, "compelling low income groups to seek higher standards principally through a more equal distribution of limited national incomes," American economic growth could serve as the engine of greater social equality without policies of mass redistribution of income. "It is the restrictionist concept of the Republicans which brings socialism about; the expansionist approach which makes it irrelevant."[40] This analysis begged more questions than it answered: how far down the socioeconomic scale did the capacity to access the economy of abundance reach? How far were social questions of equal citizenship in racial and class terms bound up with economic redistribution? And as Crosland wondered during his visit to California, how long would the tentative truce between management and unions over the relationship between productivity and wage and benefit settlements last?

It was in this intellectual and political context that the growth of the Stevenson movement and the rejuvenation of the Democratic Party in California took shape. The rise of the club movement depended in part on a political mood, a growing recognition that the zeitgeist was changing and that the old politics of business as usual was no longer enough to cope with a rapidly changing social fabric. In part, the Stevenson movement reflected the usual organizational and personality rivalries that characterized party politics in California. The head of the club organization in California, Leo Doyle, reported in August that there was "some indication that the usual quarrelling Democratic factions see this Stevenson move as an opportunity to render service to the Stevenson cause and hence gain the proverbial urge for power."[41] One San Francisco Democratic worker, Ben Heineman, was of the opinion that the whole Stevenson club movement there had sprung originally from a party faction opposed to a rival group who had come out for the presidential campaign of Tennessee senator Estes Kefauver.[42] This was a pessimistic, if not totally inaccurate, picture: the club system, however cynical its origins (and Heineman's perspective related only to San Francisco), provided a conduit into Democratic activism for thousands who had thought that the collapse of the Roosevelt and Douglas campaigns two years earlier had killed off their hopes for a new dawn for the California left. Towering figures of the party of the future: the Burton brothers, Willie Brown, Jess Unruh, Alan Cranston, all cut their teeth in the Stevenson battle. And as Willie Brown recalled, in these years before they gained power and became constrained by the compromise and chicanery of office, they were hungry for a social democratic politics around which to organize.[43]

It is important to remember that the 1952 campaign represented a political fresh start; it was not the culmination of a struggle for power among liberals, but a planting of the seed that would take another six years fully to flower. Stevenson's spirited campaign ended in failure. He received a healthy 2,197,548 votes in California, but could not come close to Eisenhower's broad appeal in a state still enamored with those who could cross narrow party lines. Eisenhower's state total was 2,897,310. The Stevenson campaign had enthused many scarred from the bruising experiences of the 1950 campaigns and the rise of a red-baiting politics that threatened to engulf all outside a narrow right-wing consensus in state politics. But much remained to be done if a six-month burst of enthusiasm for a presidential campaign was to turn into something more durable and significant.

There was no doubting the extent of the enthusiasm, nonetheless. Stevenson himself received thousands of letters during and after the campaign from Californians: there are twelve thick folders full of them among his private papers. "Your integrity, your honesty, the firmness of your intellectual grasp, the literary distinction of your speeches, and, most of all, your insistence on *talking sense* and on standing for the same principles everywhere and in all kinds of company, involved me emotionally as well as mentally in your fight and resulted in my associating myself, for the first time in my life, with the Democratic organization in my precinct," wrote a Berkeley professor to Stevenson after his defeat in November.[44] "I'm in mourning for the brains of the American people," wrote a Los Angeles woman. "Because if they're not dead, where *are* they? It grieves me far beyond the point of tears that one of the finest, most sincere men I've ever known—and I think all of us feel we know you—should be defeated, not by logic or reason, but by a fairy tale. . . . I should have done more. I'm ashamed I didn't. I should have gone down to the Stevenson Headquarters and helped. Surely there were things I could have done. Next time, in '56, I *will* do more."[45] A precinct captain in Danville wrote in a similar vein: "The tremendous popular vote you polled with your truthful and inspiring campaign bespeaks the popularity you attained in the last three weeks of three very short months. As captain of the Danville area precinct I want you to know that all the active workers are ready to campaign for you again—anytime. We feel that against any other candidate than General Eisenhower . . . the eloquent campaign you fought would have ended in victory—and will be triumphant once the General's glitter is gone."[46] If this last prediction turned out to be wide of the mark, it was nonetheless true that the contours of California politics would be far more sympathetic to his run for president four years later, and the power of left-of-center networks of activists much more entrenched and obvious.

Political Undercurrents: Race and Sexuality

The Stevenson campaign, the intellectual debate over the future of moderate left politics, and the gradual shift of organized labor fully into the Democratic camp were important reasons why the political center of gravity was shifting slowly leftward in California in the early 1950s. In order to understand the social context in which this was occurring, and to understand the peculiar dynamics in California that made the Golden State part of a political avant garde in terms of a redefinition of the relationship between economic and social citizenship, we need to examine the growing movements for civil rights on the West Coast that did not in themselves directly address definitions of social democracy but that would later shape left politics in the Democratic Party in any case. The campaign for a fair employment practices law in California, and the nascent homophile movement in Los Angeles and San Francisco, both took shape at the same time as the rise of the Democratic Party to political power, and although these phenomena were not always overtly connected, all would intersect several years later to help crystallize the ways in which social democratic ideas would operate when they gained currency in the halls of power in Sacramento.

California's booming economy and rapid population growth were set within the context of endemic and entrenched systems of racial discrimination. Over twelve million people lived in the state in 1953, and another million were expected to arrive by 1955. "Such gains, of course, must be translated into more homes, more stores, more factories, more schools, more hospitals, more prisons, and more facilities of every kind," wrote a contemporary observer in September 1953.[47] Across California, access to homes and employment was not immune from racially motivated pressures. A group of Berkeley law students in the mid-1950s conducted a study of attitudes of local real estate agents, using dummy prospective buyers of different ethnic backgrounds to assess how each would be treated and which available housing they would be shown. "The interviews reveal," noted their report, "for purposes ranging from personal prejudice to feelings of self and group-appointed guardianship of the community, local realtors are actively engaged in perpetuating the separation of the Berkeley area into segregated racial districts."[48] Willie Brown recalled that in San Francisco in the 1950s "I knew that you couldn't get housing. I knew that you couldn't get jobs. . . . The Sunset [district] was considered off-limits. As a matter of fact, there were only two or three communities in which the welcome mat was there. The real estate people would only show in certain areas of San Francisco. You still had to buy through a dummy buyer."[49] The report compiled for Adlai Stevenson's campaign team in 1952 on San Francisco stated that all "past public housing is segregated. The city has one of the worst private housing shortages for minority families." A new public housing development in Diamond Heights was planned that would be open to all, but it would not solve the racial divisions in the city's employment and housing situation. The local NAACP had had to go to court to overturn a housing authority ruling that a new housing project could not rent to African Americans because ethnic uniformity was the "neighborhood pattern."[50] The Yellow Cab Company in the city openly refused to hire African Americans. "Employment and housing are still the main problems which confront Negroes in the Bay Area," wrote the president of the Urban League in 1957.[51] "There are in California about 500,000 Negroes, 800,000 Mexican Americans, 85,000 Japanese Americans, 60,000 Chinese Americans, 400,000 Jews, over 2 million Catholics and a million foreign born," stated a report of the California Committee for Fair Employment Practices in 1955. "There are some employment restrictions against all of these groups in California. The records of the California State Employment Service in Los Angeles three years ago showed that 67.5% of all job orders were discriminatory."[52] Economic development and tacit racism appeared entwined in California life in the 1950s.

As elsewhere in the country, a movement to enact a state fair employment practices law had been gaining momentum after the nation's experience of a national law during World War II and the passage of a landmark state law in New York in 1945. By 1949 seven states had enacted antidiscrimination laws, two of them—Oregon and Washington—on the West Coast.[53] The NAACP had set up its West Coast Regional Office in San Francisco toward the end of the war, and Assemblyman Gus Hawkins had begun to push fair employment in Sacramento during the 1940s. The lobbying campaign was led by East Bay NAACP leaders C. L. Dellums and Tarea Hall Pittman, first through the NAACP itself, and later in the 1950s through the California Committee for Fair Employment Practices. Dellums was also International Vice President of the Brotherhood of Sleeping Car Porters and member of the Alameda County Central Labor Council, as well as the Alameda County Democratic Council. He thus crossed the boundaries between party activism, organized labor, and civil rights movement, and was a central figure in the formation of a statewide organization to lobby for major changes in the relationship between California politics and wider society.[54] The struggle mounted by Dellums and others for legislation to mitigate against discrimination in employment during the 1950s pointed up the growing influence of groups pushing for social change over the political process, but it also demonstrated the fact that the Republican power structure was ill-equipped to deal with the demands of the postwar era, and that a major shift in the balance of power in party politics was imminent. Underlying this political shift was an implicit recognition that the enemies of fair employment were part of a broader attack on state regulation of the economy that by its very nature was both antigovernment and racist. Whether Dellums and his allies liked it or not, their struggle was not merely one of civil rights; it was a basic fight for economic rights as well, meaning that the fair employment movement was participating in the same ideological reading of social democracy as politicians and intellectuals on the California left.

In March 1953 hundreds of Californians, among them Dellums, Pittman, Los Angeles city councilman Edward Roybal, Berkeley assemblyman Byron Rumford, and John Despol of the California CIO, gathered in Sacramento to lobby the legislature to pass fair employment legislation. Angry at the repeated failure of the Republican legislature to act on the proposed legislation, the gathering hoped that a show of solidarity and strength would force the elected representatives to change their perspective: "This session of the legislature has not distinguished itself by any concern for civil liberties," argued a sympathetic piece in the *Los Angeles Daily News*. "Rather, it has gone to the other extreme in an effort to destroy labor unions and check up on the loyalty of public employees, most of whom are conceded to be loyal. The FEPC mobilization may have had the effect, however, of convincing the lawmakers that a large segment of the population is not supine or indifferent to what goes on in the capital. It may stay the hands of the more reactionary solons and lay the groundwork for future legislation of a better kind."[55] Certainly the newly formed lobbying group the California Committee for Fair Employment Practices was keen to relay an optimistic message to its sponsors. Tarea Hall Pittman claimed that the Sacramento mobilization was "very successful. We feel that we have impressed upon members of the Legislature the importance of taking official notice of employment discrimination in California and the need for corrective action."[56]

The Committee for Fair Employment had no choice but to assume that the Republican Party was the cradle of power in California and that all lobbying had to concentrate on persuading its leadership to support the legislation. It was becoming increasingly clear, however, that the Republican establishment was not going to act. Dellums's attempts to take the matter to Washington got a polite brush-off, a representative of the Republican National Committee stating that the feeling there was that it was a "local matter." His attempts to arrange a meeting with Governor Warren in early 1953 failed. His letter in March to California GOP National Committeeman McIntyre Faries smacked of desperation: "As one who wants to see the Republican Party retain its control in 1954, I thought it advisable to seek your help. The last Fair Employment Practices Bill before the California legislature was killed in the committee on a strictly partisan vote. . . . We are very conscious of the fact that this is a Republican state and that this bill can only be put through by the Republicans, and they shall receive full credit for what is done."[57] Unfortunately for the fair employment movement, the issue was a matter of party politics: both Republican senators refused to intervene, and the Committee on Governmental Efficiency and Economy of the State Assembly, in which the FEPC bill was bottled up, was dominated by conservative Republicans, all but two of whom were from wealthy, white districts of Los Angeles. The chairman of the committee, Albert I. Stewart, represented Pasadena, not an area in which FEPC ranked high on his constituents' wish list.[58] All FEPC bills were in fact introduced by Democrats and representatives of organized labor and the NAACP: the principal effort in 1953 was AB 900, introduced by the Assembly's two African American members, Byron Rumford of Berkeley and Augustus Hawkins of Los Angeles. Dellums attempted to get the state and national Republican leadership on board in order to broaden the bill's appeal, claiming that Rumford and Hawkins had sponsored AB 900 "not because they are Democrats but because they are Negroes."[59] The very existence of an antidiscrimination movement in California, with its demand for governmental oversight over employment and economic relationships, unwittingly contributed toward a political polarization that meant party and political ideology would become more interconnected.

The fair employment campaign coincided with a growing effort on the part of business interests and their Republican allies to resist efforts to regulate the private economy in any way. Fair employment as a concept was bound up with bigger themes of economic relationships between employer and employee, between homeowner and prospective buyer, between private individuals and the state. It was simply impossible in the 1950s to disentangle economic and civil rights issues, let alone attempt to argue that party politics did not matter. The State Chamber of Commerce, Associated Farmers, and the Merchants Manufacturing Association of Southern California all spearheaded efforts to kill FEPC, and funded Republican assemblymen who killed it in committee. The California Real Estate Association, which would become an enormously powerful antiregulatory lobby group once Democrats gained power in Sacramento and attempted to prevent discrimination in house sales, understood early on the interrelationship between economic rights and civil rights. In a direct attack on the fair employment movement, an article in the Association's magazine in September 1953 observed that "tricky phrases with favorable meanings and emotional appeals are being used today to imply a distinction between *property* rights and *human* rights. . . . Expressed more accurately, the issue is not one of property rights versus human rights, but of the human rights of one person in the community versus the human rights of another." If government could interfere in private economic relationships on the side of one individual's rights to a job or a home against another's rights to decide how to disburse the fruits of his company's profits or how to sell his private home, what other new human rights would follow? "Now what about the so-called human rights that are represented as superior to property rights? What about the 'right' to a job, the 'right' to a standard of living, the 'right' to a minimum wage or a maximum work week, the 'right' to a 'fair' price, the 'right' to bargain collectively, the 'right' to security against the adversities and hazards of life, such as old age and disability?....These 'human rights' are indeed different from property rights, for they rest on a denial of the basic concept of property rights. They are not freedoms or immunities assured to all persons alike. They are special privileges conferred upon some persons at the expense of others."[60] Whether the proponents of fair employment liked it or not, their efforts for state regulation of employment law would, if successful, have economic consequences that an increasingly self-confident private business community, supported by a powerful public relations machine, was not prepared to tolerate, seeing civil rights predicated upon race as an opening wedge to broader economic redistribution of wealth outside the control of private enterprise.

Historians have recently become sensitive to the ways in which economic development became more contested terrain in the postwar years, as business public relations firms and representatives of organized labor and the New and Fair Deals vied for political supremacy using contrasting notions of freedom and individualism as tools in their rhetorical and political strategies.[61] It was becoming increasingly clear to civil rights advocates in California during the 1950s that their fight for housing and employment rights was becoming bound up in this wider struggle. It was not just the fact that Republican legislators repeatedly voted against the bill, though its repeated failure, most frustratingly in 1955 when it passed the Assembly but failed in the State Senate, was due almost entirely to Republican right-wingers from Southern California. One Santa Barbara Republican claimed citizens could not "be partially tolerant any more than they can be partially pregnant," a reference to the claims by FEPC proponents that the bill would not force anyone to give jobs or housing to particular people, demonstrating the inextricable link between the debate over economic freedom and that over civil rights.[62]

There was also the fact that the Cold War put at the center of political debate contested notions of freedom and democracy that created a more antagonistic relationship between left and right around the twin themes of free enterprise and race. The CIO in its October 1951 newsletter noted that "our national security demands all-out production of defense materials and the use of all the available manpower. But discriminatory employment practices are preventing the full utilization of our manpower resources, impeding our productive capacity, and providing ammunition for the Communists' propaganda campaign about the failures of democracy. . . . Negro chemists are still working as laborers and Negro stenographers serving as maids. . . . .We cannot aspire to world leadership in world affairs so long as we make mockery of our high-sounding talk about justice and democracy by practices of discrimination which destroy the dignity and deny the rights of millions of our fellow citizens."[63] By contrast, a new right-wing organization based in Southern California in the same year stated in its articles of incorporation that its aim, in addition to the outlawing of communism in the United States, was to "prepare and propose constitutional amendments and legislative enactments for the restoration of democratic liberties and property rights" and to "formulate, develop, and promote public interest and education in basic democratic principles, civil rights, and property rights." Those associated with this organization, known as America Plus (P for Property, L for Liberty, U for Unity, S for Strength), included state senator Jack Tenney and notorious far-right figure Aldrich Blake, who had led the fight against the recall of Los Angeles city councilman Meade McClanahan for his overt support for Fascist Gerald L. K. Smith during the war. Blake had authored *My Kind! My Country!* in 1950, a propaganda novel set in a dystopian future in which a new state of "Negroland" had been established in the United States. Its principal target was an economic and civil rights movement "officered by stooges of the Soviet Union . . . skillfully recruited from the ranks of those worst off in the social scale . . . from those among the rich and the intellectual who revel in striking a pose and in seeming to be out of the ordinary; from the emotionally upset and frustrated, including many members of the so-called minority groups," all of whose "compassion for the unfortunate has inspired them to believe falsely that the remedy lies in unlimited handouts and controls by the State."[64] Just as the Fair Employment movement was gaining strength in the 1950s, so was a popular right movement in southern California that welded together issues of private property rights, the Cold War, and racial prejudice in a manner that would have a major impact on both political debate and party political activity by the end of the decade.[65] As we shall see, Democratic party politics in the 1950s turned on the question of economic citizenship in a state in which the established channels of political patronage were being closed off, allowing the party to harness forces for economic and social change that were demanding greater representation.

When Harry Hay, Bob Hull, and Chuck Rowland first met in Los Angeles in 1950 to discuss the potential formation of a new organization to promote understanding of homosexuality, something other than their sexuality united them. All three had been members of the Communist Party.[66] By the early 1950s Marxism to these former party members was a God that had failed, and a combination of McCarthyism and a growing realization that individual sexual freedom was incompatible with communist doctrine helped men like Hay shake off any vestiges of fellow traveler status from Mattachine. Anyone who "espouses political philosophies which abrogate basic rights of the individual as set forth in the Constitution of the United States will hardly find the principles of social and moral responsibility as set forth in the aims and principles of the Society to his purpose," the committee assured Mattachine's current and potential membership in 1954.[67] Much of the new organization's early publicity material avoided discussion of ideology or political partisanship lest it become tainted by association with communism at an inopportune time. "Politically, the Mattachine Society is strictly nonpartisan," one statement read. "It espouses no 'isms' except Americanism, for it realizes that such a program is possible only in a free nation such as the United States."

In addition to the fear of political persecution homophile activists harbored at a time of McCarthyite purges of suspected gay men from public service in the early 1950s, they also faced more mundane problems of political identification that stemmed from their lack of a coherent ideological worldview into which their sexuality could fit.[68] British-born author Christopher Isherwood, who during the war had settled in Los Angeles and become a key figure in the city's gay demi-monde in these years, later recalled that by the time of his emigration to the United States he had "lost my political faith—I couldn't repeat the left-wing slogans which I had been repeating throughout the last few years. It wasn't that I had lost *all* belief in what the slogans stood for, but I was no longer wholehearted. My leftism was confused by an increasingly aggressive awareness of myself as a homosexual and by a newly made discovery that I was a pacifist. Both these individualistic minority-attitudes kept bringing me into conflict with the leftist majority-ideology."[69] When a Los Angeles journalist in December 1953 wondered openly about the political intent of the new fledgling group in his newspaper column, the reply was forthright: "There is no political aim of the Mattachine Foundation Inc. other than to fight for the rights of man. IT IS DEFINITELY AND ABSOLUTELY NON-PARTISAN. . . . They are concerned with the problems of the homosexual and only that!"[70] These "problems" for the Mattachine Society of the 1950s concerned the rights of individuals to conduct their private affairs as they wished without unwarranted legal impediment and the education of wider society to accommodate sexual difference. Chuck Rowland went as far as to say that "it was *society* which created our culture by excluding us," suggesting that the extent of political engagement on the part of early Mattachine members was to gain unrestricted entry to existing social structures, not to change those structures as any socialist would advocate. As the slogan of the 1954 convention put it: "evolution, not revolution."[71]

As the gay rights movement grew and evolved it was clear that the membership's analysis of social exclusion was predicated upon something more than just individualism, and that they faced internal pressure to take an interest in mainstream politics. To Rowland, political activism, a belonging to a concrete organization of people determined to advance the cause of social acceptance of gay men and women, provided "a pride in participating in the cultural growth and social achievements of my people, the homosexual minority." In this he claimed kinship with those advocating civil rights for different racial groups, trying to open avenues of employment and housing to all without discrimination. The Society's magazine, *Mattachine Review*, was launched in 1954 to promote "permanent advances in integration, education, understanding, civil rights, elimination of unfair practices and discrimination, and abolishment of false ideas about human sexuality."[72] Even in its very early days the founders of the organization recognized that theirs was a lobbying group with political goals, however muted and tentative they may be: "Once it has been conclusively demonstrated that variants can be unified in their own behalf, and when the time is agreed to be right for such a move," they asserted, "it is considered imperative for the Society to move into the realm of political action to erase from the law books discriminatory legislation presently directed against the sexual variant minority."[73] At the Society's 1954 convention in San Francisco the chair of the newly established legislative committee noted that no legislation of use to gay Californians had been passed in the Republican legislature, and that 1954 was an election year: "The chief factor here is the exercise of every American's basic franchise—that of voting. . . . THIS NEED FOR US TO ASSUME THIS RESPONSIBILITY OF AMERICAN CITIZENSHIP CANNOT BE OVERSTRESSED, FOR UNLESS WE VOTE, WE AS INDIVIDUALS AND AS AN ORGANIZATION HAVE NO REAL RIGHT TO CRITICIZE OFFICIALS AND THE LAWS THEY ENACT."[74]

The involvement of Mattachine in electoral politics began with the organization's creation, when the committee sent various candidates for office in Los Angeles a questionnaire soliciting their opinions on the question of making material on homosexuality available in schools. The accompanying letter attempted to demonstrate the potential electoral power of gay Angelenos, suggesting that if even only "a conservative percentage of Dr. Alfred Kinsey's testimony before the 1951 California State Legislature's Interim Committee is conceded, there are at least 150,000 such persons in the Los Angeles area alone."[75] *LA Mirror* journalist Paul Coates saw as early as December 1953 that gay rights activism had the capacity to shape the way in which political parties conceptualized social change in the postwar age. Pointing to the forthcoming midterm elections in California, Coates observed the Mattachine questionnaire gambit, describing it as a "broadside from a strange new pressure group. An organization that claims to represent the homosexual voters of Los Angeles is vigorously shopping for campaign promises." Mattachine, he noted, "pointedly hints it has the potential support of 150,000 to 200,000 homosexuals in this area."[76] It would be some time before homophile politics gained general recognition in mainstream political debate in California, and throughout the 1950s a system of legalized repression of gay bars and political meetings relating to homophile activism kept sexuality out of the political lexicon of all elected politicians. Yet Coates was right to perceive the potential for gay rights to gain electoral traction at the same time as it struck a chord with a political class developing a new program for gaining and maintaining power in the 1950s and 1960s.

The language of rights deployed by both the racial and sexual equality movements contained similar cadences and perspectives to the intellectual debate that underpinned the Stevenson campaign in California. The development of civil rights organizations set up as lobby groups to press for political rights and representation in the halls of power mirrored the establishment of clubs and societies based around the advancement of the Democratic Party in California, a state in which the terms of political debate had been set in particularly narrow terms and in which existing channels of legislative action had proved to be inadequate when questions of civil rights came into play. The years between 1952 and 1958 would see the rapid rise not only of the Democratic Party in California politics, but also a concomitant rise of the influence of grassroots political organizations that would play a role in dramatically reshaping the ideological agenda of Democratic liberalism in the second half of the twentieth century.

CHAPTER 4

A Democratic Order

The aftermath of Stevenson's defeat witnessed a dizzying period of political organizing and intellectual soul-searching among those wishing to use the still enfeebled Democratic Party as a vehicle for major social reform in California. Exhilarated from their experience in Stevenson clubs and on the campaign trail, his supporters on the West Coast had learned valuable lessons. The party still lacked both organizational and ideological discipline, and still did not have the machinery in place to ensure candidates on the ticket shared at least some political kinship beyond the party label. Politics at the national level had been reshaped during the New Deal and World War II to create a new "democratic order" that would set the parameters of socioeconomic relationships for decades to come.[1] California had not shared in this landmark shift in the political zeitgeist, at least not in party political terms. "As Democrats," remarked Attorney General Pat Brown to the Western Conference of Democratic Party leaders in October 1951 in Los Angeles, "you will obviously not feel that you are in an alien land—for out of our total voting registrations, there are over 3 million Democrats and approximately 2 million Republicans. In connection with this, I must yield to the temptation and say that our outlandish system of cross-filing many times has bewitched these figures I have just given into senseless impotence." Brown, the sole Democratic winner for statewide office in 1950, made the point that as the New Deal and its aftermath had injected a more obvious ideological cleavage into national party politics, it was imperative that California experience this debate if it was to benefit from the improvements in labor relations, welfare provision, and race relations that Democratic power elsewhere was helping to bring about. "The structural arch, as we know, of the Democratic Party is to devote itself to lessening the burdens which are imposed by these human needs. The Democratic Party does this in no patronizing sense. We are not a party superimposed upon our people. We are not a paternal party. We are the people."[2]

A growing number of activist Democrats wanted to get that message across to the electorate, a task made more achievable now that the California ballot would specify party affiliation. As many observed, it was not just that Stevenson and many other Democrats had lost in 1952: a large percentage of eligible voters did not cast their ballots. Approximately 4.5 million Californians cast their vote for U.S. senator in 1952, a turnout of not much more than 50 percent in an election in which there was no Democratic candidate. Although the 1951 census suggested that registered Democrats outnumbered Republicans by a substantial margin, fewer than 200,000 votes separated the number voting in each party primary in 1952, suggesting that a significant number of registered Democrats did not vote at all.[3] To Democrats like Brown, the party needed to configure and articulate a message for the age that would enliven political debate and make party politics important to Californians. "I think that we can make the most of this defeat by some concerted self-examination," read a statement written by one of Brown's key speechwriters as Brown prepared to attend a gathering of liberal activists in January 1953 that would change the political landscape of the state for the rest of the century. "I think that when the Democratic Party re-establishes itself in power again . . . it will be because it has developed *new, audacious, humane, and constructive* plans. . . . We supplied [Stevenson] with little more than a program which we had pulled from only the successful *past* record of the Democratic Party. . . . We did not, unfortunately, have a *new look* for our New Deal."[4] The mid-1950s saw the growth of organizational discipline and ideological debate within the party that would thrash out what form this new look would take. Furthermore, as the ferment of McCarthyism died down, California liberals appalled by the vicious attacks on standard bearers like Helen Douglas felt confident challenging the assumptions of Cold War anticommunism. They articulated a political vision that emphasized domestic socioeconomic reform and exhibited skepticism of a foreign policy that drowned out the language of social democracy in its rush to condemn Soviet totalitarianism.

The Creation of the California Democratic Council and the Emergence of Grassroots Activism

An atmosphere of excitement and anticipation filled the conference hall as hundreds of left-leaning activists, fresh from the 1952 campaign, met to work out where to go from their recent defeat. The meeting, held in Asilomar, near Monterey, in January 1953, was advertised as a forum where party activists could reflect on the lessons of the 1952 electoral disaster and decide how best to enthuse voters into going to the polls and voting Democratic. The conference program was entitled "How to End the Republican Stranglehold in California," and laid out a blueprint for a new organization, the California Democratic Council, which would mobilize members behind a specific candidate in party primaries to prevent damaging free-for-alls in contests for public office. In the final report of the meeting liberal congressman George Miller, Jr., argued that the "test of a political party" should be its capacity to "rally the people to the ideals and principles for which it stands," implying that a measure of ideological conformity was necessary in a socially diverse state like California. "We must," he wrote, "at the very outset give up all thought of simply standing on the record of the Democratic Party. Since 1940, that record, at least in domestic affairs, has been rather thin. The social gains of the 1930s are only a starting point. We must develop a new program, agree upon it, and as one voice speak out for it—in the national legislature, in the state legislature, and, indeed, in every part of California."[5]

The delegates consisted of an impressive cross-section of the party membership, from elected office holders like George Miller and Pat Brown to party grandees such as State Committeeman Roger Kent to neophyte campaigners like Phil Burton and Alan Cranston. The assembled throng also represented a cross-section of society. Burton was a scruffy city boy from San Francisco who never owned his own home and who had little time for the niceties of San Francisco society. "He didn't own any place to live," recalled political ally Willie Brown. "Maybe he had one or two suits and didn't care about those kind of things."[6] Cranston and Kent, on the other hand, were representatives of a Bay Area moneyed aristocracy that dominated the social world of Marin and the Lower Peninsula. Cranston, the first chairman of California Democratic Council (CDC) who would play a crucial role in developing an ideological conscience for the party, had grown up in a wealthy Palo Alto family and had been a journalist watching the approach of war in Europe before working for the Office of War Information during the war. A champion sprinter, he embodied the easy charm and political enthusiasm that a privileged background conferred. Kent was a household name in Marin County: his father had been a prominent progressive Republican in the Hiram Johnson era, and the family home at Kentfield was a well-known landmark in a neighborhood where discreet but obvious wealth was hardly unusual. As he later recalled, Democrats in staunch

Republican Marin were a rare but dedicated bunch as "they had to be pretty tough to survive, and they had to be pretty dedicated. I think this is a pattern that you'd see in other parts of the country, where an affluent—and oftentimes, it's a campus-type group, this not being one of those—community will generate very strong Democratic leadership. This may be because they have time enough or money enough to do some work that the poor working man would love to do if he were able to."[7]

Delegates from Southern California represented the same powerful mixture of labor Democrats from blue collar Los Angeles suburbs and wealthy suburban activists. Steve Zetterberg, who had taken on Nixon in his congressional district in 1948 and who was a major player in Democratic politics in Claremont and Pomona, represented the type of well-connected suburban professional who would form the backbone of CDC and shape left-of-center activism in the 1950s and 1960s. The Asilomar meeting, he recalled "was just bubbling over with excitement and interest and application of a lot of people to the Democratic issues. By issues, I mean not issue-issues but also program, finance, and so on. It was not just all in one big auditorium. It was a lot of separate meetings where there was a lot of participation."[8] From the same district came Carmen Warschaw, an uncompromising, straight-talking party strategist and leader who would later run for the chair of the state party and who was one of the most important women in California Democratic politics. She was no idealist neophyte, having formed a Democratic organization in Los Feliz in the 1940s, worked on Jerry Voorhis's campaigns, and who would play a key role in getting people like Jesse Unruh, the future speaker, elected to the Assembly. "We all were in Asilomar at that time," she later remembered.[9] James Q. Wilson in his 1966 study of club politics stressed the middle class, privileged background of CDC activists: "Over half were under 40 years of age, over 60% had a college education or better, most were in professional occupations, and practically no one was Catholic while nearly half were Jewish in their religious background." He emphasized the change in style of California politics that club activism would bring, bringing a greater emphasis on fighting for principle than power and a heightened sense of amateur activism over precinct organization. The Asilomar meeting, however, demonstrated that CDC, at least in its early days, was a mixture of party regulars and new activists, of working class and middle class, and that the mixture of idealism and the practicalities of gaining power defined how party politics worked in California.[10]

The Asilomar meeting produced universal agreement on two things: the need to put the power of a new organization behind endorsed Democratic candidates so that the party could gain power in Sacramento and abolish cross-filing, and the need to swing public opinion behind Democratic candidates through the development of a program of political action. Individual clubs would be formed and chartered across the state, which would solicit members in the neighborhoods and fight for endorsed Democratic candidates in each election cycle. These endorsements would be furnished at annual CDC conventions attended by delegates from every club, and endorsed candidates would gain the CDC's official seal of approval through their embrace of approved CDC ideological stances on key issues of the day. The final report of the Asilomar conference contained resolutions from all the various workshops on different aspects of public policy, including labor resolutions opposing Taft-Hartley and right-to-work initiatives and supporting FEPC. Interestingly, the labor committee had also concluded that since World War II "it has been recognized more and more that the average citizen has a right to adequate medical care. Although many health plans exist today most of them are of a piecemeal variety, and they fail to give complete protection. The committee therefore recommends that Democratic legislators introduce health insurance legislation which provides for complete medical coverage for a fixed fee, to be operated by private persons or by a public agency."[11] The Asilomar workshop acted as a testing ground for policy formation that would provide a political purpose for a Democratic Party struggling to establish a purpose in a difficult political climate.

In early 1954 the newly formed California Democratic Council held the first of its annual conventions, intended to shape the party's political agenda and to endorse candidates for public office who would be committed to that agenda. One delegate to the first convention, held in Fresno, wrote to CDC chairman Alan Cranston that he thought it "a remarkable demonstration of democracy at work." He felt that the attempt to use a gathering of the party faithful to advance a political program usefully mirrored the system of party conferences in countries like the United Kingdom. "In Great Britain," argued Joseph Harris, "both of the major parties hold annual conferences that last for a week or more. These conferences are devoted to a discussion of public issues, election of party offices, and various other social events. . . . The platform and program of the party are hammered into shape without the disturbing element of selecting candidates."[12] Another enthusiastic supporter of the new organization, Dewey Anderson, wrote Cranston that there could "be no victory for the Democratic Party in California in 1954, nor for that matter in any future year, unless its candidates . . . are true-blue liberals standing on a platform that reaches to the heart of the economic and social problems which the government must tackle and solve if we are to experience prosperity and growth. . . . No compromising with expediency, no attempts to look as conservative as possible, will wean away from the reactionary Republicans their supporters or appeal to the silent and unorganized mass of voters whose ballots are so often decisive." He appealed for the espousal at Fresno of "our common faith in a program intended to promote the welfare of the broadest possible body of our citizens."[13] The Fresno convention offered its support only to candidates who supported the CDC platform and who ran on the Democratic ticket, eschewing cross-filing deals with the Republicans.

By November 1954 party candidates could benefit from the active political and fundraising support of 425 local Democratic clubs with some 30,000 members, and there were congressional district councils affiliated to the statewide CDC in twenty-four of the thirty congressional districts. "What has happened is not a mere growth or development of the Party but its complete rebirth," wrote two observers of CDC in 1955. "Although the NEW Democratic Party is still young, it has all the potentialities necessary to make it an integrated, coordinated, disciplined, and more efficient party than it has been in a generation." The local club movement would make members "FEEL like Democrats, just as the addition of party labels made them VOTE like Democrats."[14] Creating a bond between an identifiable social base—labor unions, the unorganized poor, committed liberal activists, Democratic Party loyalists—and a major political party in California would be predicated on an ideological program that would make party politics relevant to wider society. The Issues Committee of the CDC made annual statements of policy that could be used in election campaigns, such as the 1959 statement that "the essential problem of the American economy today is to provide full employment and a more equitable distribution of the benefits of our productivity . . . without regard to a dependence upon a military economy."[15]

The CDC and its affiliates remained forever divided over the extent to which ideological commitment could flourish at the same time as organizational discipline. For the fact was that the new group was created as much to establish an organizational structure for a previously chaotic and undisciplined party as it was to breathe new ideas into the heir apparent to the New Deal. A revitalized party apparatus would help elect more Democrats to the state legislature, but this did not necessarily entail a damascene conversion to European-style social democracy. Merely getting a majority in the legislature before 1960 would allow the Democrats to control the redistricting process, redrawing constituency boundaries so as to ensure further Democratic gains. In his speech announcing that he was stepping down as CDC chairman in 1957, Alan Cranston warned that party activists "must see to it that in our zeal to have certain ideas pushed we do not push so far and so fast that we make it impossible to elect candidates who could carry out those ideas if elected. After all, we cannot achieve what we are after by resolutions, we will achieve it by winning elections." CDC convention resolutions, he argued, needed to be drafted so as to allow candidates in tough election fights to campaign "without being defensive," a clear reference to the antiliberal legacy of the anticommunist witch hunts and the climate of fear spawned by the Cold War.[16] Forming a united front in elections tended to blur the party's ideological focus, as CDC attempted to win over skeptical party regulars and labor bosses to the new strategy of mobilizing the grassroots. Cranston replied soothingly to Chet Holifield's criticism that CDC and the club movement had "created needlessly an unofficial superstructure which conflicts, confuses and dissipates our political energy in a multitude of meetings and activities." Cranston replied in October 1955 that the formation of the CDC was an idea "frankly copied" from the GOP equivalent, Republican Assembly, formed in the 1930s to circumvent the state law that proscribed official party committees from endorsing candidates in primaries. The new politics of the 1950s, far from heralding a new dawn of ideologically driven infighting, was "designed to end the habit of rival Democratic candidates killing each other off in the primary, while the single endorsed Republican candidates almost invariably won our primary as well as theirs. . . . The most casual glance at the primary returns shows that where clubs and councils made endorsements and backed the endorsements effectively, Democratic candidates ran well."[17]

Democratic State Central Committee Chairman Roger Kent had to mediate between the club movement and the AFL-CIO after the latter's George O'Brien wrote a letter in 1957 stating that a "state of war" existed between the unions and the local clubs over who controlled Democratic policymaking. "The letter indicated that our party's muscle in money and manpower came almost exclusively from organized labor," wrote Kent. "Such a position was much more accurate a few years ago than it is today," he continued, implying that no single interest group had a monopoly on party decision-making. New CDC president Tom Carvey wrote in 1961 that although an important aim of the organization was to engender "broader, grass roots participation in the party," the "overriding objective" of CDC in its early years had been "simply stated, to 'win.' This objective could, of course, be understood and applied with varying degrees of sophistication. Some wanted just to win, others wanted to win for certain principles and ideals, others wanted to win in the right way, and so on."[18] Carmen Warschaw as a party regular who believed in the mechanics of power more than ideological posturing quickly saw the potential for tension between CDC and the state party: "CDC was a great idea," she later argued, "it was just that some of the leadership ruined it. Because it originally started to get candidates through the primary so that the cross-filing wouldn't kill off Democratic candidates. And in searching for a new goal they kind of lost their way. . . . You can't do anything until you win in our political system."[19] In a state as politically and socially diverse as California, it was difficult to make a clear link between political mobilization and commitment to a coherent policy agenda.

Nevertheless, the commitment of a dedicated cadre of Democratic Party workers to expanding their electoral base effectively shifted the balance of power within the party leftward, and married the development of a grassroots organization to a political program that demanded an expansion of the parameters of New Deal welfare. Alan Cranston noted that for the first time the local club movement in California's communities had "given so many men and women a place in the party, a voice in its affairs. And these thousands upon thousands of Democrats have brought new vitality and vigor to our party." In 1958, the year of the party's sweeping electoral victories at both the state and federal levels, the Democrats enjoyed the support of 57 percent of all registered voters, including independents as well as Republicans, but, crucially, 72 percent of new registrants termed themselves Democrats. By 1964 Cranston was able to base his primary campaign for the Senate on "the waging of a new, dynamic drive against poverty" that would transcend the politics of the New and Fair Deal era: "The New Deal now lies in the dim past. So does the Fair Deal. Together, we crossed the New Frontier with John Kennedy. Now, we are called upon to climb ever higher, toward new horizons."[20] An in-depth look at how these clubs operated helps to clarify how they managed to transform the California political landscape so dramatically, and the ways in which their formation changed the parameters of political debate in the 1950s.

Club Politics in the 1950s

Democratic clubs were not new in 1953. There had been several attempts in the 1940s to rejuvenate the party through the establishment of local activist organizations, and some counties, notably Alameda, did have a local club organization, established in 1949 and strengthened by strong local African American leadership in the form of Assemblyman Byron Rumford and NAACP and labor activists C. L. Dellums and Tarea Pittman. The Alameda Council's by-laws stated that the principal purpose of the organization was to "establish and maintain continuous machinery for participation in the formulation and implementation of Democratic Party policy and for the development, training and election to public office of Democrats who will carry out party policy."[21] In Los Angeles there existed a Democratic luncheon club that invited prominent national Democrats to give talks as a way of mobilizing public interest in party politics, and this group had played an important role in stoking enthusiasm for Stevenson in 1952. Its principal organizer, Steve Zetterberg, wrote one of Stevenson's aides in August 1952 that "we are the only regularly meeting Democratic forum in Los Angeles and we afford a platform for visiting Democrats. This year our speakers have included T. V. Smith, Oscar Ewing, and Senator Kerr."[22] In 1949 attempts were made to establish a California Democratic Assembly, modeled on the Republican equivalent as a vehicle for the endorsement and promotion of candidates without falling foul of the state's electoral laws. A group of party regulars, including Pat McDonough, San Francisco strongman Bill Malone, Ed Heller, and San Jose congressman John McEnery met in September to try to hammer out a group that would "work within the realm of the regular legally established party organization." McDonough correctly predicted the problem with insisting on acting through established party grandees, a course he took principally because he had become so disenchanted with the reform forces of Jimmy Roosevelt and Helen Douglas: "those in temporary power in the State organization do not want any kind of an organization other than that which they happen to be principal officers. . . . many leaders cannot brook competition and survive because of lack of organization." The proposed Democratic Assembly never got off the ground.[23]

These efforts at party organization reflected weaknesses that did not afflict the later Democratic renaissance of the mid-1950s to anything like the same extent. The examples described above were not representative of the state as a whole, much of which did not witness attempts at greater grassroots organizing until the 1950s. Prior to 1953 all attempts at breathing life into the party came from regular party functionaries, and they mostly failed to extend the reach of political involvement beyond those already committed to the party in any case. Some key figures in the party in the late 1940s, such as Byron Rumford in Berkeley or Bill Malone in San Francisco, would actually display hostility toward the big expansion in activist politics in the 1950s because they headed solid local organizations of their own and were not necessarily bothered about extending them; these political leaders knew how to work the corridors of power, including making deals with the GOP, and ends to them were more important than means. Roger Kent painted Rumford as someone who had got where he needed to go by getting to the Assembly in 1948 and who thereafter took his political position for granted: "he just about ran the CDC and the county committee people out of his district. He said, 'Get out of here! This is *my* district! I don't want any registration effort in here!' "[24] The most important distinction of all between established channels of political patronage and the California Democratic Council after 1953 was ideological: all efforts to strengthen the party prior to 1953 centered on matters of organization, of getting all Democrats to work together, whereas CDC had an ideological agenda and was prepared only to work for people who espoused a political worldview the membership endorsed. Not everyone found this new emphasis on program a positive development, but the case studies that follow show that a thrashing out of ideological principles in different settings across the state developed the necessary enthusiasm for Democratic politics, as well as the necessary program of political principles that pulled people together at election time, necessary if the Democrats were to overturn decades of Republican power. The social, as well as political, bonding that the club movement engendered also helped bridge the divide between "high" politics and society in ways that would change the social complexion of California dramatically once the Democrats gained power at the end of the decade.

The headquarters of the California Democratic Council shared office space with the regular state party organization in San Francisco, highlighting the blurred boundaries between the party and the ostensibly separate CDC in parts of the state where the two got along. Roger Kent described the scene he found when he took charge of the state committee in 1954: "We had a walkup on Market Street as an office. One lame-brained girl in there with a broken finger [laughs] was typing." He put up his own cash to pay the rent on new offices at 212 Sutter Street and then held a hundred-dollar dinner to raise funds: "we got two hundred people to come out at a hundred dollars each! That was the first time that they ever had hundred-dollar dinners in San Francisco. Then we moved on out to that big building next to the Civic Center. We had one-dollar and five-dollar and ten-dollar seats for seeing Stevenson to speak. It was just absolutely jammed! The fire marshal closed the door five times. . . . It was great, we made a lot." The 212 Sutter operation was shared between the party members answering to Kent and CDC, headed by Cranston. The "212 gang" consisted of Kent, Cranston, their secretary, Leonore Ostrow, chief of staff Don Bradley, and Jane Morrison as chair of the Women's Division of the Northern California party, among others. They had a network of friends and supporters, including State Senator George Miller and future liberal Assemblymen Joe Rattigan of Marin and Nick Petris of Alameda. "Usually," Kent recalled, "if people stayed until seven o'clock, we would give them a drink before they went home. There would be work going on there of one kind or another at all times, party work. And . . . it was the office not only of the party but of CDC. We had the closest relationship with CDC. . . . If you walked in that office and there was a project going, you wouldn't know who was a party person and who was CDC. We were all friends, and we just did what had to be done."[25] Kent's operation was based on the principle that established systems of party organization and patronage had failed, and his new strategy required as many volunteer workers as possible, bound together by a common political cause. He reported to a Democratic club meeting in San Francisco after two years of the 212 Sutter operation that it was "strictly amateur and the glue that holds it together is only a common interest in the selection and election of honorable qualified candidates. There are no ward-heelers who do favors for people, then trot them out to vote, and there aren't any jobs to pass out if we win. In other words, you can't 'buy' votes in California even if you wanted to, and the 'organization' which we have achieved is laughable in terms of Eastern machines. . . . Any influence which we might have on the ordinary voters of California is based purely and simply on the art of persuasion."[26]

The art of persuasion required a manifesto as an instrument with which to persuade. The drawing up of the constitutions of the various CDC clubs gives clues to the general direction these programs might take. The Democratic Club of Claremont in the rapidly growing Southland drew up a constitution that contained the following statement: "In order to promote the principles and activism of the Democratic Party, and to provide for all people the highest degree of justice and social welfare, we associate ourselves together to establish the Democratic Club of Claremont." Club chairman Steve Zetterberg succeeded in replacing the second clause with "to stimulate an active interest in public affairs," seemingly because the statement as originally written suggested that the club itself would be the agent of justice and social welfare, whereas in truth clubs existed to get public opinion behind party candidates who would then make policy in the state legislature.[27] Nonetheless, the statement of intent differed in tone and emphasis from previous Democratic Party statements like that of the Alameda club of 1949, which pledged merely to support the party. The new emphasis was on supporting a political stance—social justice—and on supporting the Democratic Party in so far as it was the agent of that political worldview. The West Beverly Club in the Fairfax area of west LA, one of the most active and successful in the state, had its own political action chairman who organized get-out-the-vote campaigns, brought in political speakers to address the club, and made it the mission of the organization to "help elect the type of candidates that believe in the same things we do."[28] Issues that united these activist volunteers included bitter opposition to the House Un-American Activities Committee, support for organized labor, support for universal health insurance and an expanded welfare state, and civil rights.

The West Beverly Club is a good example of a group of activists who were helping to inject a specifically left-wing political disposition into Los Angeles Democratic Party politics in the 1950s that mixed elements of economic and social justice in a discourse that fitted with the times. The club movement in prosperous neighborhoods aimed to mobilize local activists to rejuvenate Democratic Party activity in districts the Republicans had come to dominate almost by default. Local club leaders compiled mailing lists obtained not just from voter registration forms, which included only those already on the rolls, but also from inoculation data garnered from polio and tetanus booster sessions held at the local club headquarters partially as a means of effectively mapping the district. They then wrote to local residents encouraging them to become involved in the club movement and to donate money to it. "We shall be honest," confessed president of the West Beverly Democratic Club John Lear in a form letter to potential voters and activists in 1959. "Your name was taken from the card filled out when you had your polio shot at our headquarters on October 27th. We are proud and happy to sponsor these clinics since we feel this is another responsibility to our community. But, after all, we are a Democratic Club, and as such, we must strengthen ourself for next year's presidential election. We are therefore conducting a membership drive pointed at young people who live in our immediate neighborhood and who can assist us in obtaining 'Victory in '60'." Since its creation in 1952 the West Beverly club had established a permanent headquarters, holding monthly meetings "at which time varied programs are presented. . . . We also have theater parties, dinners and outdoor social events during the summer, some of which double as fundraising events. . . . We repeat that we need active people to help us get out the vote and to do all the other important jobs during election campaigns."[29] The club mobilized support through the use of community-minded initiatives, but also needed a political rationale with which to engender commitment to the organization, thus the vague reference in John Lear's letter to "varied programs" that could form the basis of their meetings.

The issues and ideas that underlay the club's monthly meetings included a commitment to a welfare state and employment opportunities to the underprivileged, but they also represented wider issues of social inclusion and identity politics that would appeal to the more affluent constituency in the West Beverly-Fairfax area of Los Angeles. Clubs like that of West Beverly did not necessarily need to deliver local victories to Democrats: in November 1958 local representative James Roosevelt gained 83 percent of the vote in the district and governor-elect Pat Brown won 79.8 percent.[30] Local club leaders like PAC chairman Saul Reider saw their role as one of delivering large turnouts of Democrats to help maximize statewide Democratic margins. They also sought to develop a political agenda locally that would both influence state-level Democratic policy and create a network of local committed activists and fundraisers who would propel the state party to further victories. The West Beverly-Westside Democratic network launched the political careers of a number of Democratic politicians who came to national prominence as congressmen who would maintain the party's links with reform politics in the lean years of the late 1970s, 1980s, and 1990s: Henry Waxman, Anthony Beilenson, Howard Berman. It also helped create a political reform coalition that would end the rule of conservative Democratic mayor Sam Yorty and elect the city's first African American as mayor of what was soon to become America's second largest city.[31] By the end of the fifties the West Beverly Club was one of several hundred local organizations with a well-organized membership and a budget of hundreds of dollars a year with which to run registration drives, social events and political meetings.[32]

"After years of eclipse in California," announced the March 1959 issue of the *West Beverly Bray*, newsletter of the West Beverly Democratic Club, "the Democratic Party surged to victory in 1958 because of the well cared for seeds which had been planted in the Club movement earlier. The Democratic Party returned to its grass roots, and its grass roots returned it to power."[33] But what were the issues mobilizing the grassroots in a middle class Jewish Los Angeles neighborhood? An important issue was simply the need for Westside activists to control the policy levers of the state Democratic Party: "To the extent that you fail to participate in a party, you are responsible for the imperfections in our party system," warned the state's Young Democrats in a newsletter in the early 1960s. In a sense this adherence to the two-party system neutered the ideological unity of Los Angeles liberals: the newsletter went on to say that liberalism to Young Democrats entailed "positive government action and energetic government. This basic philosophy of the Democratic Party has largely freed our Party from blind adherence to dogma and rigid programs."[34] Perhaps, though, a more sophisticated reading of the political development of California Democrats in the 1950s and 1960s would be that local organizing allowed for the development of a range of mobilizing issues that could appeal to the particular social setting in which the local activists were working, all of which could be understood as emerging from the mainspring of Western social democracy.

At the same time California liberals increasingly saw the Cold War as a distraction from the ongoing battle for social justice at home and abroad. In February 1959 the West Beverly club meeting heard three supporters of Fidel Castro's revolutionary movement discuss his recent ascent to power in Cuba. Israel Tapanes was a member of Castro's army, while Victor Lazano had been arrested in nearby Lynwood for producing machine guns for export to Castro's rebels. The following year a memorandum circulated in the local congressional district party offices was entitled "Cuba as an Issue in the Campaigns," and contained several pages of material sympathetic to the Castro rebels.[35] In early 1963 the *Bray* carried a scathing attack on "the powerful military-industrial complex that has a stranglehold on our government and our economy" as "a monstrous Frankenstein which may in the end destroy us." The March 1964 CDC convention voted to make U.S. policy in Latin America one of the four topics for discussion at the 1965 CDC issues conference, in addition to "automation and jobs, taxation, [and] social welfare," all of which was reported enthusiastically to the West Beverly club.[36] The emergence of a middle class leftist element in California politics mirrored the growth of new left activism in universities and fringe parties, with the important difference that local Democratic clubs were working to shift the center of gravity of mainstream party politics to the left to achieve concrete legislative results.

The club movement thrived in the late 1950s partly because it reflected the attraction of Californians to joining groups as a way of making sense of their position in a sprawling, rapidly changing social milieu, and it also reflected the desperate need many Californians felt for political engagement in a state in which political debate since 1952 had become a trend-setter on both left and right.[37] Clubs acted very much like the communist cells that had proven so popular in California in the 1930s, or like local groups of Mattachine homophile activists who had come out of the communist movement in Los Angeles, or like local committees dedicated to the passage of FEPC.

The link between the political message and the social involvement that made local clubs successful can be observed by comparing clubs with local chapters of the ADA in the 1950s. By the mid-1950s the California ADA was in crisis. Chapters in Los Angeles and San Francisco had collapsed, despite several attempts to resurrect them. National ADA leader Sheldon Pollack concluded in July 1956 that the fact that ADA policy was being made in Washington and disseminated to local chapters just did not work in Southern California, and that local Democratic clubs "absorbed all of the political interests of people who had been active in the [ADA] chapter." CDC clubs made their own policy, participated in the drawing up of a political agenda at annual conventions, and had a direct stake in the election of a California Democratic Party to power, rather than a generalized commitment to liberalism espoused by a distant ADA high command three thousand miles away.

Just as importantly, the very ideology that formed the core raison d'être of ADA was out of step with the California scene. Pollack suggested that the reason for ADA weakness was that "the initial enthusiasm generated by a new organization and the turmoil of the post-war world has subsided, and the issues we support, while apparently important, do not seem as vital, nor of such immediate consequence. . . . Liberals are willing to support them but not so willing to actively work on their behalf." This defeatist statement contrasted starkly with the vigor with which California Democrats were organizing and growing in the 1950s. Nor did Pollack understand the power that the link to the party gave clubs as they recruited members: the advance of the Democratic Party gave the membership a goal, a more relevant consideration than Pollack's criticism that the club movement had become so enmeshed with the party that there might be "more room for an independent organization that would keep the party people mindful of issues."[38] Later events would prove that too close a connection between party and club movement could lead to schisms and disillusionment, but it also made a commitment to political participation more concrete, and the divisions between parties over policy more clear-cut and important.

Some ADA observers of the California scene were more aware than Pollack of the importance of what was going on there in the 1950s. "Continuous defeat in state and local politics in the past made difficult the growth of responsible state-wide party organization," reported Paul Seabury, a Berkeley political science professor involved in the local ADA chapter, "but it has made it possible for the newly emergent Democratic organization in the state to be far more responsive to the forces of 'modernity' within the party. . . . By and large it is something new in American politics: a broad movement of well-educated liberals whose political cohesiveness derives not from ethnic, or narrowly based economic interest, but from a deep 'concern' with political issues transcending the 'self-interest' of the movement itself. The 'great issues' of American politics and international affairs for them have been overriding." Seabury noted the insularity of the club movement, which did not have much traction outside the state, but felt that perhaps ADA could provide the bridge from state to national politics: "Perhaps the very 'freshness' of our Western political milieu may produce here part of the vigor and intellectual initiative so greatly needed in national politics."[39]

This was unlikely to happen so long as the east coast ADA leadership remained obsessed with communism and the Cold War at a time when clubs like the West Beverly one were prompting a reappraisal of the entire basis of Cold War liberalism. Indeed, the origins of the Democratic renaissance in California lay in its popular front past and a widespread revulsion at the impact of domestic anticommunism on California politics. Many members of clubs in southern California had fellow traveler and communist pasts, and were moving into mainstream politics on the basis that the issues-oriented clubs were shifting the parameters of California party politics leftward. Sheldon Pollack wanted to use ADA to "counteract the infiltration of the Democratic clubs" and characterized activists at the CDC Issues conferences as "commies and fuzzies," but he simply missed the point of where the strength of the clubs originated.[40] ADA national organizer Nathalie Panek in 1954 put her finger on the answer even as she was condemning the fact that "fuzziness among decent liberals out here seems almost endemic," the term "fuzzy" apparently meaning less than hysterically anticommunist. She had been told "by sane and respectable people that the Democratic Party here is really a united front outfit—old style—and that some of the blossoming Democratic clubs have been or are in the process of being taken over by the CP. To round out the picture I should tell you that in the two months I have been here I have had more stupid pre-ADA type of arguments on whether we can work with Communists than I have had in the last five years. And I don't think one of the arguers was a knowing fellow traveler."[41] Most in the club movement, including CDC leader Alan Cranston, had never been communists or fellow travelers, and others, like Saul Reider, had exchanged communism for Democratic activism: all were united in disgust at the California Republican Party's immolation of Helen Douglas and Jimmy Roosevelt at the altar of anticommunism, and all were dedicated to the establishment of the Democratic Party on the basis of issues of relevance to Californians in the 1950s, not the dark years of the late 1940s when Cold War liberalism had conspired with the right to all but destroy not only the remnant of popular front politics but the entire structural basis of liberalism in California.

The socially responsive, cell-like structure of the clubs, and their link to the official Democratic Party hierarchy in California, had another important benefit ADA observers tended to miss: they acted as a useful fund-raising outfit that both provided valuable financial resources to Democratic campaigns and furnished the membership with a day-to-day task that energized activists striving to use politics as an organ of social networking. Democratic clubs were not talking shops, but were by 1956 part of an integrated web of regular Democrats, Young Democratic Clubs, CDC clubs, and unions, which all contributed funds to the statewide party. The CDC participated in a statewide "Dollars for Democrats" campaign for the 1956 elections as its part of the fund-raising effort. "An estimated 15,000 volunteer workers will be ringing doorbells tomorrow in the Democratic Party's nation-wide effort to put campaign fund-raising on a small contributor basis," reported the Northern California Stevenson-Kefauver committee in October 1956.[42] That year all but eight counties out of 50 in the northern half of California participated in the Dollars for Democrats drive, raising tens of thousands of dollars in door-to-door campaigns. Alameda Democrats raised $13,945.75 in the October 1956 push for funds, and Marin raised the significant sum of $3,905.64 or 15.6 cents per registered Democrat, a decent tally considering that in the late 1950s Marin remained a Republican county.[43] In 1958 new CDC leader Joe Wyatt sent out a memo to members urging them to support a repeat of the 1956 effort, predicting that his army of volunteers could raise over $250,000 if every club was properly motivated and managed.[44] Steve Zetterberg, commenting on the participation of the clubs in this effort to renew the Democratic Party, said that the campaign of fund-raising and doorbell ringing "was getting things from the grass roots rather than just having it done from the top down. I think we were renewing the spirit of the Democratic Party, in that sense."[45]

Dollars for Democrats raised funds that were then distributed to those running for office in winnable districts. "We just went to the clubs," Roger Kent recalled, "and explained the fact that on a certain weekend they were to post people on the streets to go from door to door. . . . It was a remarkably successful way of making money." CDC's clout in this process was enhanced because their conventions endorsed candidates: "it was perfectly obvious that the regular party took the CDC convention *very* seriously," said Kent. "For a statewide candidate to be endorsed by CDC, I suppose, would be worth somewhere between ten thousand and twenty-five thousand dollars in every district and every town because where there was a decent CDC organization, a central headquarters would be opened, and the candidates would be told, 'Look, you can come in here, you can put a telephone in here, you can get desks, you can put your literature in here, and you can meet people here, and you can distribute literature.' . . . Then, presumably, this was the nucleus of the political organization."[46] Through CDC candidates for office could recruit canvassers and precinct workers, establish a Dollars for Democrats operation, and hold parties and rallies. The fact that fund-raising coincided with a broader political agenda to involve people in the political process made Dollars for Democrats far more effective than its rival, Dime a Day for Democracy, run by party regulars who solicited money from established party backers including a "1% leadership group," those the DDD people felt were party grandees who could spend $3 a month.[47] It was also more effective than paying people to vote, a tactic employed by Jess Unruh and party loyalists in blue collar parts of Los Angeles.[48] Clubs combined organization, ideology, and a community sense of belonging that made them powerful political and social structures, at least for a while. When Anthony Beilenson first arrived in west LA in the late 1950s and got involved with the local party politics, he found a district in which the "CDC was basically the mainstream grassroots representative of a portion of Democratic politics on the Westside, and some other areas of California as well. . . . Elected officials were elected largely because of the clubs, and we tended to stay close to them."[49]

The rapid rise of the club movement was bound to irritate some of the regular party leadership who had worked for years to carve out a niche for themselves. "The clubs and the CDC are a target of almost universal dislike among the longtime party workers," observed a political PR company working on the Stevenson campaign in 1956. "The complaints are sometimes that they are novices pushing ahead of the people who have been devoted for years. The complaints are sometimes that the clubs are too ideological and in some cases infiltrated, but in any case more interested in discussing program than politics." But then came the vital point: "But along with all the complaints, no one wants to abolish them. In many places, e.g., San Diego, they are credited with doing whatever work is being done."[50] Carmen Warschaw as a party regular was a case in point, complaining that in some cases "the CDC unfortunately sometimes was sponsoring candidates against an incumbent who really wasn't bad. We don't need to fight each other that much." Yet she also admitted that in the Claremont area there was "this tremendous club; we used to hold meetings here and we used to have two hundred, three hundred people at every meeting."[51] An examination of Democratic campaigns for the assembly, governor, and president in 1954 and 1956 reveals that much more united the California Democratic Party and its supporters in this period than divided them, contributing toward an astonishing transformation in the balance of power in state politics in these years.

"A Virile and Meaningful Democratic Left": The Rise of Phil Burton

"If you think that Phil's ultra-liberalism offends his constituents in the twentieth Assembly district," remarked San Francisco resident Orrin Cassmore of Phillip Burton, representative of the city's downtown and poor South of Market in the state assembly and now, in 1963, candidate for Congress, "you are profoundly mistaken. Desperately poor people, pensioners, working men, minorities eat it up. For them, the New Frontier does not exist: the fights along the old frontier which were won for most of us in the thirties are the ones that are still important to them, for they have not really participated in the gains we won." Cassmore argued that not only was Burton strong in his own assembly district, the Twentieth, but the Eighteenth, farther west toward the Castro and Haight-Ashbury, was "even more favorable for him." This was a district where a then unknown African American, Willie Brown, had in 1962 come within a hairsbreadth of defeating incumbent long-serving Democrat Ed Gaffney.[52] Burton's successful effort to build a local fiefdom for himself and his left-wing political views in a locality that in 1954 still elected Republicans to the state legislature forms a useful case study of the way in which party politics interacted with the social structure of urban California.

Burton's campaigns for public office in San Francisco in the 1950s exemplified how a direct appeal to local constituencies and organizations of citizens could overturn the political dominance of a small party elite. By the time of his first campaign for the state legislature in 1954 Burton was already a hardened campaigner—president of the Young Democrats of San Francisco, member of the State Central Committee, tireless worker for Helen Douglas's 1950 Senate fight—but he was also a controversial interloper into city politics, refusing to wait his turn or play the cross-filing game between local Democrats and the powerful state GOP. He also unashamedly described himself as of the left. He described his decision to run in the Democratic primary for the city's Twenty-third Assembly District in 1954 as a realization that there were many liberals in the party "who felt, as did I, that it was time to attempt to increase the 'measure' of the more liberal wing of our party in the Assembly. . . . I intend to run an aggressive campaign on the issues, including taking an emphatic position in opposition to the so-called 'loyalty oaths,' in favor of Health Insurance, and the rest of the positions that spell out the specific application of the New-Fair Deal philosophy." Burton was indeed specific in framing his campaign literature to underline the "implications of a virile and meaningful 'Democratic left' program in this country."[53] One campaign leaflet advocated a large state public works program to eliminate unemployment, a liberalized pensions system, state health insurance, universal unemployment insurance, more state child care centers, tax relief for working mothers, adult education facilities, and other state-sponsored measures that formed the hallmarks of the social democratic state in countries like Sweden.[54] Burton's campaign took these themes directly to the doorsteps and public meetings of San Francisco, bypassing an established party hierarchy that made clear its enmity toward Burton from the outset, throwing its support behind incumbent Assemblyman Cliff Berry even though he had in fact died early in the campaign. The late Mr. Berry won 55 percent of the Democratic vote and a respectable 30 percent of the Republican primary vote; Burton managed 25 percent of the Democratic vote and refused to contest the Republican primary. The fact that Burton had mounted a leftist campaign with almost no official party support and come second in the primary suggested that an appeal to grassroots voters excluded from the cozy world of machine politics might well yield results, as the 1956 elections would prove.[55]

In July 1956 Burton upset a thirty-two-year tradition by winning his own party primary in the Twentieth Assembly District, based on downtown San Francisco and Chinatown. Previously, Republican Assemblyman Thomas Maloney had won both primaries handily, as his reasonably liberal record and political networking had persuaded influential city Democrats to support him. The key to Burton's primary victory, which later would be duplicated in the general election, was his campaign's ability to mobilize previously unregistered voters, and to persuade key constituencies that his voice in Sacramento would help to advance a liberal agenda in California. Local Young Democrats formed a PAC and targeted their resources in Burton's prospective district, conducting intensive preelection clerical work to identify and register new voters sympathetic to Burton's views. They estimated that between the primary and general elections in 1956 the Young Democrats assisted in adding over 10,500 new voters to the rolls in the city, over 5,000 of those in the Twentieth District, helping to ensure Burton's eventual 659-vote margin over Maloney in a district that had scarcely ever seen a Democratic candidate.[56] Burton's successful campaign bypassed the County Democratic Central Committee, whose members loathed him, and failed to win the endorsement of the AFL's campaign arm, the Labor League for Political Education, which endorsed Maloney for his pro-labor record (though most CIO locals supported Burton). Still Burton managed to eke out a narrow victory before going on to build an impregnable Democratic bastion in the city. In 1956, "for the first time," proclaimed the *San Francisco News*, "the GOP label is Maloney's biggest handicap. In the 40-year era of California's non-partisanship, he encountered no difficulty under the Republican banner, for labor in this state, too, was largely Republican. Now there is a sharp awareness of party affiliation. Labor has shifted to the Democratic column and Maloney stands almost alone in the State Capitol as an elderly liberal still wrapped in the mantle of the Grand Old Party."[57]

The key to Burton's political success rested on his ability to conduct a face-to-face, precinct-by-precinct campaign that tied his personal candidacy to a specific ideology that could justify his running against a relatively liberal, popular Republican. In a political system built on personalities, unknowns needed to define an ideological space for themselves in order to be relevant. Once elected, Burton had to forge a record in the legislature that would represent the social geography of his district and bind key social groups to his mantle just as labor and social democratic parties did in other industrialized countries.[58] Unlike in parts of the country that had forged Democratic machines in the New Deal era and had built up solid Democratic constituencies based on labor union membership and political patronage, in California Democrats like Burton were running against patronage networks and were instead creating Democratic bastions out of a commitment to a particular political program. In later campaigns Burton would use his liberal record to emphasize the links between liberal Democracy and the social structure of his constituency: "I am proud of my efforts in behalf of working men and women which have earned for me the endorsements of AFL-CIO COPE, Machinists Non-Partisan League, ILWU, the Railroad Brotherhoods and many independent local unions. As chairman of the Assembly Committee on Social Welfare I have fought for important improvements in the laws affecting our aged, blind, disabled and needy children."[59] Putting across legislative achievements in ideological terms was essential to California liberals, as suggested in a Democratic Central Committee memorandum on the African American vote in 1956: "California has no catalyzing agent like PAC, which uses top Negro strategists and union officials to 'deliver' the Negro vote as in the industrial areas of Detroit, Akron and Cleveland, nor does it have the patronage organizations of Philadelphia and Harlem. California politicians, even in their wildest dreams, cannot envision the invincibility of Chicago's south side. . . . The Roosevelt-Truman New Deal-Fair Deal record with its strong civil rights flavor and its economic benefits to working and lower middle class Americans, to which most Negroes belong" was the key factor to creating a Democratic majority in California.[60]

Burton created personal links with significant sections of the community based on his commitment both to the day-to-day issues of his constituency and on broader political concerns that could be furthered through legislative action. Through his contacts in his constituency Burton informed gubernatorial candidate Pat Brown in early 1958 that he had gauged which issues "have primary importance in my district" and listed them in order of priority as being jobs and unemployment, pensions, a Fair Employment Practices Committee, and the inequities of the 1952 McCarran Immigration Act, a Cold War measure that attempted to restrict the residency rights of persons classed as political radicals. Campaign material and press releases in several languages, and particularly in Spanish and Cantonese, flooded district homes and businesses, keeping Burton's name in the limelight between elections.[61] A prominent welfare rights advocate commented in 1963 in the wake of the massive changes in California's welfare laws promoted by Burton that his political concerns "are peculiarly suited to the district he represents. The twentieth district is among the most variegated and fascinating in the whole state. It embraces San Francisco's Chinatown and Fisherman's Wharf; the colorful beat of the Mission District and the bohemian 'beats' of North Beach. . . . In short, Phil Burton's constituents include many of the city's underprivileged, and perhaps even a few of its overprivileged; they represent a kaleidoscope of nationalities, minorities, and hard realities," a kaleidoscope of interests on which a commitment to social democratic ideas could be based.[62] Having narrowly won his seat in the legislature in 1956, once the Democrats gained control in Sacramento two years later Burton worked to mobilize large majorities behind his candidacy and succeeded: in 1960 his margin of victory over his Republican rival was a huge 14,148 votes in an area in which the Democrats had received 72 percent of new registrants and where only 14.5 percent of residents were homeowners, 43 percent earned under $5,000 per annum, and nearly half the voters were members of minority groups.[63]

CHAPTER 5

Turning Point: California Politics in the 1950s

Democrats were assisted in their efforts to become the majority party in California by the Republican Party's self-immolating lurch to the right in the landmark 1958 elections; placing anti-union shop "right to work" initiatives at the center of William Knowland's campaign for governor had the immediate effect of rallying the whole of organized labor behind the Democrats.[1] Yet their rise to power was taking place well before the state GOP decided on an antilabor initiative: in 1952 the Democrats won only 11 of the 40 State Senate seats and 26 of 80 State Assembly seats. Two years later, with the introduction of party labeling on the ballot and vastly superior organization through the CDC, Democrats won 16 State Senate seats, including the election of Richard Richards to the single Los Angeles seat previously held by arch-Republican Jack Tenney, and 32 Assembly seats. In 1956, the year of Phil Burton's spectacular triumph in San Francisco, the Democrats took exactly half the Senate seats and 38 Assembly seats to the GOP's 42.[2] Burton may have been a master campaigner and electoral strategist who would go on to have one of the most important careers in congressional politics arguably of anyone in the twentieth century, and he may have had a unique relationship with his district that allowed him to triumph repeatedly without the assistance of a major support organization. "He just ran the whole operation," recalled Willie Brown of San Francisco politics in the late 1950s and 1960s. "He did all the thinking and didn't suffer from the need for advice or counsel. He made the decisions and sold them to us as the proper way in which to do it."[3] These figures demonstrate, however, that his victory was part of a much bigger political phenomenon transforming the landscape of California politics. Democrats were gaining power and political influence all over the state. And Burton was far from a political loner, running for national chair of the Young Democrats in 1959 and strongly supporting CDC and his friends in the labor movement.

Stirrings: The 1954 Campaigns

In many ways the campaigns of 1954 that followed the formation of CDC represented the turning point in Democratic Party fortunes, building confidence that would push activists toward further victories in 1956 and 1958. Initial portents did not augur well for the Democrats. The campaign of incumbent governor Goodwin Knight, appointed to the post after Earl Warren's elevation to the U.S. Supreme Court the year before, benefited from the support of virtually the entire state media network, as well as the American Federation of Labor. Knight's campaign employed the services of notorious public relations firm Whitaker and Baxter, made famous by their successful campaign on behalf of the American Medical Association against federal health insurance in the late 1940s. Richard Graves, the Democratic nominee endorsed by CDC, had only recently defected to the party from the Republicans, and lacked experience of the kind of brutal media campaign to which he would be subjected, though ironically it was partly by reason of his distance from the party regulars that he had been nominated. Several local Democratic campaigns for Congress, notably those of Jimmy Roosevelt and Robert Condon, were tarnished by scandal, damaging the statewide ticket as it struggled for political legitimacy. Yet the 1954 campaigns pointed up the need for a widening of the terms of political debate that would galvanize liberal activity as the 1956 campaigns got underway.

The Whitaker and Baxter campaign to elect Knight demonstrated the growing chasm between the record of the governor, relatively friendly to labor and supportive of his predecessor's centrist agenda, and the rightward lurch in the Republicans' campaign strategy that would only intensify as the party's right wing increased their influence over election tactics during the 1950s. Knight's campaign treasurer, a San Francisco banker, assured one potential donor that "an intelligent and hard hitting campaign has been carefully planned which will utilize every medium of public expression to win the fight."[4] Whitaker and Baxter could rely not only on the supine acquiescence of the state press, but also on a vast reserve of campaign finance, dwarfing the Graves campaign budget of roughly $80,000, much of this raised by an offshoot labor committee that rebelled against the dominant AFL's endorsement of Knight.[5] While every move of Knight's schedule of engagements was reported in the press, Graves was rarely mentioned. Reports ranged from widespread predictions that Knight would win both party primaries to the most anodyne of reports in small-town dailies exemplified by the following report in the *Delano Record*, headlined "Governor Knight has pleasant visit here." Knight, the report proclaimed, "a big man with a pleasant countenance, visited Delano for more than an hour yesterday and by the time he left his infectious smile was reflected by nearly all of the several thousand persons who greeted him. . . . As for the people of Delano, Knight said: 'You are smiling, happy, prosperous people. All people in this country should have a similar spirit.'"[6]

Knight's issue-light campaign reflected both the extent of GOP dominance of the electoral landscape in California and the limits of his own political worldview. Before his election as lieutenant-governor in the 1946 GOP landslide he had never held political office. Born in Utah, Knight had moved to Los Angeles as a child and had worked his way, via Stanford and Cornell Law School, to a judgeship in 1935. His principal access to Republican politics in California had come from his considerable wealth, accrued when he bought a gold mine in the Mojave Desert that had turned out to be well sited for the purpose. Knight possessed an easy charm and affable personality that seemed in part a product of his good fortune, at least if one believed the story that he had once stated, "With my luck, who needs brains?"[7] To his political supporters and campaign managers he possessed useful attributes for a career in Golden State politics in the years before the development of serious two-party races: he toed the party line, made few enemies, and had enough bipartisan appeal to provide plentiful uncontroversial copy for the GOP-friendly press.

Occasionally Knight made policy statements during his campaign. At a campaign luncheon for Democratic and Republican women in San Francisco he "cited the fact that the State budget was balanced without new taxes; that jobless workers have received an increase in their unemployment benefits and that a drive has been intensified to prevent chiselers from raiding the unemployment fund."[8] More often, however, his campaign team encouraged him to keep away from controversy, adopting the tried and tested method of keeping their candidate above the fray and attacking and discrediting his opponent. A campaign aide to Leone Baxter wrote her in late March confirming that "in line with your instructions at luncheon Tuesday, we have accumulated a considerable amount of anti-Graves material, which will be submitted to you as soon as digested and organized."[9] Some of this material was put together by various individuals posing as supporters at Graves campaign rallies in order to gain information on the type of people supporting him. One such mole reported to Whitaker and Baxter that a rally at the Cow Palace in San Francisco "fell flat on its face. It was badly organized, late in starting, and just wasn't the sort of thing that would whip up enthusiasm for any campaign. The Graves talk was very short, rather pontifical, and was received very coolly. The overall impression I got from Graves' speech was that lacking any sort of program he is counting on the fact that the political affiliations will be listed in the ballot to carry him through. There was no noticeable enthusiasm for this idea at the rally."[10] These observations could be fed to the press. Press stories featuring Graves were unearthed and pored over for damaging material, including the story in the *San Francisco Chronicle* from October 1953 in which Graves argued "mass transit must be publicly owned—whether we like it or not."[11]

Allegations of this nature were then extrapolated into a broader attack that Graves and other Democratic candidates, including Senate candidate Sam Yorty, were captives of the extreme left. Whitaker and Baxter encouraged the formation of a renegade Democratic organization, pointedly titled the "Democratic Conference Against Radical Party Leadership," a front organization through which to launch attacks on Democrats as dangerous radicals. Its leader, a complete unknown called Gregory Harrison, wrote National Committee chairman Stephen Mitchell that the "Democratic Party in California faces another year of disastrous defeats unless we are able to break the grip of the radical Coffey-Condon-Miller machine which now controls party affairs here." State Senator George Miller, CDC Chairman Alan Cranston, and State Committeewoman Elizabeth Snyder had to deny allegations that Graves and Yorty, as well as controversial congressman Robert Condon, were tools of the far left, accusing Whitaker and Baxter of fabricating the smear.[12] The Knight campaign zeroed in on local Democratic campaigns that had nothing to do with Graves, but which were causing controversy and could paint a picture of his opposition as untrustworthy. Whitaker and Baxter gathered material from HUAC files and on Robert Condon's background in the Progressive Citizens of America for use in Knight's campaign. They got hold of Democratic National chairman Mitchell's comments withdrawing the national party's endorsement from Condon because of his classification as a security risk due to his association with Democratic state committeeman from Contra Costa and former communist Bert Coffey, and also from Jimmy Roosevelt, who, according to the *California Eagle*'s reading of Mitchell's comments, was undergoing "marital difficulties in which James is accused of infidelities with a dozen women." This was not how Mitchell in fact framed his criticism of Roosevelt, but it formed a useful hook on which to hang some of Knight's campaign themes. He appeared at a Seventh Day Adventist church in San Francisco to hear delegates to a convention claim that "moral laxity before and after marriage is one of the greatest threats to the American home."[13]

The lack of a serious engagement with socioeconomic issues in the campaign was reinforced when AFL leader C. J. Haggerty decided to keep a large percentage of the labor movement behind Knight's campaign. Whitaker and Baxter established a "Labor for Knight" committee and funded campaign literature that included a piece by Haggerty himself entitled "The Record of Richard Graves," attacking Graves's Republican past and claiming he was less progressive than Knight on labor issues.[14] This question had dominated the California Federation of Labor's endorsement convention, and although Knight gained the support of the preprimary gathering in San Francisco in April, the debate demonstrated the fact that a left-right ideological split was opening up in California politics over the question of labor relations. "I think the basis of this decision for Knight is supposed to be practical politics and realism," said one delegate. "But I think sometimes realism is mistaken for opportunism, and sometimes we are throwing away our real power in hoping to trade for a few promises." The connection between political ideology and race was also becoming clear as a result of African American labor representatives turning against the leadership over Knight. "I don't believe that any delegate could assume that I would go back to my respective community where I am attempting to carry a labor program . . . in the minority areas and present to them a reactionary Republican candidate in the person of Goodie Knight," argued a delegate from the Dining Car Employees Union. "In looking over the other endorsements we find that 27 of the 30 Congressional candidates are Democrats."[15] The battle over Fair Employment legislation was increasingly becoming entwined with a bigger political battle over the direction of the Republican Party, as one newspaper observed in April when it claimed that Knight's "stand on FEPC completes a record which includes opposition to an anti-depression program and all progressive social legislation. Surely strengthening the labor movement by eliminating discrimination and developing a political alliance with the Negro people are more important to labor than the game of political footsy played with Knight by a few AFL officials."[16] The California AFL was in a state of complete confusion owing to the rapid pace of political change: the convention endorsed Butch Powers for lietutenant governor even though Los Angeles city councilman Ed Roybal, the Democratic challenger, was a militant labor man. The membership mutinied over the reluctance of Haggerty and his cronies to support Richard Richards for the LA Senate seat, Haggerty having claimed that Richards's membership of the ACLU made him politically suspect to a leadership keen to assert its anticommunist credentials. Widespread hatred for arch-Republican incumbent Jack Tenney was enough to defeat this absurd notion. There was controversy, too, over Phil Burton's challenge to Cliff Berry.[17] It was a simple case of the California AFL coming to terms gradually with the changing complexion of California politics.

At the California AFL's August meeting to prepare for the November elections the Knight controversy had not gone away. Many had expected Knight to win both primaries, but Graves had managed to stay in the race. Vice president Ash of the Oakland Central Labor Council observed the shifting tectonics of California party politics and predicted the gradual divorce of labor and the GOP: "Whereas on the one hand the Democratic Party platform is very close to the policy that has been established and is being established by the Convention of the California State Federation of Labor, and on the other hand there is very little in the platform that the incumbent Governor is pledged to support that was adopted on the same day in Sacramento by the Republican Party. . . . Mr. President, I can't understand, I still can't understand, the reason, the psychology, behind this recommendation of the incumbent Governor. . . . I don't think that there is a thing that the Republican Party has to offer us as trade unionists."[18] While this sentiment was widely shared, a lack of enthusiasm for Graves prevented a mutiny over the AFL's continued association with Republican candidates.

The continued existence of this unhappy marriage between labor and the Republican establishment helped to perpetuate the marginal status of farm workers in California politics. Labor's support for the incumbent governor followed logically from the AFL's gradual retreat from the farm worker cause in the early 1950s, as the desire to head off antilabor legislation trumped any sense of class solidarity. "Governor Knight," Ernesto Galarza later recalled, "discarding neutrality between labor and management, publicly endorsed the false information reported to him by the Farm Placement Service."[19] Yet Knight's close ties to agribusiness and the state machinery of agricultural regulation not only limited the capacity for the former NFLU, now called the National Agricultural Workers' Union (NAWU), to gain any traction in Sacramento, but it also ended up damaging organized labor more generally.

The Farm Placement Service's main office in the state capitol gathered information on farm union activities for growers, manipulated official figures on farm labor needs in California to justify the continuation of the bracero program, and indirectly supported the right-to-work campaign in 1958. Its director, Edward F. Hayes, a Knight appointee, acted as advisor to the Farm Bureau and Associated Farmers, who openly backed draconian limits on union power.[20] It was hardly surprising that an alliance of organized labor and an enfeebled and poorly resourced group of dedicated organizers in the NAWU could never really take root: the latter was too poor and lacking in political connections to act as an effective lobbying organization, and the potential benefits of improving the farm workers' lot were outweighed by the political fallout that could result for the State Federation of Labor. "No issues were raised [by California labor leaders] concerning the growers' offensive against domestic farm workers" during the 1954 campaign, Galarza recalled bitterly.[21] The cozy relationship between labor and Knight kept discussions of the capacity of government to provide security for all within very limited parameters.

It was for this reason that much activity in rural Latino communities—and much later historical analysis of the farm worker issue—remained focused on grassroots organizing outside the realm of party politics.[22] Cesar Chavez cut his political teeth as an organizer in the Community Services Organization (CSO), affiliated with Saul Alinsky's Industrial Areas Foundation (IAF). The IAF had mobilized blue collar residents of a poor Chicago neighborhood, and the CSO aimed to imitate the IAF's grassroots organizing and reaching out to religious organizations and labor unions to politicize Mexican Americans in California. Under the tutelage of CSO leader Fred Ross, Chavez learned the art of working neighborhoods around San Jose door to door, registering voters, hosting house meetings, setting up citizenship classes, and establishing Latinos as a political force in the South Bay. Some twenty-two new CSO chapters sprang up in San Jose in the 1950s, and by 1959 Chavez was executive director of the organization. Yet the age-old problem of how to translate successes in an urban setting to the countryside remained: Alinsky thought the organization of farm workers impossible, and tensions within the group prompted Chavez to quit in 1962.[23] Without the cooperation of the political establishment to end the bracero program and thereby engender greater commonality of purpose among farm workers, it was hard to envisage how the house meeting strategy would work in the fields.

Even in San Jose itself, a city in which Democrats were making major inroads during the 1950s, the new generation of Anglo liberals was having trouble relating to Latino activism. "This is an area about which local Democrats have done almost nothing," wrote a visiting Democratic strategist as late as 1961, "because they really didn't know where to turn in the Mexican American community for leadership." By the end of the 1950s the CDC had granted club charters to ten "Mexican American clubs in the San Jose area, set up under Hector Moreno and Robert Kaiser (MAPA) and they are all paper and apparently have never met. The Central Committee would like to revoke the charters (which they should never have issued in the first place) but fear to do so because they think (rightly) that such a move would be misunderstood in the Mexican Community."[24] The fact that Democratic activists were having difficulty interacting with one of the most significant political movements in the region sounded a warning note for both club Democrats and CSO organizers, as it left a gaping hole in the drive to make California politics truly responsive to grassroots efforts to challenge the long-established prerogatives of business elites. While it was comparatively straightforward to slot demands for fair employment and general economic justice into a liberal bid for political power, the creation of a genuine coalition between white liberals and minority activists was still in its infancy in the 1950s, and plagued by mistrust and inexperience.

Despite the fact that the odds were so heavily stacked against the Democrats in 1954, right-wing Republican Assemblyman Harold Levering predicted that California politics was becoming more competitive. The *Los Angeles Times* reported in early June that Levering had warned GOP supporters that "they had better 'run, not walk' to the polls next Tuesday or wake up with a headache the morning after. The Democrats, he says, are very well organized this time and every Republican vote will be needed."[25] Graves managed to win his party primary despite the fact that he had been plucked out of thin air at a time when Democrats held only one statewide office and possessed very few strong, experienced leaders. He was not a massively prepossessing figure, struggling to find a voice given his recent switch from one party to another. He told the AMA in April that "as a true liberal" he was "opposed to having government do publicly what can be done privately and in the public interest . . . Specifically, I oppose the direct extension of government into the area of private medical care."[26] He was, however, a poster boy for a growing movement for political change in California that needed a campaign, even a losing one, to get them started.

Other campaigns that year were successful: the winning of the Los Angeles State Senate seat was an enormous coup, and demonstrated the growing power of the Democratic clubs in Los Angeles as well as the steady shift of labor locals into the Democratic camp. And the Democratic platform of 1954 demonstrated a degree of ideological commitment that overrode the factional and political divisions within the party. The platform reflected the rapid economic development of the state in the 1950s that required regulation to maintain social stability: civil rights and health care were central, as was a call for "full utilization of the national full employment law and for adoption of similar legislation for the people of California. We believe in the prompt and early use of useful public works as a means of restoring full employment; and we believe that both the state and federal governments must consciously and conscientiously work toward not only the restoration of full employment, but the goal of providing adequate jobs at decent wages insuring the future of our growing population."[27] Despite the Republicans' well-funded, relentless campaign onslaught this message had at least mobilized the faithful if not the uncommitted: Graves's margin of defeat was half that of Roosevelt's four years earlier, and Senator Tom Kuchel, a popular liberal Republican appointed by Warren after Richard Nixon became vice president, won by 260,000 over Sam Yorty, not a spectacular margin.[28] While the Democrats lost Condon's House seat in the East Bay, they picked up a House seat in the Central Valley, and came close to taking others that had been impregnable in 1952.[29]

The increasing self-confidence of the left-of-center forces in the Democratic Party in 1954 can be observed in Jimmy Roosevelt's Twenty-Sixth District in West Los Angeles. The Republicans had gerrymandered it to take in as much hostile territory as possible to protect neighboring Republicans, but even then it had not been considered a Democratic fortress when the lines were drawn. In Roosevelt's campaign for Congress he could rely on two campaign headquarters, one in the Sixty-First Assembly District and one in the heavily African American Sixty-Second District; three large Democratic clubs, the West Beverly and the West Pico in the Sixty-First and the Miramonte in the Sixty-Second; and the Hollywood branch of the Young Democrats. Overseeing the whole operation was a Twenty-Sixth District Democratic Council, whose chair, Rosalind Wyman, appointed coordinators to distribute literature to the clubs and local HQs, advise candidates on campaign strategy and secure speaking engagements for them, and dedicate teams of workers to each candidate for each different office.[30] Once the local party organization had taken the decision to endorse Roosevelt despite his marital difficulties—and in 1954 all local clubs were required to vote to endorse one candidate and not allow a free-for-all in the primary—this formidable organization virtually guaranteed his election. Roosevelt's links to the left in the late 1940s and his unashamedly leftist campaign for governor in 1950 endeared him to the big players in West and South Central Los Angeles, and his announcement of his candidacy won over those in the newly created district uneasy about incumbent Sam Yorty's commitment to the liberal cause: "I will campaign on the basis of the liberal Democratic philosophy which I have supported all my adult life and if elected to Congress will do my utmost to put that philosophy into effect."[31] The extent to which the national political scene would impact upon the dynamics of California Democratic politics would be tested when Adlai Stevenson returned to the campaign trail in 1956.

The Second Coming of Stevenson

California was Stevenson's first major campaign tour of 1956, and the situation he found there differed in a number of respects from four years earlier. For one thing, the most important part of his visit in early February would be his address to the California Democratic Council Convention in Fresno, testimony to the power that the club movement now possessed.[32] The groundswell of support for Stevenson in California in the fall of 1955 had been powerful enough to help Stevenson make up his mind to run: as one Democratic supporter in Oakland put it in October, "if he wins the California primary he'll overshadow all other candidates and not be considered the choice of the 'smoke-filled room.' . . . Believe me, Stevenson will win if he really fights for the nomination here in California."[33] Attorney General Pat Brown, who would head the Stevenson for President effort in California, gave the assurance that Stevenson "need have no fears whatever" that he would be able to defeat his principal rival, Senator Estes Kefauver, with only a "minimum" amount of campaigning in a state that was rapidly becoming the most electorally important in the country.[34]

The California "draft Stevenson" movement involved not only Brown but National Committeeman Paul Ziffren, Roger Kent, then vice chair of the State Central Committee, Elizabeth Snyder, state chair, and Alan Cranston of the CDC. So important were these figures in California politics by 1956 that they had already enlisted the services of a public relations firm to boost Stevenson's candidacy, commissioning a statewide survey of party support for Stevenson that had cemented the support of thousands of party members, four congressmen, eight state senators, ten state assemblymen, two-thirds of state county chairmen, and nearly three hundred California Democratic Club presidents. Stevenson's campaign managers took California very seriously when they decided to enter him in the presidential primary there, as they had worked out that November that a campaign lasting from December to early June would cost his campaign $317,854, including $137,060 just on TV ads. In Southern California alone there were nearly 2.8 million television sets in 1956 and seven television stations. Viewers in the Bay Area watched three major and two minor TV networks on well over a million TV sets.[35] That the spending of such a large amount of money—and these sums were considerable for just a primary campaign in the 1950s—on a media-driven campaign in a state that had been of marginal importance just a few years earlier was approved demonstrates how the landscape of American politics was changing in these years.

Stevenson's campaign budget highlighted another way in which California was important: it was a symbol of modernity that was moving Democratic Party politics in new directions, a fact that would impact significantly upon Stevenson's campaign. In just one year between 1951 and 1952 the official population of California had grown from 11,100,000 to around 11,550,000. The areas of fastest job creation were in commercial and service sector industries, and the pressures on public services, including water, transportation, and public power, were major issues that transcended party political divisions and made the articulation of a political message challenging, recalling Tony Crosland's interest in West Coast affairs during his 1954 visit. A CDC brochure entitled "The Consumer in the Modern Market Place" argued that the "potential market for all types of goods and services is so great in California because average income is higher than the average national income (one-fourth higher); population expansion is in the group heavily dominated by active buyers, that is, eighteen-to-forty-five-year-olds; employment is high; business climate is good in the sense that the demand for housing, for highways, for other services and goods is expanding." The overriding question of the brochure asked how "can the Democratic clubs and Democratic party assist in the fight to protect the consumer interest?"[36] A California AFL-CIO leaflet produced in late 1956 and later revised and reprinted was headed "Consumer, Beware! A Guide to Installment Buying," which attempted to advise California workers how to cope with rapidly burgeoning levels of available credit and debt in the nation's fastest growing economy, by 1960 one of the world's ten largest.[37] Historians have in recent years crafted detailed studies of the emergence of this "consumers' republic" in the United States both in terms of the political import of consumption to consumers and workers themselves and in terms of the development of a militantly pro-business, antiregulatory movement that it encouraged in places where rapid population and economic growth offered opportunities for business elites to dominate the political process.[38]

In California, economic concerns predicated upon consumer interests and rapidly growing pressures on public services pushed the Stevenson campaign and the Democratic Party in the opposite direction to the antistatist dynamic at work in Sunbelt states. A confidential report compiled by a PR company working for Stevenson in California before the crucial primary clash against Estes Kefauver stated that "the issues of credit, jobs and inflation should in some way be underlined. . . . An informant in the consumer credit business explained that the average indebtedness in Los Angeles and other rapidly growing parts of California is far higher than the nation as a whole. These communities of small new homes, depending on the automobile for transportation and oriented towards California style easy living are overhung by the shadow of monthly payments and mortgages. . . . Perhaps this is the time for a new New Deal focus on a tremendous increase in productivity and the leisure that goes with it. . . . A psychiatrist told us that his patients here show far more than the usual anxiety about earning enough to keep up in the rat race." The report urged Stevenson to "show the voters that he cares for the things they care about by describing in concrete and emotionally charged language the problems from which they are suffering." There was not as much popular interest in health insurance or the injustices of Taft-Hartley as might have been expected, stated the report, but the "New Deal-Fair Deal as a whole has not lost its glamour. A New Deal program is what the Democratic voters want, and other forms of welfare legislation are popular. . . . There are other things . . . such as job stabilization, consumer debt, and above all, a rapid increase of living standards." The report concluded: "What this adds up to is a kind of New Deal package. Aside from pointing out a few issues which should be de-emphasized most all that is said above adds up to noting a widespread groping for a vigorous restatement of a New Deal approach on bread-and-butter matters, coupled with foreign affairs, civil rights and an occasional unifying pep talk to the active Democrats. The bread-and-butter package should appeal to the rapidly growing lower middle-class suburbs and might include such items as schools, water, taxes, and consumer debt."[39]

This conclusion found support in responses by local Democrats to a questionnaire sent out by Stevenson's campaign team in order to build up a statewide picture of issues that mattered to Californians. One question asked respondents for evidence of the status of local schools, housing, hospitals, and welfare. The response of the San Francisco party was that "our schools are excellent; housing is growing old, needs redevelopment; hospitals good but getting old; general health, good; social security, fair. We have thousands of old, lonely men and women living a meager existence in cheap apartments and hotels on skid road, South of Market. Better provision for them would be a boon to the community as well as themselves. Governor Stevenson should tour our Howard Street flophouses and point up the human misery. . . . He should visit our Hunter's Point 'temporary' housing where negroes live because they can't get good private housing at rates they can pay. He should dramatize his interest in these problems." Another question read: "what do you consider to be the key issues in your city and area in 1956? At what points is the Republican record strongest or most vulnerable to attack and at what point do you believe the Democratic position is strongest or weakest?" The response: "in four years Governor Stevenson can consolidate and *advance* the Democratic gains in social and old-age security, health preservation . . . health insurance (this need not touch the doctor-patient relationship but can cover all the costly incidentals of catastrophic illness such as hospital, laboratory, drugs, nurses, technical therapies), farm security, housing, SEC."[40] Gerald O'Gara, a veteran of San Francisco Democratic politics, argued in April that "Governor Stevenson to win must punch harder. As of now, the contrast between him and Eisenhower is too pale, too vaguely defined. Governor Stevenson must put on the mantle of Wilson, Roosevelt, and Truman and wear it boldly and proudly. . . . If he is not the apostle of the Democracy that crusades for labor (by which I mean all work for wages), for the small farmer, for the old, the sick, and the jobless, for children, for Negroes, for peace, for the small businessman, for a better life for all Americans (especially the little fellow) without a ceiling, either permanent or temporary, and a vigorous, unremitting fighter for the better life—then he is nothing as a Democratic candidate in 1956."[41]

The social democratic edge to Democratic Party thinking in California in part reflected the increasing influence of club activists and left-of-center thinkers in the party's affairs; it also formed a reaction to the increasing antiregulatory business control over Republican Party strategy. Central, however, to the left turn in Democratic politics during the 1956 presidential primary contest was the place of civil rights in party discourse, made vitally important not only by the growing pressure for a state FEPC but also because Estes

Kefauver made race an underlying rationale behind his run for president. Even after Kefauver withdrew from the race in July 1956, Stevenson's team remained concerned that his political enemies nationwide "will seek to cut down his lead and ultimately defeat his candidacy primarily by attacking his alleged position on civil rights. They will contend and argue that he has equivocated on the civil rights issue, that he seeks to accommodate the southern wing of the party and that he will not be a liberal president who will forthrightly face the issues in this critical area of our national life."[42] Stevenson had made serious mistakes during the primary season, asserting in Minneapolis in March that northern states had to put their own house in order before "we cast a stone at Alabama." A New York supporter called this speech "sheer political ineptitude," and Walter Reuther at a press conference tactfully replied to a question about Stevenson and civil rights that "I think that maybe if I were making speeches, I would say things differently than perhaps Mr. Stevenson says them."[43]

In California Stevenson's PR advisers were categorical: "Any new boners on the civil rights and desegregation issues—that is, any further actions on which Stevenson sounds indecisive, unindignant, or cool about the whole thing could be catastrophic for the Negro vote."[44] Not only that, civil rights was increasingly forming the new central issue for left-wing elements in the Democratic coalition, white as well as black. "Kefauver has benefited in California from a misunderstanding of the 'moderation' point and from his relatively more vigorous positions on such issues as natural gas and civil rights," wrote one Stevenson informant after having met with prominent state Democrats, including Roger Kent, Paul Ziffren, Richard Richards, and Peter Odegard.[45] The far left elements of the California Democratic Party were increasingly latching on to civil rights as their principal cause after the collapse of communism in the United States: "A large part of the energy behind the Kefauver campaign comes from pinks and fellow travelers, not to mention out and out Communists," claimed Stevenson's public relations consultants in California.[46] Stevenson's speech to the CDC convention at Fresno in February, at which he followed Kefauver and gave a lackluster speech, was widely seen as a major setback to his campaign. One correspondent begged Stevenson to make his speeches "inspired, provide definite benefits, frightened by black and definite evils and dangers—not gray shadows of possible disadvantages."[47] The increasing power of civil rights as a theme in California politics—and San Francisco passed a citywide fair employment practices ordinance in 1956—added a social citizenship dimension to the party's agenda and forced those running for office to take much more forthright stands on issues than was often the case elsewhere.

This is not to argue the Democrats were a united, integrated machine that worked harmoniously together in 1956. The party was, however, forced to come together around issues and personalities because of a growing feeling that the political tide was turning their way. The Stevenson campaign's interest in setting up a Stevenson for President Committee independent of the official Democratic party machinery and the clubs demonstrated the national campaign team's exasperation at the complex, unwieldy nature of state party politics, and reflected the advice they received from prominent party figures on the West Coast. Stevenson's campaign adviser Jane Dick reported during a long visit to California that Pat Brown, then still the only statewide office holder in the state party, "says that the Democratic Party loses a large segment of its conservative wing at every election. The conservatives don't like the Club movement 'which they feel is dominated by wild-eyed young people—wouldn't be caught dead at the Fresno Convention.' Most of these conservatives won't work with the regular organization either, so Brown feels the solution to getting them back is an independent organization for AES." She argued that it was "evident . . . that the Clubs do consist, in large part, of young people and that they are the most liberal element in the party. In considering a California SPC, the two-way North-South split and the three-way Organization-Clubs-Old Guard split must be taken into account."[48] In April Dick told fellow Stevenson national agent Wilson Wyatt that "there are so many cross currents there involving clashing personalities, old political feuds, power struggles, etc, that I don't believe it is possible to achieve anything beyond a sort of working arrangement which will develop out of the exigencies of the campaign."[49]

This prediction turned out to be accurate: the Independent Stevenson Committee brought together rival personalities such as Bill Joyce and Paul Ziffren in Los Angeles, and Roger Kent and Don Bradley in the Bay Area who were never friends, but who were able to turn out an impressive primary vote in June. Stevenson racked up 1,139,964 votes in the Democratic primary, nearly double the Kefauver vote and only 200,000 behind the Eisenhower tally in the uncontested Republican primary. Fred Dutton, a major player in Los Angeles Democratic politics, reported on the "startling and welcome" results in which African American precincts, corralled by an efficient Stevenson grassroots organization put together after the civil rights panic of the Fresno convention, had gone to Stevenson "by four and even five to one." San

Francisco had gone for Stevenson by 3–1 and LA by 2–1, "which was frankly much better than anybody expected for a population as un-Stevensonian as Smogville. . . . In the old folks' neighborhoods in southern California Stevenson did very well."[50] The coming together of the various warring factions to secure a Stevenson victory in the primary quickly came apart at the seams afterward. Roger Kent reported to Stevenson later in June of a party meeting in Monterey to appoint a man and woman to national committee posts ahead of the Chicago national convention that had been "about as bitter as any I've ever been in."[51] The tensions between rival factions and between regular Democrats and the clubs remained an issue, as did the fact that the Stevenson campaign could not manage to translate a near two to one registration advantage into a victory over a popular president.

A look at the race of Los Angeles State Senator Richard Richards for the U.S. Senate demonstrates, however, that the power of the club movement was pulling the various factions of the party together behind liberal candidates to create a party apparatus more clearly aligned to the left of their Republican rivals. Richards had won over the increasingly powerful CDC with his sensational victory in the state senate race in 1954, and he had a reputation as someone committed to the CDC's left-of-center agenda. His principal rival, Sam Yorty, had run for the U.S. Senate in 1954 against popular liberal Republican Tom Kuchel, and represented the conservative wing of the Los Angeles Democratic Party, who distrusted the club movement and who in 1960 would back Nixon over Kennedy and claim that during his second try for the Senate in 1956 "the Communists started a stop-Yorty movement. The CDC is the far left of the Democratic Party and not representative of the Democratic voters."[52] Both men knew in 1956 that they needed CDC endorsement in order to win the primary, an extraordinary fact given that the organization was but three years old. The Convention in Fresno wound up a turning point in shifting the political center of gravity within the party: Yorty failed to get the endorsement, the vote going overwhelmingly to Richards, who then trounced his rivals in the primary. Yorty stormed out of the meeting in fury, calling CDC "captive Democratic clubs," and claiming that the CDC "besmirch and defeat all Democrats who refuse to knuckle under to their political bossism. They're more like the old Independent Progressive Party, which was infiltrated by Communists."[53]

The extent to which the party had changed was indicated by the fact that many regular Democrats as well as organized labor fell in behind Richards. Carmen Warschaw, no particular fan of CDC as a loyalist to the Los

Angeles regular organization, "broke with Yorty" over his behavior at Fresno, claiming his supporters had spread scurrilous red-baiting material about Richards.[54] The AFL-CIO were split on the question, but in the end supported Richards because of the clout of CDC.[55] At their postprimary meeting in San Francisco labor's leadership endorsed Stevenson for president "on the basis of the intention of the Party platforms," and listened to Richards as he dissected the lessons of the primaries: "without cross-filing, your campaign for the office of United States Senator amassed more than one million votes on the Democratic ticket alone. . . . We amassed the largest number of counties carried on the Democratic ticket (and we were not on the other ticket) since 1944."[56] Richards did not in his moment of euphoria mention that his Republican opponent, who had cross-filed, garnered nearly half a million votes in the Democratic primary, more than Yorty had managed, in addition to 1.3 million in the Republican primary. Richards, like Stevenson, could not turn the tide in a Republican year.[57] The Republican Party continued to act as the default option for many in a state still unused to issue-driven party politics. There was no doubt, however, that the prevailing wind of California politics was shifting in the Democrats' direction just four years after their 1952 meltdown in a Senate race they had lost in the primary. In 1956 party loyalty was far more common, and the political message far more robust and clear-cut.

"There isn't any question in my mind," Roger Kent asserted some years later, "but that we would have carried California if it hadn't have been for the Suez crisis. We were running a very good campaign. The campaign was enthusiastic for Stevenson. The people were for Stevenson. It was going our way."[58] It is impossible to factor in such imponderables, but the signs in California were suggestive. Democrats won enough seats in the state senate to produce a tie with the Republicans; they were just three seats short of gaining the Assembly. Phil Burton won his Assembly seat with a strongly left-wing campaign against a popular incumbent Republican. More important, a coalition of economic and social rights advocates that encompassed labor, civil rights groups, and those pushing for a consumer-oriented social democratic politics was gradually coalescing into a major political force, with the Democratic Party as its lynchpin. Though this phenomenon had a particularly Californian flavor thanks to the growth of the clubs and the legacy of popular front influence that made civil rights and economic rights together especially potent on the party's left-wing, there were signs elsewhere that new Democratic strength was building in areas where the contours of 1950s social problems were influential. An example was South Dakota, where George

McGovern used worry over farm income and concern that the Cold War was leading the United States toward a real conflict to breathe life into a moribund Democratic Party. "Farmers' share of the consumer's food dollar has shrunk more than 10 cents since 1947," he reported to his constituents in January 1956. "The spread between farm and retail prices widens. Yet farmers do not have the conviction that their city cousins on mainstreet are prospering."[59] Former Connecticut Democratic congressman Chase Going Woodhouse argued in 1957 that the "Democrats need a new line. . . . I have tried out the idea of 'conformity,' of the need for 'angry young men' such as were around Roosevelt. . . . The changes in American life towards conformity and 'tranquillizers,' the attitude of the Eisenhower administration in not telling the public anything that might disturb them etc has troubled people. Few were courageous enough to speak out when McCarthy et al. were strong but now they would like to be associated with people who did."[60] The landmark elections of 1958 would change the political landscape of both California and the nation dramatically, demonstrating the extent to which a new political order was on the horizon, with enormous consequences for the economic and civil rights of California citizens.

CHAPTER 6

The Liberal Moment

The midterm elections of 1958 transformed the electoral landscape of the United States in ways that would resonate for decades to come. After the disaster of 1946 that had swept aside the New Deal coalition of the cities, suburbs, and the South in Congress the Democratic Party had become beholden to its still monolithic southern base, which had provided the margin of victory in its narrow victories in 1948, 1950, 1954, and 1956. Congress had failed in these years to repeal much of the anti-New Deal legislation of the Republican 80th Congress, in particular the Taft-Hartley Act. After 1958 a significant change could be discerned. It was not just the sheer scale of the Democratic victories: 13 gains in the Senate and some 48 in the House, gains that would establish a substantial majority for the party for years to come.[1] Many of the new Democratic members on Capitol Hill were northern liberals who had not come of age politically in the febrile years of the very early Cold War, but had come to office committed to an agenda that would form the basis of the Great Society in the 1960s. The Democratic Study Group was formed in the aftermath of the 1958 elections to establish a left-of-center powerbase in the House and exploit the greater influence urban and suburban liberals from outside the Deep South would have over policymaking. Significant Democratic victories at the state level, including in California, would create a Democratic bias in redistricting that would impede the Republicans' ability to recover from the disaster that had dramatically reduced their strength in urban America. The year 1958 would be the last time key districts in Berkeley, West Los Angeles, and many other American cities would be talked about as competitive. And the scale of the northern Democratic majority would pave the way toward the creation of Medicare, the passage of the Civil Rights and Voting Rights Acts, and the expansion of Social Security and welfare programs. It is certainly the case that the electoral success of Democratic candidates was far from irreversible, and only ten years later Kevin Phillips was making his influential argument predicting a new Republican majority in American politics.[2] Nevertheless, the response of the voters to the Eisenhower recession set the scene for the dramatic change in the political zeitgeist in the 1960s.[3]

Nowhere was this political transformation more apparent than in California. Democrats committed to an agenda that combined a commitment to economic and social citizenship seized power at every level of state politics from the governorship to state controller, and established majorities in the legislature that would only briefly be interrupted over the next twenty years. The victories of Democrats across the state were particularly remarkable given how inconsequential the party had been just a handful of years earlier. The 1958 campaign gave Democrats the chance to articulate their political worldview in clearly defined terms, using the campaign against the state's right-to-work Proposition 18 as a foil against which to set out their broader agenda of equality of opportunity, enlargement of the public sector, and the promotion of civil rights legislation. The Brown campaign's articulation of a language of rights set the stage for an expansion of the state that would encourage the inclusion of previously marginalized sections of society into mainstream society. Their electoral success that year represented the culmination of a process of political self-definition that had gathered pace in the decade since World War II and established California Democrats as trendsetters for the emergence of a left-of-center program for the later twentieth century.

The attention of political historians of California has often focused upon the 1950s and 1960s as a time in which a right-wing coalition of antiregulatory business organizations and a grassroots conservative movement established a foothold on state politics ahead of the later successes of Barry Goldwater and Ronald Reagan as standard-bearers of a new right politics.[4] Important though these studies are, they can serve only as partial explanations for the particular path right-wing politics took in the postwar era insofar as they do not examine the role that the creation of a powerful left-of-center alternative played in the establishment of a clear left-right tension in modern Californian politics. Far from being a new phenomenon, right-wing antiregulatory politics was the default position in California in the 1950s, and the emergence of the Democratic alternative as a force to be reckoned with formed the basis of a competitive political dynamic in state politics that helps to explain the increased organizational and ideological zeal on both sides of the political spectrum. The "right-to-work" referendum that framed the 1958 gubernatorial campaign in California represented the end of the cozy Republican consensus in state politics and provided Democrats with a way of legitimizing their political worldview and redefining the terms of debate in ways that would have long-term significance.

The "Big Switch" and the Creation of a New Free Enterprise Ideology

The attempt of prominent business leaders to brush aside the New Deal compact between management and labor that had been gathering pace since World War II reached its height with the sponsorship of "right-to-work" statutes in California and Ohio in 1958. These initiatives, which allowed states to outlaw the union shop and drastically weaken the influence of labor unions in the workplace, had since the passage of the Taft-Hartley Act in 1947 been made law in several states, but the Ohio and California measures were the first to reach the ballot in industrialized states with a high percentage of union members in the workforce.[5] In California the situation was complicated by the fact that Senator William Knowland not only spearheaded the right-to-work campaign, but did so in an attempt to elbow aside sitting governor and fellow Republican Goodwin Knight and unite right-wing business groups behind his campaign for the governorship, presumably with the aim of using the governor's mansion as a stepping stone to even higher office.[6] To the extent that the 1958 California elections are known to historians, they represent the story of a disastrously misjudged forced job swap between Knowland and Knight that split the Republican base, completed the divorce of the GOP and organized labor in California, and created a groundswell of opposition to Republican candidates in an already difficult year for the GOP that resulted in defeat for the California party at almost every level and delayed the construction of a new right majority in the state that came to prominence under Governor Ronald Reagan.[7]

Far from being a brief hiatus in an otherwise uninterrupted natural development of a conservative hegemony in California politics, the clash between Knowland and Knight in fact symbolized the replacement of the idea of Republicanism as the natural political order with a radical antilabor campaign that essentially portrayed Republican antistatism as an insurgent force against a leftist political ascendancy. Knowland's right-to-work campaign in effect handed political legitimacy to a Democratic opposition that had been steadily building up its command of its own base but which before 1958 had remained unable to translate its increased organizational and ideological self-confidence into widespread electoral success. Starting with the events of 1958, left and right forces in California politics defined themselves and their respective political worldviews with reference to each other, something Republicans had not always needed to do before then. Right-to-work was more than just a tactical blunder in California: it pushed the terms of reference of political debate onto the rhetorical and ideological terrain of the liberal Democrats, creating a new left versus right dichotomy in a state in which Republican candidates had previously been able to monopolize power.

Knight was not alone in feeling exasperation at Knowland's decision to enter the race against him in September 1957. Knight's campaign managers, Whitaker and Baxter, though hardly opposed to a bold statement of pro-business, antiregulatory arch-Republicanism as symbolized by Knowland, were convinced his intervention would be a disaster. They had perfected a campaign strategy for Knight, and for Earl Warren before him, that successfully portrayed them and the political world they inhabited as representative of all California. Anyone who opposed them was an extremist or someone alien to the political culture of the state, but, as we have seen, the key to Whitaker and Baxter was to deny these opponents any exposure or political legitimacy lest the debate be opened up and the range of options available to the electorate made apparent. The ideological underpinning of the Whitaker and Baxter strategy was the concept of individualism, a notion designed to advance the legitimacy of private enterprise as the engine of order and progress but which also encompassed labor union members who could be convinced that the "free enterprise system" under Republican stewardship remained the only political show in town. Whitaker and Baxter's carefully crafted response to Knowland's announcement that they provided for Knight's use was a restatement of this technique. "I have a deep and abiding faith in California's climate of tolerance among business, labor, agriculture and government," the text read. "It is this mutual understanding of a common interest in a stable and prosperous economy which I firmly believe has permitted us to meet the challenge of our phenomenal growth. I assure the people of California that I will not stand idly by and see this cooperative spirit, which has benefited us so greatly, destroyed by extremists of either the left or the right."[8] Later, after he had switched to run for the Senate, Whitaker and Baxter provided a keynote address for Knight entitled "This is what I believe" which argued that Knight believed "in the inherent dignity of the individual. I believe in government which is honest and efficient and which—while preserving public order and protecting civil rights—least restricts the liberties of the individual. I am an enthusiastic champion of the free enterprise system. . . . We must not, ever, sacrifice the individual initiative system which made us prosperous and free for the very totalitarian methods we abhor."[9] The message of the Whitaker and Baxter operation never suggested that alternatives to the pro-business, antitotalitarian consensus established under Governor Knight were especially powerful, nor were any opponents mentioned. The intention was to make Knight and the Republican Party as constituted the default political choice, and all opponents somehow outside the mainstream.

Knowland's approach to political campaigning differed in both tone and emphasis. His candidacy had received strong backing from key figures in the state Chamber of Commerce, National Association of Manufacturers, and the Chandler newspaper empire, all of whom had observed the growth of the political center-left in California and the increasing politicization of the state's labor organizations and who were demanding a major antilabor drive to crush opposition to private sector prerogatives before it could gain any more strength. Lemuel Boulware of General Electric (GE) saw the 1958 elections as a platform upon which to take his education program out of the company boardroom and into the wider political arena. He was convinced that a concerted effort to convince elected politicians to support a pro-business agenda was a crucial next step in his campaign to roll back union prerogatives, claiming in a letter to Raymond Moley in April 1957 that his "recent contacts in Washington indicate the legislators and administrators there don't know any businessmen anymore, don't know that they are even interested in what's going on, don't know what businessmen want and why, and don't sense that businessmen have any interest or ability in changing the course of politics." Boulware wanted the campaigns of friendly candidates for political office to reflect his GE educational drive and flag up "the concept of business really involving *the many* and, thus, anything affecting business affects the voting majority, whether or not that majority has yet been alerted to that fact."[10] A National Right to Work Committee was established in Washington in the mid-1950s to "do all that we can to bring it about that every American citizen shall be fully informed with respect to the evils of compulsory unionism in the confident belief that an enlightened public opinion will soon banish from our national scene this menace to traditional American liberties."[11]

The committee provided a national focus for the various state-level campaigns to implement Section 14b of the Taft-Hartley Act, and one of its core leaders was also executive vice president of the Kansas Right-to-Work effort, the only successful initiative of its kind in 1958. Reed Larson would soon become right-to-work's roving ambassador throughout the 1960s and 1970s, addressing a variety of audiences ranging from civil rights groups to chambers of commerce on the dangers of compulsory unionism. Yet his analysis of his successful experience in Kansas gave clues as to the problems inherent in Bill Knowland's Senate campaign in California. He emphasized in his memo to right-to-work committee members entitled "How Right to Work Was Adopted in Kansas" that he did not feel that it was because Kansas was not a major industrialized state: "Kansas is more industrial than agricultural," he wrote. "Organized labor is strong and aggressive." He argued instead that the key to victory in areas of Kansas that had supported the referendum was obtained "when business leaders come out from behind the cloak of anonymity afforded by business organizations to let it be known that they, as individuals, believe in freedom from compulsory unionism." In Kansas City, where right to work did not win a majority of votes, "Right to Work had almost NO public support from business men." In Wichita, by contrast, "businessmen and other community leaders courageously let their position be known. The head of nearly every Wichita firm wrote letters to all employees stating frankly that he, the writer, was supporting Right to Work, and explaining why. Among the active business people were executives of Boeing Plane Company, Cessna Aircraft, the Coleman Company, Vickers Petroleum Company, Kansas Milling Company, Southwest Grease and Oil, Love Box Company, and many others." Larson's strategy was to portray these individual corporate leaders as individual citizens, part of a broader coalition of "the company president and the lathe operator . . . the doctor, the lawyer, the farmer, the housewife," that would enter battle against the impersonal force of "labor."[12] The organization was kept carefully separate in public discourse from party politics, and indeed as 56.3 percent of Kansans were voting to pass a right-to-work initiative they were also voting in a Democratic governor. Although the right-to-work effort was intimately bound up with Republican Party politics in Kansas as elsewhere, the public face of antiunionism was, like Whitaker and Baxter's management of Goodie Knight in California, a stage-managed appeal to universal democratic values.

In California, by contrast, right-to-work became a tool in a battle for control of the state Republican Party. L. R. Hart of the Sebastopol Fruit Growers Association made clear his frustration at Governor Knight's pro-labor policy, seeing Knowland's candidacy as the perfect vehicle for an attack on union prerogatives in the Golden State. "The Governor's complete leftist attitude in endorsing and supporting labor . . . has also severely damaged the Governor," he wrote. "The Governor's repeated statement that he would veto any 'Right-to-Work' legislation is another factor that has lost him Republican support throughout the state." Yet business leaders were divided over the value of right-to-work as a political issue in 1958: Hart was responding to a mass mailing to business leaders on behalf of Knight by a director of Delta Airlines Inc., who feared the implications of a right turn in the state GOP that would only strengthen the previously moribund Democratic Party.[13] "California is becoming the most important state in the Union," argued a political pundit on a radio debate entitled "Governor Knight—Did He Jump or Was He Pushed?" on KQED San Francisco, "and the conservative element is not willing to let it be a liberal state. They couldn't trust Knight to be conservative. Knight has been all things to all men." Knowland had tapped key business allies for support, promising them he would push a right-to-work ballot proposition to the center of his campaign agenda, something Knight refused to do. In the eyes of the radio show pundits, Knowland's "gamble on the right-to-work law paid off in consolidating the Kingmaker group behind him." This group of "fifty Destiny Makers," headed by newspaper barons Norman Chandler and Joe Knowland and Chamber of Commerce leader Charles Blyth, had in the eyes of *Newsweek* bureau manager William Flynn operated in the interests of Vice President Nixon as he eyed the presidency himself: "He saw a chance to give both Knowland and Knight 'the deep six.' He would put Knight in the cooler for six years, and if Knowland is beaten he is out as a presidential threat to Nixon." Nixon had put pressure on the business elite to tell Knight he had to abandon the governor's race or face losing all political funding. "It was a case of a disgraced officer being given a loaded revolver and left alone in a room," argued Flynn.[14] Whoever was behind the decision to force Goodwin Knight out of the gubernatorial race, it was clear that they were motivated by the belief that defending the status quo was not sufficient. A new political strategy of rolling back all that remained of the political economy of the New Deal was required at a time when powerful sections of the state's business leadership were flexing their political muscles.[15]

In order to sell right-to-work to the electorate it was necessary for the Knowland campaign to depart from the tried and tested campaign script that had guided Republican gubernatorial campaigns up to that point. Individualism and free enterprise were no longer the natural order of things, but were suddenly under threat from powerful and dangerous subversive forces hell-bent on destroying the American economic system. Far from ignoring his opponent, Attorney General Pat Brown, Knowland's campaign speeches seemed almost to assume Brown and his allies were in power and that he, Knowland, was the insurgent. "There are forces in the world so senseless and perverted," Knowland proclaimed in a near hysterical tirade at San Bernardino Valley College in September 1958, "that they are busy selling men that the age-old system of slavery is new because they have put new garments on it. They would tell us that the heavy hand of government regulation is new instead of something that mankind in its struggle has been attempting to throw off for years."[16] Whereas previous Republican campaigns in California, as well as Knight's 1958 Senate race, had portrayed Democratic liberalism as new and untried in California, Knowland seemed to suggest that it was well on its way to power. Referring to the tax implications of the "New Deal-labor boss combine that has taken over the Democratic Party in California," Knowland warned a crowd in Santa Monica that Brown "would turn back the clock in California, lead to state controls of your wages, prices and production and scare away the new industry and business California needs to continue its program." He told a partisan audience of the Republican Assembly in Stockton that Brown was "the captive candidate of the political bosses who have accumulated a one and a half million dollar slush fund from their members in an all-out attempt to seize power in California. . . . This is the road away from free enterprise and toward state labor socialist controls. . . . he would lead California down the road of state OPA type controls."[17] In every speech Knowland lambasted his Democratic opponent and organized labor for being "power-mad men" seeking to gain control over the levers of political power in California. Rarely did he mention his own program beyond a commitment to roll back trade union prerogatives and reinforce private business control over economic activity.[18]

Knowland's campaign strategy was little different from the public education campaigns of the business leaders who were bankrolling him, notably GE, whose Public Education Department had been preaching the virtues of business executive control over corporate decision-making for years. It also resembled the right-to-work campaigns in the 1950s in over a dozen other states. Initially Knowland also seemed to have the advantage, with a poll in fall 1957 suggesting the initiative had a 57 percent to 30 percent margin of support, and four small California counties had passed county right-to-work initiatives by 1957.[19] What made California different, and Knowland's campaign ill-advised, is that California had a strong union presence and a long history of industrialization, as well as an entrenched Republican establishment that had managed to accommodate the realities of a complex and rapidly evolving industrial economy. In the Bay Area, union membership in July 1956 stood at 542,300, an increase of some 25,000 from 1954, the largest increases occurring in food production, transportation and warehousing, and wholesale and retail trade.[20] Knowland's strategy risked legitimizing a political other that had heretofore rarely troubled Republicans' hold on power, and also seemed tailor-made to render antilabor Republicans as the extremists and outsiders and the Democrats as the purveyors of inclusiveness and common citizenship.

Whitaker and Baxter, veterans of the California political scene, made it clear that they believed that handing political legitimacy to Knowland's opponents by admitting the existence of a big debate over political economy was a mistake. "As a matter of principle," they wrote, "we are opposed to the idea that a man should be compelled to join a union either to get a job or to hold it. But practically, we feel that it would be a mistake to submit the issue to the voters of California at this time, and that those in the business community who favor the Right-to-Work principle 'missed the boat' in not fighting this battle to a decision years ago before the union shop became as thoroughly entrenched in many of our major industries as it is today. We have serious doubts as to whether a Right-to-Work campaign can be won at this year's election, due to many complicating factors, we also feel it would create bitterness and turmoil as to endanger the whole Republican ticket."[21]

Their alternative strategy for Knight in his run for Knowland's Senate seat placed their candidate's worldview at the heart of the experience of all Californians. In a "suggested editorial" circulated to the pro-Republican press, Whitaker and Baxter's team of copywriters outlined Knight's "nonpolitical, nonsectional leadership" and argued that he had been "supported by every segment of the population—proof that they recognize he stands for equitable treatment for ALL of California, and represents ALL of California." Knight's nonpartisanship was not an apolitical statement: his speeches and campaign material referred repeatedly to the need for tax cuts to stimulate a stalling economy and to the dangers of "pump priming measures of expedience" and "leaf-raking projects which will not create prosperity."[22] He refused, however, to join the right-to-work bandwagon because he saw the danger it posed to his party's control over the terms of political debate. He also bore the wounds of the betrayal he had suffered at the hands of Knowland's political allies, having "had his head amputated and served up on a platter for the entertainment of two powerful, ambitious fellow Californians, names Nixon and Knowland."[23] The *New Republic* commented gleefully on the disintegration of the previously mighty Republican machine, noting that "Knowland, Nixon and other GOP California politicians in Washington are now threatening Republican Senatorial candidate Knight with dire consequences (such as refusing to distribute his campaign literature) if he doesn't overlook the blood he's still coughing up from the beating they gave him last Spring and help elect Knowland Governor. Knight says he differs with Knowland on right-to-work and will have none of it."[24]

Knowland's team ploughed on with its increasingly shrill campaign to cast California as part of a vanguard of states friendly to business investment and hostile to labor unions and regulation of the private sector. The movement to elect Knowland formed part of a broader campaign on the part of corporate America to remove the policy legacy of the New Deal from the political landscape. GE ran pro-right-to-work advertisements in California and stepped up their junior executive political education programs. "If we are lulled into further stupid political silence and inactivity, we are licked," commented GE's by now famous PR guru Lemuel Boulware. "It's as simple as that."[25] The business lobby's umbrella group "Californians for Yes on 18" ran a careful campaign, replicated in Ohio, Arizona, and a number of other states, that tried to reassure voters that right-to-work did not seek to destroy unions, only to introduce choice into the industrial relations process. "You'll find NOT A WORD threatening the existence of ANY UNION," promised one pro-18 leaflet. "Its purpose is clear—to give wage earners the RIGHT TO JOIN or NOT TO JOIN a union as they see fit. That's all!"[26] Knowland himself was tempted into a different approach in his increasingly desperate drive to turn the election his way. "Wielding the mighty sword of hate in the mailed fist of compulsion," he thundered, "the Goliath of uncontrolled union dictatorship has strode among us, daring us to send out our champion. . . . To place in the hands of a few the power of economic life and death over any individual, without his consent, is *wrong* by every moral standard acceptable to man. It was wrong for the Pharaohs; it was wrong for the Caesars; it was wrong for Hitler; it is wrong for the Kremlin, and, by everything which I believe, it is wrong for America."[27] His team circulated a booklet entitled "Meet the Man Who Wants to Rule America," a slanderous attack on Walter Reuther by Joseph P. Kamp, described by the *New Republic* as a "well-known pseudo-fascist . . . who served a jail sentence for contempt and caused the late Senator Taft to declare that he was 'particularly disgusted' with Kamp's mailings."[28]

Knowland's wife Helen approved the distribution of the leaflets from her position in the highest echelons of the "Rollin' for Knowland" organization, and she contributed material to the campaign, including an article in right-wing periodical *Human Events*.[29] Her strident, paranoid interventions further distanced the gubernatorial race from the rest of the party in California. "The reason behind Billy's decision to run for Governor is the frightening, successful inroads the Labor-Socialist movement has made in our country. . . . Knight is hand in glove with the Labor Bosses. . . . What motivates the Browns, the Knights and those who think Government should not only compete with but supplant private business?" Her apocalyptic tone was at odds with the more measured "Yes on 18" approach that attempted, like Knight's campaign, to adopt the consensus approach. "How well Billy knows," she wrote, "that even now the time may be late for California. That perhaps California might be the last hope of saving our country from the Piggy-back Labor-Socialist monster which has latched on to the Democratic Party and to some Republicans as well, 'poor Goodie' being a perfect example." She claimed union leaders were determined to "destroy" her husband.[30] Although her tone seemed at times to be intemperate, her concerns were widely shared in a broader national conservative campaign against organized labor. Barry Goldwater made the point during a visit to Michigan, a strongly unionized state that stood in stark contrast to his increasingly corporate-controlled home state of Arizona, that many Republicans feared "that what is happening here is all too much like what happened about fifty years ago in England when seasoned political bosses from the labor unions moved in behind the façade of the Liberal Party, and took it over."[31] Former New Deal brain truster and by now arch-conservative commentator Raymond Moley wrote an article for *Newsweek* headed, "Crisis in California," in which he sketched an apocalyptic vision for the nation in the event of a Knowland defeat. "Our two-party system, already weakened, would crumble. . . . The Democratic Party would fall more deeply into captivity to the AFL-CIO COPE political machine." Democratic control over redistricting would "swing the ideological balance in the House for ten years. This margin . . . would assure more inflationary spending, progressive invasion of the states and of economic life, drastic weakening of Taft-Hartley, and ultimate Welfare Statism."[32]

This sort of approach to questions of mid-twentieth century political economy worked to a degree in states with strong, centralized private business organizations and weak labor movements where a new "Sunbelt" strategy of attracting investment was taking shape. Arizona had passed a right-to-work law and would reelect Barry Goldwater to the Senate in a difficult year for Republicans. In California, however, strong labor representation and a diverse, decentralized political system in which regulation of economic power had strong roots made Knowland's campaign out of step with the political current.[33] In Arizona the relationship between the newly powerful Republican Party and the business community was being formed virtually from scratch, but in California GOP dominance of the political process had a longer pedigree and was more broadly based, and so GE's Lemuel Boulware's argument that "the major labor problem of the country is not with the few bad union officials but with the many so-called 'good' ones" encapsulated an agenda that was difficult to sell in the Golden State.[34] The apocalyptic tone of GOP attacks on organized labor and its ties to the Democrats also sat awkwardly with a political culture that privileged appeals to issues that transcended party. Earl Warren's refusal to embrace party loyalty and Nixon's appeal to anticommunism had both in their different ways associated their candidacies with universalist American values of democracy that could appeal to a wide cross-section of the electorate. Pat Brown also embraced this strategy, reaching out to Moley in June in an attempt to head off blanket negative coverage from the East Coast conservative press by offering to talk politics with Moley, before later responding angrily to the *Newsweek* piece. At the bottom of his typed letter branding Moley's article "very unfair" he scrawled in pen "and *you know it*," venting his frustration at what he perceived to be a portrayal of a "captive" Democratic Party and his own campaign that simply did not reflect the realities of California politics.[35]

The self-portrayal of the Knowland forces as an oppressed minority fighting valiantly against a socialist plot, quixotic at first in a hitherto Republican stronghold, gained increased currency when the primary results pointed to the extent to which California's balance of power had changed in the 1950s. Whereas four years earlier Richard Graves had eked out a win in his own primary, in 1958 Brown garnered 1,792,621 votes in the Democratic primary to Knowland's 388,712. Knowland won his own party primary handily, but Brown managed 322,886 votes in the GOP primary, and managed a lead when both primaries were added together of over 600,000 votes, the first Democratic lead in overall primary voting in state history. The state Republican high command blamed the poor figures on apathy and poor organization, but also commented upon the "better organization" of the Democrats thanks to the California Democratic Council, as well as the concerted effort of the AFL-CIO to register their membership: "It is reported that CIO-COPE checked their membership for registration, found it at about the 35% level. Through the very simple device of requiring proof of registration . . . before dues could be paid (i.e. no dues, no 'card'—no card, no job), CIO-COPE raised the registration level of their members to about 70% They plan to push it closer to 100% for the November elections. There are approximately 1,725,000 union members in California."[36] The primary results revealed to the *New Republic* "a new pattern of voting along semi-straight party lines—strange to California." It observed that to the "distress of Republicans, in fact, little in California politics seems as it was before. . . . Pat Brown . . . has divided the usually monolithic daily press and has on his side many respectable businessmen and Republicans who can afford to contribute generously."[37] More significantly still, the decision of Knowland and his allies to place class and ideology at the heart of their campaign, portraying the Democratic platform as "the most destructive, class conscious, socialist-directed program ever offered the people of this state," encouraged the Brown campaign to define its own program in stark opposition to the Republicans, completing the transformation of the California Democratic Party into an organ of left-of-center politics on the West Coast.[38]

"Government with a Heart": The Political Education of Pat Brown

Pat Brown was the obvious choice for the Democratic nomination for governor in 1958. He was a proven statewide vote getter, having been elected attorney general in a year, 1950, that was generally ghastly for Democratic candidates. Brown was an unusual breed: a native Californian who could trace his family's connection to the Golden State back two generations on both maternal and paternal lines. Born in 1905 in San Francisco, Edmund Gerald Brown would make the city his lifelong home, except for the eight years he spent in the governor's mansion in Sacramento. A graduate of San Francisco Law School, he quickly established his own small private practice in the city, and had a precocious start to political life when he ran unsuccessfully for the state assembly as a Republican at age twenty-three. The horrors of the Depression converted Brown to the party of FDR, just in time for him to assist with one of the California Democratic Party's very few state-level successes prior to his own in 1958: the election of Culbert Olson as governor in 1938. His experience as head of Olson's fund-raising committee in San Francisco and the speakers' bureau for Northern California left Brown hooked on state politics, and he ran twice for the office of San Francisco district attorney, winning at the second attempt in 1943. In 1946 a run for attorney general foundered on the rocks of a heavily Republican year, but his fortunes changed four years later when the GOP incumbent, Fred Howser, became mired in scandal and thus hampered his replacement's campaign.[39] Brown was gregarious and a good glad-hander whose affable personality earned him few enemies in the party. He was an enthusiastic supporter of the CDC and the club movement without ever becoming overly associated with the left of the party, battling manfully to keep the different factions of the Democratic endeavor working as one. As one club liberal put it, "you're never quite sure where he's going to end up on an issue. Although he's always on the right side, you're never quite sure how he got there. You ask, 'where's the big money? Where's it coming from?' OK, Brown's getting a lot of it—a lot. Liberals being the sort of people they are, they're suspicious of it." Another described him as a "lone wolf" during his 1950 race, determined to avoid too much identification with the collapsing Roosevelt and Douglas campaigns.[40]

The Knowland and Knight debacle convinced Brown, as it did Congressman Clair Engle in his decision to run for the Senate, that races that looked difficult in mid-1957 suddenly looked winnable. "That was the touchstone," recalled Roger Kent. "That was what made it possible that we field such a strong team." The strength of that team was reflected in the primary result, which prompted sudden national interest in the political earthquake occurring on the West Coast. Kent, who happened to be in Washington on primary day, held a press conference "and two hundred people there were absolutely astounded, because the Eastern press had just not picked up what was going to happen out here at *all*. . . . We felt very secure. And as soon as you have that kind of security, money begins to come in. People want to bet on a winner . . . so we got *plenty* of financial support."[41] Brown's ability to represent a diverse range of interests during his political career allowed him to tap various sources for funds and even to gain the support of many Republicans angry at Knowland's bitterly partisan campaign while still winning the overwhelming endorsement of the CDC and organized labor, both sensing that a major change in the political terrain of the Golden State was imminent.

Though historians have picked up on the contribution of the Republicans' mistakes in shifting the political center of gravity at the end of the 1950s, less has been made of the ideological underpinnings of the Democratic campaigns that year that both propelled them to victory and contributed to a long-term change in political identity in California. The labor-led campaign against the compulsory open shop was the principal issue of the election, but it also acted as a catalyst for the broader politicization of the labor movement and the increased political confidence of the Democratic Party as it put together its campaign message. At a basic level Knowland's embrace of right-to-work completed the break between labor and the California Republican Party. Though C. J. Haggerty forced the executive committee of the CLLPE to remain loyal to Knight by just a one vote margin, the rank and file of the endorsing convention rebelled and insisted that Clair Engle be endorsed as well. In so doing they were only taking the advice given to them earlier in the proceedings by the AFL-CIO's national political director James McDevitt, when he advised members to "express yourselves politically or you die by their [right-to-work forces] weapon. There is no way of divorcing the economic side from the political picture." He argued that "for the first time in the history of American politics the program is clearly outlined. You see on the one side 'the average man and woman'—as against the powerful interests of this country on the other side."[42]

The labor campaign against right-to-work had deeper political implications: the notion of the working person pitted against the barons of industry created a more significant political message underpinning labor's education program directed at its membership. Organized labor was assuming the mantle of the defender of economic citizenship for its members, using campaign techniques that linked labor rights to the rights of all Americans as members of a shared community. A television educational program sponsored by labor's political wing and produced by labor's Bay Area PR consultant David Selvin was entitled "Every Other House" and was designed to ram home this message to viewers on two Bay Area TV stations. "Do you realize," intoned the narrator as the camera panned across a suburban neighborhood, "that every other house on this block—and every other block around the Bay Area—is occupied by a union family, a family with at least one person belonging to an organization which represents them in their dealings with their employer? . . . Labor unions are people—people working together to accomplish desirable goals. And the people are your neighbors, the man living next door—the girl across the street." The narrator then proceeded to chat to a carefully scripted cross-section of society to build up a picture of labor unions as representative of the broader community.[43] The program was designed to provide a "solid Labor Day message for Bay Area TV viewers" by "introducing in a non-controversial manner a background for judging the compulsory open shop bill or measure."[44] Selvin's strategy was to wrest from the GOP command of the default option in California politics and make pro-union economic citizenship the new consensus. The No on 18 campaign tied opposition to right-to-work to a broader social democratic political agenda. A radio advertisement aimed at housewives argued that the rationale behind opposition to the open shop concerned "her family and home—her household budget and living standards. A NO vote will protect California's high wages and salaries—keep them going up, ahead of living costs. . . . A NO will protect our good working conditions—our forty hour week, job safety, paid vacations, job security."[45] An anti-18 leaflet claimed that the open shop "would create a dog-eat-dog competition for jobs. Without unions and union contracts, jobs would go to the low bidder. . . . Wages are lower, hours are longer in 'right-to-work' states. . . . Health and welfare plans, pension plans, paid holidays and vacations, sick leave for millions of California workers depend entirely on union contracts. Weaken the contracts and the unions that stand behind them and the foundation of these benefits is seriously threatened."[46] Just as GE's PR department argued that it was "an essential part of good corporate citizenship" to educate the electorate in the benefits of the open shop, so now labor's high command saw the benefits of using political education to articulate a vision of the working man and woman as defenders of social justice.[47]

The anti-open shop campaign cemented the political direction of organized labor and its relationship with a confident, well-organized Democratic organization. A labor committee for Democrats against right-to-work was set up in the wake of the dramatic primary victories, making the case that "we have to make sure, too, that our flanks are protected—that we elect state officials and a legislature who share our firm and vigorous opposition to any form of 'right to work' legislation. Outside the labor movement itself, we're convinced the strongest support we can find is in the Democratic candidates—every one of whom has publicly and unqualifiedly declared his opposition to the compulsory open shop."[48] The massive labor campaign to register voters—three hundred volunteer deputy registrars enlisted by the San Francisco Labor Council were working around the clock in that city alone through August—took place alongside a massive organizational campaign by Democratic clubs and the Brown campaign to galvanize voters behind their political efforts. Hordes of precinct workers were dispatched to take the issue of the open shop to the streets and to people's homes.[49] A polling company noted the extent to which the right-to-work issue had brought together organized labor and Democrats to form a powerful electoral machine. Predicting a "clean sweep" for the Democrats in the November general election, the report noted that since January 1958 "when it appeared reasonably certain that '18' would qualify for the ballot, organized labor and the Democratic clubs have been engaged in an intensive, well-organized drive to get all out voter registration and vote turnout." Of new registrants in 1958, 72 percent had registered as Democrats.[50] Democratic candidates were careful to point up their support of labor and the broader political program that their support of the labor cause entailed. "Assemblyman A. Phillip Burton has received the endorsement of every branch of organized labor (AFL, CIO, Railroad Brotherhood, independent unions) in his bid for reelection," proclaimed a press release from Burton's campaign team in San Francisco. "Burton, a fearless champion in the cause of the working men and women of this state, has a perfect labor voting record . . . Burton advocated increasing the unemployment benefits, extending the coverage and the length of the benefits period and to accelerate a public works program." Burton extended the concept of labor rights to include a broader definition of economic citizenship: "I take pride in my legislative support of the new laws which guarantee equal pay for equal work (for women) and the improvements enacted for our needy aged and blind."[51]

Pat Brown used the formal kick-off of the general election campaign around Labor Day as an opportunity to set out his stall for a radical overhaul of the public sphere in California. "Meeting the needs of a growing state like ours requires a vigorous and progressive public spirit," he announced in a broadcast on Los Angeles TV station KTTV. "Our population increase, for example, will require that 600,000 new jobs be created during the next four years. And every day of every week for those four years, 23 classrooms should be opened in our public schools." He outlined an eight-point plan to enlarge governmental responsibility for providing public services and to manage the state's economic development. He proposed the creation of a state Department of Economic Development "to attract new industries, new jobs for our growing population." He attempted to develop the consumption angle to modern liberalism suggested during the 1956 Stevenson campaign by advancing the idea that a "public defender for the consumer interests" would be needed "to fight high prices, borderline lending practices, high utility rates and the impact of inflation on family spending."[52] He linked economic citizenship to an equal rights agenda by endorsing "legislation with enforcement powers to assure equal job opportunities for all Californians without regard to race, creed, or color." His opposition to right-to-work was contextualized in broader political terms when he described it as "a return to the ugly and destructive law of the economic jungle." He noted the importance of the guiding hand of the state to the provision of water to Southern California, and to the provision of education opportunities. He concluded the announcement of his political program with a stark differentiation between the worldviews of his opponent and himself: "I believe Californians have a clear-cut choice this year between progressive leadership interested in people and determined to look forward or ultra-conservative leadership grimly determined not to let an incumbent Republican governor or anyone else stand in his way of national ambition."[53] Brown exploited the creation of a left-right binary in political debate to establish his own party's political worldview as representative of the popular will. "At a political level," he informed an audience at a hundred-dollar-a-plate fundraiser in San Francisco in October, "this campaign and this election prove the maturity, the unity, the responsibility, of the Democratic Party in California. We are demonstrating that with steady progress, the Democratic Party in this state is more vigorous than ever before—and more representative of the community of California than ever before. . . . The truth is: this California campaign is closing the national political spectrum on the extreme far right."[54]

Brown's attempt to transform the parameters of political discourse in California utilized specific policy commitments to tie Democratic Party values to the particular social concerns of the late 1950s. California's economic infrastructure simply could not cope with the demands of the state's population growth without the guiding hand of government, particularly at a time of sharp recession. Brown was confident enough of the changing political climate to argue for "a bold approach" to economic planning, "something that could stimulate the economy. The freeways—before they're completed they won't handle the traffic load. I think government should make things a little more comfortable."[55] He waded in to a debate over whether the federal government or Pacific Gas and Electric should manage a new water project on the Trinity River to divert surplus water to the Central Valley, comparing his view that public power was a public sector problem with Knowland's dismissal of public water projects as "another Tennessee Valley Authority."[56] A policy draft prepared by Brown's campaign team entitled "The State's Responsibility for Urgent Problems of Urban Expansion and Improvement in California" listed various problems of urban infrastructure including transport, overcrowding, the provision of water and power, the lack of open spaces, and noted that "*all* of these problems are obviously more and more in the lap of the State, not only because the State is called upon to remedy past mistakes, but also because the *State itself*—through its freeway and water programs, agricultural policies, housing and subdivision controls, public works development, and so on, *has a tremendous influence on the pattern of urban development*, for better or worse. But at present there is no effort to coordinate these State programs and policies, to insure a sound pattern of overall growth" (emphasis original).[57]

The use of governmental authority to promote economic development had become a national political issue during the 1950s, and public figures including Leon Keyserling, John Kenneth Galbraith, Arthur Schlesinger, and Walter Reuther regularly set out their visions of how the state could act as an agent of economic and social change.[58] Schlesinger wrote in a 1956 article that Brown read and filed away that the issues for liberals of the 1950s "have to do with education, with medical care, with more equal opportunities for minority groups, with the better planning of our cities and our suburbs, with slum clearance and decent housing, with the improvement of life for the sick and aged, with the freedoms of speech, expression, and conscience, with the bettering of our mass media and the elevation of our popular culture—in short, with the *quality* of civilization to which our nation aspires in an age of ever-increasing abundance and leisure."[59] Robert Nathan, national chairman of ADA, testified before the fiscal policy subcommittee of the Joint Congressional Committee on the Economic Report in May 1958, putting forward the view that there was "no need to wrestle over the false dilemma of choosing between public works and tax reductions as means of combating the recession. . . . A large federal deficit rising out of the recession is inevitable."[60] Hubert Humphrey had visited San Francisco in September 1957 and had noted "the new spirit of enthusiasm growing among Democrats in California," before observing that the "same spirit is sweeping the country—and it's sent rock-ribbed Republicans scurrying out of Washington to the hustings all over the land."[61] Yet the debate over economic citizenship under the direction of government had particular resonance in California, a state that combined a vast, complex economy, a diverse and rapidly growing population, an unquenchable demand for natural resources that were not indigenous to the region, and a political backdrop that was only just beginning to reflect genuine ideological divisions over how the demands of a modern industrialized state were to be met.

Brown's campaign team repeatedly highlighted this theme of California as the archetype of a modern economy that demanded a new politics of state-led development. CDC Democrat and adviser to Brown Steve Zetterberg prepared a report entitled "Medical Care and California Issues, 1958" in which he argued that "compulsory health insurance will be an issue (albeit secondary) in the 1958 gubernatorial campaign, whether the Democrats want it to or not." The report noted the popularity of contributory schemes in California, a contention supported by the fact that Governors Johnson and Warren had supported state health insurance schemes during their tenure in Sacramento. "Medical expense has risen and will continue to rise," claimed Zetterberg. "This burden of cost is growing too fast to fail to have political implications." This prediction would prove to be a prescient analysis of the way in which the political debate on the American center-left in the 1950s would impact upon the Kennedy and Johnson administrations in the 1960s, and would also impact upon the way in which the Brown administration once elected would expand the reach of the public sphere. Zetterberg also noticed the way in which opposite political perspectives on issues were serving to define political worldviews as each campaign used caricatures of the other to establish their own image. The "Democratic candidate may expect to be on the spot on the issue of 'Socialized medicine' and 'health insurance.' He had better be informed." The best way to respond to such brickbats, Zetterberg claimed, was to embrace the differences between right and left and run enthusiastically on a program: "The Democrats should go at least as far as Governor Warren, Hiram Johnson, and Teddy Roosevelt, in working out a health plan."[62] Zetterberg formed part of an advisory group putting together position papers for Brown on key issues that formed a left-of-center policy agenda. Other members included Joe Wyatt of CDC and Warren Christopher, San Francisco attorney who would much later become Bill Clinton's first Secretary of State. While their policy advocacy did not ensure change would happen in the labyrinthine world of state governance, the fact that they were given extensive access to Brown during the campaign, holding a health insurance briefing with him at Palm Springs with a view to forming a legislative committee once elected to power, indicated that a Brown administration would move to expand public access to economic security once elected.[63]

Brown's speech writers and campaign team utilized their role to make Brown a mouthpiece of a specific political vision that combined a commitment to economic rights and civil rights. Brown's speeches heralded the advent of a new era in California and national politics. A key example was a speech entitled "Government with a Heart," which made an explicitly social democratic argument that the role of government was to distribute the riches of an undeniably wealthy state to ensure social harmony. "Public welfare," Brown argued, "involves the state's obligation to the aged, to needy children, to babies without homes, to the alcoholic, to wayward youth, to the mentally and physically ill, to crippled children and adults. These are the unfortunates who need our outstretched hand. . . . IT IS COMMON SENSE to assist the needy of the State on two bases: humanitarian considerations, and the ability of the State to pay the bills. . . . I will fight for government which respects the dignity of every last citizen in our State, including and down to the humblest and the poorest."[64] In a speech in Oakland Brown used Knowland's antilabor campaign as a way of framing his own political ethos: "Unlike my opponent, I do not believe in trickle-down economics or trickle-down social status. To me it is supremely important that every one of our citizens enjoys every privilege and advantage that our state has to offer. . . . I don't like to see class pitted against class, employer against employee, neighbor against neighbor. . . . I have pledged that in my first message to the legislature I will call for passage of an enforceable statute for equal job opportunities for all, without regard to race, creed, or color."[65] Another speech described the "progressive spirit" Brown claimed to embody by contrasting his own political outlook with that of Knowland. "The many serious disagreements stem from a difference in the fundamental attitudes of the two men toward government, toward the people—a difference in basic political philosophy." Having charted the achievements of the progressive and New Deal eras, and having noted how state governments had acted as the laboratories for economic and social policy experimentation, Brown developed an idea that had been increasingly evident in left-of-center debate in California but not yet clearly articulated. An ideology that used government to promote a common citizenship in terms of access to economic resources together with basic civil rights had the flexibility to expand these terms to encompass new challenges: "beyond today's problems there lies the crucial role of the Progressive philosophy. It will help us answer the question that has not yet been asked. It will provide a constructive approach to tomorrow's problems."[66]

It is easy to dismiss Brown's rhetoric as merely the exuberant outpourings of a confident campaigner on the hustings, not yet exposed to the rather more complex demands of government. Yet his long-standing commitment to enacting fair employment legislation, and the rationale upon which he based his support for it, suggests that the drawing up of political battle lines over the question of access to employment, housing, and public services had long-term significance. There was no doubting Brown's commitment to civil rights for all in principle: Franklin Williams of the NAACP affirmed that "the guy is 120%" on civil rights, and Loren Miller, the NAACP's legal counsel and key player in Los Angeles, called Brown "this new kind of Catholic whose conscience is touched by [civil rights issues] . . . whose position is rooted in his faith. . . . He goes beyond making mere affirmations."[67] But Brown saw more at stake than just the nation's moral compass: he and his advisors saw the civil rights of men and women to a job and to union membership and to a decent home as part of a package tied together by a social democratic notion of economic citizenship. "I believe it is self-evident," stated Brown, "that the rights of a man to work, and to a home for himself and his family are primary." Discrimination in employment and housing had social costs "in taxes to all of us who must ultimately pay the price for juvenile delinquency, high crime, disease bred by the slums, and the loss of human effort and creativity that encompasses all mankind."[68] In his address to the CDC convention in 1958 Brown attacked "the trickle down economic theories" of the GOP and Dixiecrats that would "leave most American Negroes, and most other Americans, only the crumbs on our economic table. There is need for reminder that along with our civil rights, equal job opportunities—and genuine prosperity—must be assured at the base, not just at the peak, of the economic pyramid."[69]

Knowland and his supporters defined common citizenship in terms of economic freedom from government regulation, and historians have charted the ways in which corporate capitalism and its political allies utilized rhetorical strategies of individualism and the "American Way" to reinforce their political influence.[70] Knowland in his refusal to make "promises to the racial minorities of this state" as to do so would, in his own words, "set them apart as a special interest group seeking special legislation" set the boundaries of common citizenship within the context of existing economic relationships. In other words, people in rapidly growing suburbs had the right through their ability to purchase those homes to live their lives as they chose, discriminating in choosing their neighbors if they wished.[71] The commitment of California Democrats to civil rights legislation not only committed them to the regulation of economic relationships—one of Brown's first acts as governor would be to enact a state FEPC—but it also committed them to a dramatic expansion of the public realm that would have long-term implications for the rights of others currently excluded from mainstream society, including single parents and gay men and women. These developments were still in the future, but the 1958 campaign set up the terms of the broader debate and the parameters of Republican and Democratic power that would have relevance for decades to come.

Brown's road to the governor's mansion was no repeat of Upton Sinclair's End Poverty in California campaign of 1934, and his assault on entrenched power structures required money and media coverage that necessitated a broad church approach to campaigning. The incompetence of the Republican campaign had turned many unlikely people into Brown supporters, many seeing him as a winner and therefore as someone who might need to be bought: even in arch-Republican La Jolla, Brown's local campaign director wrote that wooing voters was "not a completely hopeless task, since more and more Republicans are losing sympathy for Knowland and his program."[72] A Doctors' Committee for Brown was formed to raise campaign funds from a potentially lucrative demographic, asking each committee member for twenty-five dollars up front to pay for a series of letters to doctors endorsing Brown and to defray other campaign expenses. Of course such support came at a price: Brown addressed the California Medical Association Council in February and was careful to state that he felt "very, very strongly against any state medicine or socialized medicine of any kind, nature, or description."[73] Dewey Anderson of the Public Affairs Institute restated what most California politicians knew well: "California is a very difficult state to organize politically because of its great physical size, the large population to be reached, the diversity of interests of its several localities and its people. California is many states in one. Any candidate has to be able to present a many sided character to make any great impact on voters."[74] Brown's chameleon quality as an already successfully elected politician served him well as he quietly but efficiently raised hundreds of thousands of dollars in funds from interests that spanned the political spectrum, but his broad church campaign reinforced the sense that he was walking a political tightrope that would test him in office. Even his confident opposition to right-to-work that helped galvanize his campaign rested on shaky foundations at a time of bitter controversy over the place of labor unions in national life: Roger Kent had to beg Senator John F. Kennedy in May not to allow the McClellan committee investigating labor racketeering to come to California and potentially provide a "circus . . . which would be vastly overplayed by the Republican press."[75]

The demands of fund-raising and of a state already used to slick, carefully orchestrated campaign extravaganzas made Brown's election effort more of a thrill ride than a profound state conversation on the future of society. His campaign team prepared for their candidate's visit to Fresno in February by hiring "four VERY ATTRACTIVE GIRLS" to hand out Brown stickers and buttons. Some 15,000 buttons, 4,000 lapel stickers, 2,000 balloons, and 5,000 bumper stickers were delivered to the campaign headquarters in Fresno, and the young ladies chosen for the job of handing them out to the gathering throng wore matching shorts and brown sweaters, posing with Brown at a press conference and beaming as the flashbulbs popped around them. His major campaign appearances were orchestrated to the last detail: his appearance on the speaker's platform that evening was carefully choreographed, Brown running up onto the stage six minutes after the start of the show with his wife by his side, grinning and waving wildly as a girl placed a large campaign button on his lapel. Brown spoke for exactly two minutes in a style scripted as "personal, warm, informal," introducing his wife, Bernice, before sweeping out of the venue through the crowd.[76] It was a far cry from political campaigns elsewhere, as the *New York Times* noted in an article in October 1958 headed "A Political Convention in Britain: Issues, not Ballyhoo, Hold Stage," in which the journalist observed that the "complete absence of high pressure ballyhoo is the first thing that strikes the American visitor. There are no bands, no carefully calculated demonstrations, no frenzied outbursts of mass hero worship. . . . These policy debates mean a tremendous amount to the delegates. To them the conference is not a paid vacation but a yearly opportunity to 'build Jerusalem in England's green and pleasant land.' Their sentences are sometimes clumsy, but their faith is strong to the point of arrogance."[77] Brown's campaign may have been rather more media-savvy than those of parties overseas still coming to terms with an age of television, but the sheer number of speeches he gave on economic and social issues, together with the contrast his campaign painted with the staunchly pro-business message of his opponents, suggested that his election in 1958 would mean more than just the changing of the political guard.

California Democrats and the Battle of Ideas

The importance of the battle between Knowland and Brown over the future direction of state politics is further highlighted when we examine the wider context of party politics in California and what it tells us about the strength and tactics of Democrats across the state and at all levels of the ticket. The right-to-work issue did not just enthuse organized labor; it also provided a rallying cry to the CDC and its network of clubs. Pat Brown's rousing address to the Fresno convention in January, one of his earliest speeches of the campaign, demonstrated the importance CDC now held in the eyes of senior party members. CDC acted as a trial balloon for Democrats, passing resolutions at its conventions that could then be tested in the court of public opinion as the campaign unfolded. It became clear at the Fresno conference that right-to-work was acting as a catch-all issue around which a broader political agenda that appealed to the middle class activists as well as organized labor could be established. The report of the resolutions committee described right-to-work as "legislation which is designed solely to undermine the organized strength of labor and its ability to bargain effectively for the welfare of the wage earners of this state by depriving unions of the representation of all workers whose interests unions seek to protect." The resolution linked the labor question to Knowland's wider worldview, noting that "by his unfavorable votes on Social Security, minimum wages, unemployment insurance and disability insurance and on public housing [he] has shown himself to be no friend of the working man."[78]

Clubs used right-to-work as a way of bringing together clubs and the regular party and labor unions in a coordinated campaign for Democratic candidates. The West Beverly Club invited Sig Arywitz of the garment workers' union to address club members in March 1958 on right-to-work, and used the issue as a way of mobilizing the local community to register to vote and to support Democratic candidates. The West Beverly club took credit for the huge Democratic vote in Los Angeles in the primary, its president stating that the result "has just demonstrated to the entire United States the value of the club movement, and the California Democratic Council, which we have been building for the past six years. This was our biggest victory to date, and we should all be proud. . . . You too will be rewarded because you will help elect the type of candidates that believe in the same things we do." The club aimed to raise over a thousand dollars for campaign expenses in the general election for office space, a telephone, and campaign literature, and provided eighty volunteers for precinct work and telephone canvassing.[79]

Right-to-work provided a unifying focus for the different parts of the Democratic coalition, but it did not entirely paper over the differences within the party over exactly what constituted a candidate who "believes in the same things" as club Democrats. It was becoming evident that the late 1950s were witnessing a definite shift away from the earlier certainties of Cold War liberalism in the Democratic Party nationwide, and that the battle lines of the 1960s over both domestic and foreign policy were already being drawn in 1958. Most Los Angeles Democratic clubs and district councils had established legislative committees of their own by the late 1950s so that they could send well-briefed representatives to the CDC Convention, and several of them, buoyed by the impressive primary results for Democratic candidates, put together a legislative issues conference to be held at the Amalgamated Clothing

Workers Auditorium that August. Ed Lybeck, Jimmy Roosevelt's right-hand man, warned his boss that "some notorious extremists" were serving on the legislative panels and that "it is being bruited about that the chief subjects of discussion are to be recognition of Red China and denunciation of the Administration for sending troops to the Middle East. Guys like Bernie Selber, who is CDC Director nowadays, and Paul Posner, who got 'em the hall, are having catfits, for fear that the publicity will damage the Democratic ticket."[80] The Los Angeles issues conference was not as controversial as Lybeck feared, stressing unemployment, benefit levels, the need for public works, right-to-work, and the indicative but hardly revolutionary statement that "diplomacy, that is bargaining, treaties, conferences and economic understanding must take precedence over the military emphasis."[81]

There was little doubt, however, that a combination of the vestiges of the old left in Los Angeles and the increasing influence of the young in southern California politics who had not come of age politically in the 1940s was pushing the club movement toward an anti-Cold War stance, and that the California Federation of Young Democrats, in particular, was calling out for a radical change in U.S. foreign policy toward greater accommodation with China and communist nations in general.[82] At their 1957 meeting at Monterey it produced a statement arguing that "this country has put relatively too much emphasis on pacts, treaties and international diplomacy, and too little on measures to promote the growth of stable, effective and democratic societies abroad—societies which will remain in the free world not because they have been coerced or bought but because they are politically healthy and mature." Regarding the recognition of Chiang Kai-Shek's government in Formosa as China, the convention resolved that it had "become increasingly obvious that this policy does not conform to reality."[83] What clubs and Young Democrats thought about foreign policy was hardly headline news in the late 1950s, but the potential such views had to cause schisms in the Democratic order being developed in California was manifest. State Senator Robert McCarthy of San Francisco referred disparagingly to CDCers as "the hot-rod set" of the Democratic Party, deprecating both the radical style of the insurgents and their policy program of a larger welfare state and opposition to inflexible anticommunism.[84]

The controversy at the CDC Convention over the choice of candidate for the Senate nomination pointed up the line party activists walked between practical politics and principle as they prepared for power. Clair Engle, the frontrunner, was a popular, gregarious congressman who represented a sprawling district high in the Sierra Nevada Mountains. He was a New Dealer but as a member from a predominantly rural district had supported Taft-Hartley and was very much a congressional insider. His supporters made the same case that had helped sell Pat Brown easily to the assembled delegates in Fresno: he had plenty of experience winning elections. Also in the running was Peter Odegard, a professor at UC Berkeley and prominent club advocate, as well as member of the local ADA chapter. A strong advocate of civil rights and social welfare, he was strongly opposed to right-to-work and his supporters self-consciously styled themselves as idealists unsullied by the compromises of elected office. A hunger for victory and a sense that Democrats were on the verge of a historic triumph allowed Engle's legions of supporters in the state party to emerge with the crucial CDC endorsement, but die-hard club member Mary Ellen Cone of West Los Angeles professed to a "heartfelt defeat . . . when Clair Engle's well-organized supporters wiped the CDC convention floor with those who thought Peter Odegard had something real and new to offer the Democrats and the country. Don't misunderstand me, we love Clair Engle and think he's a wonderful candidate. But he's not Peter Odegard." Jimmy Roosevelt spoke for many regular Democrats when he contrasted Odegard's inexperience with Engle's practical ability that, Roosevelt felt, would serve him well in the Senate. He warned Cone gently that "on most of the fundamental and real issues we, as liberals, must stand together and work together and not get split up just because on some details or questions of personalities we may from time to time differ. This habitually has been the weakness of liberals, to the delight of the reactionaries. I am sure we won't let this happen to us, will we?"[85]

A perceived division between principle and practical politics was not unique to California, as Arthur Schlesinger touched off a lively debate in the *New Republic* when he railed against the Democratic Party's choice of machine politicians over principled intellectuals in Senate races on the East Coast, calling the primary results "a revolt of the lowest-level professional within the party organization against the New Deal and post-New Deal leadership of the Democratic Party." Schlesinger argued that these old-style pols hankered after a return to the party of the twenties, "a dreary alliance of Northern city bosses and Southern bourbons" in which intellectuals "played a wholly decorative role. It was a party without ideas, program, energy or zeal. . . . A Party which seeks to qualify itself for responsibility in an age of national and international crisis is not well advised to begin to do so by blowing out its own brains."[86] One respondent made a point that possessed in rhetorical flair what it lacked in pinpoint accuracy and which could apply loosely to California in the late 1950s: "American politics is a coalition of the over-educated and the under-educated against the half-educated. If the 'over-educated' want to continue to play a role very disproportionate to their numbers, it is best that they understand this relationship."[87] In 1958 the diverse coalition of interests that made up the California Democratic Party did stand together and deliver a stunning political upset to the Republicans across the state, but the seeds of future political strife had clearly been sown.

The remarkable fact about the Democratic successes in California that year was how dominant the campaign theme of a common citizenship through governmental action was in races across the state. In the East Bay, for instance, Democratic congressional candidate Jeffery Cohelan bridged the divide between labor, regular Democrats, and club activists with his left-of-center platform. Cohelan was secretary-treasurer of the Milk Drivers and Dairy Employees Local 302 of the Teamsters and was therefore in the vanguard of politicians encouraged into elected office by the labor issue but aware of the broader implications of the Democratic renaissance. The Central Labor Council of the Alameda AFL-CIO established a new political action committee in January in its bid to defeat not only Knowland but also the right-wing Republican congressman, its executive secretary noting that 1958 was "a crucial year in politics for all of us because we are not only confronted with a 'Right to Work' initiative measure, but we are confronted as well with the important task of electing candidates favorable to labor. Many of us believe that the fight to defeat 'Right to Work' law and the task of electing candidates to office are one and the same. . . . if we fail this year it will be a long time before we recover."[88] Cohelan's campaign support depended upon the right-to-work issue but was not limited to it. The *New Republic* saw Cohelan as one to watch among the crop of promising congressional Democrats, noting that his "appeal seems to be equally strong in the low income Democratic strongholds and in middle class suburbs. Cross-filing on both the Republican and Democratic ballots, he polled 49 percent of the total district vote in the primary. So far Cohelan has centered his campaign on the recession issue, emphasizing Democratic answers to the widespread unemployment in the Seventh District." He also stressed his support for a fair employment practices law in the district in which the Committee for Fair Employment lobbying effort had been born at the end of World War II, and used his support for the state party's "government with a heart" message to encourage "a clearer demarcation between the political parties" ahead of the big legislative battles to come over social programs and civil rights.[89] His victory over incumbent Republican John Allen ended twelve years of GOP representation in the most urban part of Alameda, and would be the last time in the twentieth century that a Republican candidate was a contender in the district.

Across the Bay in San Francisco Democrats continued to push the center of gravity of local political debate remorselessly leftward. Crucial to this effort was Assemblyman Phil Burton as he cruised to easy reelection in his own inner-city district and strengthened his command over local political activity, but it was not confined to his patch. Frank Brann, the party's Assembly candidate in the Twenty-Second District in the wealthy, more Republican Sunset neighborhood was declared in his campaign literature to be "a Democrat, pledged to the far-reaching and progressive program of his party." His support for FEPC and a putative Human Rights Commission, and his endorsement of medical assistance for the elderly and pump-priming measures for the economy were rolled together into a political outlook that would "extend human rights to all."[90] The massive labor drive in San Francisco bolstered the confidence of local Democrats that a campaign stressing social justice was viable: in mid-September five hundred volunteer workers organized by the San Francisco Labor Council's Committee on Political Action began "an intensive house-by-house campaign throughout San Francisco in an effort to direct attention to Proposition 18," and the strategy of these foot soldiers was to associate opposition to right-to-work with a desire for "a society in which the average working man and woman and his family may through his union achieve a decent standard of living, a decent home, insurance against the crippling costs of illness, and security in old age."[91] Phil Burton carefully tailored his campaign literature to labor's broader political agenda, underlining his sponsorship of "proposals to increase minimum wages to $1.25 per hour, increase the state pension to the elderly, a Fair Employment Practices law to eliminate discrimination in employment. Also, he co-authored a bill to provide pensions for elderly non-citizens, which passed both Houses but which was vetoed by the Governor, and co-authored improvements and liberalization in the Workmen's Compensation and Unemployment Insurance programs."[92]

San Francisco and Oakland were both cities in which strong local labor organizations made a reshaping of the contours of party politics in response to right-to-work relatively straightforward. Willie Brown later sketched out the history of the establishment of Phil Burton's political patronage system in San Francisco in the late 1950s and early 1960s and argued that it depended to a large extent on extensive funds from organized labor.[93] This was a far cry from the situation in Orange County or in San Diego, where a tradition of hostility to organized labor and a strong Republican establishment and antilabor media made the area one of the few to support right-to-work by a large margin and to remain immune to the Democratic tide. A poll of Californians undertaken in August and again in early October noted a clear shift in public opinion in the Bay Area against right-to-work but a much less clear-cut picture in the Southland: northern California was 37 percent to 54 percent against but the south polled 44 percent in favor and 45 percent against.[94] Yet the scale and durability of the Democratic gains in 1958—they would control at least one part of state government for all but a handful of years over the next half century—should encourage us to reflect upon the success of a coalition of labor, activist clubs with avowed left-wing aims, and Democratic politicians in creating a new political order that held together urban, suburban, and some Central Valley agricultural districts to set the legislative agenda in vitally significant ways, as will be demonstrated in the next chapter.

A final Dollars for Democrats drive in the fall of 1958 coordinated by the CDC demonstrated the statewide effectiveness of the volunteer activist part of the grand Democratic coalition. In Northern California Alameda brought in the highest total, but several thousand dollars was raised in San Francisco, San Mateo, Santa Clara, Sacramento, and Marin. The only large county with a low tally, Contra Costa with $1,500, was a county with a high proportion of labor union members who were contributing to the campaign through the labor fundraising drive. The total raised in San Mateo was nearly as high as in the presidential election year of 1956, some $4,465, and pointed to the fact that although the peninsula and South Bay Area remained home to large numbers of Republican voters, these communities of rapid suburban development and high technology industries were politically more volatile and more receptive to the appeal of consumer liberalism and economic citizenship than the inhabitants of Orange County who have received so much attention. Even in Southern California, Los Angeles County raised $27,000 for Dollars for Democrats that fall, and was home to more CDC clubs and fundraising efforts than anywhere else in the state.[95] In Jimmy Roosevelt's West and South Los Angeles district a massive telephone and door-to-door registration drive coordinated by the Sixty-first Assembly District club helped produce an enormous primary advantage for Democratic candidates: Brown gained eight times as many votes as Knowland in the Democratic primary in the Twenty-Sixth Congressional District but only three times fewer in the GOP primary.

Roosevelt garnered similar tallies in his primary against African American Republican Crispus Wright in a race in which the African American candidate stood for balanced budgets to "encourage the growth and expansion of free enterprise" and Roosevelt was described as a "recognized champion of civil rights, pensions, social security, labor, and small business."[96] Roosevelt had the support of both active CDC clubs and organized labor—the International Brotherhood of Electrical Workers contributed to his campaign—and this joint effort on behalf of shared political principles was reflected in the scale of the Democratic victories and the diversity of the socioeconomic strata that contributed to those victories.[97]

The 1958 election results were a stunning reversal of decades of Republican dominance in California, and a terrible upset to the Grand Old Party across the nation. The Democrats won the governorship and the open U.S. Senate seat by landslides: Brown received over three million votes, 59.8 percent of the total in a state in which his party had been on life support only six years earlier. They captured eight state senate seats to break the deadlock there and take control by 28 seats to 12. In the Assembly races Democrats captured another nine districts to take control for the first time in decades by a margin of 47 seats to 33. They gained three Republican congressional seats—one in the rural north stretching down the coast to Marin, one in Berkeley, and one in Nixon's former district in suburban, East Los Angeles County—to assume a majority of the state's representation in Congress. The right-to-work proposition was roundly defeated by almost a 60–40 margin.[98]

The party would go into the 1960s ready to reshape legislative boundaries to cement their control over state politics, redrawing lines to make districts like Jeffery Cohelan's seat in Berkeley safe and creating new seats in rapidly growing Los Angeles that would elect more Democrats. Crucially, as Totton Anderson stated shortly after the election, the Democrats "did not 'surfboard in' on a national tide running for their party. . . . The party and its auxiliaries have been revitalized with intelligent leadership, acceptable candidates, adequate financing, and a program which has rallied the support of its own majority in the electorate."[99] In the Twenty-Fifth District in East Los Angeles County the Republican candidate spent the most money of any congressional candidate in the state in 1958 to hold the seat held by Nixon in the late 1940s, but he could not escape defeat, and this in a district seemingly perfect territory for the "suburban warriors" of neighboring Orange County. The Republicans regained the seat in 1960 but lost it again in 1962, and they also lost an Assembly district locally in 1958, and another, the Forty-Fifth, next door in Monterey Park. The winner of this Assembly seat, George Brown, would join the Assembly Committee on Governmental Efficiency and Economy and vote to pass FEPC in February 1959, demonstrating that suburban voters had a more complex role to play in shifting the terms of debate over civil rights and social citizenship than has sometimes been assumed.[100]

The scale of the Democratic victories and the diversity of the party's political coalition pointed to potential weaknesses in this grand alliance. Both organized labor and the CDC had been able to use right-to-work as a launch pad for a broader conceptualization of economic citizenship that encompassed a commitment to civil rights and the regulation of capitalism. Now that the Democratic Party held power at all levels these principles would be tested for the first time, potentially exposing fissures between different factions over how to prioritize the different strands of the party's rights agenda. The CDC, previously an integral part of the party's vote-getting machine, would now have to redefine its role as the left-of-center conscience of a party no longer in opposition. The Brown administration would have to defend its complex legislative agenda from attack from implacable enemies of mandated racial integration and the redistribution of wealth and the growth of the state. And whereas the business-led right-to-work forces had a relatively simple message—opposition to government power and support of the prerogatives of management and the owners of capital—the volunteers and activists who had propelled Brown and his allies to power had put together a nuanced, ambitious program that had the capacity to expose the competing demands of numerous rival interest groups and destabilize the party's political dominance. Musing on the possibility of California turning into a regular two-party state in the wake of the 1958 battle, James Roosevelt sensed that "California will still be the home of many political independents and the maker of political upsets for sometime yet to come. A state which has produced a Hiram Johnson, an Earl Warren, and a Culbert Olson, not to mention a Richard Nixon, and the rising star of Edmund G. (Pat) Brown, hasn't been a dull place in the past."[101] The mammoth legislative and political changes of the following eight years of a Brown administration, with the successes and reversals they witnessed, were to prove Roosevelt a prescient observer of the California scene.

CHAPTER 7

Democratic Politics and the Brown Administration

At the end of the 1959 session of the California legislature, the state AFL-CIO leadership looked back on the achievements of the preceding year. "Undoubtedly," wrote C. J. Haggerty in his foreword to labor's guide to events in Sacramento, "1959 will go down in state history as the year in which California undertook the protection and extension of equal rights of its citizens." Pointing to the extension of unemployment insurance, disability insurance, workmen's compensation, and the landmark civil rights laws in the form of the passage of a state FEPC, the prohibition of discrimination in the provision of goods and services, and in public housing, Haggerty argued that the legislature had "produced the most impressive array of legislation in my experience as [AFL-CIO] legislative representative which was as satisfying as its disappointments were disturbing and basic."[1] The years between 1959 and 1963 were to see a radical transformation of the political landscape in California, with landmark legislation in fields ranging from civil rights to higher education to natural resources and to the rights of welfare recipients. The Brown administration and its allies in the legislature enacted an impressive legislative program that dramatically expanded the reach of the state and sharpened the divisions between statist Democrats and business leaders and most Republicans over key questions of economic and social citizenship that were to define political debate for the rest of the century and beyond. A number of historians and political biographers have detailed these legislative accomplishments and the debates that surrounded them.[2] Others have analyzed the limits of legislative and political change at the national level, mindful of the fact that much of the nation's welfare, labor, and regulatory infrastructure had altered little since the New Deal.[3] My purpose here is to argue that the political changes of these years in California were important in shaping politicians' understanding of social relationships and what constituted the normative in society in ways that had long-term significance even if the actual policy changes proved less durable. Policy innovations in the realms of civil rights and economic rights forced politicians to re-evaluate the boundaries of social inclusion and entitlement in ways that opened up debates over gender, sexuality, and race and the relationship of these categories to government regulation. This chapter and the next will use case studies of policymaking during the Brown years to show how policy debates before 1964 raised new questions of social citizenship and the place of the individual in wider society that set the stage for the rights revolution of the later 1960s and 1970s and tied the Democratic Party irrevocably to the social movements that spawned that revolution.

FEPC: Race and Economic Citizenship

The twenty years after World War II saw a dramatic change in willingness of state governments to regulate the relationship between the individual and the marketplace: almost half of all states in these years passed legislation forbidding employers from discriminating on the basis of race when handing out employment contracts. These state laws, pioneered by New York in 1945 and finally passed after spirited debate in the California legislature in the spring of 1959, explicitly associated the rights of individuals to freedom from discrimination with governmental regulation of the economy. As James Rorty explained in his analysis of the experience of New York's State Commission against Discrimination (SCAD) in 1958, "SCAD's experience has demonstrated nothing so clearly as that the problem of discrimination is an indivisible aspect of the total national economy and culture. Discrimination in housing is inseparably linked, not only with discrimination in employment and education—South and North—but also with the low income status and relative immobility of the nonwhite minorities; it is also linked with trade union policy and control, with local, state and national politics, and, of course, with our international responsibilities as leader of the free world."[4]

In California proponents of the FEPC bill framed their arguments for the new law in terms of the rights of all to economic citizenship. "We in California are faced with a tremendous problem," stated African American Assemblyman Byron Rumford in February. "There are 5,000,000 in our minority groups. This will protect their rights. It represents the full flowering of the Democratic [sic] process." Rumford elaborated on his deliberate use of the capital D in his press release by noting that all five votes in the Assembly Committee on Governmental Efficiency and Economy against a favorable report on the bill came from Republicans, and that it was the new Democratic majority that had forced the bill onto the Assembly floor. The Republicans represented wealthy white districts in Los Angeles, Pasadena, San Jose, San Diego, and Van Nuys; the Democrats represented a cross-section of the state ranging from wealthy Westside Los Angeles to San Francisco and, crucially, to Garden Grove in a lower middle class section of Orange County.[5] It had taken the political earthquake of the 1958 elections to force FEPC through the committee and then through the legislature as a whole. The political geography of the state demonstrated the growing schism along party lines over governmental regulation of private enterprise: the bill sailed through the Assembly by 65 votes to 14, and of the 14 no's only 2 were rural Democrats and 11 were Republicans from Southern California, with one GOP assemblyman hailing from San Jose. The debate on the Assembly floor also demonstrated the ideological divide, as San Jose Republican Clark Bradley claimed that it was impossible to "legislate against discrimination," while Democrat Ed Gaffney of San Francisco cast the legislation in terms of "the right" of a citizen "to earn his living" free from discrimination based on racial or religious criteria.[6] Freshman Congressman Jeffery Cohelan (D-Berkeley) reported to the House of Representatives on California's recent experience in his testimony in support of a federal FEPC law, explaining that in passing FEP legislation "the California State Legislature . . . has made it quite clear that we realize enforcement of civil rights cannot be left to the private citizen alone. In California we have recognized . . . that civil rights are not enjoyed in a consistent manner and to the same degree in all areas when the burden of enforcement is placed upon private citizens."[7] California was hardly a trailblazer in this respect, but the bill's passage in April 1959 coincided with the accession of power of a Democratic administration whose political program had been shaped in response to the political pressures of the 1950s, melding a concern for economic rights with a growing realization of the problems posed by a diverse and rapidly growing population.

The new Fair Employment Practices Commission, given enforcement powers to investigate complaints of unfair hiring practices with financial sanction, represented one part of a bigger legislative program to regulate economic relationships in California. Future speaker Jesse Unruh wrote into the state code a new clause forbidding discrimination in the provision of goods and services, a small but potentially very significant revision to state law that made government a powerful player in the private economic marketplace. Several bills for a large increase in the minimum wage, and the inclusion of men as well as women for the first time, were placed in the hopper. Assemblyman George Brown made the connection in left-of-center Democrats' sponsorship of economic regulation and civil rights legislation: "Civil rights can be defined as the right to equal treatment in our society; the right to be free from discrimination, to have access to all those things, values, or goals, which are generally sought after, without regard to extraneous factors such as race, color, sex, language, religion, politics, national or social origin, property status, age, etc. . . . In the U.S., and in California, much remains to be done if every person is to have available, even on a minimum basis, all that he needs for a free, healthful, productive and dignified life." Antidiscrimination laws were the first step; economic entitlement was a complementary agenda: "The right to full employment and to social security when unemployed has become of increasing importance in our industrial society."[8] The California FEPC worked with organizations like the National Urban League (NUL) to promote this dual agenda in their educational drives, exemplified by the use of a NUL propaganda film "A Morning for Jimmy" in 1961 that "dramatizes the plight of a Negro teenager, apparently in a Northern city, who is discouraged by his rejection for a part-time job. . . . A friendly teacher takes him on a tour of industries and professions to meet successful Negroes, and he decides to do his best to become an architect." The educational film, which never mentioned antidiscrimination laws at all, was framed so as to point up the economic, rather than the legal, side of the fair employment debate: "the message is essentially that of merit employment."[9] The film, described by the FEPC's education officer as "realistic and touching," was in fact trite and prone to racial stereotypes of its own, but it demonstrated the way in which new organs of state government, in cooperation with outside interest groups previously excluded from the corridors of power, were reshaping the debate over the relationship between government and individual rights in the marketplace.

The fact that the publicity drive and the debate in the legislature over fair employment emphasized African Americans and all but ignored Latinos suggests that the capacity of the new administration to tackle deep-seated economic inequality remained severely circumscribed. Domestic workers were excluded from the new law, and attempts by Los Angeles Congressman Gus Hawkins to extend the federal minimum wage to farm workers on an equal basis met with stiff opposition.[10] The fact was that forcing employers to accept people of color as employees, the stated aim of the executive officer of California's Fair Employment Practices Committee, was not the issue at stake for Latino farm workers. The FEPC's educational drive was intended to shame employers into revising their employment practices, on the assumption that "word gets around the office, plant, or industry when employment policies are revised, and . . . the introduction of minority group workers is watched with much interest."[11] Such a statement made no mention of the fact that the farm question was one of the right to fair pay and working conditions, not just of access to employment. The whole language of fair employment was one of racial integration within an industrial and commercial economy, and possessed no terms in which to frame a much more complex debate over the state and nation's dependence upon a limitless supply of legally imported indentured labor to provide cheap and plentiful farm produce. The state FEPC held two conferences in 1960, one in San Francisco and one in Los Angeles, on the topic of legislative civil rights priorities for 1961, and all three identified areas for development related to housing and the provision of goods and services under the Unruh Act. There was no mention of farm workers.[12] Attempts to eliminate discrimination in public and private housing, together with questions of police brutality and safeguards for people displaced by urban renewal that were also mentioned, did not disturb the workings of existing economic structures to any great extent.

When the NAWU lobbied Brown to fire Farm Placement Service (FPS) head Edward Hayes in May 1959, they were met with silence. The state Department of Employment did begin to assert some control over the FPS, and later in the summer demoted Hayes after discovering the extent to which the FPS had excluded domestic workers from jobs to encourage the continuation of the bracero program. Brown promised in August that "the present administration will not rest until our farm placement program functions for the people it was created to serve—our domestic farm workers." Yet that very month over 8,000 braceros were hired for peach picking in California at wage rates far below the basic minimum wage.[13] The farm worker question exemplified perfectly the close relationship between economic and civil rights, and yet policies to inject an element of racial justice into the employment and housing markets could not touch a rural economy that remained outside the confines of the cozy relationship between industrial capitalism and labor established under the New Deal.

If many California politicians remained too wedded to the financial patronage and economic clout of the growers, it required federal action to eliminate the bracero program in 1964, paving the way for major advances in the rights of domestic farm labor in the later 1960s. The election of a raft of new

Democratic liberals to Congress in 1958, including Chairman of the Migratory Labor Subcommittee of the Senate Labor and Public Welfare Committee Harrison Williams (D-N.J.), together with the formation of the legislative program of the Kennedy-Johnson administration in the early 1960s, opened up the possibility of integrating the farm labor question into the broader liberal agenda. Senators like Harrison were not beholden to Western agribusiness interests, and saw farm workers as a crucial component of the Great Society. Not only did the heavily Democratic 88th Congress fail to extend the bracero program beyond the end of 1964, cutting the number of imported bracero farm workers in California from well over 100,000 in 1964 to 20,000 a year later, but it also attempted to extend poverty program provisions to farm labor.[14] Both houses reported antipoverty bills during 1964 and 1965 containing migrant labor provisions, and the Senate Committee report characterized migrant farm workers and their families as "an almost forgotten group of the poverty stricken . . . trapped, by lack of education and harsh economics, on a treadmill of poverty."[15] It was easier to identify the problem than to solve it, but the elimination of the bracero program alone allowed the secretary of labor to impose stringent restrictions on growers' ability to import foreign labor below prevailing wage rates, raising wage minimums dramatically and giving groups like the United Farm Workers much greater leverage in their campaign for bargaining rights. As would be the case with the national grape boycott later in the decade, the farm labor question required national pressure to help force the economic rights of dispossessed Latinos into a debate that could too easily slide into a simple defense of individual civil rights.

In any case, the California FEPC bill—limited in scope as it was—had a tough time in the state senate and had to be rushed to the governor for his signature before the end of the legislative session. The Brown administration's program faced stormy opposition in its attempt to challenge private sector prerogatives, however tentatively. At the same time as California was expanding the reach of government regulation and its role in managing access to economic resources, other states hungry for inward economic investment were advertising their states as offering economic opportunities unencumbered by restrictive red tape.[16] As we shall see in the case of fair housing legislation, widening the parameters of social inclusion through legislation directly challenged the control of powerful business interests over the management of the state's economic affairs. It was not that business elites were overtly racist, and in some cases businesses recognized that opposition to racial discrimination could be good for the company's public image: Carmen Warschaw, who served on FEPC from 1959 to 1964, argued that Bank of America, for example, one of California's largest employers, "did change their practices and they were anxious to try to comply, and not give the appearance of being discriminatory."[17] However, the lengthening reach of governmental control over the day-to-day management of businesses in California had the effect of widening the gulf between liberal Democrats and right-wing Republicans and their business allies during the Brown years, and raised the thorny question of how to achieve social equality without arousing the hostility of major economic players who had the option of doing business elsewhere. The implications of these issues notwithstanding, the Brown administration chose to make social citizenship—equal access to jobs, homes, social welfare, and the protection of the law—a key part of its legislative agenda, with consequences for politicians' understanding of normative social relations that went beyond the particular issue under consideration.

Health, Welfare, and Social Citizenship

The Brown administration's establishment of a new program of social and civil rights legislation contributed to a mushrooming of legislative support staff, advisory committees, and pressure groups dedicated to promoting the expansion of social policy entitlements in the early 1960s. The enlargement of the state government workforce coincided with the establishment of the Issues Committee of the CDC as the intellectual and policy conscience of the state Democratic Party. One of the first acts of the new administration was to establish a Governor's Committee on Medical Aid and Health to investigate health care provision and to recommend ways in which the state government could act to improve public access to health services. The extent to which the Brown administration could tackle deep-seated inequities in the state's health system would be limited. Nevertheless, an important reason for investigating the health care debate is that it demonstrates the ways in which a combination of state welfare professionals, state legislators, and amateur activists all used an issue like health to articulate their broader political agenda and to gain valuable legislative experience that would serve them when enacting more far-reaching welfare reform in 1963 and when establishing Medicaid and Medicare at the state level in 1965. The initial health care task force included an interesting mix of government professionals—from the state Department of Public Health, the California Division of the Social Security Administration, the state Department of Social Welfare, and the state Department of Mental Hygiene—and party activists, including Steve Zetterberg, who had advised Governor Brown during his election campaign and who had experience as an intern at the then Social Security Board, but whose main qualification was as a CDC point man who bridged the divide between government and party apparatus. He later described his experience on the task force as "one of the best seven or eight months I ever had," and he also served on the fully state-funded nineteen-member committee that followed the initial taskforce, this time with health care professionals as well as government employees and activists as members. The chair of the committee was Roger Egeberg of the University of Southern California Medical Center, and the committee reported in December 1960.[18]

Though the report, compiled as it was by people with a range of perspectives, was carefully worded so as not to suggest too radical a departure from accepted practice, its publication marked the legitimization of the Democratic left's ideology of social citizenship through governmental involvement in the provision of key services. The introduction to the report noted that the "problems presented by the rapidly expanding amount of information, techniques and procedures related to health; the increasing population; the rising medical costs; the difficulties of meeting health manpower needs; the necessity for new equipment, new hospitals and other institutions; the desire to provide medical and surgical care for older men and women; and the need to raise the standards of care for seasonal agricultural labor, require planning if there is to be adequate supply, adequate service and appropriate distribution of health services." The authors of the report were quick to qualify their use of the term "planning" by stressing their commitment only to "more voluntary cooperation at the community level, where desire to help the aged, the indigent sick and the crippled is often born."[19] But the report was published at a crucial time as it formed part of a much broader public interest in the question of health care and as such validated the underlying ideology of social inclusion. It also came at exactly the moment a new administration was about to take power in Washington, D.C., and establish a range of new federal measures—Medical Aid for the Aged among them—that would free up federal funds for state governments willing to implement new assistance programs.

Even medical professionals in California realized the need to tap government funds to correct financial imbalances in the system that threatened to slow the growth of private health care products. California suffered the problem of a rapidly rising population combined with a lower than average level of health insurance coverage. "More than half of all families in the state have total annual incomes of under $5000, the figure generally accepted as the minimum requirement for a healthy and decent standard of living," reported Dr. E. Richard Weinerman at the Annual Meeting of the American Public Health Association in San Francisco in October 1960. "About 12% of all families are still below the $2000 bracket while 50% of persons over age 65 are under this meager level. How realistic are the chances of financing, on an individual payment basis, the expansions and improvements in medical service needed in this burgeoning state?" He noted that the state government "was now the largest single purchaser of medical care in California," as half a million Californians were in receipt of public assistance, three million received some form of compensation insurance, 58,000 were in mental hospitals, and 60,000 had remediable incapacities. The development of a state insurance plan for state employees, together with possible federal financial incentives that would require state matching funds, would increase this public bill further. The 60 percent of Californians covered by private prepaid insurance schemes was substantially higher than the 1951 total but much lower than the 73 percent average for the United States as a whole, and preventive medicine and rehabilitative care were rarely included in the coverage. "Social physicians" were needed in California, Weinerman concluded, "mindful of the unrealized potential of the social application of full medical capacities to the health needs of all of the people."[20] In other words, the overall welfare of society required an underlying commitment to social justice on the part of the state as well as the maintenance of the private profit motive in the provision of health services.

The question of health care formed the perfect theme for a major Issues Conference held by the California Democratic Council in Santa Monica in February 1961. Since the abolition of cross-filing by the Democratic legislature in 1959 and the promotion of the Democratic Party to power the CDC had needed a new rationale to justify its continued existence as what president Tom Carvey termed "an instrument for collective political action." There were people, he noted, who had joined since 1958 "and who really don't know what it was like not to be 'in.'"[21] Major issues of the day would, it was hoped, galvanize club members into continued interest in state and national politics. "We expect about 400 people to take part in the discussions on medical care," wrote Steve Zetterberg to an employee of the state Department of Social Welfare, hoping to gain legislative and professional involvement in the conference, "and most of the discussions will be in relatively small discussion groups with discussion leaders and resource people. . . . The end result of this study and discussion will be the formulation of a recommended Democratic policy for the Democratic Party."[22] Zetterberg later recalled that the Issues Conference sprang directly out of the official Governor's Committee investigation, inviting the same experts and policy specialists to Santa Monica and thus bridging the divide between government and party. "At this point," he said, "the California Democratic Council was very powerful, as impecunious lobby groups go. But it represented roughly 70,000 members throughout the state. . . . And the recommendations from the California Democratic Council did get to a lot of the state legislators who were, many of them, in office because of the California Democratic Council." The Issues Conference drew upon expert testimony and composed a statement of intent that could act as a trial balloon for state legislators as they assembled a political program. "The most interesting, intellectually, for me was listening to all that stuff on the governor's study committee and being able to put together conceptually a statement on health care; and the CDC medical issue conference," he recalled. CDC activists, who later entered the legislature and Congress themselves, such as Henry Waxman, used their experiences at the 1961 conference in later legislative battles over health care. "The thing that really stands out in my mind is that everybody agreed that every person in California, without regard to ability to pay, should have access to health care. That is what we are still wrestling with on the national scene."[23]

The statement on medical care exemplifies how the energy and zeal of liberal activists in the early years of the Brown administration provided them with a new political language of social inclusion that would reshape the terms of political debate over rights in California even if the specific policy proposal remained unimplemented. The language of the CDC resolution on health defined a broader agenda of social citizenship that asserted that all individuals had the right to a certain quality of life, an idea that would influence later debates on the left about welfare, the nature of the family, racial equality, and sexual politics. The health policy document made specific recommendations: there was a call for access to medical care based on need, not financial resources; for "services of high quality as a matter of right and not as a matter of public assistance or charity"; for easy access to preventive medicine; and, crucially, for the inclusion of "those most in need of health insurance coverage. . . . The old, the sick, the poor, the disabled, the member of the minority group, these are least able to get coverage at present, and they should be first to be included."[24] This early 1960s foray into the needs of the elderly and the poor heralded the landmark Medicare and Medicaid legislation of 1965, but it also set the terms of debate over social inclusion and individual rights that dominated the politics of the decade. Historians have clearly delineated the limited scope for any challenge to the dominance of private health insurance providers over the American health system.[25] What is important for our purposes is to note how the language of universal rights to a decent standard of living formed the backbone of Democratic policymaking in California in the early 1960s, and would have important consequences for welfare state building and for legislative reordering of individual rights later in the decade.

The extension of Social Security provision to long-term noncitizen residents of California in July 1961 also highlighted the dynamics of the link between civil rights and an economic safety net in this period. Assembly Bill 5, shepherded through the legislature by Phil Burton, offered old age and disabled assistance to all who had lived in the state since before 1 January 1932.[26] This had been a key goal of CSO activists since the early 1950s, as it would greatly strengthen the marginal economic situation of hundreds of thousands of working and elderly noncitizens who formed a significant part of the California workforce. The new law created a groundswell of enthusiasm for the Brown administration in urban Latino communities. In the run-up to the 1962 election, Napoleon Tercero, Jr., of a Latino social club in Los Angeles reported that his neighborhood was "'sold out' for Mr. Brown" because of AB 5, and wrote Brown in Spanish that in "the name of all the aged persons who receive pensions without being American citizens, I express directly to you their blessings."[27] Unfortunately, however, such celebrations in Los Angeles could not hide the disappointment out in the fields of the Central and Imperial Valleys. Tinkering with the Social Security Act did not change the fact that the entire basis of that social safety net excluded those not on the payroll of a regular employer in the industrial and commercial sectors of the economy.

In the wake of the 1962 election, in which Brown had promised to deal with the farm worker question, his legislative secretary saw the issue of economic insecurity in the fields as one to be circumvented, not tackled directly. "Obviously, we cannot support the $1.50 minimum wage [for farm labor], the extension of unemployment insurance to farm workers, and other such proposals," he wrote the director of the state Department of Finance. "It seems to me that we should do something in this area, however, and perhaps the best thing that we could do, in the long term, is to support the proposal to provide $135,000 as an augmentation item for child care centers in farm areas." Such centers would help children "overcome the meager environment of their home," an assessment that combined the heavy-handed rehabilitative ethos of early 1960s welfare policy with a determination to use welfare as a prop to support the existing private market in human labor: adequate child care would allow farm workers to continue to work in the fields. This view carefully avoided the clear evidence that only a fundamental reordering of the agricultural economy—the end to the importation of cheap labor, the integration of domestic labor into the industrial economy through unionization and access to a minimum wage and health and welfare services—would lessen the huge financial chasm separating the rural and urban populations. Indeed, Brown's assistant explicitly argued that he advocated the child care measure precisely to head off calls for more far-reaching state intervention in agriculture. "If we could support this measure," he wrote, "it would also offset some of the pressures that are being brought to bear for social legislation in this area."[28] The marriage of civil and economic rights that formed the backbone of the administration's program in the early 1960s broke down when it came to areas of the economy outside the protective embrace of New Deal era labor law.

In any case, the unquenchable thirst of the Golden State for resources to nourish its phenomenal economic and population growth created policy dilemmas for the Brown administration that did not always point toward a smooth path to a progressive future. Pat Brown was not the first governor to have to balance a commitment to social equality with the demands of a growth agenda, but his implementation of the Central Valley Project to solve the Southland's perennial water shortage represented one of the biggest capitulations before the altar of economic expansion in state history. In one sense the $1.75 billion bond issue on the November 1960 ballot was a model of liberal statecraft, using vast reserves of taxpayers' money to construct a state-run water system to divert the Feather River down the Sacramento River into the Central Valley delta. There an artificial channel would suck water from the delta and pump it ever southward toward enormous reservoirs in the Los Angeles basin. It was a public works project on an unheard of scale, providing an unshakeable bond between government and the needs of agriculture, industry, and Southern California's mushrooming citizenry. In order to make the plan workable, however, Pat Brown had to abandon his earlier commitment as attorney general to the federal limit of 160 acres as the maximum size of any one agricultural holding to benefit from federal water projects. As Brown's biographer neatly summarized, "the fact remains that for nearly two decades Brown's beloved water project provided enormous wealth for some of the state's largest agricultural interests, corporations with no legitimate claim to assistance. If that bothered him greatly, he never let on."[29] Greater Los Angeles did not at the time need the huge increase in supply that the project provided, and so the Metropolitan

Water District sold excess water to San Joaquin Valley farmers at a massive discount, farmers who as often as not were in fact huge corporations like Standard Oil and the Southern Pacific Railroad. As *Ramparts* magazine later argued, "Pat Brown was fully aware that the plan meant additional billions for the state's richest men, yet, over the opposition of all of organized labor and virtually every liberal group in California, he pushed it through the legislature, trumpeting in Churchillian rhetoric its vision and grandeur."[30] The control wielded by liberal policymakers over the public purse raised new questions over how to share the bounty of a wealthy economy while continuing to stoke the fires of economic growth.[31]

Finding a Language of Liberalism: The Dilemma of the ADA

The coming to power of a Democratic administration in California did not just prompt the CDC to reappraise its role in the articulation of a political program in the early 1960s. Americans for Democratic Action joined the debate in California over where next to take the liberal agenda. The national leadership managed to reestablish an office in San Francisco in 1960, cognizant of California being "an increasingly important political state," and assigned ADA's national director of organization to northern California. The *ADA World* explained the purpose of the new California chapter as a sort of intellectual conscience for Democrats and liberals: "Taking cognizance of the growth of the Democratic clubs in California and their role in involving liberals in election campaigns and grassroots organizations, the new chapter will not engage in direct political action nor hold regular membership meetings. Instead it will function as an idea and issue organization acting on behalf of the National ADA on national political strategies."[32] California ADA leader Sheldon Pollack was adamant that ADA could provide a much-needed bridge to the national political scene in a state in which CDC had become an accepted part of the local political landscape and threatened to pull the California Democrats away from the mainstream. He termed the CDC Issues Conference in Santa Monica "a debacle" as he felt that the "commies and fuzzies were well at work . . . and it took the Lt. Governor, Alan Cranston, and Richard Richards to get the China resolution changed and equally top notch leadership to handle several other changes at the last minute." New CDC Chairman Tom Carvey had defeated ADA-allied Nancy Swadesh with support, in Pollack's view, "from the far out element, for the most part." ADA, by contrast, would continue the work undertaken by the likes of Arthur Schlesinger and John Kenneth Galbraith of conceptualizing a new vision for liberalism: "I believe that what we are developing at the state level comes close to finding the new issues. In a sense they are the ones that affect the quality of the life we are going to lead—planning, metropolitan government, open spaces, recreation, housing, governmental structure. The old ones of labor, civil rights, welfare programs, unemployment, workmen's compensation are ones that we will largely ignore. They have strong proponents and basically they need toying with to bring them up to date, modify, etc." Given the bitter struggle over right-to-work and the fact that the welfare state remained patchy and limited in scope, this seemed a rather questionable judgment, oblivious to the political realities of the late 1950s both in California and elsewhere. Pollack conceded that the Democratic Party in California was in the avant garde of policy formulation, but believed that this made ADA's intellectual role even more important: "Where they are in power and can effect legislation they need an intellectual arm to stimulate, create and push and we can show results."[33] According to the *Los Angeles Times* Pollack and fellow ADA figure Ned Eisler were "intense, articulate and enthusiastic liberals of the new generation which puts the New Deal and the Emancipation Proclamation in the perspective of ancient history."[34]

The reappearance of the ADA in California pointed up both the strength and the weakness of the movement for political reform on the left in California in the 1960s. On the one hand, ADA's focus on California demonstrated the growing political importance of the Golden State and showed how a fervent debate over the intellectual mainsprings of left-of-center politics was helping to guide Democratic Party policy formulation into new areas of social and individual rights and to make California a political laboratory of new ideas in the early 1960s. Though the divisions between CDC and ADA reflected the latter's formation at the height of the Cold War and its passionate commitment to reflexive anticommunism, in many senses the two organizations shared a commitment to individual rights and social equality that transcended divisions over foreign affairs and provided the California Democratic Party with a powerful intellectual raison d'être. On the other hand, however, the existence of overlapping and rival groups all staking an uncertain claim on Democratic Party legislators and on the formation of government policy gave credence to the argument that the 1960s would witness a gradual weakening of the Democratic Party in California politics and the growth of multiple factions and interest groups all clamoring for political influence at the expense of a strong, centralized unit that could act as a disciplining force.[35] In addition, the continuing casual use of terms like "communists," "fuzzies," and "far out element" demonstrated the difficulty faced by many self-described liberals in articulating a clear, coherent ideological worldview when they lacked obvious recourse to a vocabulary of explicitly left-wing terms. If the 1960s witnessed the gradual coming together of various Democratic Party and leftist factions behind a shared commitment to individual rights and a shared citizenship under the protection of government, as will be argued here, it took a long time before many politicians and grassroots activists realized the fact, hamstrung as they were by personal and factional animosities, not to mention a lack of ideological clarity over questions of economic justice.

The 1962 Elections and the "Politics of Reacting to the Reactionaries"

Pat Brown's dramatic and convincing reelection victory over Richard Nixon in November 1962 achieved a certain degree of notoriety, not least as a result of Nixon's extraordinary outburst in front of the assembled media throng after his landslide defeat. The significance of this election in consolidating the political program of the California Democratic Party and in establishing a clear delineation between the parties on ideological grounds and preparing the ground for a major assault on inequities in access to economic resources has been less studied. This is probably because we know that in 1966 Ronald Reagan's victory over Pat Brown signaled the beginnings of a dramatic shift to the right in state and national politics, and so the attention of historians in recent years has been on the background to this seismic shift in conservative political fortunes in California and elsewhere.[36] For California Democrats, however, the victory in 1962 seemed initially to validate the Brown campaign's strategy of tackling the radical right head-on and trying to build on the legacy of 1958 in making Democratic liberalism the center of political gravity. In so doing, Democrats laid the groundwork for an array of legislative activity in 1963 designed to redefine ideas of economic and social citizenship and to identify the party more closely with the notion of individual rights in society. Even if we accept the argument that Reagan's rise to political prominence marked a "decisive turning point" in American politics, we must also concede that the legislative program of California Democrats in the 1960s marked another decisive turning point: the association of a majority of the party with interest groups and political ideas predicated upon the entitlement of all individuals to certain rights without regard to outdated definitions of race, gender, and sexuality. This process was not a linear one, and this chapter seeks as much to identify ideological tendencies in campaigns and legislation as it does to make bold claims about major political realignments that did not, after all, happen overnight.

The Democratic victories of 1958 and the consolidation of the party's control over the state legislature in 1960 had convinced senior party officials that evidence of far-right-wing political activity in California could be used to complete the legitimization of Democratic liberalism as the center of political gravity. "Recent unpopular excesses of right wing groups, particularly in Southern California, afford the Democratic Party an historic opportunity to take the offensive and make major political gains on a front which has long been a source of intra-party friction," wrote Roger Kent in a confidential memo to Pat Brown headed "A Note on the Politics of Reacting to the Reactionaries." The memorandum, which essentially laid out a blueprint for Brown's 1962 reelection strategy, argued that the growing strength of John Birch Society members in Orange County and elsewhere allowed Democrats to claim the political center ground and neuter some of the party's internal divisions over the extent to which the Brown administration's policies had radicalized state politics. "It now appears that at least a partial reunion of liberal and conservative Democrats on the questions of Americanism and Communism is feasible," wrote Kent. "The basic change in the situation is the movement of the reactionaries' center of gravity to a point beyond the limits of comfortable toleration by the large center group which comprises the majority of the general public. . . . *We should now exploit the dilemma of the conservatives by public emphasis on their association with the lunatic right wing.*" He highlighted two key themes for the 1962 campaign: "1. Ours is the truly American approach. 2. We are the real, the effective anti-communist party."[37]

In part Kent was sharing in a perceived change in the national political zeitgeist that the election of President Kennedy had inaugurated, namely that the dark days of McCarthyism and a Republican ascendancy were over and Democrats could confidently propose legislation that expanded the reach of government without concern that a massive backlash would occur. In a separate election strategy document Kent laid out what he termed "the liberal position," which he described as the belief "that the United States is big enough, rich enough, and wise enough to assure every child a good education, every family a decent place to live, every worker a job at a fair wage . . . every sick person good medical care, proper drugs and hospitalization, every old person a comfortable and dignified life. We won't tolerate hunger or discrimination." He concluded that the liberal "knows and accepts it as a fact that on this overcrowded planet there must be a vast amount of regulation if people are going to be able to live peaceably and happily together."[38] This articulation of an ideology that placed the state at the heart of an agenda of ensuring social harmony was implicitly social democratic and used the right-wing alternative as a foil against which to establish Democratic liberalism as the dominant political order in California.[39] In a radio broadcast during the election campaign Kent was keen to point up the association between dynamic legislative activity and the popular will: "Governor Brown's 1962 legislative program was probably the most forward looking and progressive ever presented to a state legislature. It went far beyond the 1958 and 1960 program in its interest and concern for consumer protection, civil rights, conservation, education, social welfare, urban problems and human rights."[40]

The confident championing of a left-of-center political vision in California stood in stark contrast to the politics of other Western states in the early 1960s, many of which were witnessing the emergence of a militant pro-business, anti-regulatory agenda that would pave the way for Barry Goldwater's run for president in 1964. California's Republican Party in many senses remained trapped in the anticommunist mindset of the early 1950s and was relatively slow to appreciate the extent to which it had since the 1958 debacle lost control of the political agenda. Nixon's career had been built on the confident championing of anticommunism at a time when spy scandals such as Whitaker Chambers's exposure of Alger Hiss and the sense that Democratic liberals had failed to stand up to the Soviet threat dominated the headlines. By 1962, despite the arrival of the Cuban Missile Crisis that October, the domestic political situation had subtly changed. An editorial in a Texas liberal newspaper noted that "Texas and California have long been the greenhouses of the radical right in America, but even in Texas we do not hear major candidates for governor debating over who is the more anti-communist. California politics seems to have degenerated into chronic anti-communist paranoia; Nixon's current line is predicated on the fact." The editorial observed the confidence of the Brown campaign's engagement with the socioeconomic complexity of his home state: "Sometime this year California will pass New York in population. Brown is defending his job-making, anti-discrimination, water-conserving, school-building welfare state and promising to extend it." Many in the GOP high command, by contrast, were bankrolling Proposition 24, a ballot measure that would force any organization or individual found to be communist by a grand jury or superior court to be officially labeled as such.[41] Nixon distanced himself from the convoluted and unworkable measure, but he was forced to tie himself to an agenda that privileged anticommunism above all else, in part because of his efforts to woo an increasingly powerful Southern Californian right wing that had initially rallied behind Los Angeles State Assemblyman Joe Shell, a supporter of the John Birch Society and bitter opponent of big government in all its guises.[42]

Whether or not the wranglings within the California Republican Party in 1962 represented the stirrings of a developing leviathan in state politics, the tenor of the GOP campaign mobilized Democrats into political action and helped to reinforce a left-right binary in California politics that had been noticeably absent ten years earlier. "I have been out on the road a bit lately," reported CDC President Tom Carvey to Brown in September, "talking to clubs and councils, and have come off of it quite pleased about the enthusiasm about the campaign—especially the job that you are doing. Right across the board, people have a good feeling about your campaign and the way it's being run." Part of this enthusiasm, Carvey observed, stemmed from Nixon's campaign strategy: "I think Nixon pulled perhaps the biggest blunder of his career in this 'communist menace' issue of his. . . . Within 48 hours of his opening day statement of this type, I had over a dozen completely independent and rather non-political people come by my office . . . holding their noses and saying that okay this did it, Nixon was out as far as they were concerned. In contrast to his behavior, your very solid plugging away at the issues which really confront California is truly beginning to take effect."[43]

The optimism of the party translated into a state platform and campaign style that utilized the legacy of the Brown administration to date and the promise of further policymaking to come as a way of tying Democratic candidates to the rhetorical notion of the popular will. A press release put out in Brown's name in August to launch the state party platform pointed proudly to the labor plank as "further proof that our party is the party of all the people, dedicated to the betterment of their lives." In fact the platform as a whole was a wildly optimistic wish list of government-led legislative activity, promising a $1.25 minimum wage, the rehabilitation of injured workers unable to return to their former jobs, improved disability and dependency benefits, more generous access to unemployment insurance coverage, the extension of state benefits to more citizens, including to farm workers, and a host of other specific measures to reform, improve, or extend policies protecting labor and recipients of social welfare. Though the administration's progress on the question of farm labor rights had been hesitant at best, the 1962 platform made explicit reference to the need for "reforms in foreign labor importation programs to protect domestic labor," a nod toward the growing pressure at both the state and federal levels to end the bracero program.[44]

Some of these policies, as we shall see, were enacted in Brown's second term; what is also important is the impact of the ideological thrust of the campaign that would help to set the terms of West Coast liberalism in ways that would long outlast the Great Society era. "A system of public education that is twenty-five years ahead of the rest of the nation," boasted Brown to an AFL-CIO convention in Long Beach during his campaign. "Historic improvements in unemployment and disability insurance and workmen's compensation. The first FEPC in the history of this state. A more secure life for the blind, the lame, and the elderly. A minimum wage for women and children in agriculture. The first Economic Development Agency to bring new industries and payrolls to California. The first Office of Consumer Counsel to protect your families from fraud in the market place. . . . Together we have made California the best place to live, work, and raise children." He cast his administration as guardian of the rights of citizens to a quality of life, and contrasted his agenda with what he portrayed as the penny-pinching economic anarchism of his opponent: "Is [Nixon] proposing to cut unemployment insurance—classroom construction—pensions for the elderly—beaches and parks—salaries of our state employees?" He concluded his address by synthesizing his program into a simple linguistic trope that associated individual rights with the common good: "We must tell [voters] that California—which will become the largest state in the nation this year—is also the first state in education, economic opportunity and equal rights for all. . . . We must tell the worker that average factory pay in California is more than $113 a week—far above the national average—and a gain of 16 percent since I took office."[45] Another press release proudly declared that fair employment and antidiscrimination measures constituted "the most significant advances in civil rights laws in California history. Their enactment and successful administration make California the leader among the enlightened states in the struggle for equal opportunity and human dignity for all." The governor explicitly linked the question of antidiscrimination in employment to that of economic security, calling FEPC "a milestone in the long fight for equal opportunity and freedom from poverty."[46] The Brown campaign of 1958 had attempted to portray Democrats as the natural defenders of the majority of California citizens; in 1962 his reelection effort used his legislative record to reinforce that message and to tie together what had in the early 1950s been a loose coalition of interests and factions into a unified, policy-driven entity.

The confidence with which the Brown campaign tackled Republican dirty tricks and negative campaigning demonstrated the change in the political complexion of California since the early fifties and also showed a lack of imagination in state GOP tactics that contrasted vividly with its self-confidence in states in which it was the rising power. It was almost as if the political omnipotence of California Republicans earlier in the century was impeding their capacity to reinvent their agenda. A leaflet appeared claiming to be from the "Committee for the Preservation of the Democratic Party in California," bemoaning the influence of CDC in the party's affairs and exhorting party members to "throw off the shackles of this left-wing minority, now so powerful it can dictate the course of our Party." The front organization used an address on Market Street in San Francisco and used language copied directly from an attack made by *LA Times* hatchet man Kyle Palmer in which he claimed CDC were "more representative of the extreme left than of the general body of Democrats" and that the CDC had "wangled itself into a position of such strength it would now be extremely difficult for a Democrat to win nomination and election if the CDC turned thumbs down." Further enactment of the Democrats' legislative agenda "not only would effect basic changes in our governmental forms and policies but would set in motion various influences designed to effect still more radical modifications."[47] The implicit association of Democrats with a totalitarian left was in many ways a replay of earlier California campaigns, and pictures that accompanied the printed material were still more explicit, picturing Brown in a doctored photograph talking to Khrushchev, above a caption that read "we who admire you and applaud you . . . welcome to California." Roger Kent and his team quickly leapt into action, discovering that over half a million of these mailings had been paid for in bulk, "so we knew that this had to be a Republican mailing. There couldn't be that many Democrats that were *that* mad at CDC that would put up what we figured was seventy-five to a hundred thousand dollars for this gambit. We immediately commenced working on the complaint, and the restraining order, and the temporary injunction."[48] The Democratic campaign, competently staffed, well-funded, and politically confident after four years of power, was a world away from the dark years of the early Cold War.

More importantly, the Republicans seemed unable to recast their message for the times, unlike in neighboring Arizona, where a coalition of business leaders and Republican politicians were successfully formulating their own version of the strategy employed by California's Democrats of outlining a political message that placed their worldview at the center of a self-styled consensus.[49] The *Los Angeles Times*, like much of California's print media, had long been a scourge of Democrats and anyone remotely on the left, but in 1962 under the new editorship of Norman Chandler's heir Otis, it divorced itself from Nixon's campaign. Chandler claimed after the election to have been unimpressed by the

GOP's simple antiradical strategy, telling Brown "in all sincerity that I admired your effective and forthright campaign. . . . We on the *Times* are certainly not chagrined or upset that we have a Democratic governor in Sacramento. I think we have a good relationship and I know it can be even more beneficial to both sides in the future."[50] The backbone of the Nixon campaign was not the cadre of highly motivated entrepreneurs who were reshaping party politics in Arizona or who would command the Reagan campaign four years later, but rather a rag-tag army of Southern Californian John Birchers and far-right elements only partially converted to Nixon as their standard-bearer and still obsessed by the antistatist anticommunism that had defined so much of the renaissance of right-wing politics in the 1950s. One sympathetic Orange County resident thought far-right extremism to be Brown's "right-to-work issue of 1962. . . . In my judgment the key to your campaign is the middle of the road Democrat, who instinctively reacts against immoderation of any kind. 'Nixon,' therefore, must be made synonymous with 'extremism.' For if he attacks right-wing conservatism, many Shell Republicans won't bother to vote in November. But if he does not attack it, you will then be in a position to assail his tacit acceptance and thereby ensure the votes of middle Democrats and perhaps Warren Republicans as well." The correspondent went on to list several prominent Orange County Republican powerbrokers, including John Rousselot, John Schwartz, and Congressman James Utt, and argued that despite their electoral popularity in their home districts their political message could be poisonous elsewhere.[51] Certainly by 1962 Orange County was already synonymous with right-wing activism and a powerful Republican establishment, but the dominant political message coming out of prominent local political organs such as the *Register* was a particular brand of antitotalitarianism that assailed the United Nations, foreign aid, the collection of taxes, and "the power of the government to direct or control private industry."[52] It was not the same as a concerted assault on the halls of power of the type that would occur with the Reagan campaign of 1966 or in several of the Sunbelt states over the next two decades, and which had a much more sophisticated understanding of the role of government in shaping economic growth and in associating American citizenship with free markets.

This is not to argue that the grassroots right in southern California was not growing in political influence, but it is important to remember that in 1962 many liberals did not rate the right and were more confident in the way they shaped their worldview than they had been before. The extent to which the development of the burgeoning suburbs and the rapid economic development of California in the early 1960s made its political geography contested terrain in ways that cannot be adequately understood by an analysis of Orange County can be seen by an examination of the South Bay region around San Jose and San Mateo. By the early 1960s the 101 freeway cut a swathe through an increasingly densely populated series of communities that spread southward from San Francisco to San Jose, sandwiched cozily between the Santa Clara mountains and San Francisco Bay. Home in the early 1960s to a burgeoning array of high technology and manufacturing industries, and to the 1.5 million people who worked for these companies, shopped in the new malls, and who placed increasing pressure on the local services and infrastructure of the area, the South Bay and San Mateo peninsula seemed an archetype of the suburban America that threatened to swamp the old nation of the New Deal era.

This region, like much of the Bay Area in the 1960s, was in the words of a Santa Clara Democratic Assembly candidate "acquiring more than a slight resemblance to the LA pattern. That is, a pattern of freeways, endless urban areas, little or no public transportation, long drives to and from work in slow, creeping, nerve-wracking traffic and a city without the benefits of a central core." It was not, however, the same as Southern California in its politics: William Stanton was successful in his Assembly race in the Twenty-Fifth District, and his Democratic campaign focused on the need for an activist state government to ameliorate the social ills caused by rapid and unplanned economic expansion. "Peace is of course the paramount issue facing all of us," he asserted in a campaign leaflet distributed to local residents by an army of eager volunteers. "However, not far behind in importance to the residents of Santa Clara County and California are those which have arisen as a consequence of the tremendous population growth of the county and state. The population increase of Santa Clara County alone is more than 50,000 persons a year. . . . It will be necessary to bring new industry to our county, diversify our local economy, lessen our economic dependence upon defense industry and provide retraining programs for those who have lost jobs and are unemployable without new skills." Economic and population growth required active state management in order to ensure their sustained development, and the Brown program was designed to provide it: "I support, and would if elected act to implement Governor Brown's programs on consumer protection, education, social welfare, civil rights, workmen's compensation, unemployment insurance, economic development, state government reorganization and water development."[53] Stanton's success in San Jose was not preordained: one visiting Democratic strategist in late 1961 found "more disorganization, more 'personnel' problems, and less understanding of cooperative effort in Santa

Clara County than any other I have been in." She noted the "virulence of the right wing" and evidence of divisions within the Central Committee. Nevertheless, there was also evidence of vibrant Democratic Clubs in Palo Alto and Los Gatos and the existence of a large 100,000-strong Latino population in San Jose, which would "constitute a permanent voting majority for us in the 25th Assembly District and the 9th Congressional District if registered and got to the polls."[54]

The campaign gave the region's Democrats a mission that seemed to overcome some of their inbuilt handicaps in local politics. To senior Santa Clara Democrats, a commitment to social welfare and civil rights was a commitment to efficiency and a theory of modernity that associated economic growth with social cohesion and a quality of life for local citizens. The chairman of the Santa Clara Committee to Re-elect Governor Brown, John Racanelli, took aim in a campaign speech at Nixon's attempt to win over voters with a promise to slash welfare spending. A press release reporting Racanelli's comments stated that he had attacked "Nixon's remark that mismanagement of the state's welfare program must be measured in terms of character, moral fiber, and self-reliance . . . Racanelli indicated that one of the basic purposes of the welfare program is to preserve those very same human qualities. 'Mr. Nixon's charges are a slap at welfare workers and law enforcement agents throughout the state . . . who every day are working conscientiously to make the welfare program more efficient and effective in building self-reliance and usefulness to society.'"[55]

This idea that enterprise, efficiency, and social inclusion were interrelated formed a centerpiece of the Brown campaign at the state level that symbolized a self-confident liberal mission in California in the early 1960s. That Democratic strategists thought it would resonate in Santa Clara suggests that the party had assumed a position of political dominance in many communities in the years after 1958 that had made it confident to portray itself as the guardian of political inclusion and consensus. Democrats captured both the Assembly district and the U.S. House seat from that part of San Jose that year, and enjoyed successes in a number of other suburban districts around the Bay Area.[56] The crucial issue was the failure of leading state Republicans to identify themselves with a new agenda, together with an enthusiastic association of Democrats with a notion of modernity that made social justice part of a commitment to economic growth. "Beyond question, the most perplexing social, economic, and political problems confronting California are those associated with our population explosion, labor force expansion, and growth generally," argued the secretary-treasurer of the California Federation of Labor to the Platform Committee of the State Democratic Party in advance of its 1962 Convention. The party had to orient its platform "toward planning for growth, and recognition of the responsibility state government must assume for stimulating private enterprise and unlocking human initiative."[57] Intriguingly, the underlying premise of using state power to encourage enterprise actually united labor-liberal Democrats in California with a new generation of pro-business Republicans; the inclusion of increased infrastructure and welfare spending provided the big political division and the electoral endorsement of the Democratic program in 1962 suggested a window of opportunity for a social democratic vision that would shape Democratic politics for a generation even when changing political currents revitalized the antiwelfare, laissez-faire agenda in later years.

One vital factor in tying Democrats to the spirit of 1962 was the energy of the candidates and their volunteer supporters in pushing for victory, an energy that left a visible imprint on the politics of the party. Enthusiasm for local candidates blurred the boundaries between activist and party regular and between different shades of political opinion among those loosely grouped under the "liberal" umbrella. Campaigns for local offices were community affairs: in the Fifty-Ninth Assembly District, which included Beverly Hills and part of West Los Angeles and Venice Beach, freshman candidate Tony Beilenson went door-to-door with his wife distributing literature, enlisting the help of the local clubs to provide funds and manpower. Some of his campaign techniques were innovative: he handed out three or four thousand specially designed cookbooks to people who endorsed him and provided a lasting reminder of his candidacy. Some residents, he later recalled, "still have the cookbook and still remember me because of it. I mean, it's a real book. You know, hardcover book, and it's nothing that anyone's going to throw away, unlike some of the junk that sometimes people pass out when they're running for election."[58]

In the Eighteenth District in San Francisco African American Willie Brown challenged the long-term incumbent Assemblyman Ed Gaffney in the primary, using the issue of the proposed freeway through Golden Gate Park as an issue around which to unite a coalition of local residents and politicians behind his notion that the district needed fresh blood and a more dynamic political agenda. Though he narrowly lost, he won two years later and used his 1962 run to put in place his team of local activists like Frank Brann, who had run for Assembly four years earlier, and Joe Williams, Phil Burton's African American law partner. "We got the Democratic Club endorsement of course," Brown recalled. "We got the endorsement of the ILWU and the pension people. . . . We didn't run a good get-out-the-vote operation. But the 1962 campaign became the seed for the 1964 campaign. . . . It was geared to the Hispanic community, it was geared to senior citizens and it was geared to families of organized labor and what we can loosely identify as the liberal left, social activists, environmental groups . . . It eventually became a majority but it was not always a majority."[59] Brown's run came a year after a liberal coalition had gained control of Berkeley City Council for the first time, and a year after Jose Sarria's quixotic but symbolic run for a seat on the San Francisco Board of Supervisors as a key figure in the city's queer demi-monde. His campaign literature reproduced the proclamation engraved on the city's Hall of Justice, a commitment "to the faithful and impartial enforcement of the laws with equal and exact justice to all of whatever state or persuasion."[60] These races were significant straws in the wind, not necessarily of an emergent Democratic majority statewide, but rather of an emerging ideological and political sensibility of social inclusion that would come to dominate the party.

They also represented a sign that the party's radical edge would not tolerate policy fudges, a fact that would have repercussions for state politics for the rest of the decade. In August 1962 CDC's leaders called the faithful back to Asilomar, site of its founding in 1953, to debate where to take the organization next. The majority view seemed to be that CDC should "continue to participate in the political process but as a partner with the regular organization and labor's political arm, rather than as one of several contenders for power and influence within the loosely-structured entity we call the Democratic Party."[61] CDC Chairman Carvey certainly went to considerable lengths to keep CDC working as an arm of the official Brown campaign, arguing in a campaign bulletin that CDC and Brown stood "shoulder to shoulder" and that alleged divisions between the two over ideology had been overplayed. "No sensible person will believe Governor Brown is 'left-wing' any more than they will believe that the Democratic club members, County Central Committee members, State Committee members, officeholders and nominees (which happens to be the CDC) are a bunch of 'extremists.'"[62]

There were signs that the imprecision of the political vocabulary of politicians and the inevitable gulf between idealist activists and elected representatives attuned to the day-to-day realities of power were starting to put pressure on the Brown campaign. He received a large postbag in the summer from activists concerned that he was distancing himself from CDC and from his more ambitious policy ideas. One correspondent from Venice Beach warned Brown that "if you are going to repudiate the California Democratic Council or the CDC you won't get my vote, nor the vote of many of my friends and neighbors. Oddly enough, the Democrats I know are all *liberals*."[63] Another wrote that Brown had offended a luncheon audience in Ontario, California, by mentioning "the Left Wingers in the CDC and you suggested they should go into the 'Socialist Party, that is where they belong,' etc. Governor, there are many former honest Socialists in the Democratic Party and are sincere workers to elect Democrats in California as well as all other states. They act and work like good Democrats. . . . Former President Eisenhower had to apologize to the Swedish people for his remarks against Socialism. Did you know all the Scandinavian countries are headed by 'Social Democrats'? Hugh Gaitskell of England, Willy Brandt of West Berlin, Paul Spaak of Belgium and many other countries, all Socialists and in constant conferences with President Kennedy. . . . Remember Socialism is not Communism."[64] Brown claimed his speeches had been taken out of context by the press, and tried hard to keep CDC on his side, in part because he was aware that he needed them: they were the most enthusiastic foot soldiers of the campaign, and represented a leftist politics that no longer seemed as politically untenable as a few years earlier. "My concern," Steve Zetterberg wrote Democratic Senate candidate Richard Richards in July and which he copied to Brown, "which led me to cook up all this good advice is: You are a creature of CDC. If it hadn't been for CDC you would not have had the nomination. . . . CDC is the Democratic Party in California. It includes amateurs, professionals, think-people, work people. They have divergent views. They are united on you (as with Brown, etc); they do not ask that you be 'their creature' intellectually; only that you be the guy that they have come to support."[65]

In truth, CDC was not the Democratic Party tout court, but it was a device by which to expand the reach of the party into much of the state that had previously been poorly organized. The 45th FAssembly District east of Los Angeles, for instance, contained six local clubs, all of which raised money and manned the district headquarters for the Democratic slate. "It was entirely through their unselfish efforts the headquarters and precinct organization was a great success," wrote the chair of the local CDC to Brown after the party's victories in the November elections. "The entire project was completely voluntary, carried out by the 'grass roots' Democrats."[66] The CDC's Southern California Get-Out-the-Vote Committee reported after the election that its volunteer operation in Los Angeles County had resulted in very high Democratic turnouts across the county: in the Forty-Fifth the rejoicing CDC had not only garnered a Democratic turnout of 78.58 percent but had also elected a new Democratic assemblyman. In Beilenson's Fifty-Ninth district 81.17 percent of registered Democrats turned out to vote, and almost every one of those voted for Brown for governor. In heavily Republican districts in which CDC had run a volunteer operation, still they managed Democratic turnouts of near 80 percent with a high Brown loyalty factor. In two Assembly Districts in Speaker Jesse Unruh's patch of South-East Los Angeles, the Thirty-Eighth and Fifty-Second, in which Unruh had approved the use of an entirely paid operation in which cash was handed out in exchange for voting, Democratic turnout was reasonable—74.83 and 73.02, respectively—but party loyalty was not: the Brown vote as a percentage of Democratic registration was 62.94 in the Thirty-Eighth and 60.18 in the Fifty-Second. "Not only did a substantial number of Democrats get out and vote for [Brown]," noted the report of Los Angeles Democratic voting, "but over 5,500 volunteers in all districts of this single county gave freely and enthusiastically of their time to work for the election of Governor Brown and the Democratic slate. The 57th Assembly district is an excellent, because extreme, case in point. In 1960, with bare 50% Democratic registration, the district came within 800 votes of electing a Democratic Assemblyman against a Republican incumbent. . . . Now note that the 57th AD ranks third in the county in both Democratic turnout and Brown loyalty vote in the recent election. Following intensive pre-election day precinct work, 400 volunteers covered 319 precincts for the election day Get-Out-the-Vote Drive." This was without the benefit of a local Assembly candidate, who had withdrawn after his appointment to a federal government post.[67] These grassroots activists provided both organizational energy and ideological zeal, building on a long legacy of left-wing agitation and an affinity for community politics that defined California's distinct political culture. Such energy also suggested dangers ahead, for an uneasy truce between everyday politics and ideological purity would come under severe strain during the massive social upheavals of the later 1960s.

Nevertheless, the emphatic victories won by Democratic candidates in an off-year election for the party provided the political launch pad for the major legislative efforts in welfare and civil rights that would take place in 1963, setting the terms of debate between right and left over the relationship between economic rights and social citizenship for the rest of the century. Brown's victory over Nixon of some 300,000 votes was not quite the landslide he had secured against Knowland, but it seemed to be a ringing endorsement of his record of the past four years. Thanks to the Democratic-controlled legislature's reapportionment efforts, the party had extended its control over the legislature and had created new safe districts in Congress, including the state's first black majority district in Los Angeles, won by long-time Assemblyman Augustus Hawkins. Twenty-four Democrats from California sat in the House in the 88th Congress in January 1963, compared to sixteen in the 87th, a triumph of the team led by Phil Burton in ensuring the eight new districts assigned to California would go to Democrats. The only disappointment was Richard Richards's failure to unseat popular liberal Republican Senator Tom Kuchel, a sign that state politics remained driven by individual personalities and candidates as well as by party.[68] The victories the party secured allowed them a considerable degree of power in shaping the legislative agenda in 1963, but it also provided many Democrats with an electoral mandate for the gradual redefinition of their underlying ideological attachment to a politics of social inclusion that would form the basis for 1960s liberalism. As the co-chairs of the Committee for Women's Activities in Southern California, one of whom was party regular Carmen Warschaw, announced in a press release in April, "we want every woman to know that the Brown administration is an administration with a heart that is responsible for the finest insurance program in the nation for the aged, the needy, the sick and the unemployed."[69] A new pressure group called Californians for Liberal Representation endorsed liberal candidates for new congressional seats around the state in order to "assist in the election of Congressmen who will devote themselves to translating liberal ideas and ideals into national policy."[70] The extent to which the Democratic mandate would translate into a major overhaul of governmental policy, with important ramifications for the relationship between the state and the regulation of society, can be measured by an examination of the landmark overhaul of the California welfare state in 1963.

CHAPTER 8

Welfare Reform and the Idea of the Family

"This is indeed a crucial time in public assistance," reported assistant secretary of Health, Education, and Welfare and long-time federal Social Security administrator Wilbur Cohen in a speech in Boston in November 1961. "I can venture to say that the welfare programs have never been so thoroughly studied as they are being studied under this administration. And they have never been the object of so many independent evaluations by such highly qualified people."[1] In California a number of factors coalesced in the early 1960s to put the welfare state at the center of the political agenda. First, the passage of several federal bills, ranging from Social Security for the disabled in 1956 to the Kerr-Mills Medical Assistance to the Aged bill in 1960, offered federal funds on a matching basis to states that implemented new state programs of categorical assistance. The election of President Kennedy ushered in a period of high political expectation that new entitlement programs would be on the agenda, and the president's temporary allowance of AFDC benefits to unemployed parents as an economic stimulus measure raised the possibility that a major expansion of entitlements at the state level would not necessarily cause ructions in Washington. Third, the early years of the Brown administration had witnessed a dramatic enlargement of the state government, and an increasingly ambitious and influential state Department of Social Welfare sought to capitalize on the favorable political climate and enlarge its control over a multilayered and bureaucratically complex welfare apparatus. Fourth, the state legislature was by the early 1960s solidly under Democratic control, and the chair of the Social Welfare Committee was the extraordinarily talented and driven champion of the poor and dispossessed Phil Burton, who possessed such powers of legislative legerdemain and singularity of purpose that he would almost single-handedly revolutionize California's welfare state without arousing the suspicions of many of his opponents until it was too late.

Finally, the reelection of Pat Brown in 1962 gave the political green light to the most enthusiastic supporters of a more generous welfare system, and gave Brown the electoral capital he needed to throw his weight behind one of the biggest spending sprees in the history of any single state.[2] While the story of the major amendments to California's welfare system in 1963, usually referred to under the umbrella Assembly Bill 59 that brought them about, is important in itself, the underlying story of the ideological impact of welfare state building on the Democratic Party in California is a less-understood narrative that had a major influence on politicians' understanding of how society did and should function in later years. Efforts to define welfare as a right to all needy people and not just those who met a particular moral standard opened up new opportunities for marginalized interest groups to integrate themselves into the political mainstream through involvement in the campaign to eliminate the morality-based foundations of public policy. At the same time, debates over welfare suggested growing tensions within liberal politics between notions of individual rights to freedom from state oppression and questions of economic rights that required the state to regulate people's private lives, tensions that would come to define the political climate by the 1970s.

AB 59 and the Reshaping of the Welfare State

The enlargement of the federal welfare state at the close of the Eisenhower presidency combined with a significant rise in the profile of the California Department of Social Welfare at the start of the Brown governorship to sharpen debate on the West Coast over the scope and purpose of public assistance. Though the state's inability to tackle a fundamental class imbalance in the distribution of economic resources was very real, the political debate on these themes, utilizing intellectual arguments about class and welfare, advanced a mainstream political awareness of racial and gender issues that set up the terms of reference for later social and political struggles to redefine the normative in American society. "Today there is a new climate at all levels—legislative, departmental, and executive," asserted Harry Girvetz in a memo to Brown's legislative assistant in April 1960 on the question of the elderly in California. "The time is opportune for a comprehensive statement embodying an inclusive program and philosophy. Necessarily such a statement must concentrate on the needs of the lower income groups and indigent among the aged." Girvetz noted that "old age is the great leveller," and that it represented a useful subject for uniting voters behind a program of state action, "acting collectively and through legislation" that would inevitably come to include all of society once they reached retirement age.[3] Girvetz was not alone among advisors to the administration in recognizing the appeal of a collectivist politics that targeted issues of universality. "In the true sense, State government is a consumer program," noted one of Brown's assistants in 1960. "Roads, schools, mental institutions, hospitals, forestry conservation, beaches and parks, fish and wildlife, etc., all are consumer programs with the purpose of serving us as taxpayers to achieve a way of life we have determined upon. Consumers looking hopefully to this new office have identified the most pressing consumer problems today as medical care, housing, public utilities, insurance, and what I will call the 'need to get a fair shake in the marketplace.'" The state would serve to evaluate and monitor the private economy, but would also "provide needed services that cannot be provided privately."[4]

Jacobus tenBroek, a California welfare policy expert who would become a key witness in the state's successful effort in 1963 to expand assistance to needy children to two-parent families, was another policy thinker who, like Girvetz, bridged the divide between government advisor and intellectual.[5] In 1959 he and a coauthor published *Hope Deferred: Public Welfare and the Blind*, which argued that the "blind as a group are mentally competent, psychologically stable, and socially adaptable; and that their needs are therefore those of ordinary people, of normal men and women, caught at a physical and social disadvantage." The key question for tenBroek was that of "whether [welfare] provides services as rights due to citizens or as the charity bounty due to wards and indigents. . . . The welfare of the blind is a social responsibility. . . . It underscores the obligation which exists in any democratic society to assure equal rights to life, liberty, and the pursuit of happiness to all its members." Crucially, the "shift in the economic setting from depression to prosperity" was one factor that had widened the debate over public welfare from one of ameliorating conditions of pauperism to one of reintegrating the disadvantaged and socially marginalized into civic life: "The principle that the recipient [of aid] is free to conduct his own life and manage his own affairs must be maintained at all costs against caseworkers whose advice becomes direction, whose services are supplied with a sanction, and whose investigation and handling of recipients' problems become psychoanalysis and treatment." The debate over the welfare state was to the authors a universal question of individuals' rights as citizens "to be free to make their own decisions with respect to spending, living arrangements, and personal matters."[6] As with the debate over aid to two-parent families, amendments to aid to the needy blind to liberalize entitlement and attempt to lessen bureaucratic interference with lifestyle choices forced political actors to reconfigure the relationship between the individual and the state even as their struggles to expand the welfare state and state oversight of civil rights continued to meet with widespread opposition.

This intellectual debate dovetailed with legislative action to implement the new Medical Assistance to the Aged bill in California and to liberalize existing social welfare programs, underpinned by the bureaucratic expansion of the Department of Social Welfare and a reconsideration of its investigative role in policing welfare recipients. The legislature's social welfare committee had been able to force through the Rattigan-Burton Act in 1961 that gained federal funding for hospital stays for the needy elderly of longer than thirty days, and had also expanded the reach of unemployment and needy aged relief by removing the restrictive "responsible relatives" clauses that placed much of the burden for supporting the poor on cash-strapped relatives, and by extending some welfare provisions to noncitizens. But these limited successes showed up significant weaknesses in state provision that propelled both legislators and welfare administrators to seek further improvements in the state's welfare programs. The gradual liberalization of programs forced politicians and welfare bureaucrats to conceptualize what it was they were tying to achieve, and this both furnished welfare experts with new influence in state politics and gave welfare advocates in the legislature a rationale through which to pursue further expansion of public assistance programs. Rattigan-Burton had, for instance, left short-term medical care for the elderly as a county responsibility, and it was clear that this was untenable, not only because county revenues were so low but because the federal act specifically allowed states to seek federal resources for both short- and long-term care: in restricting its program California was missing out on federal money. It was also missing out on an opportunity to recast the debate over welfare provision for a post-New Deal age. "The Department of Social Welfare which has the major share of responsibility for the needy aged has been inhibited by statutory restriction from functioning as a coordinating agency," stated Girvetz in his memo pushing for a major expansion of the state's welfare program. "It has also been limited by traditional notions concerning welfare which our more liberal legislature and Administration have discarded, thereby freeing the Department to plan in a positive way for the overall benefit of the needy and dependent."[7]

The head of the State Department of Social Welfare, Jack Wedemeyer, worked with Democratic legislators throughout the 1961 legislative session to implement this overhaul of state oversight of welfare programs, in part due to a realization that a more modern conception of familial relationships was not only morally desirable but financially necessary if new sources of funding were to be tapped and a fair system of benefits that reflected actual family relationships was to be implemented. An effort in the State Senate in 1961 to pass a bill to make a male breadwinner who was not married to the mother of needy children liable for their upkeep reflected in Wedemeyer's words "an attempt to codify as statute a regulation which sets forth the method whereby at least part of the income of the stepfather or assumed spouse is determined to be available to meet the needs of the children. . . . The fact that the partners are not legally married raises the question of whether the limitation of legal liability of the assumed spouse to the wife's community interest on his income does not, therefore, relieve this assumed spouse of all liability."[8] This particular bill was an effort to force parents, rather than the state, to assume a greater financial burden for their children's upkeep, but in order to do so it required the Department of Social Welfare as drafters of the legislation to engage with what constituted normative social and familial relationships in ways that would have important repercussions on both bureaucrats and pro-welfare politicians. The governor's interim committee on welfare reform in its initial report in December 1960 underlined clearly how proponents of an enlarged welfare system saw an engagement with social conditions as they really were as a vital way of combating welfare opponents who used caricatures of familial relationships and the myth of the nuclear family to attack welfare programs. "The state Aid to Needy Children program has been the subject of widespread criticism by grand juries, boards of supervisors, representatives of taxpayer associations, chambers of commerce, and others. Isolated examples of fraud and statements concerning illegitimacy and immorality have been used to give weight to the position of those who advocate a restriction of the [Aid to Needy Children] program," stated the report of the committee, whose chairman was Phil Burton. The committee refused to consider the question of cost without "also considering the substantial social good which is done by the program," a program that by 1959 benefited some 71,000 California families.[9] By the time of the 1962 election the stage was set for a major overhaul of the state's welfare system: the electoral mandate, the careful planning and deliberation on the part of the Governor's Commission on Welfare and the state Department of Social Welfare, and the desire of Brown, Burton, and their allies to take advantage of federal funding and leave a lasting policy legacy all came together as the legislature prepared to start a new legislative session in 1963.

The American welfare state in the late 1950s had changed relatively little since the passage of the Social Security Act in 1935, and much recent scholarship has emphasized how the social and political assumptions of 1930s policymakers engendered inherent inequalities in provision and entitlement.[10] By the early 1960s many of California's Democratic legislators had seized upon the issue as a means of further strengthening their political advantage, combining control of the redistricting process in 1962 with an ideological campaign to tie many of the state's socially disadvantaged to the Democrats. It had become clear from the deliberations of the governor's welfare commission that the aid to needy children program would form the centerpiece of legislative change, as it best exemplified the loaded social assumptions of the policymakers of the 1930s. The application of the program, argued welfare policy expert tenBroek in 1961, "is selective and discriminatory." The original Act had provided for aid to mothers with children in cases where the mother had been widowed or abandoned, assuming, in effect, that all "deserving" mothers were widowed and that women who were in relationships could depend on the male for support. The state undertook to ensure that all claimants were genuinely on their own: "Interrogation on nothing more than suspicion or gossip, detectives operating in teams, night raids, simultaneous approaches to the back and front of the house, guns conspicuously displayed on hips, unceremonious entry, inmates interrogated at length and notes taken, the entire house searched without any particular care to secure permission, men and sometimes ANC mothers arrested and hauled off to jail—all of this in the presence of the children to many of whom the episode must come as a frightening and even traumatic experience." Professor tenBroek further noted that the legislation was used by the state to prescribe particular norms of social behavior: indicted welfare cheats could be "ordered as a condition of probation not to indulge in extra-marital relationships," and the law used as a weapon "to disarm and discredit the welfare worker and arm the prosecutor and policeman to the teeth; to arrest, to raid, to threaten, to crack down, to punish." He saw the Democrats' 1958 victories in California as potentially heralding a new direction in the theoretical and ideological underpinnings of public welfare: "Social problems of inequality and instability require social planning and legislation, as specific and broad-scaled as the need to be met."[11]

Local welfare officers' caseload demonstrated the ways in which the state's need to demonstrate value for money in its welfare budget encouraged stringent policing of the lives of those receiving aid to needy children benefits. Los Angeles area deputy of the Department of Social Welfare Ralph Goff had the responsibility of investigating AFDC applications and allocating funds on the basis of how welfare mothers lived their lives. "Your application for restoration of Aid to Needy Children was denied July 16th 1963, because the County was unable to determine the real nature of the relationship between you and Mr. Bryant," he wrote to Mrs. Tammie Stephens in late August 1963, after the passage of AB 59 but before its implementation into law. "Your children's eligibility for assistance is dependent on you, what you do, and what your living arrangements are." To another claimant he wrote: "According to information received from the County, it has been determined by that agency that there is a continuing relationship between you and Mr. Lewis. On May 10, 1963, for instance, he was observed picking you up in front of the District office in his car. We realize that this was some time ago and there is the possibility of your and Mr. Lewis' relationship being different at this time. However, it does appear that you are in touch with Mr. Lewis."[12] One welfare recipient, who was outlining her experience of claiming aid to the disabled, described social workers as "mostly young dictators who are trying to run other people's lives and tell them what to do as adults and grownups. They are very ill-mannered, nosey, and ask too many questions about private lives. . . . That is why poor people are fed up. It is not Welfare at all. It is Hellfare."[13] California was not unusual in using its welfare programs as a form of social control to try to force recipients to conform to a particular pattern of behavior that was seen as rehabilitating the poor and underprivileged and would justify to a watchful state government the expenditure of funds. What was distinctive was the dramatic shift in the underlying rationale of the welfare state that Phil Burton and his allies brought about in a few dramatic months in 1963. It did not completely transform how welfare recipients experienced the day-to-day process of living on welfare, but it did transform how liberals engaged with questions of social behavior and social difference.

The huge growth in the number of those who qualified for public assistance in the years after World War II, together with the not unrelated rehabilitation of the Democratic Party in the late 1950s across the United States, gave politicians like Phil Burton a legislative issue with which to cement his party's electoral base. "The so-called 'soaring sixties' are liable to be exactly that with respect to public welfare programs and costs," predicted William MacDougall of the County Supervisors' Association of California at a meeting of the County Welfare Directors in November 1961. "Those who view our public assistance and other welfare programs as a mammoth monster are going to have to wake up to the fact that the monster cannot be slain."[14] Jacobus tenBroek argued that Phil Burton's ethnically variegated and working class constituency made his chairmanship of the assembly's Social Welfare committee a perfect route to political invincibility by using his power to reshape the political language of welfare in a more inclusive direction. Burton, by the time of the passage of his mammoth welfare reform bill in 1963, had "placed [his] knowledge and expertise at the service of an idea—or, more exactly, of a set of ideas—concerning the proper scope and purpose of public welfare. . . . The dignity of man is not lost by virtue of poverty and the receipt of welfare benefits."[15]

Assembly Bill 59, in Burton's words "almost a textbook of advanced social welfare theory," had the effect when gradually molded into shape during 1963 of strengthening Burton's political base in the legislature and his constituency while also providing an issue platform with which liberal Democrats could claim political legitimacy in an age of rapid social change.[16] It represented a defining moment in Burton's career before he moved into national politics the following year, as the passage of AB 59 not only flagged up his reputation as a crusader for the rights of the poor and for the equal treatment of all citizens in the eyes of the law but it also demonstrated his extraordinary command of the legislative process that would later come to be seen as legendary. He had already shown himself to be a gifted operator in the halls of the state capitol, masterminding the reapportionment process in 1961 and displaying a rare understanding of the electoral picture of every district in the state.[17] Roger Kent, personality-wise as far away from the mercurial and street-fighter Burton as it was possible to be, described him as "damn near a psychopath sometimes. But he's a *tremendously* smart politician. He doesn't think or breathe or eat anything but politics, twenty-four hours a day, and hasn't for twenty years. . . . Phil is really almost impossible. He can be so mean and so paranoid; his eyes just bug out like this, you know. But he knows more about welfare, and he knows more about election techniques than anybody in Congress."[18] He nursed a burning resentment at the economic and social inequalities of society and at the indignities suffered by recipients of state welfare, and knew that the new legislative session offered him the opportunity to change the way in which the state regulated its welfare system, and also to take advantage of federal funding streams into the bargain. The impact of AB 59 on the California political scene would far exceed its impact on welfare provision: it would provide the basis for common ground between mainstream legislators and an array of social groups beginning to clamor for political recognition in the 1960s.

The ideological imperative of the legislation was to define welfare as a right.

The bill's authors attempted to remove anachronistic notions of deserving and undeserving poverty from liberal policymaking, and to limit the extent to which government could dictate how welfare recipients lived their lives. The biggest change to the state's needy children program took out the provision that the male in the household had to be absent before a family could qualify for relief; after 1963, the unemployment of a child's "parent or parents" was sufficient, a clause that both allowed for the notion of a female breadwinner and also promoted the concept of a "living wage," providing relief if a family's earned income was below a certain threshold even if either parent was in work. These provisions embedded in law the idea that the provision of government funds, rather than the withholding of them, could promote better integration of the poor into wider society: the governor's welfare commission concluded that the lack of "suitable provision for maintenance of decent living standards" of California's unemployed "has strong and direct tendencies to promote family disintegration and moral degradation."[19] Section 1523.7 of the new Act took the principle of welfare as a right rather than an emergency stop gap to another level: it established criteria that constituted "good cause for refusal" of employment. No longer would a welfare recipient have to take any job that was on offer to remove them from the relief rolls: the employment had to offer a wage higher than the relief payment; the relief recipient had to be fit to undertake the job; he or she could refuse the employment if the vacancy was caused by a labor dispute; and, most controversially, the job could be refused if acceptance "would be an unreasonable or inconsistent act because of hardships imposed upon the person or his family due to illness, hours and working conditions, or remoteness or inaccessibility; interruption of a program for permanent rehabilitation or self-support; or conflicting with an imminent likelihood of re-employment at his regular work."[20] The bill also attempted to ameliorate the burden on the welfare applicant of the intrusive and stigmatizing eligibility process by requiring counties to apply a rule of "presumptive eligibility," speeding up the process of granting welfare checks considerably. Welfare was no longer defined as a port of last resort, but was now a legitimate secondary source of income for families through which the state protected its citizens from arbitrary and antisocial working conditions in the private sector.

Even if few politicians dared spell it out in these terms, the amendments to California's welfare laws represented classic social democratic thought. The state was to provide income transfers to all those unable to provide for their families by private means. The changes to ANC formed part of a sweeping program of reform: the definition of disability was amended in the omnibus bill so as to remove the requirement that the recipient of disability relief required continuous supervision and help with his or her daily regimen, allowing instead for provision for a disability which "substantially precludes the individual from engaging in useful occupations within his competence, such as holding a job or homemaking."[21] The bill thus widened the definition of the disabled, but at the same time it removed a loaded understanding that disabled meant helpless by providing community work experience and vocational training opportunities for those able to benefit, "so that they can become self-supporting, tax-paying members of the community and State."[22] AB 59 included medical assistance for the aged including thirty days in a county hospital, and prohibited the taking of liens by county authorities against property of those receiving aid in all qualified categories of assistance. In addition, AB 5 in 1961 had repealed the requirement that the Old Age and Survivors Insurance apply only to U.S. citizens. The ideological underpinning to all these changes was clear: the state should play an active role in the welfare of its citizens, and not merely act as a prop for carefully compartmentalized categories of the destitute.[23] Equally important was the underlying assumption of the new law that the socially marginalized should be recognized as full citizens and have their "economic rights and welfare protected."[24] This theme represented the culmination of the state Democratic Party's process of redefinition of the previous decade, and had implications for politicians' understanding of gender and race that would extend beyond the subject of welfare.

The fact that many of the important changes to California's welfare system required what one journalist termed "enviable legislative gymnastics" in order to be passed reminds us that liberal Democrats did not enjoy anything close to complete freedom of action in the legislature nor unequivocal support in the state at large.[25] Many legislators remained wedded to the view expressed by the California Taxpayers' Association that it was "downright dishonest and immoral to take [taxpayers'] money to pay it out to support indolence, idleness, illegitimacy and welfare cheats and chiselers." The Kern County Board of Supervisors opposed the new laws for reasons that demonstrated the widening gulf between the worldviews of social democrats and antistatists in the 1960s: families qualifying for aid to dependent children "should be required to maintain an adequate home environment conducive to the moral and physical development of their children."[26] It was mainly Phil Burton's skill at manipulating the legislature's arcane procedural rules that got the omnibus bill through to gain Brown's signature. He knew that he could introduce a relatively uncontroversial bill, one that initially provided that recipients' earned income and interest on savings would not be deducted from their grants. He would then sneak amendments in, knowing that although they were highlighted in strike-through text and in italics those highlighted sections disappeared in subsequent amended versions, making it easy to hide controversial sections confident that most legislators would not have the patience to keep track of everything that was going on. He organized lobby groups that included Catholics, farm groups, and disabled charities to come to Sacramento and put pressure on legislators. He manipulated key members of Assembly and Senate committees to quietly push the bill past chairmen hostile both to the provisions of AB 59 and to Burton personally.[27]

His cunning and persistence, together with the key support of legislative allies and the staff of the State Department of Social Welfare, paid off in spectacular fashion: a massive welfare bill that many had thought would take years to bring to fruition was passed by large majorities, 30–9 in the Senate and 56–19 in the Assembly.[28] An overriding factor in addition to that of Burton's skill was the fact that although welfare expenditures would increase dramatically, for the first time federal funds would take up a large proportion of the burden and county expenditures would actually decrease. The state Department of Social Welfare estimated that in 1964–1965 counties would save some $27 million while the state would pay out an extra $17.3 million on welfare and the federal government an extra $52.6 million to California.[29] Even Ronald Reagan's tenure in the governor's mansion would not see a repeal of the state's new enlarged welfare system. The ideological premise that welfare should not reinforce outdated notions of normative social behavior would come under sustained attack in the decades that followed, but its legacy was to force welfare's proponents to engage with the varieties of social experience in new ways.

The sheer scale of the new law touched off a passionate debate over the purpose of welfare that set the stage for a larger public discussion over the structure of society. On one side, the emboldened state Department of Social Welfare saw the welfare state in a post-AB 59 world as providing social stability and ensuring the economic productivity of the socially marginalized. "For many Californians," stated director Jack Wedemeyer in the Department newsletter in December 1963, "AFDC is the difference between lingering and marginal starvation and the basic necessities of life. . . . until the economy can use these people productively so that they can earn their own way, they must not be permitted to languish without food, shelter, clothing, and hope. Most important, the children in these families deserve the opportunity to improve their circumstances. . . . The state cannot be guilty of stunting their growth."[30]

On the other side of the debate was a collection of interests headed by the California Taxpayers Association, which saw the new law as prohibitively expensive, with a distorting impact on the labor market and an incitement to delinquency. "Welfare costs in California are already prohibitive and the state's Give Away program over the years has attracted too many moochers already," wrote one angry taxpayer to Brown. "Probably a majority of unemployed parents would be unwilling, undesirable or unqualified to hold other than the most simple jobs."[31] The Kern County Board of Supervisors stated in January 1964 that it "vigorously opposes any moral abuses which reportedly occur in some AFDC homes."[32] As in the case of fair employment or fair housing, the economic debate masked a bitter public contest over the right of the state to regulate and influence social relationships, and this controversy had embedded within it value judgments about the marginalized. Were the poor by nature unable to contribute productively to society? These were not new debates, but they gained new salience with the dramatic enlargement of government in the early 1960s, forcing state welfare advocates to reach for ever more ambitious arguments in favor of the welfare state and establishing the parameters of the rights liberalism that would gain ground in later years.

In September 1964 members of the welfare department and legislators held a meeting on the role of welfare in relation to the new Economic Opportunities Act, the centerpiece of President Lyndon Johnson's Great Society program. One research assistant to Assemblyman Jack Casey who attended the meeting described Wedemeyer and certain other state agency figures as the "philosophers" of welfare who used welfare programs to articulate a vision of society. Wedemeyer, for instance, claimed that the Economic Opportunity Act "is a challenge to Welfare and to community resource skills to reorient their thinking on some very old problems through 'mass effort of a total body politic.' . . . Half [the poor] are families of children who really can be helped if we, in a community plan, can get rid of group thinking of the clichés and stereotypes that say 'the poor will always be with us,' 'the poor are ne'er do wells,' 'to deny aid makes people independent,' and that the poor *want* to remain on welfare as a way of life." He concluded the meeting by reminding the assembled politicians and administrators that "social welfare has been guilty of interpreting 'downward' instead of upward. . . . Other countries supplement underemployment of large families in order to protect the family structure for the future strength of the child and the nation."[33] Though his department maintained and reinforced an insistence that welfare recipients be made to work, often in poorly paid farm labor programs, as part of an enduring ideology of rehabilitation and government direction of those benefiting from the public purse, Wedemeyer articulated an idea of social inclusion and respect for the individual that had a powerful impact on California politics in the 1960s.

Legislators and policy advocates had to walk a tightrope between a commitment to tackling poverty and a broader commitment to individual economic rights that transcended class boundaries. In the 1960s they turned to the social theories that had shaped the shift in liberal emphasis in the 1950s, as exemplified by the material made available to the California legislature's State Welfare Committee. Associate professor of social work Martin Rein published an article in 1965 that was circulated to members of the committee and their administrative staff as they met for a workshop on welfare in Santa Barbara in July of that year. Rein's article, entitled "The Strange Case of Public Dependency," explicitly borrowed its thesis from the work of Richard Titmuss, the prominent British social policy expert, and argued, as had Titmuss in numerous academic works and essays published since 1950, that "we can make welfare serve social justice and humanitarianism by using the criterion of *common citizenship*, in which need, not virtue, determines aid. . . . We need to extend the principles of socially accepted dependency to the poor."[34] He argued that Western welfare states had tended to prioritize social insurance and contributory mechanisms that allowed for the acceptance of middle class dependency but not the redistribution of funds to poorer citizens. This fact had embedded notions of deserving and undeserving in society, had guaranteed the alienation of those excluded from insurance programs, and had built waste and lower productivity into the economy by marginalizing sections of the potentially productive population.[35] This was an argument that could long have been made in the American case at least, but the fact that the California committee of legislators, headed by Democratic Assemblyman Jack Casey, wanted to discuss the issue demonstrates the changing political lexicon of mainstream politicians in positions of power, even if their ability to change the status of welfare as the poor relation to social insurance was limited. The briefing paper for legislators and staffers meeting in Santa Barbara to discuss "social services for public welfare recipients" noted that the

> 1960s have seen a new emphasis on services to recipients in addition to financial support. . . . Some believe that these services are a necessary supplement to aid, which otherwise becomes a mere dole and a means to perpetuating an inadequate way of life. Others are now question-

> ing whether or not such services, by focusing on the problems of the individual recipient, tend to ignore those causes of dependency which originate in the racial and economic organization of society. . . . According to this view, we should separate economic aid and social services, rather than considering the aid grant an inseparable part of the rehabilitative process.[36]

In the mid-1960s it was far from clear in California that the Titmuss-inspired route would be possible: Republican members of the committee, and some Democrats, were too wedded to a paralyzing fear of the "dole" to allow a reconfiguration of welfare policy into a genuinely universal and redistributive system. In addition, the election of Ronald Reagan to the governor's mansion in November 1966 forced left-leaning members of the Legislature to spend much of their time opposing and watering down attempts to roll back the welfare state.[37] Yet the intellectual and political maturation of liberal thought on citizenship and the state between the late 1940s and the mid-1960s led to the linking of social entitlement and universal human rights, with important consequences for other areas of American life outside the scope of actual welfare policy.

Queering the Welfare Debate

Since the groundbreaking work of John D'Emilio in the early 1980s there have been numerous studies that have historicized the experiences of gay men and women in the United States.[38] We now know a huge amount about the steady growth of homophile organizations in the 1950s, the fight of these early activists for respectability, campaigns in San Francisco against police repression of gay bars and spaces, the growing pressures on established homophile organizations from a new generation of queer activists with a more radical, nonconformist ideology, and the eventual integration of queer political interests into local mainstream politics through the successful campaign of gay politicians like Harvey Milk for city office in the late 1970s.[39] The emphasis of this historiography is on the agency of gay men and women in shaping their civil rights agenda, and the interface of homophile activism with other political organizing is often portrayed, not inaccurately, as troubled.[40] Yet the story of how gay rights came to interact with liberal politics more widely is an important theme in helping to conceptualize why the gay rights agenda took the form that it did. Crucially, it was just at the moment that the Burton alliance was mounting its bid for political supremacy in city and wider state politics through its espousal of a left ideology that the struggle in San Francisco for gay rights entered a new and dynamic phase. In 1964 the Society of Individual Rights (SIR) was created in San Francisco, the brainchild of key figures in Mattachine and Daughters of Bilitis in the 1950s, including Don Lucas, Phyllis Lyon, and Del Martin, and together with the Tavern Guild and the Committee on Religion and the Homosexual (CRH) formed a group of interrelated new organizations that placed sexuality at the center of a burgeoning rights discourse in the state.[41]

The formation of SIR coincided with the establishment of a human rights commission for the city and with *Life* magazine's sudden discovery of homosexuality as a way of life in an influential feature article "Homosexuality in America" in June 1964 that flagged the issue of sexuality for society at large. Though this article, and two small precedents in the *New York Times* and *Harper's* the previous year, retained a traditional notion of gay men and women as a "problem" with which wider society had to engage, all three accepted that sexual difference was not a pathology and, in the words of the *New York Times* piece, while "homosexuality is not the preferable condition, . . . there's nothing morally wrong with it . . . [and] one has to make the best of the situation" and that "out of this desire to make the best of it grows a gay community with a social structure specially adapted to homosexual needs."[42] This separation in public discourse of the "moral" question from the question of the right of individuals to be accepted as members of society was a way in which the politics of sexuality resembled the politics of welfare: proponents of the rights of welfare recipients and the rights of gay men and women both attempted to shift the focus of debate away from questions of sex and relationships and onto the terrain of economic and civil rights.[43] In so doing both welfare organizations and groups like SIR actively sought to engage mainstream party politics in order to gain greater recognition in public policy as equal citizens. A political committee of SIR was established to lobby politicians and participate in campaigns and voter registration drives.[44] The purpose of SIR's political activities was to lobby for the greater acceptance in law of the idea that "homosexuality is as necessary, just and desirable as heterosexuality, that human beings, all of them, are of value intrinsically, and that the question is not *the act*, it is the man." This was an implicit attack on the overcautious and uncertain politics of the society's forebears in the 1950s, reinforced by the SIR committee's attempt to articulate a vision of political power that transcended mere understanding and tolerance of sexual difference.[45]

Emboldened by the Tavern Guild's successes by 1964 in protesting police persecution of gay businesses and by the political scandals of the Wolden affair, the Gayola revelations of police corruption, and the proliferation of new organizations devoted to gay civil rights, leaders of the movement faced the thorny question of how to stake a claim on wider political debate.[46] An obvious way to do this was to follow the rhetorical strategy of the broader civil rights movement that had been gathering pace over the previous decade and emphasize the human rights of all individual citizens. An early form letter from SIR's president and secretary to solicit support for the new organization argued that "there are certain freedoms connected with being a man which are, despite peculiarities of color, of creed or of sexual orientation, guaranteed to all men." In calling for an end to discrimination against gay people in their private sexual relationships and in their access to jobs and their freedom of association, SIR's leaders framed their demand for a "political mantle" in terms of the "guaranteeing to the homosexual the rights so easily granted to others."[47] The organization's statement of purpose attempted to plug into the constitutional language of freedom and democracy that had so often formed the lynchpin of successive campaigns for citizen rights in the United States: "The outline of directions for SIR in 1965 is based on the realization that we are fortunate to live in a society which has a history of consistent statements of belief in the premise that Society must give heed to the needs and aspirations of the individual."[48] The founding conference of the CRH at the end of May 1964 also conceptualized the problem of sexual freedom in terms of human rights that related, as in the case of many appeals against racial prejudice at the time, to the notion of the individual human being's value in the eyes of God. As CRH founder Del Martin wrote in a summary of a group discussion at the conference, it was "felt that homosexuality is not unnatural, that the homosexual is a human being who is not excluded from God, that he is entitled to the same rights and freedoms as other citizens of the larger community."[49]

This discourse of individual rights had dominated the agendas of gay rights organizations since the creation of Mattachine in 1953, but it was becoming clear that such a strategy had limitations for a movement interested in raising its political profile in the city at a time when few recognized homosexuality as a natural state of being that could be legitimized through recourse to an appeal to civil rights. Mindful of the pitfalls of the assimilationist strategy of Mattachine in the 1950s, the SIR briefing document asked "whether SIR is to assume a public image of studied middle-classism, a posture of 'We're just like the rest of you Philistines, so why not get off our backs,' or whether we are to redefine our positions and rediscover alternatives to this uneasy state of hypocrisy and double dealing."[50] The fourth annual convention of Daughters of Bilitis in San Francisco on 20 August 1966, was structured around the theme of "San Francisco and Its Homophile Community—A Merging Social Conscience," and the different sessions of the one-day conference attempted to paper over the emerging divisions over identity and strategy within the gay rights movement by emphasizing the broader relationship of the sexual equality struggle to other social movements. One session was entitled "The Homophile Community and Civic Organizations—How They Relate," and speakers included Robert Gonzales of the Mexican American Political Association and Bernard Mayes of San Francisco Suicide Prevention. This was followed in the afternoon by "The Homophile Community and Governmental Agencies—Can They Relate?" at which the speaker was Dr. Joel Fort of the San Francisco Center for Special Problems.[51] The convention represented an attempt to define a political agenda for gay activists that had resonance in the wider polity at a time of considerable social and political upheaval.

The importance of finding some sort of entrée into mainstream liberal politics that was predicated upon more than just individualism and civil rights was highlighted by the attempts by gay civic leaders to canvass support from candidates for office in the city. SIR quickly immersed itself in political lobbying after its formation, sending a questionnaire to candidates for state and federal office in San Francisco before the November 1964 elections asking their views on matters relating to the right to sexual privacy and police harassment of gay bars and businesses, but received very few responses.[52] The politics of sexuality were not central to any politician's electoral prospects in 1964, but it was clear that gay rights activists were developing into an increasingly organized interest group that could, with the right strategy, push for political recognition in city politics. In a November 1964 speech to SIR, Rev. A. Cecil Williams of the Glide Memorial Foundation, an important center of community activism in San Francisco and whose members like Phyllis Lyon formed the backbone of CRH and SIR, argued that homophile organizations "must find ways to deal with the people who can effect change, basically: the power groups which really make the decisions in our society."[53]

Beginning with the campaigns of the Burton brothers in 1964 SIR involved itself heavily in electoral campaigns in San Francisco, running candidates' nights, flagging up candidates and issues in its monthly newsletter, *Vector*, and coordinating its activities with those of CRH. "The goal of our committee," stated a report on the new SIR political committee in January 1965, "is to organize a substantial block of at least 50,000 votes so that, in the future, we will be able to elect those people to office that will be most effective in helping us to realize our aims."[54] Nancy May, head of SIR's political committee, reported in September 1965 in advance of the group's candidates' night for those seeking election to the Board of Supervisors that the year had "brought a markedly increased interest in politics among the members of the community. Several organizations have volunteer deputy registrars who will be registering voters until the close-off date on September 9th. Among the represented organizations are Daughters of Bilitis, Tavern Guild, Mattachine Society, and of course, SIR."[55] SIR held a candidates' evening in April 1966 that was attended by State Senate candidate and Burton protégé George Moscone and Twenty-Third Assembly District hopeful Everett Hedrick, who both gave talks and answered questions, before a discussion was held concerning a putative protest against the treatment of gay servicemen in the Armed Forces.[56] Phil Burton had started turning up to meetings of the key gay organizations since their inception, and befriended Del Martin and Phyllis Lyon in the early 1960s.[57]

A crucial factor in establishing homophile activism as a political force in San Francisco much earlier than in many other parts of the state and nation was the fact that in the mid-1960s the movement acted as a meeting ground in the city between civil rights and economic rights. This was the language that reformers like the Burtons and their allies in organized labor and left-liberal circles in San Francisco had been using to provide an ideological framework for their campaigns for office, and it formed part of gay rights activists' attempt in the mid-1960s to hitch their flag to the same mast. A briefing paper for SIR in 1965 promoted the use of what the author termed "sensible ideologies, acceptable and pertinent to the realities of the new cultural, political, legal and economic forces now emerging in our society." The arrival on the national scene of the Great Society and the increase in tempo of civil rights as a federal issue heightened pressure on San Francisco activists to integrate issues of social justice into their program. "Special action projects like a halfway house, a homophile community center, cultural programs, events and contests, grants and scholarships" were viewed in the report as useful tools for raising the profile of sexual freedom. Engaging with economic and social programs framed by Great Society liberalism would help ensure "that pressure may be exerted on the dynamics of these processes to alter and mold them to human exigencies," a clear indication that the leadership of SIR had become alert to the capacity for a discourse of social rights that eschewed easy moral judgments to encompass all sorts of social groups.[58]

The idea of a halfway house, promulgated by Williams of the Glide Memorial Foundation, an interracial church and centerpiece of CRH, in collaboration with SIR and Mattachine, was formulated explicitly to tie gay rights to the notion of social inclusion. A briefing letter from SIR stated that the house would be "a place where a man, specifically a homosexual man, who is jobless, broke, hungry, dirty, tired, emotionally sick, on dope or drink, in short who is out of it by conventional standards" would be fed and looked after on a temporary basis "just because he is a man" by charity workers who "believe that all men should have at least a few of these comforts once in a while during a lifetime." The halfway house would "help the homosexual take care of his own, the first step he must take if he is ever going to reaffirm his place in society."[59] Thus the focus of the search for respectability was shifted toward the dispossessed, seemingly a more politically palatable subject in Great Society America, and away from the individual rights of gay people generally: if gay activists could harness the language of social inclusion, it was argued, they would adopt the language of mainstream liberalism as a means of legitimizing their cause.

The campaign in San Francisco in 1965 and 1966 to establish a halfway house soon expanded into a push for the inclusion of the Central City and the Tenderloin as a target area of the local Economic Opportunity Council's (EOC) antipoverty funding. From the moment of their arrival in the city the Great Society programs had exhibited many of the tensions often ascribed to the schemes nationally: the areas targeted (Hunter's Point, Chinatown, Western Addition, and the Mission) were chosen on the basis of the assumption of an association between poverty and race, and there were overlapping and rival programs and administrations.[60] A coordinated effort by members of the local Mattachine Society, the Society for Individual Rights, and an umbrella organization, the Central City Citizens' Council, forced the local Office of Economic Opportunity (OEO) to consider the Central City as a target area for funds.[61] The Citizens' Council was composed of prominent gay activists as well as antipoverty campaigners, and represented an important example of the growing linkage between antipoverty and antidiscrimination discourses in San Francisco politics. Central City campaigners included Hal Call and Don Lucas, founder members of Mattachine, Mark Forrester, founder of SIR, and Phyllis Lyon, the prominent lesbian activist.[62] A report entitled "The White Ghetto," with Forrester as one of the authors, argued that the Tenderloin, a crime-infested neighborhood downtown, demonstrated "a terrifying need for some sort of program directed toward helping these outcasts of society, these young people who are unloved and unwanted because they don't seem to fit into society's general idea of productive citizenship." The report linked social dislocation caused by poverty with issues of sexual difference: "If [Tenderloin youth] feel it impossible to be adequate as an adult in our society, they may feel compelled to be adequate in their sexual relationships with their partners, their peers." The argument set out a program of education, social outreach, halfway houses, and employment schemes that entwined questions of sexual and economic marginalization. The Mattachine Society also submitted a separate report on similar themes to the local EOC in early 1966.[63]

These reports, and the arguments that framed attempts in San Francisco to widen the debate over poverty and its alleviation, formed the culmination of a gradual process of the enlargement of the parameters of economic and social citizenship in left-of-center discourse in California since World War II. Though the EOC dragged its heels over the integration of the Tenderloin and Central City into its San Francisco program, the campaign was ultimately successful, and Don Lucas became a member of the EOC in San Francisco.[64] Just as significant is the similarity of the rhetorical strategies of those fighting for the inclusion of the central city and those wishing to widen the safety net of the AFDC program: the sponsors attempted to argue for the moral worth of the poor and for the potential of government aid to allow them to live productive lives, as the authors of the "White Ghetto" stressed when they stated that "it will have to be recognized that a majority of these young people are homosexuals who either will not or cannot change their sexual orientation. This must not become a barrier to a helping relationship. As in every case, the effort should be made to help them become more self-accepting, happy, affectionate, spontaneous and creative persons—in short, to help each person to become the best he is able to become."[65] Like the campaign to widen the scope of the state's welfare program, the Central City campaign harnessed a coalition of local interest groups, a central state bureaucracy (in this case the city's OEO), and local politicians to effect a far-reaching legislative change. Both campaigns attempted to highlight economic marginalization and the putative economic value of assisted integration of welfare recipients into active economic life. Both campaigns provided a political strategy for politicians seeking to tie their fortunes to a multifaceted coalition of social groups that seemed to hold the balance of power in San Francisco politics. One hopeful for a seat on the Board of Supervisors in 1965 credited SIR with "at least 20,000 votes of the 30,000 which he received."[66]

The debate over the fate of the socially marginalized, whether unemployed parents or underprivileged gay youths in downtown San Francisco, flagged up serious questions about the coherence and durability of the joining of questions of poverty and sexuality. A broad political debate over the social rights as citizens of the poor and disenfranchised empowered liberals in certain areas and showed the potential for questions of class and economic rights to highlight other forms of social marginalization, including the issue of sexual difference. In so doing, however, a serious cleavage in state politics was becoming apparent, with those who stressed the moral degradation of society through activist government policies gaining a new wedge issue that would gain momentum during the violent social upheavals of the mid-1960s.[67] In addition, the debate within liberal circles over social and economic citizenship highlighted the fragility of the coalition between the diverse range of interests with a claim on policymaking. The Central City Citizen's Council for instance was an almost all-white group with an explicit goal of spreading the resources of the OEO more thinly across the city, directly challenging the race-centered priorities of the Great Society program in San Francisco. Over 80 percent of residents of the Central City target area were white, and nowhere in the citizen's committee lobbying material was race mentioned.[68] It may have been true that the aim of the citizen's council was to attempt a race-blind approach to tackling poverty, as in Calvin Colt's question to the EOC of whether the Great Society was "a program which enables all the poor to lift themselves out of poverty, or is this a program which further isolates men from one another in blocks of power built on hatred?"[69] Yet the question of race, the fact that the issue of the distribution of limited economic resources remained controversial, and the tentative nature of the liberal left's hold on power all suggested stormy times ahead for those seeking to advance a reformist agenda in San Francisco and California in the mid-1960s. Colt attempted to cast his group's ability to secure the support of established local antipoverty organizations like the Mission Community Action Board for the Central City project as a demonstration "to attackers of San Francisco antipoverty programs that there is unity among the city's poor," and that they were "dedicated to eradicating poverty wherever it exists in San Francisco, not in just a few specialized locations."[70] Yet the Central City Project was diverting limited funds and aggressively entering into the patronage network of competing community organizations all jostling for the attention of federal aid agencies, hardly the basis for a coalition of the socially marginalized.

Just as problematic was the question of how gay rights activists in the

Central City Citizens' Council, SIR, CRH, and Mattachine were making the connection between sexuality and social marginalization. As in the case of welfare reform, a debate on economic rights threw up issues of political power and the moral worth of the dispossessed that intersected uneasily with the rights of individuals to live their own lives. The intended targets of Central City anti-poverty funding were youths of the Tenderloin, often homeless or living in overcrowded walk-ups, and the idea that countercultural gay youths were somehow "compelled to be adequate in their sexual relationships with their partners, their peers" because of their economic and social marginalization practically pathologized their sexuality, hardly a helpful strategy for organizations ostensibly interested in the legalization of gay sex.[71] The organizations that sponsored the Central City project remained wedded to a normative construction of sexuality that stressed respectability and assimilation into mainstream society. Many of those leading the Central City campaign were themselves well-off and well-connected, and though their commitment to a wide range of liberal causes, including the expansion of the welfare state, was doubtless heartfelt, the irony of their association of sexual politics with a welfare politics that explicitly excluded those not in dire economic need from the attention of policymakers seemed lost on them.

Nevertheless, the intersection of gay rights, welfare politics, and the building of a liberal bastion in San Francisco had major implications for the development of liberal politics statewide in the 1960s and 1970s. Though San Francisco was in some senses a special case, the question of the linkage between economic rights and civil rights was fast becoming a major fault line between liberals and conservatives that would play out in debates over taxation, social policy, and sexual equality at the state level in later years. And the liberal policymakers at the heart of these debates, led by the Burtons, formed a broader legislative phalanx of politicians whose constituencies ranged widely across the state, an important consideration when we observe that the late 1960s saw a major reordering of legislative districts in favor of rapidly growing Southern California. San Francisco might have the legislative know-how, but Los Angeles had the votes. In the battles to preserve and extend the achievements of the Brown administration in the mid-1960s, the question of the durability of the brand of liberal politics gaining prominence in the City by the Bay, but still alien elsewhere, would take center stage.

CHAPTER 9

Culture Wars, Politics, and Power

California has always been a political outlier. As most of the United States was waking up in November 1964 to a Johnson landslide and massive majorities for Democrats in Congress and in statehouses across the land, Californians awoke to a new Republican senator, the repeal of the state's fair housing law by way of Proposition 14 on the state ballot, and the spectacle of a state Democratic Party rapidly descending into a deeply factionalized, impotent mess. Even if Democrats could take comfort from Johnson's huge victory over Barry Goldwater, historians have recently demonstrated that the Goldwater movement represented the stirrings of a powerful right-wing sensibility in state and national politics that would help elect Ronald Reagan governor in 1966 and a return to a Republican majority coalition nationally in the years after 1968.[1] Reagan's successful campaign in 1966 demonstrated that the state GOP had learned from the mistakes of 1962, and also benefited from damaging divisions within the Democratic Party and the political wounds inflicted on the Brown administration by the Watts riots and the social turmoil that seemed to characterize the mid-1960s.[2]

This chapter will advance several propositions that complicate this picture of California politics in the 1960s. First, the case study of the battle over fair housing demonstrates that the economic battle over government interference in the market, infused as it was with the politics of race prejudice and antistatism, is an example of how successful liberals had been in reshaping political debate to take much greater account of the diversity of society. The backlash was very real, but California Democrats had successfully placed questions of social citizenship and equality at the center of state politics to the extent that the State Supreme Court had the opportunity to overrule Proposition 14 and change the legal standing of minority groups in a way that would have enormous consequences for political life in California. This argument tackles head-on the thesis that there was some sort of liberal heyday prior to the 1960s, when too many interest groups entered political life and ruined the Democratic Party and liberalism generally. It also finds much to criticize in the work of anyone using the term "consensus" for the period between World War II and the 1960s: as I have tried to show, the period between 1945 and the 1960s was in California a time when a modern era of political party cleavage over major issues of ideology came into being.[3] Second, though full account is taken here of the devastating internal debates within Democratic Party circles in the 1960s, I also analyze the extent to which different shades of leftist politics coalesced in the period to shape the character and dominant political themes of the Democratic Party in its post-Cold War liberal form. Many politicians in California whose careers took off in this period went on to influential positions of leadership and influence, and their political teeth were cut in debates over abortion, the Vietnam War, gay rights, women's rights, welfare rights, and managed economic growth that would shape the Democratic Party even if they would have less traction in the nation at large. It is not at all clear that California entered the 1970s a less liberal place than it had been ten years before, and in any case we can see in the political struggles of the mid-1960s the makings of the contemporary Democratic Party.[4]

Fair Housing and the Rise of the Culture Wars

In 1963 prospective home buyers in the East Bay might have found themselves drawn to a home for sale at number 7940 Winthrop Street in Oakland. For an asking price of $18,950 it was possible to buy this "nice family home, hill view, beauty pleat drapes . . . covered patio." An electric stove was included. There was one drawback if you happened not to be white: the real estate listing stated "Caucasians only."[5] Though the liberal block in the legislature had passed a raft of legislation between 1959 and 1961 establishing a state FEPC, outlawing discrimination in the provision of services, and forbidding discrimination in the allocation of public housing, the regulation of the private economic marketplace remained deeply controversial. Housing was a particularly hot topic, as to try to restrict the seller's freedom of maneuver struck at the heart of many Americans' sense of economic well-being and self-sufficiency: what if, one would hear from white Californians in the early 1960s, prospective new residents drove down the price of property, or made it more difficult to sell when someone changed jobs and wanted to move quickly? A Latino real estate agent reported in summer 1964 that he had taken his client "to purchase a home in Monterey Park and the owner told me that they would not sell to Mexicans and, apologizing, that he did not have anything against the Mexican-Americans but that he was concerned with what his neighbors would say." When the agent spoke with one neighbor, he "was quite vocal and told me that he didn't like Mexicans because they would come into the neighborhood, bring in their trashy cars and lower the value of his property."[6] The economic basis of both sides in the housing discrimination debate in California exposes the ideological schism between left and right that was emerging thanks to the rise to power of reformist Democrats in this period.[7]

Certainly one of the major underlying forces behind the Fair Housing Act of 1963, often known by the name of its chief sponsor, Assemblyman Byron Rumford of Berkeley, was the idea of economic citizenship through governmental regulation of the private marketplace. Back in 1958 a National Commission on Race and Housing, formed as an independent citizens' commission consisting of a diverse group of seventeen wealthy and influential figures including Henry Luce, Clark Kerr of the University of California, and prominent academics and businessmen, had produced its report. The report investigated the housing conditions and access to the housing market of African Americans, Latinos, and Asian Americans, noting that housing remained "the one commodity in the American market that Negroes and persons belonging to certain other ethnic minorities cannot purchase freely. A complex of forces and pressures operates to exclude members of these groups from residence in the majority of the nation's urban and suburban neighborhoods." Crucially, the report's authors identified two entwined "social trends" that were acting as engines for the promotion of equality in access to the private housing market: "the rising economic status of the minority groups and the reawakened concern of the general public with the problem of racial inequality. These trends have provided stimulus to action and a growing public readiness to accept changes."[8] As different ethnic groups took their place as consumers in the rapidly growing and diversifying American economy of the postwar era, the argument went, so the state would be needed to ensure their equal access to economic resources. The idea of civil rights, wrote Bayard Rustin about the national picture in early 1964, "is now concerned not merely with removing the barriers to full *opportunity* but with achieving the fact of *equality*. From sit-ins and freedom rides we have gone into rent strikes, boycotts, community organization, and political action."[9] The notion that economic rights formed a vital component of the civil rights struggle had been evident in California for a number of years. Alan Cranston as chair of CDC had visited Mississippi in 1957 to demonstrate his organization's awareness of the race question, and the idea of equality of access to economic resources had characterized the debates that had preoccupied senior Democrats as their party clambered toward power during the 1950s. The economic rationale for civil rights law ran through the text of the Rumford Act.[10] Discrimination had social and economic costs that had adverse effects upon wider society. In the words of the text of AB 1240, "because of discrimination in housing, many persons in this State live in segregated sections under substandard, unhealthful, unsanitary, and crowded conditions; that these conditions have caused increased rates of crime, disease, fire, and juvenile delinquency in certain sections of this State; . . . discrimination is incompatible with, and contrary to, the welfare, health, and peace of the people of this State."[11]

The passage of the Rumford Act through the state legislature demonstrates the acceptance of arguments for governmental management of economic outcomes for a growing number of Democratic legislators in the 1960s, as well as the countervailing power of antistatist voices in California politics outside the legislature. Although wrangling between Assembly and Senate delayed the passage of a final version until the last day of the legislative session in June 1963, the numbers spoke for themselves: 63 Assemblymen voted in favor and only 9 against, and 22 state senators, all Democrats, voted to pass the bill, with 13 Senators voting against. The lop-sided Democratic majorities in both Houses was not the only reason Assemblyman Rumford was able to push his bill through: since the debate on FEPC and discrimination in public housing between 1959 and 1961 pro-civil rights Democrats had built up an impressive coalition of legislators from a diverse cross-section of the state willing to put their names to antidiscrimination bills, including militant liberals like Phil Burton but also speaker Ralph Brown of the Central Valley and establishment Democrat Jesse Unruh. In addition, buoyed by their big 1962 wins Democratic floor leaders had packed committees with Democrats and had taken the unprecedented step of allowing freshmen Democrats from liberal urban districts to join the most prestigious committees. Tom Rees of Westside Los Angeles moved from the assembly to the state senate in the new 1963 session and immediately joined the powerful Finance Committee in a move designed, in the words of Senate Majority Leader Hugh Burns, to "recognize urban areas," areas growing in electoral power in the early 1960s with landmark Supreme Court cases on political representation in legislatures.[12] Some activists felt that progress in Sacramento was slow enough that they occupied the State Capitol overnight in May despite Rumford's concerns that the action might do more harm than good in the halls of power, but it was clear that Rumford and his allies, determined to add a human rights dimension to the working of the free market, had more power in the state legislature than ever before.[13]

Outside Sacramento, however, the political balance of power looked to be somewhat different. After Governor Brown signed the bill into law the California Real Estate Association (CREA) immediately announced its plan to fight to repeal the measure by putting a proposition banning state interference in the private housing market on the ballot in the 1964 election. The well-financed campaign formed the lynchpin of a coordinated attempt by an enraged right-wing portion of California's business community and its allies to recapture the political initiative in state politics that would start with fair housing and extend to the 1966 gubernatorial election. The language of the anti-fair housing campaign took its cue from similar antistatist efforts in states like neighboring Arizona, designed to establish a left-right split over economic policy and to portray unfettered free markets as a genuine defense of individual liberty. "The Rumford Act is another step in the socialization of this state, one which should be eliminated just as quickly as possible," fulminated the executive vice president of the San Francisco Real Estate Board over the radio in July 1964. "A man's home is literally his castle, and the decision concerning the sale or rental of his home is strictly the business of the renter."[14] Readers of the *Antelope Valley Ledger-Gazette* received a Christmas message from the editor: "So far the Rumford law fans have come up with vague generalities in support of their stand—something to the effect that 'human rights are above property rights.' Such a remark is typical of the socialist mentality. The collectivists are completely incapable of comprehending the human relationship to property—probably because the whole idea of human beings owning property is repugnant to them." This editorial was one of several included with a letter from the president of CREA to members at the end of 1963 to solicit signatories for the ballot initiative and cash for the campaign.[15]

The campaign quickly adopted the technique of portraying supporters of Proposition 14 as defenders of an American way under attack by an all-powerful state, a strategy the Knowland forces had adopted in 1958 but this time with the advantage that the liberal forces were actually in power and so the threat of the erosion of American "freedoms" could be seen as very real. "If there is a single issue that marks the last bulwark against a flood of socialistic and freedom-reducing laws, that issue would have to be the current campaign to spell out private property rights in the state constitution," intoned a radio announcer in a paid radio spot on behalf of Proposition 14. "Failure . . . will signal the end . . . of the hope of a large segment of the American public that the trend of this nation toward the left—and a Fascist-police state—could be halted short of violence." Leaders of the campaign were careful to appeal to a sense that politicians had lost touch with the majority, instead seeking "political profit in giving special privileges to strong minority groups."[16] It was significant that nowhere in the CREA Proposition 14 campaign was communism or a red scare highlighted: the terms socialism and "the left" abounded, and even Fascism crept in, but CREA and its allies sought to learn from perceived mistakes in previous campaigns that had suggested antistatists in California were somehow extremists and mired in the struggles of the past. This is not to say other right-wing organizations did not use the communist issue and even openly racist appeals to whip up support for Proposition 14 among the faithful.[17] But Proposition 14 represented the widening of the right's political base and its move toward respectability as part of California's new political order. Consequently a party that stressed collective responsibility stood against one that stressed individualism and the sanctity of private sector prerogatives. A new political spectrum, constructed when left-of-center Democrats challenged the ideological sponginess of state politics in the 1950s, had come of age: the Republican renaissance was not a challenge to a status quo, but rather the completion of a process of political affiliation in which party identity carried ideological freight. The right had captured control of the California Republican Assembly—CRA leader Nolan Frizzelle justified Proposition 14 by saying that "freedom to be unequal is really our national purpose,"—and had established a new power structure in United Republicans of California (UROC). As the political scientist Totton Anderson put it at the time, the "real California story is that the Ultra-conservatives stepped in when the old guard (Richard M. Nixon, William Knowland, former Governor Goodwin Knight) bowed out. This UROC organization . . . is well-financed and intelligently led."[18]

Supporters of the Rumford Act quickly organized their own campaign group, "Californians Against Proposition 14," but their effort suffered from several weaknesses, including a lack of funds and the fact that the proposition itself was confusing to voters. The financial crisis became acute the moment the proposition qualified for the ballot. "We have an immediate need for money—money for billboards, television, radio, and newspaper advertising, brochures and bumper stickers," pleaded one mailer. "Can you send us

$250,000 right away? That is our immediate cash need for securing our contracts for billboards and television time. Our total campaign media budget is for $750,000." The anti-14 campaign leaders had a mammoth task: it cost $2,000 just for one billboard for a month, and $1,300 for a one-minute prime-time TV advertisement. CREA could, like the AMA had done in its successful campaign against federal health insurance in the late 1940s, simply levy charges on its membership and raise hundreds of thousands of dollars overnight, given the fact that there were some 40,000 CREA members statewide.[19] Even when the money started to come in, formulating a campaign message that would make good advertising copy was tricky: to be "for" fair housing was to be "against" Proposition 14, and the question of how to instruct voters how to vote often drove to distraction those attempting to explain the complex California ballot to those faced with a bewildering array of initiatives as well as a long list of candidates for public office.[20]

The ambiguities of the anti-14 message also caused the proponents of fair housing difficulties, and sent out a warning message about the potential pitfalls facing civil rights politics in the future. It may have been true that the rewriting of the state constitution to enshrine in law a citizen's right to sell a home to whomever he or she chose "would stamp California . . . with one of the most reactionary dictums to be found outside the Union of South Africa."[21] Jack Hall of the ILWU in Hawaii bitterly attacked CREA members arriving in Honolulu for a conference after the November elections, arguing that next time "they leave the confines of segregated California for a convention or conference may we recommend they choose either Alabama or South Africa, where temporarily the 'natives' are under control."[22] The *New York Times* also stressed the Southern-style segregation theme of Proposition 14, musing that it seemed "a strange year in which to push for even greater segregation. . . . that California can even consider imitating the unhappy state of Mississippi is of concern to all of us."[23] To compare California to the Deep South at a time when massive resistance and rampant violence and disorder in states like Mississippi and Alabama dominated the national headlines did not win over white homeowners to the fair housing cause.

Proponents of fair housing like Byron Rumford and Assembly Speaker Jesse Unruh had to hold together a diverse coalition of interests that had converged over the issue of the right of government to intervene to regulate market forces, but which threatened to come apart over the racial implications of a regulated economy. Unruh attempted to eschew emotive appeals that made reference to the Deep South, claiming that "rights of property are not and never have been absolute. This is why I say the California Real Estate Association is guilty of sophistry. To paraphrase Orwell—they believe wholeheartedly in fair housing, it's just that they think some of it should be fairer than others!"[24] Rumford tried to underline the economic and social necessity of a law to permit the spread of urban populations out of racial ghettos that encouraged "crime, delinquency, and certain ill-health considerations with which the legislature has been concerned."[25] A report for the Berkeley Bureau of Public Administration had noted that between 1940 and 1960 the African American population of the Bay Area had increased twelve times to almost a quarter of a million, and that "many of the problems of intergroup relations in the Bay Area in the years ahead will stem from the fact that Negroes and other non-whites, but especially Negroes, are concentrated residentially in a few sections of the large cities."[26] As the FEPC later pointed out, fair housing was not a Southern-style reconfiguration of state law to undo decades of in-built constitutional segregation of races, but was an attempt to codify in law the economic right of those with capital to live where they chose. "No property owner who is covered is obliged to lower his standards of selection among prospective tenants or buyers," the Commission stated. "He need never accept an undesirable or fiscally unqualified tenant or purchaser. . . . The members of this Commission believe strongly in the importance of home ownership and in a competitive market in housing. We believe that *all* Californians should be able to compete equally, within their economic means, in that market."[27] This statement came in the wake of a State Supreme Court decision striking down Proposition 14 in 1966: during the proposition campaign itself proponents of fair housing had not been able to get across the idea of racial justice that simply allowed equal access for all to the marketplace.

Advocates of Proposition 14, by contrast, had a ready-made appeal to individual rights and property ownership that transcended class boundaries and set the stage for the invigoration of the pro-business right in California in the late 1960s. The proposition was carried in November by more than a two to one margin, with more than four million voting in favor.[28] Though Lyndon Johnson easily carried California in his landslide victory, it looked as though the Golden State's age of liberal reform would turn out to have only lasted a handful of years. "Evidently," stated Pat Brown resignedly in a remark that signaled a rather simplistic and patronizing view of his fellow citizens, suggesting that a turbulent election cycle lay ahead in 1966, "a majority of whites in the state don't want Negroes living in the same neighborhood with them. They wanted Proposition 14, but also wanted President Johnson, despite the president's stand on civil rights."[29] The contradiction was not hard to understand when we consider that the thorny question of race had come to the fore of Democratic policymaking at a time when the Democratic Party had established itself as a governing party, and that all the inherent divisions and complications within it were becoming apparent. The Democratic Party would never return to its pre-1950s form, and would remain a party that was left-of-center on economic and social legislation, but it would have to endure a period of internecine warfare over its soul and tactics before its status as a political equal to a rejuvenated Republican Party could be cemented.

Meltdown: The 1964 Senate Race and the Breakdown of Democratic Discipline

The battle over fair housing came at a moment of bitter strife within the California Democratic Party that did much to take the political initiative away from proponents of the liberal state. That moment was testimony to the impact seemingly random events can have on politics. In 1963, Senator Clair Engle fell seriously ill with a brain tumor. A victor in the 1958 landslide and a congressman before that in the sprawling Sierra Nevada district of northeastern California, Engle was not a huge figure in the Senate but he was a reliable party man who satisfied everybody: his career predated CDC and so he was a friend of the old time party pros, but he was a good enough operator to know how to keep the insurgent element happy and gain their trust. Nobody in the party had much concern that he would not win reelection in 1964 easily, and that he would work assiduously to keep California issues on the agenda in Washington. The tumor was rapidly interfering with his capacity to function but for which there was no proven treatment or definite prognosis. This tragic and yet on the surface politically insignificant situation was to prove devastating to party harmony and morale, as various factions and personalities began to plot how to take control of the situation for their advantage. Looking back, Roger Kent saw Engle as the lynchpin that held the diverse factions together, and had he lived, "it could have been a dynasty, a Democratic dynasty that would have gone on a good deal longer." Instead, the political rivalries to take his Senate seat during 1964 "just absolutely destroyed the party, practically."[30]

The countdown to the deadline for filing for the 1964 elections was ticking away: would Engle possibly be able to recover and file for reelection, and if not, would he withdraw? Party loyalists were determined to stick with

Engle, whose wife was adamant that he would recover. Many were horrified that some in CDC were plotting to replace him ahead of the CDC endorsement convention in February and the party primary in June. "They were just screaming for him to resign, and to admit he was dead," recalled Carmen Warschaw, who would be instrumental in denying CDC's preferred candidate Alan Cranston the lion's share of the primary vote in Los Angeles County.[31] Still, the problem was very real: if Engle's prognosis did not improve, the party could go into a general election campaign already colored by the fair housing battle with a candidate who would not live to return to Washington, thereby handing the Republicans a way back from the political wilderness and a useful wedge issue with which to advance their agenda. And unlike in the late 1950s, Democrats now benefited from nearly six years in power, meaning there was a proven track record of victories and a growing number of high-quality candidates in a variety of public and party offices who relished the chance to jump into national politics at an unexpected but opportune moment. It was likely to be a Democratic year, and California's other Senate seat was held by an extremely popular liberal Republican who seemed impervious to political challenges, having seen off Richard Richards in an otherwise Democratic year in 1962. It could have been years before another chance came up.

Unsurprisingly, therefore, the CDC endorsement jamboree saw the first significant challenge to a Democratic incumbent officeholder in the organization's history: in addition to Engle, who had not withdrawn, CDC voters had a choice between Cranston, the group's first leader and clear favorite, Jimmy Roosevelt, five-term congressman from Westside Los Angeles, and George McLain, the long-time pensions advocate who had been around since the Upton Sinclair days. There were other potential primary candidates, too, who did not take part in the CDC event as they knew Cranston and Roosevelt were just too powerful in those circles; these included Attorney General Stanley Mosk.[32] The Long Beach meeting of CDC was vitally important, as it represented the flexing of the political muscles of a left-wing of the California party who wanted recognition at the national level for the first time, but it also showed that while bitter factional divisions remained very real within the party, those divisions manifested themselves at the level of personalities and quests for power more than in terms of significant ideological schisms.

There was no question that Cranston's decision to run for the CDC endorsement was based on both personal ambition and a calculation that the idealist volunteer wing of the party now had the clout to win command of a major political office. "Together, we have made CDC the most effective grassroots political structure in the United States," he told the assembled delegates immediately following his nomination as CDC candidate, elbowing aside the ailing Engle. "Together we have transformed California into a stronghold of the Democratic Party. Now we must move on together to new heights of achievement. . . . To me, civil rights is the burning issue of the age. . . . To me, too, the waging of a new, dynamic drive against poverty is imperative. . . . We must do more for the aged, so many of whom live in poverty. . . . One vital step to this and other ends would be the passage of the medicare bill which has languished so long in Congress." The rhetorical capstone to his address summed up the status of CDC as a political avant garde of the California party: "The New Deal lies in the dim past. So does the Fair Deal. Together, we crossed the New Frontier with John Kennedy. Now, we are called upon to climb ever higher, toward new horizons."[33] He consciously directed his campaign toward the volunteer CDC faithful who would, he felt, provide the balance of power in Democratic primaries in the 1960s. "I challenge the thesis that ours is an affluent society," he claimed in a speech to a Latino political meeting in Los Angeles to launch his candidacy. "It is not. Many millions of Americans live in poverty. Many millions more live on poverty's edge. . . . The great danger is that our country will become two nations—the employed and the unemployed, the rich and the poor, the hopeful and the hopeless."[34] In another speech he tied his flag firmly to the mast of big government for a modern, technological age, stating that "tens of thousands of those who cross our [state] boundaries every year are low income families. In most cases, they cannot pay their own way in state taxes for many, many years. . . . Our economy must generate 200,000 new jobs a year—just to keep pace. We must build highways, freeways, and streets for 250,000 more cars a year—just to keep pace. . . . And one of the things that we are going to have to learn together . . . is that the role of government in coping with the needs of this new society is getting larger, not smaller." The 1964 Senate primary was to Cranston "another climax in the unending struggle to preserve the character, strength and security of the Democratic Party in California."[35] What this meant in practice was that Engle's illness had allowed Cranston and CDC rank-and-file the perfect opportunity to elect one of their own to high office, mindful of the fact that so far in CDC's eleven-year existence they had acted only as supporting actors rather than stars of the political stage.

It was this question of what to do about the CDC and volunteer leftists that created a division between the Cranston forces and party regulars led by Assembly speaker Unruh. The rivalry between Unruh's faction and CDC had been building for some time. Unruh in many senses modeled himself on a boss politician of the old school: he was a physically imposing, cigar-chomping, womanizing political bruiser who used the art of backroom deals, the doling out and withholding of patronage, and a network of loyalist party functionaries based around his home patch in eastern Los Angeles County to impose his authority on the legislature and on the party at large. An increasingly tense rivalry had built up in Los Angeles during Brown's reelection campaign between the Unruh operation and CDC over who had delivered the region to Brown, and Unruh had attempted to damage the clubs by introducing a resolution that would ban communists "or any other totalitarian group" from membership of any organization with the name Democrat. During 1963 Unruh's demand for political authority in Sacramento had brought him into conflict with the party's radical wing, led by Phil Burton, for control over the political agenda, and this had also caused increasing tensions between Unruh and Brown, the latter feeling that he had to push the legislature hard to enact his program given all the support the club movement had given him in 1962. The Engle affair was the final straw for Unruh's people. Engle had been a loyal and successful Democratic politician since the New Deal, and his reward was to be thrust aside against his will. So adamant were Engle's supporters that he should not give in that they even made a doctored tape to demonstrate he was fit to run again.[36] His broadcast to the CDC convention was a disaster: he sounded horrible. To Unruh loyalists, the public airing of his illness was in bad taste, and the final result—Cranston won endorsement with 1,197 votes to Roosevelt's 727, Engle's dismal 281 and McLain's 6—testimony to the treachery of CDC leadership and its inability to take orders from the people who had built the party long before CDC came into existence. The CDC vote itself showed the potentially damaging schisms within the party: Engle held all the votes of his home turf in the Sierras, but also won in the African American district of Gus Hawkins in South Los Angeles, an area where the clubs did not really penetrate. Cranston and Roosevelt cleaned up everywhere else, Roosevelt winning in his home territory in much of Los Angeles and running Cranston close in San Francisco, but Cranston winning the rest of the state handily.[37] There were increasingly two parties between which California Democrats had to choose: the regular party and the club party. They had always coexisted uneasily, but now the break threatened to fracture the Democrats' hold on power.

Fresh from the wounding experience of the CDC Convention in Long

Beach, Unruh and his allies refused to let the matter rest. Club endorsement was not the end of the story: the official party primary was not until June. No one of any stature within the state party could run against Cranston, as a defeat could rule them out of serious contention for high office for years to come. So Unruh turned to Washington. Though Brown and President Johnson were on reasonably good terms—Johnson asked Brown to make a nomination speech for him at the Democratic National Convention in Atlantic City that summer—the disciples of Camelot certainly were not, mindful of Brown's disastrous handling of his state delegation at the 1960 National Convention. Brown had run as a favorite son candidate and had secretly pledged that he would quickly release his delegation to vote for Kennedy, but in the end had failed to control them and had lost almost half the votes to a Stevenson surge.[38] Unruh's growing enmity toward Brown gave him traction among followers of the fallen president, and it was not long before Kennedy's former press secretary and erstwhile *San Francisco Chronicle* reporter Pierre Salinger arrived in California and announced he was entering the race for the Democratic Senate nomination. Salinger was temperamentally as removed from the spirit of California Democratic politics as it was possible to be, at least in its post-1950 club manifestation. He had acquired political experience in the Kennedy White House in an atmosphere of Cold War crisis: the Berlin Wall, Bay of Pigs, and the Cuban Missile Crisis to him were testimony of the continued seriousness of the Soviet threat and of the certainties of the foreign policy outlook that had crystallized in the late 1940s. Though there were some in the California party who shared these concerns, and many, like Unruh, who were prepared to use antileftist barbs for political advantage, the soul of the California Democratic Party was occupied elsewhere: the bitter battle against Proposition 14, the legacy of the party's popular front past, and the growing criticism of Cold War foreign policy and of reflexive anticommunism in the clubs and Young Democrats lent the party a very different sensibility to many elsewhere in the country.

It was not that Salinger's candidacy did not have many supporters: the assassination of JFK was still a raw wound in the nation's psyche, and Salinger's candidacy seemed to many a good way of purging the bitter memory of the Engle affair by choosing someone untainted by the CDC endorsement fight and associated with the martyred president. His campaign strategy, however, served to inject a divisive note into the campaign specifically designed to expose political splits within the party that need not have been critical in an otherwise strongly Democratic year. The California Young Democratic convention in Fresno in May offered Salinger an opportunity to make the most of his Kennedy Cold War liberal credentials, as the delegates had called for the recognition of Red China and its admission to the UN, the resumption of diplomatic relations with Cuba, and the dissolution of anti-Soviet military alliances such as NATO. Salinger publicly repudiated "the forces of the extreme left which forced an astonishing group of policy statements through the State Young Democrats last weekend," and called on Cranston "to repudiate these stands and to join with me in an effort to stop this dangerous infiltration in our Party," comparing the left of the Democratic Party to the Republican right in its obsession with ideological purity over political realism. He argued that Cranston was "working closely with these zealots who would attempt to remake the goals of the Democratic Party into their own brand of extreme political philosophy. . . . I ask him how he can be so confident of his own virtue that he can ally himself with this sort of extremism without seeing that followed to its logical extent it would mean a policy of surrender all around the world."[39] Foreign policy had served since World War II as a fault line to create a political division among liberals for tactical reasons; it also now reflected a dividing line between the Cold War liberalism of the 1940s and 1950s and the post-Castro liberalism that dominated club politics in California. "We said it was a struggle between the citizen participant and the pro, between broad-based decision-making and machine control, between image politics and issue politics, between the club movement and the fat cats," stated an editorial in the *Liberal Democrat* in its June issue. "This dichotomy has sharpened as Salinger has moved to the right, and Cranston has developed an increasingly liberal posture on the issues and on matters of organization."[40]

Cranston embraced the challenge of using Salinger's campaign as a way of uniting his own base. He also worked strenuously to gain the backing of organized labor and African American leaders to create a progressive coalition and preserve the integrity of the forces that had established the Democratic Party as a force in California. He endorsed the labor wish list for public works, Keynesian demand management, a large expansion of Social Security entitlements, a federal health care system, and support for civil rights went on for pages, and suggested that there was some possibility of a repeat of the grand alliance of leftists, labor, and mainstream Democrats that had pushed the party over the top in 1958.[41] To an African American audience in Los Angeles he highlighted his strong civil rights record and excoriated Salinger as a political stooge for Unruh and his attempt to rein in the volunteer movement. "Jesse is working underground but overtime to defeat me and the forces I represent in the Democratic Party," he thundered. The question was "whether the rank and file Democrat will continue to have a voice in his party's affairs, or whether a rigid party hierarchy will take command."[42] He attempted to use Salinger's foreign policy tactics to reaffirm his own progressive agenda, which he felt would play well with his CDC club base. "We must start by admitting to ourselves that it is a dangerous folly to regard foreign aid largely as a deterrent to Communism," he told a rally at a high school in late May. "We must instead regard foreign aid as an investment in the economic stability of poorer nations—a stability that will eventually produce new markets for the export of both American products and American concepts of freedom."[43] He expounded a social democratic vision of state involvement in the domestic economy, committing himself to supporting "a joint federal-state assault on the economic and social roadblocks to full employment. . . . With the weapons available to us in President Johnson's War on Poverty, we must now move forward to end the folly and cruelty of four million unemployed in the richest nation in the world." He proposed the extension of the minimum wage to agricultural workers, a nod toward an issue rapidly gaining political momentum in California in the 1960s. He made reference in a speech to black Baptist leaders in Los Angeles to the need to frame the civil rights debate at the center of state and national politics in 1964 in economic terms.[44] Cranston's campaign built upon the groundwork laid by CDC activists in reorienting the political foundations of liberalism to embrace economic management, civil rights through social citizenship for all, and the downplaying of Cold War foreign policy concerns, a process that had been gathering pace long before the oft-cited Vietnam crisis in the party in 1968.

The bitter divisions in the California party between the clubs and the Unruh forces killed off any hope for a united front in the general election campaign when on 2 June, primary day, Salinger eked out a narrow victory over Cranston by 1,177,517 votes to 1,037,748. Ominously for the Salinger campaign, Republican front-runner George Murphy, a song-and-dance performer with little political experience but a solid conservative outlook that was acceptable to the faithful, had beaten his main challenger by nearly two to one and went into the general election campaign with his party united behind him. The crucial result had been in Los Angeles County, where Unruh, Carmen Warschaw, and the regular party machinery in the east of the county had delivered the crucial margin to Salinger: 508,432 votes to Cranston's 343,487.[45] Unruh's supporters were jubilant, feeling they had firmly put the club activists in their place, but the narrowness of the Salinger victory left neither side able to vanquish the other. Indeed, the sense that the Cranston campaign had almost prevailed despite the injection of a dose of Camelot magic only heightened the determination of club activists to make their voices heard and to ignore appeals of the Salinger forces to get behind the party leadership. "In the foggy morning of defeat of a senatorial candidate one contemplates the victories achieved in a campaign," wrote the chair of the Claremont Democratic Club to Cranston the day after his defeat. "We must redouble our efforts to bring to the Democratic voters the philosophy we believe in." The campaign had forced club activists to "evaluate a philosophy, to examine goals closely, to sharpen one's commitments—and then to expand efforts to invest oneself in the campaign in such a way that these motivating beliefs will prevail." There were hundreds of letters of this sort to Cranston in the days and weeks after his primary defeat, written by those who saw Cranston as their candidate and were bewildered as to what to make of a primary loss after a decade of CDC endorsements that had meant certain election in the primary.[46] It was hard to find anyone involved with the club movement or in the Northern California Party who thought the political tone of the Cranston campaign had been misjudged. Roger Kent, himself no leftist firebrand and a total pragmatist when it came to elections, fixed upon Salinger's name recognition as a member of the Kennedy team and Cranston's tendency to take financial help from people and then rebuff them when they asked for political favors.[47] The primary result did not put an end to party infighting: if anything, it intensified factional animosities.

The year 1964 also signaled the completion of the Democratic left's takeover of San Francisco politics and the establishment of the city as the spiritual capital of the party's most social democratic advocates in elected office in California. We have already seen how Willie Brown and John Burton launched their careers in the Assembly in 1964 by piecing together a coalition of civil rights interest groups and organized labor, paving the way for the emergence of new liberal pressure groups like the Society for Individual Rights as influential shapers of local Democratic politics. The sheer scale of the victories of the Burton organization, together with the evident power of the ideological message these candidates were sending out, made them important players in Democratic politics statewide and also in national politics. His supporters in his massive win in the special election in February 1964—he garnered 26,269 votes to his nearest rival's 12,748 votes—were left in no doubt as to what he stood for. To the *Service Union Reporter* Burton represented "the rights of working people, the retired, minorities, consumers—all the people.

He won because he stood for freedom, equality, protection from poverty and a fair share of prosperity. . . . His record of achievement for human rights, consumer aid, veterans, social insurance and in other matters of importance to the people is impressive."[48]

Burton's press conference announcing his candidacy showed him to be a bridge between New Deal era liberalism and the new social movements that were redefining liberal politics in the 1960s as opposition to the old certainties of the early Cold War era came to the fore. "Civil rights is a major issue," he said. "I will give vigorous expression to the struggle for human dignity and human rights. Medicare is another major concern. Health insurance under Social Security is a pressing problem for the elderly of our city, state, and nation. My background as Chairman of the Assembly Committee on Social Welfare places me in a unique position to contribute to the passing of this needed legislation." His articulation of his political vision as that of a "fighting liberal Kennedy Democrat" aroused much comment from both left and right, the radical left arguing that would mean support for involvement in Vietnam, "the perpetual serfdom of the Latin American people, the continued racial policies of the Union of South Africa . . . and . . . the continuation of paying lip service to the southern Dixiecrats," and the right arguing that his opposition to loyalty oaths and support for anti-Cold War policies such as lifting the ban on travel to Cuba rendered him "diametrically opposed to the majority of Democrats."[49] Such rhetorical confusions aside, Burton's election to Congress, and the election of Willie Brown and John Burton to the Assembly together with the grooming of a whole slate of allies such as George Moscone, established San Francisco as a bulwark of the party's left in state and national politics.

Si Casady and the Breakdown of CDC Discipline

The period between 1964 and Reagan's election as governor in 1966 saw major convulsions in state and national politics and society. In late 1964 supporters of the Free Speech Movement at Berkeley had occupied university buildings, and the governor eventually lost patience and ordered California Highway Patrol officers to join the local police department in emptying Sproul Hall and carting students off to jail.[50] In August 1965 a random traffic stop in South Los Angeles sparked off some of the most devastating violence in the city's and state's history, with parts of Los Angeles reduced to a virtual war zone in rioting that went on for days as state authorities were powerless to stop it. To many Californians the middle years of the decade represented a breakdown of social order and a sign that the halcyon days of economic growth, benign good government, and social evolution without revolution were over, and that the Brown administration had lost its drive and command of the political scene.[51] The escalation of U.S. involvement in Vietnam during 1965 also heightened a sense of political crisis that encouraged different sides of the political spectrum to sharpen their rival perspectives and develop oppositional rhetorical strategies that played to the faithful and abandoned appeals to shared values. Both the Vietnam issue and the question of social order affected the Democratic Party and its affiliates deeply, but the debates of the mid-1960s reflected more than a reaction to specific events and controversies. The coming of age of the California party system that had been building since the 1950s was virtually complete by the time Reagan took the keys to the governor's mansion. We need to see the political convulsions of these eventful years as part of a longer process of political identity formation. An expanded language of civil and economic rights espoused by a key section of the California Democratic Party narrowed core distinctions between liberalism and leftism and created a modern individual rights discourse that has shaped state politics up to the present.

The agonies of the Proposition 14 battle, the demoralizing end to the student occupation at Berkeley, and the seeming impotence of the once-proud CDC to work its magic at election time were still raw wounds when President Johnson's rapid escalation of troop deployment to Vietnam touched off another stormy and potentially crippling battle within the state party in early 1965. At the CDC Convention in Sacramento in March the approximately 1,800 delegates chose a new leader: Si Casady, a semi-retired newspaper publisher from San Diego. Casady exemplified many of the peculiarities of the California left. Like many who had risen to statewide prominence via the club movement, he was extremely wealthy, living in sun-kissed splendor in the exclusive San Diego hillside suburb of El Cajon. He owned and piloted his own plane, and moved in social and business circles where Democrat was a dirty word. Democrats could win inner-city precincts in state and national elections, but these districts were encircled, from beachfront La Jolla in the north to eastern neighborhoods like El Cajon, by Republican bastions home to an active right-wing business community. Local congressman Bob Wilson was past president of the San Diego Junior Chamber of Commerce and was vice president of a major local advertising and public relations consultancy. Like other politicians, including Mayor Frank Curran, Wilson received the patronage of Westgate-California Corporation boss and future indicted criminal C. Arnholt Smith, known as "Mr. San Diego" for his economic power in the Southland.[52] The city was a coastal gateway to the Sunbelt southwest, a glittering testimonial to the power of entrenched corporate interests and unrivalled economic growth.

Yet its wealthy enclaves also functioned, as in many exclusive and upper middle class parts of Los Angeles, as centers of CDC club activity for liberal-minded, white, often rich locals who saw the clubs as an opportunity for networking and as a way of cementing their liberal political identity in an area generally thought to be hostile. Casady had no real experience of the grubby world of party politics, as the Democratic Party was historically very weak on his home turf, and in any case he came from a social milieu in which heated debate on issues and world affairs was more important than precinct organization and electoral mathematics. To the wealthy "angels" of Southern California who bankrolled many of the clubs and sat on statewide committees, the election of many more liberals to elected office from their patch was a tall order, whereas their capacity to inject a healthy dose of idealistic issue-oriented debate on the big issues facing the nation was more obvious, and made men like Casady feel involved in political action at a time of global political crisis.

At the convention Casady placed himself publicly on record as hostile to Assembly Speaker Jesse Unruh in an escalating war over control of the Democratic Party, arguing that Unruh was "more of an irritant than a danger," and that "provided he keeps out of our way we won't need to pay any attention to him." He battled to radicalize the demoralized club faithful by supporting a raft of left-leaning resolutions on civil rights, the student protests at the University of California, agricultural labor, and taxes, and also tried to force through a statement that would prove popular in the club meetings of San Diego but bitterly divisive in California at large: a demand for an immediate unilateral ceasefire and withdrawal of troops from Vietnam. He was supported by the Burton brothers—Phil attended the Sacramento meeting and pushed for the resolution—and President of the California Federation of Young Democrats, Josiah Beeman, who argued that the U.S. "position in Vietnam is morally indefensible. The President is harassed by military forces that seek escalation." Though the CDC Convention debated the issue from the Friday afternoon through Saturday and until 2 a.m. on Sunday morning, delegates could not agree to support such a radical statement, settling on a form of words that urged President Johnson to halt bombing of North

Vietnam and initiate a move to a negotiated settlement.[53] To Casady and his supporters, the Vietnam War represented a key issue separating grassroots activism from the nation's political leadership, and was therefore a way of rallying club activists and distancing them from the Democratic power players like Unruh, whom he despised.

Casady was not ready to let the issue rest after the 1965 CDC Convention ended, and his decision to make Vietnam the centerpiece of his campaign to invigorate the club movement and reestablish its political independence pointed up serious schisms in the broad church that was liberal politics in California. Casady used his platform as state chair of CDC to launch a sustained public attack on the Johnson administration's Vietnam policy, accusing the president of acting illegally in gaining congressional carte blanche for a major U.S. military operation in Indochina. Barely had the Sacramento convention disbanded when Assemblyman Philip Soto of the Fiftieth District in eastern Los Angeles County angrily wrote Casady that "you favor peace with the Communists—war with other Democrats. . . . You hamstring the President in his conduct of foreign policy by disapproving of his strategy in Vietnam, while you approve of the Free Speech Movement at Berkeley without taking a position on the four-letter word movement. In short, your actions and words are consistent with the CDC policy of creating a program which is embarrassing to Democratic incumbents and impossible for Democratic aspirants. I am pleased that I am no longer a member of this Democratic suicide squad."[54] By the fall Governor Brown himself, under pressure from Johnson to do something, wrote Casady demanding his resignation as CDC leader. "As a private citizen, you certainly have a right to voice your opinion on any subject. As President of the California Democratic Council, however, you have a responsibility to represent the views of your membership on major public issues. I am sure the members of the CDC did not intend, by electing you president earlier this year, to launch you on a statewide crusade against President Johnson. I am equally certain that your membership does not accept your appalling statement that burning a draft card is a display of courage."[55] Casady had committed an unpardonable sin: he had taken the resolutions adopted at the CDC Convention as a manifesto that he had an obligation to present publicly rather than subsume beneath a commitment not to rock the boat in the run-up to crucial elections in 1966. In any case, the Vietnam escalation was in its early stages, and the majority of public opinion had not yet turned against the war. Crucial was the key issue of whether CDC had a duty to act as the foot soldiers of the official California Democratic Party, or whether it was an independent organ with its own policy positions and political strategy independent of the party. "The abyss lay exposed," wrote Malibu CDC activist Lou Shaw. "There was no way of bridging it. The question had been asked and answered. Was the CDC to be an independent political organization or the darling of the Democratic Party, well controlled, free as a great big poodle on a leash?"[56]

The question of Casady's future as CDC leader immediately opened up the factional wounds in the California progressive movement that had barely begun to heal after the damaging battles of the previous year. A group on the CDC Council, led by Northern vice president Roy Greenaway and Southern vice president Charles Gant, submitted an "explanation of charges relating to the competency of Simon Casady as President of the California Democratic Council" to its board of directors on 24 October. They were careful not to make the charges against him purely about his Vietnam views, as a majority of CDC had endorsed those views at the Convention and would pass another antiwar resolution the following year. They alleged instead that he was an incompetent leader who had not solved the organization's financial and membership problems and had not presented a good image to the public. Vietnam could not be ignored. In his criticism of Johnson and the war, they charged, "by making personal attacks on those who disagree with him, [he] has largely negated any value resulting from his bringing the issue to the public forum." They also alleged that his deliberate distancing of CDC from the official party threatened to reduce the club movement to an impotent irrelevance.[57]

Cranston joined the anti-Casady bandwagon, perhaps mindful of the time when he had led CDC and it had worked effectively as a vote-getting machine and he had been rewarded with a place in office as state controller. Casady had, he said, made "destructive comments about Vietnam, draft card burning, President Johnson, the Governor and the Democratic Party. Besides that, he's been a poor administrator. CDC will be finished as an effective instrument statewide as long as he's there."[58] Casady's opponents pointed up the fact that the Democratic Party in California had been rebuilt in the 1950s on the bedrock of a strong commitment to a domestic program, downplaying the obsession with foreign policy and anticommunism that had done so much damage after World War II. To rake up foreign policy now was to risk replaying the fratricidal wars of the late 1940s, something that could only benefit their conservative opponents.

Predictably, many in the club rank-and-file rallied to Casady's defense. Those on the CDC Council supportive of Casady composed a reply to the statement of charges that did not even mention Vietnam but rather went straight to the heart of the dilemma facing the organization at a time of state and national crisis. Having noted that CDC had been conducting open warfare with key party officials such as Unruh and Senate President Hugh Burns for some time without internal controversy, the respondents stated that it had been "decided long ago . . . that the CDC is unique among party organizations. It is not just a weapon of the party to be noticed and employed every two years. It has been the conscience of the party and a liberalizing force in the development of party platform and policy."[59] The crisis within CDC over Vietnam and Si Casady represented the culmination of a struggle to reconcile a mainstream state party, an injection of new recruits and ideas, and a long legacy of popular front leftism in California.

Defining the 1960s Left: The Case of Berkeley

The Democratic Party in California came under siege from both left and right in 1966. The left challenge came in the form of the club rebellion—the CDC endorsed only ten Democratic congressional incumbents, twelve assemblymen, and five state senators in 1966—and the challenge to Berkeley congressman Jeffery Cohelan in the primary, and the right was represented first by the challenge of Mayor Sam Yorty of Los Angeles to Brown in the gubernatorial primary, and finally by the vibrant and successful campaign of Republican Ronald Reagan in the fall.[60] The right challenge was very real, and represented the coming apart of the tenuous electoral coalition that had propelled Brown to victory in 1958. The left challenge was more complicated, and requires us to delve more deeply into the Berkeley primary election to assess what was happening to Democratic Party politics in the 1960s.

"My district encompasses the City of Oakland, where a heavily commercial and industrial complex was over-extended during World War Two and where the subsequent decline has left a heavy aftermath of poverty and unemployment," wrote Congressman Cohelan to a South Carolina colleague during his bitter primary election battle against *Ramparts* foreign editor and peace activist Robert Scheer. "A third of the population here is Negro, and unemployment is twice the national average (among the Negroes even higher). . . . in Berkeley the dominant feature is the University, with its 27,000 enrollment and a high liberal, intellectual component. . . . My own strength has come mainly from labor groups, from strong supporters within the University, and from Civil Rights groups. . . . Strong opposition to the war in Vietnam now erodes the University support . . . and disaffections with the War on Poverty threaten to weaken the Negro support as well."[61] The Seventh Congressional District was unusual: the Berkeley campus of the University of California had been rocked by the explosion of student protest under the free speech movement umbrella, and Berkeley was by now becoming known for its youthful electorate and its radical chic politics.[62] Yet the battle between Congressman Cohelan and Bob Scheer for the Democratic nomination highlights crucial patterns in Democratic infighting in the run-up to Reagan's gubernatorial triumph: the impact of the Vietnam War on politics; the growing realization by leftist groups that the Democratic Party was the central locus of political activity that mattered on a broader canvas; and the breakdown of organized labor's ability to deliver a block of votes.

As Cohelan himself indicated in his brief sketch of problems facing his district, the primary campaign forced onto center stage the twin issues that bedeviled the Democrats in 1966: what sort of a foreign policy was appropriate for a "liberal" party, and to what extent were Democrats in Congress and the State Legislature delivering on social and economic policy. It also exposed the way in which a tradition of left-wing popular politics in California was encouraging, as had been the case in the 1940s, an odd and uncomfortable marriage between the left and the Democratic Party in certain districts in which conditions were right. Berkeley was a perfect location to serve as a testing ground for the relationship. Home to the Free Speech Movement, an increasingly radicalized campus, a number of left labor unions, and the Vietnam Day Committee (VDC), Berkeley was becoming almost a caricature of sixties radicalism, a microcosm of the social turmoil and experimentation that characterized the decade. Bob Scheer was well placed to represent the spirit of the challenge to establishment politics. A major figure in the VDC that had organized huge protests against the Vietnam War in the city, Scheer had coauthored a book on the Cuban revolution, had visited Vietnam in 1964 and written a pamphlet on U.S. involvement there, reflecting his horror at the impact of American policies on the people of South-east Asia. Bearded, earnest, and only thirty, he exemplified the trajectory of the California Democratic Party, having worked in the Stevenson campaigns before heading left and then reentering Democratic politics in order to use it as a vehicle for radical antiwar politics.[63] His campaign also demonstrated the way in which in California the issue of the war and disappointment with the achievements of sixties liberalism acted as catalysts for the reemergence of a radical leftism that was not new but had lain dormant during the upheavals of the 1950s and was now finding a new outlet. Critics of the Scheer campaign quickly noticed this trend: "The majority of names on the letterhead announcing the Scheer campaign were well-known old left figures: three unions which officially endorsed the campaign were Mine, Mill and Smelter, the Longshoremen, and the United Electrical Workers, unions expelled as communist dominated by the CIO and still part of the emotional and intellectual heritage of the old communist left."[64] Scheer readily accepted the involvement of communists in his campaign, cognizant of their organizational usefulness, and gathered together an impressive coalition of antiwar students, radical unions, communists, and Democratic clubs disillusioned with Cohelan and disenchanted after the dismissal of Casady as CDC Chair.[65]

The Scheer campaign pointed up a perennial problem for any observer of a California political scene in which so many shades of political opinion vied for space in mainstream party politics. In order to assess the significance of the challenge to Cohelan in Berkeley contemporaries were forced to define what sort of politics he represented and what this meant for the Democratic Party. Commentators from outside the state were prone to display the imprecision of definition that had long bedeviled followers of the California scene. The "tactics used by bearded, bespectacled Robert Scheer, the leftist candidate, against Rep. Jeffery Cohelan are typical of New Left politics," declared the *Washington Post* after the primary in a column with the headline "A New Left Near Win." It was "a ruthless kind of politics, certain to be duplicated by radicals across the country and wholly different from traditional politics in this country." Scheer's campaign against "liberal Democrat Cohelan" was "nothing less than an effort to destroy him with a bewildering array of Marxist-style campaign literature."[66] In this brief article appeared the terms "leftist," "New Left," "radicals," "traditional politics," "liberal," and "Marxist-style," with no attempt to explain what any of them meant. The same newspaper had made a similar intervention during the primary campaign, commenting in February 1966 that "the drive to weld far left organizations into a political front is reaching alarming reality. . . . What this amounts to is a leftist wrecking crew injecting a sinister new element into American politics."[67]

More enlightening is an examination of Scheer's campaign material, which shows his campaign themes to be very much along the lines of a CDC-style Democratic activism one could observe in any club newsletter from the late 1950s onward: "Instead of burning Vietnamese villages, we should reconstruct our own cities. If we really care about freedom, let us use our enormous energies, not to destroy Vietnam, but to break out of the cycle of discrimination and poverty that shames America." Scheer supported the repeal of antiunion shop provisions of Taft-Hartley, a public works program, a $2 minimum wage, a 30-hour week, a guaranteed income of $3,600 "as a right, not as welfare," access to day care centers for families, increased social security payments to seniors, the end to racial discrimination in housing, and various other measures that represented a standard left-of-center Democratic wish-list.[68] His criticisms of Great Society liberalism have become standard critiques: "The 'War on Poverty' gives too little money and *it gives it to the wrong people.* The money is administered by City Hall politicians who are afraid of change. Change will only come when money goes directly to finance the programs designed by local communities of the poor." His views on the Vietnam War were rapidly permeating into Democratic Party discourse as the war began to drag on with no end in sight: "The United States spends more in 1 HOUR in Vietnam than it spends in a WHOLE YEAR for the 'War on Poverty' in Oakland and Watts."[69] The diversity of the Scheer coalition did not obscure the fact that his campaign, like the battle over the 1964 Senate nomination, reflected the extent to which personalities and style could influence how a campaign was viewed: Scheer's style was radical, and his supporters saw themselves as outsiders storming the corrupt and remote world of party politics. The message, though different in tone, emphasis, and the extent to which it engaged with idealist absolutes, from that of Cohelan, was hardly unusual in California, nor was it new. The Berkeley campaign represented a culmination of pressures coming out of these questions of ideological affiliation that had been developing since the days of the popular front and the formation of CDC.

What was new about the Scheer campaign was the extent to which it represented the coming together of Democratic Party politics and old and new left organs in an open alliance in the mid-1960s. Club politics had exhibited these trends earlier—a brief look at the West Beverly Club is illuminating—but in a post-Joe McCarthy world the extent to which a popular front legacy resonated in the rejuvenated Democratic Party was never openly addressed until the antiwar movement forced the issue in 1965 and 1966. Some new leftists grew disillusioned with the Scheer campaign as it grew more successful during spring 1966 and even looked as if it might topple Cohelan, thus aligning radical protest with the pursuit of power through orthodox electoral means, but early on even they saw merit in a campaign that "would serve as a vehicle for community organizing while providing a framework within which to educate the organizers. Moreover, by focusing its opposition on a liberal congressman, the campaign would broaden the protest against the war to a critique of liberalism itself, and in so doing, link foreign policy to domestic concerns." These critics, members of Berkeley Students for a Democratic Society (SDS), argued in *Studies on the Left* that in the end the commitment to an electoral campaign under a standard party umbrella was counterproductive, as in "attempting to square its commitment to 'developing and ongoing, articulate political movement' with its effort 'to get as many votes as possible' the campaign was requiring its volunteers to work at two different paces on two separate timetables." Yet they noted the remarkably broad coalition that had lined up behind Scheer even as they decried the implications of a rainbow left that embraced the ballot box and the Democratic Party as vehicles for advancing social change. "For their part, the adherents of the old left wanted to build an electoral machine rather than a community organization. . . . They agreed with the liberals that important gains could be made by moving Cohelan to the left, and they realized that the campaign coalition could best be maintained by giving first priority to the election."[70]

These SDS activists were too young to realize it, but their analysis of the dynamics of Democratic electoral politics could apply to any number of electoral contests in California over the previous thirty years. Many VDC and SDS members broke with Scheer over his decision to enter the Democratic primary, but their understanding of the implications demonstrated the ease with which different political forces moved in and out of electoral politics on the west coast: "To run an 'effective' political campaign in America today means that one must be willing to set up very highly structured organizations similar to those of the Democratic and Republican parties," wrote SDS activists Carolyn Craven, Buddy Stein, and Dave Wellman. "This includes such mundane and undemocratic structures as precinct organizations with their captains and 'workers.'"[71] In Berkeley, however, radical politics *was* mainstream: the site of welfare protests, the home of the fair employment campaign, and a place in which rival conceptions of liberalism and leftism could be played out through a Democratic primary. The radical sensibility of democratic politics in the Bay Area shaped the dynamics of the electoral process there for the rest of the twentieth century. "The primary purpose of the campaign is to speak out for peace in Vietnam," stated a Scheer for Congress form letter. "But this is not the sole purpose of the campaign. We intend to speak about everything from the War on Poverty, to hot lunches in ghetto schools, to the problems of taxes in a war economy."[72] These themes would continue to resonate in Berkeley politics long after the Scheer campaign, helping to elect a radical city council in 1967 and a radical congressman in Ron Dellums in 1970. They sprang from a long tradition of insurgency politics in California, and had far deeper roots than the explosion of new left and student protest in the early 1960s.

The upheavals in California politics in the mid-1960s were taking place in a wider context. Michael Harrington, already famous as the author of *The Other America* and leading figure in the Young People's Socialist League (YPSL) and in leftist intellectual circles in Greenwich Village, argued that the early 1960s were witnessing a major transformation in the international political landscape.[73] Harrington's concession in a speech to the Harvard-Radcliffe College chapter of the YPSL in April 1967 that the "overwhelming bulk of forces for social change in the United States are in the liberal wing of the Democratic Party" was an attempt to integrate the U.S. into this international picture of social democratic politics, mindful that American politics did not lend itself to an obvious comparison with other industrialized democracies. His description of how democratic socialists could engage with liberal Democratic politics was an exact description of the Scheer campaign. "The levers of social change are [in the Democratic Party], and it seems to me that that is where every socialist, every democrat, every person concerned with social change should be. . . . In saying this, I am not saying that people of my persuasion should 'infiltrate' the Democratic Party. . . . I think programs such as the Freedom Budget, the emergency works and reconstruction program being proposed by liberal congressmen . . . are what socialists would have in common with liberals. . . . And it seems that the first step toward that new majority is going to be made in the left wing of the Democratic Party."[74] This idea of presenting a left-wing program through the vehicle of Democratic primary elections was very much the model of the Berkeley election of 1966, encouraged not just by the particular political context of that city but by the larger context of California Democratic politics since the formation of CDC.

"A New and Appealing Liberalism": Alan Cranston and the Politics of Respectability

Even at the state level, Alan Cranston's successful run for the Senate in 1968 demonstrates the capacity of liberals to engage with the rising political clout of the right and even to take on directly the issue of how to create a coalition of urban liberals and the suburban middle class. As the founder of CDC who had played a major role in reinvigorating the left wing of the Democratic Party, his election to Congress marked the coming of age of the activist politics of the past fifteen years as one of its progenitors became part of the political establishment. His move onto the federal scene flagged up serious questions about how CDC and liberal policy positions on questions ranging from the Vietnam War to civil rights would resonate in a statewide election after the social upheavals and liberal setbacks of the mid-1960s. The Casady affair had left deep wounds in CDC, and had caused many to wonder how far an ideology of the left could map onto mainstream party politics. This question gained even greater resonance when observers considered the election of Ronald Reagan to the governorship and the increasing power of a "law and order" conservative wing of the California Republican Party. The Senate race between Cranston and right-wing Republican Max Rafferty is an important example of the increasing division between left and right in state politics over the economic and social changes of the postwar era. The race and its aftermath highlighted the impact that the new social movements, the frenetic growth of suburbia, and the decline of the postwar economic boom had on the strategies of California's political class.

Cranston attempted to harness whatever parts of New Deal liberalism remained viable at a tumultuous time for his party in the wake of Robert Kennedy's assassination and the breakdown of party discipline around Hubert Humphrey's presidential candidacy, if only to create some tactical space between himself and Rafferty. He mined the Great Society phrasebook for its most popular nuggets, including the expansion of Medicare to cover prescription drugs and eventual universal coverage, and a commitment to the union shop and to the unionization of sectors of the economy still resistant to organized labor.[75] He made the right noises at the AFL-CIO convention in Sacramento in September, claiming to hope for a nation "committed to curing the underlying causes of much of our violence. An America committed to economic justice for all our people. In California, the Democratic Party is united, as never before, to do just that."[76] Cranston's team knew that they needed to court elements of the traditional New Deal coalition: one memo warned that African Americans needed personal appearances and attention with the observation that they "couldn't imagine many blacks voting for Rafferty, but guess what happens if they all stay home."[77] Another survey noted that in Alameda County the UAW campaign headquarters was the "busiest and best organized" Cranston outfit in the county, and labor remained a bulwark of Democratic strength in California in Humphrey's presidential campaign.[78] In some ways the dynamics of the Senate race in 1968 resembled those of earlier liberal versus conservative bouts: labor and minorities were gathered under a Great Society umbrella on one side, with discontented "law and order" homeowners, business leaders, and radical right activists on the other.[79] In addition, the creation of "Gopacrats for Cranston," a tool to recruit anti-Rafferty moderate Republicans, mirrored the Rockefeller break with Goldwater in 1964.[80]

Yet the tone and emphasis of the 1968 campaigns, not to mention the electoral popularity of the candidates, had undergone important changes since the early 1960s. The rise of suburbia and the ongoing social pressures of campaigns for gender, sexual, and racial equality were putting severe pressure on the social fabric of the nation.[81] While the impact of these debates on the right is well documented, the coming of age of the qualitative liberalism envisioned by Tony Crosland back in the 1950s remains only partially explored, a liberalism that would encompass civil rights interest groups and quality of life issues in an era in which the old nostrums of New Deal regulation were becoming ever harder to sustain.[82] A county-by-county analysis of Cranston's campaign structure and Democratic Party organizing, conducted by his team immediately after his narrow win over Rafferty, demonstrates the continued search on the part of California politicians of all ideological persuasions for a resonant strategy in such a diverse and rapidly changing social setting. Cranston operative Bud Curtis wanted to enlist "greater representation from growing suburban communities. In too many of these areas political ties are weak and identification of candidates vague. . . . These areas hold immense and increasing power, and, for the most part, are concerned with taxes, schools, transportation, urban planning and other issues which directly touch the household and the pocketbook. By and large, these are issues on which forthright and identifiable political platforms can be built. Blue collar militancy largely has been swallowed by suburbia and homeownership." The recruitment of "youthful suburbanites, particularly housewives," was essential, Curtis argued. These citizens had close ties to community organizations such as PTAs and could provide a bridge between suburban living and party politics. Coffee mornings could become "significant discussion groups" that might form part of a continuous pattern of events between elections rather than "de facto volunteering" only at election time. In order to cement the involvement of such people, "a new and appealing liberalism" was required. "A vital new platform is needed, one looking toward the 70s, not back into the 50s. Many of liberalism's older goals, if not met, are at least being met," Curtis argued. "A fresh platform must be advanced. . . . Some quiet philosophizing—

away from the hurly burly of daily politics—is required. Earnest consultation with professors, labor, business, church leaders—a steadfast pursuit of new vistas and ideas—should be undertaken."[83] Such sentiments seemed almost a carbon copy of those expressed at Asilomar over fifteen years earlier, suggesting that liberals in California remained ahead of their time in recognizing the tensions between welfare state liberalism and the quality of life issues that preoccupied middle-class suburbs.

The Reagan Challenge

Another major political aftershock that followed the events of 1958 and after was the choice in 1966 of Ronald Reagan as the Republican Party's gubernatorial candidate and his subsequent landslide victory over Pat Brown. The GOP had for some time been building a successful political infrastructure in Southern California through organs like United Republicans of California, and had been openly courting the business community with a clearer message than had been possible before the Brown administration had clarified the direction of the Democratic Party. Soon after Jeffery Cohelan's narrow 3,000-vote primary win Los Angeles Assemblyman Charles Warren wrote Cohelan to express his concerns that the Democratic Party needed to abandon the luxury of infighting and turn to the Republican threat. "Even now the Republicans have zeroed in on several congressional, assembly and senatorial Democratic incumbents," he wrote. "Their so-called 'California Plan' for capturing control of the Legislature by the time of reapportionment is on schedule. Their party has been united. Ours has been torn by endless factionalism. Their party raises funds sufficient to finance the campaigns of their candidates."[84] The Democratic State Central Committee, by contrast, was bitterly divided, torn apart by Los Angeles mayor Sam Yorty's challenge to Pat Brown in the Democratic primary and by the bruising fight between Charles Warren and Carmen Warschaw, both southern California symbols of factionalism, for the post of state chair. Warschaw lost the race, but noted later that her "pride was hurt to a degree, but I never really wanted to win it, because I felt Pat Brown *could not win* in '66. I just thought that whoever was chairman was just going to have a losing campaign."[85] Roger Kent agreed that the party was a mess in the wake of the Casady affair and the Watts riots.[86] The party's finances were also in bad shape after the bruising primary and general election clashes of 1964.[87] After eight years of legislative power in the Golden State, the Brown administration and its supporters were facing the same predicament that had bedeviled their GOP opponents in the late 1950s: how to unite behind a winning message that would resonate with the electorate at large when so many of the state's problems could easily be laid at their door?

Such problems seemed manifold in the summer of 1966. The Republican antigovernment message that had seemed quaint in 1958 now had resonance after nearly eight years of a massive expansion of state capacity in higher education, transportation, welfare provision, water projects, and a myriad of other programs that were inadequately financed as a result of Californians' reluctance to raise state taxes that were already among the highest in the nation. "California now has the highest total state and local taxes per capita in the nation, estimated at $343.16 for 1963," a Republican State Central Committee newsletter for the 1964 campaign had stated. "Next year, a large tax increase will be necessary to prevent complete financial chaos, but nobody knows where to go for the additional money. This predicament is the result of a six-year spending spree by Democrats in Sacramento."[88] In the wake of the Watts riots in August 1965 the sense that vast tax revenues were failing to solve California's social problems and were perhaps even making them worse became a major campaign issue for Republican candidates and conservative commentators. A radio broadcast on KNX radio Los Angeles shortly after the worst of the rioting had died down attacked "voices from the left" that "*defend* the rioters and the snipers in South Los Angeles on the ground they are poverty-stricken and hopeless. . . . Only a year ago, the governor of California was saying again and again that white people are prejudiced, biased and bigoted. . . . Only a few weeks ago, State Controller Alan Cranston castigated individuals and associations who oppose some civil rights programs. He called them bigots. This kind of political talk gives respectability to the Negro belief that white people are his enemy. What else can he think?"[89] The social citizenship ideology that had defined the FEPC, fair housing, and welfare state legislation of the Brown years had been turned on its head: tackling questions of racial division and poverty head-on through government action simply highlighted divisions in society and encouraged social discord.[90] Democrats in Los Angeles knew omens for the 1966 campaign were not promising: "Some of the radio/TV editorializing is getting rough," stated one memo to Jimmy Roosevelt. "As you commented—wonder what they will do at election time, this one hitting at Cranston etc. is certainly campaigning."[91]

The emergence of Reagan as the GOP's gubernatorial candidate soon added to the Democrats' woes. Not only did he turn out to be a skilled and experienced political campaigner, but he was also well-financed through a network of Southern California friends and business associates and backed by one of the most effective PR machines in the state, that of Stu Spencer and Bill Roberts. Reagan had only switched his registration to the Republican Party during the Nixon gubernatorial campaign, but his many years' experience of beating the drum for corporate conservatism in the educational department of GE and his easy charm as a Hollywood leading man made him a powerful performer on the political stage. His speech to the GOP convention in San Francisco in 1964 and his subsequent televised reprise of what became known as "The Speech" just before the election cemented his reputation as one of the most articulate promoters of antistatist individualism and market forces as mainstays of the American Way.[92] His background as a B-movie actor furnished Reagan with another advantage that only became fully apparent with his landslide victory over Pat Brown in November 1966: he was often underestimated, dismissed by political opponents and even at times by his campaign strategists as a neophyte who knew how to articulate a simple right-wing ideology but who could not possibly get to grips with the complexity of issues affecting California without careful, painstaking coaching. Democrats were especially prone to misread the political winds in 1966 as it seemed at first that the election would be a rerun of four years earlier in a state with a two to one Democratic registration and where the far right seemed to have a hold over GOP strategy. After Reagan's announcement of his candidacy on 4 January, an eloquent appeal to voters' fears concerning crime, civil disorder, and the priorities of government, Democratic State Chairman Robert Coate dismissed Reagan as a caricature of a John Birch Society clone. "I have called this press conference," intoned Coate the following day, "because yesterday we witnessed the most incredible performance in California's political history. . . . Reagan is not only a man of the radical right. He is also a man who is radically wrong. I charge that Reagan is wrong on welfare, wrong on industrial growth, wrong on unemployment, wrong on taxes, wrong on tidelands, wrong on crime, wrong on education, wrong on water."[93]

Senior Democrats were similarly dismissive of conservative Democratic rumblings of discontent. In response to the formation of a new group, California Moderate Democrats Inc., Roger Kent stated that "these people are so stupid that they have adopted almost exactly the same program of the phony 'Committee for the Preservation of the Democratic Party in California.' . . . In the case we won in court it was proved that $70,000 of the money they used came from the ill-fated Nixon campaign and only $236 from a one-half million mailing to Democrats."[94] Unfortunately for Kent and other senior Democrats, this was not a repeat of 1962. The challenge within the party to Brown was not just a Republican-financed gimmick, since Sam Yorty garnered nearly a million votes in the Democratic primary. And Reagan was not just a poster boy for a radical fringe in California, but was an accomplished operator with influential friends in Los Angeles society. Reagan's "Kitchen Cabinet" included Holmes Tuttle, Southern California's largest automobile dealer, Henry Salvatori, an oil company executive, Alfred Bloomingdale of Diner's Club, and Walter Annenberg, owner of *TV Guide* and numerous other profitable publications, who often hosted meetings of this coterie of wealthy Reaganites at his desert estate at Palm Springs. Reagan's campaign managers, Spencer and Roberts, were themselves moderate Republicans, masterminds of Tom Kuchel's Senate reelection campaign of 1962 and of Rockefeller's near-upset of Goldwater in the 1964 California presidential primary, but they were big players in the media-driven world of California political campaigns, and were won over by Reagan's powerful financial backing and his willingness to take advice.[95] This political expertise and massive war chest combined with the aftermath of the Watts riots and the deep political divisions within the Democratic Party to create an almost impossible political situation for Pat Brown and his allies. "They were just going to throw the rascals out," recalled Roger Kent of the election. "We happened to be the rascals."[96]

With the benefit of hindsight, Reagan's victory in 1966 by almost a million votes has been seen as a turning point in the American political zeitgeist, paving the way for a significant right turn in state and national politics in the late 1960s and 1970s.[97] In terms of bringing about a radical overhaul of state government and dismantling the massive state programs of the Brown years, the Reagan administration would prove to be less of a "decisive turning point" than its political spin doctors wanted Californians to believe. The 1966 election did, however, represent the coming of age of a new party system in California in which each of the two main parties would become associated more categorically with a particular political worldview. Though dissidents in each party remained—Sam Yorty would continue to serve as Los Angeles mayor and perennial thorn in the side of Democratic strategists until 1973—the old order in which parties acted as vehicles for personal advancement often only tenuously linked to a particular program or set of values was no longer viable. Party politics in California would subsequently act as an arena for the playing out of battles over the development of capitalism, the rights of a variety of interest groups clamoring for social equality, and the provision of core public services and amenities. This was not a completely new development, and the thesis of this book is that a process of political affiliation linked to the dramatic social and economic changes in the Golden State had been gathering pace since the 1940s, but the particular social struggles over social citizenship, civil rights, and the rights of business interests to shrug off governmental regulation and taxation would come to a climax as California entered the 1970s.

CHAPTER 10

The Legacy of the Democratic Party Renaissance

"California," wrote political analysts Michael Barone, Grant Ujifusa, and Doug Matthews in 1975, "just a few years ago the most noticeably right-wing major state, has now become a leftish state politically."[1] In fact, California remained as unpredictable as ever in political terms, electing Ronald Reagan governor in a landslide in 1966 and a Republican assembly and senate in 1968, but also electing Alan Cranston senator that same year against arch conservative Superintendent of Schools Max Rafferty, and then in 1970 throwing out Rafferty, the Republican legislature, and GOP senator George Murphy while reelecting Reagan. It is true, nonetheless, that left-leaning Democrats statewide managed in the late 1960s and early 1970s to make the state's legislative system work for them to pass landmark social rights legislation, to limit the capacity of Governor Reagan's administration to roll back the welfare state, and to launch the careers of a new generation of Democratic politicians who would maintain California as the home of the most uncompromisingly progressive members of the party in the nation. The strengthening of the links between new social movements and liberal politicians in the Bay Area and Los Angeles helped to make party politics a meeting ground for a diverse range of interest groups that bridged the divide between welfare politics and social equality politics, but it also encouraged a proliferation of competing voices for political patronage that made it increasingly difficult to speak of one liberal movement. The rise of radical right causes and the growing economic crisis of the early seventies also threw up major obstacles to the continuation of a benevolent state government. This chapter will analyze case studies of Democratic political and legislative activity during the Reagan governorship to shed light on the extent to which the rise of the Democratic Party in

California between the early 1950s and the 1970s had in fact established the party as the promoter of a particular ideological and programmatic focus, with lessons for the more recent past.

The Limits of the Republican Ascendancy: The Supreme Court

The legacy of the policy innovations and political changes of the Brown administration was substantial. This was due not simply to the political know-how of party strategists and activists but also because the structure of state institutions encouraged an idea of social citizenship to become embedded in law. Legal and political historians have long recognized the importance of judicial activism in shaping the contours of governmental power and public policy.[2] In the mid-1960s the California Supreme Court's liberal majority played an important role in throwing the weight of constitutional jurisprudence behind the concept of equal rights that had framed the policymaking of the Brown administration and liberal legislators. According to the *Wall Street Journal* in 1972, the California Supreme Court "over the past twenty years has won a reputation as perhaps the most innovative of the state judiciaries, setting precedents in areas of criminal justice, civil liberties, racial integration and consumer protection that heavily influence other states and the federal bench." Associate Justice Matthew Tobriner argued that the Golden State's highest court was "a dynamic institution" that needed to "respond to and reflect the society in which it lives." Tobriner's version of sociological jurisprudence was shared by a majority of Court members in the mid-1960s, a Court that included former Brown Attorney General Stanley Mosk, arch-liberal Raymond Peters, and Chief Justice Roger Traynor. The *Wall Street Journal* noted that "many judges outside California pay them close attention because of their reputation for clarity and sound scholarship." The California Court had "more opportunity than most to break new legal ground because of the large number and wide variety of cases it hears," and was a trailblazer in the field of class action suits, enshrining in state law the idea of social rights for the community as a whole as well as for individual plaintiffs.[3] One legal scholar argued that the California Court under Roger Traynor became "the most prestigious state bench in the United States," where "the individualistic spirit of the common law has been giving way to an entirely different spirit, which emphasizes the welfare of the community, even at the cost of individual rights of property, contract, and the like."[4] The Court kept the rights agenda alive even as the party political landscape became more difficult to negotiate by the end of the decade. An examination of the Court's overturning of Proposition 14 demonstrates the extent to which judicial decision-making reinforced the power of the state government to regulate social relationships and to enshrine in law the idea of social equality.

The Mulkeys had sued an apartment owner in Orange County under the terms of the Rumford Act for alleged racial discrimination in refusing to rent the apartment to them. The county court adjudicated after the passage of Proposition 14, which had established the right of property owners to sell to whomever they chose as Article 1, section 26 of the state constitution, and the court found that this clause in the constitution necessarily invalidated the plaintiff's case. The case found its way to the State Supreme Court, arriving on the justices' bench in early 1966. In a landmark verdict, a clear majority of justices found that Article 1, section 26 violated the equal protection clause of the Fourteenth Amendment, concluding that "the article involved affirmative action on the part of the state to change its existing laws from a situation where discrimination was legally restricted to one wherein it was encouraged."[5] In placing in the Constitution the clause that "the state shall not limit the right of any person to sell or lease his real property to such person as he, in his absolute discretion, chooses," advocates of Proposition 14 had, in the opinion of the Court, mandated the state to sanction open discrimination, providing individuals with a legal frame for their actions that left people like the Mulkeys with no legislative or legal recourse, nor any possibility of gaining it in the future. The justices were careful to note that their opinion was not an endorsement of the Rumford and Unruh Acts, nor that antidiscrimination legislation was an inevitable by-product of their ruling. Individual discrimination was one thing, something that had existed prior to Proposition 14 and which had been subject, rightly or wrongly, to state legislative regulation during the Brown years. Constitutional proscription of antidiscrimination legislation and civil suits was quite another, placing the weight of state power behind practitioners of racial discrimination and shutting down access for potential victims to their right to due process and legislative protection. The addition of the judicial branch to the ranks of those endorsing the use of state legislative power to guarantee the access of all citizens to economic resources (in this case housing) represented a powerful political advance for the forces that had been building a state-centered approach to social equality in the 1950s and 1960s.

The landlord in the Mulkey case appealed and on 29 May 1967 the U.S. Supreme Court upheld the California Court's ruling in a much narrower 5–4 opinion. Speaking for the majority, Justice Byron White noted the change in the constitutional status of homeowner rights in the wake of Proposition 14, arguing that those "practicing racial discrimination need no longer rely solely on their personal choice. They could now invoke express constitutional authority, free from censure or interference of any kind from official sources." Article 1, section 26 was, in White's words, "intended to authorize, and does authorize, racial discrimination in the housing market. The right to discriminate is now one of the basic policies of the State."[6] Justice William O. Douglas wrote a separate concurring opinion in which he went further, arguing that state endorsement of discrimination on the part of real estate brokers was hardly different from actual state policies, such as restrictive covenants and racially motivated zoning laws. "Zoning is a state and municipal function," he wrote. "Leaving the zoning function to groups which practice racial discrimination and are licensed by the States constitutes state action in the narrowest sense in which Shelley v. Kraemer, supra, can be construed." In addition to the fact that real estate agents were licensed by the state, he argued, government financing for housing also made it a public matter that could not support a blanket constitutional ban on state regulation of sales and rentals.[7] The importance of Justices White and Douglas's majority opinions to the agenda of civil rights and social justice campaigners in California was obvious: the state was legally entitled to legislate to discourage discrimination in the private marketplace, but not entitled to restrict the right of individuals to seek legislative and legal recourse in cases of alleged discrimination. The ruling had broad implications for the scope of governmental authority over private economic transactions that went beyond the question of race and housing.

The arguments of the minority opinion, penned by Justice Harlan and joined by Justices Black, Clark, and Stewart, also pointed to the significance of legal opinion in shaping a more activist state in the realm of social citizenship, guaranteeing the right of individuals as citizens equal access to the marketplace. All "that has happened," wrote Harlan, "is that California has effected a pro tanto repeal of its prior statutes forbidding private discrimination. This runs no more afoul of the Fourteenth Amendment than would have California's failure to pass any such antidiscrimination statutes in the first instance." But this was clearly not so: the California legislature had not repealed the Rumford Act; the voters had instead through a ballot referendum enshrined the right to discriminate in the state constitution. Unable to challenge the civil rights legacy of the California legislature in the Brown years through legislative action, opponents of the regulated housing market had been forced to resort to the referendum, ensuring that the question of state involvement in the market economy would become a legal as well as party political question, with enormous implications for the future of California politics. Harlan noted this when he argued that the concept of "state action" as discrimination by proxy in the "form of laws that do nothing more than passively permit private discrimination could be said to tinge all private discrimination with the taint of unconstitutional state encouragement."[8] The rights legislative agenda of the Brown era had placed on the table huge questions of individual rights, economic rights, and state regulation of society that had transformed the political landscape since the 1950s and demonstrated that the reach of legislative and judicial power over questions of social equality had been unalterably extended, regardless of the changing fortunes of liberal and conservative forces in state politics. California was soon to see new legislative activity in the realms of gay rights, the rights of the disabled, welfare recipients, and those whose first language was not English, that would demonstrate the truth inherent in Harlan's concern that opposition to discrimination, real or imagined, was rapidly becoming a lynchpin of California's political and legal structures by the beginning of the 1970s.[9]

Integrating La Huelga into Liberal Politics

In important ways, the social landscape of California was shifting in directions that demanded the rethinking of the language of party politics. For one thing, the emergence of the Mexican American Political Association (MAPA) and the spread of labor strife to California's agricultural heartland with the boycott of the state's grape industry led by Cesar Chavez and his United Farm Workers (UFW) union demonstrated that the entwined issues of race and class remained far more complex than the black and white civil rights discourse that had often framed sixties mainstream political debate. Scholarly treatments of the rise of agrarian radicalism in California in the 1960s have highlighted both liberalism's narrow angle of vision and also the continued importance of racially linked class struggle as a feature of California's economic growth. The complex dynamics of grassroots organizing, appeals to ethnic, cultural, and religious symbolism, and coalition-building with organized labor and the wider civil rights movements of the sixties in building *la Causa* and in making its legacy far more durable than earlier efforts have received wide attention.[10] The success of Chavez, Dolores Huerta, and other leaders of the UFW organizing campaign and nationwide grape boycott between 1965 and 1970 in changing fundamentally the relationship between worker and employer in the fields kept the question of economic justice at the heart of progressive politics, and provided the model for other political movements later on. By 1972, the UFW had contracts with some 150 growers and an estimated membership of between fifty and sixty thousand, of whom half were year-round workers, a huge advance on the failed organizing efforts of the 1940s and 1950s.[11] Also important was the way in which *la Causa* interacted with Democratic liberal politics and with welfare liberalism, ensuring economic citizenship remained part of the political lexicon of elected politicians—not just grassroots activists—as they entered the 1970s.

The relationship between Democratic politics and economic rights viewed through the lens of farm labor is more complicated than is suggested by the oft-cited vignette of Governor Brown stealing away in fear with Frank Sinatra after refusing to meet a large UFW crowd at the culmination of their 300-mile march to Sacramento on Easter Sunday in 1966.[12] At the national level, Bobby Kennedy saw the value of the UFW to his presidential campaign early on, but so did a number of California politicians who supported Kennedy in 1968 and also saw the grape boycott as part of a bigger project to sell the idea of economic citizenship to a wider public. Phil Burton spearheaded this effort, making sure Chavez addressed the House Labor and Education Committee during their visit to the heartland of the dispute in Delano, California, in August 1968. Chavez used the language of economic dignity common to labor and welfare rights movements of the sixties, language that had launched Burton's career. "We are struggling for higher wages," Chavez told the committee, "better working conditions, and recognition as a union. We are also struggling to be recognized as men and treated with dignity by our employers . . . for justice equal to that accorded other workers in the United States."[13] Burton tried to throw the weight of legislative action behind the grape boycott, using the commerce clause of the Constitution to frame a bill to curtail the sale and distribution of grapes produced on nonunionized farms.[14] More important, he and likeminded colleagues made the boycott part of a wider publicity campaign for the economically disenfranchised. His successful lobbying for the reversal of a freeze in federal payments to AFDC recipients in 1969 was hailed by the executive director of the National Welfare Rights Organization (NWRO) as clearing "the way for positive action toward a *Guaranteed Adequate Income* for every American," and farm labor unionization was but another tool in reaching that goal.[15]

The fact that many of the farm workers affected were Latino, the fastest growing ethnic group in the state by the 1970s, added another layer to the increasingly unstable tower of interests clamoring for inclusion in the coalition of liberal politics. Cranston's campaign informant in San Francisco in 1968 reported that relations between the Burton-dominated County Central Committee and MAPA leaders Robert Gonzales and Herman Gallegos were "vastly improved" since party officials had begun at least to recognize the new power block in city politics, but still needed "constant attention."[16] Gonzales would later challenge Phil Burton in a congressional primary, a reminder, if any were needed, that elected politicians needed to pay attention to a broader mosaic of ethnic and social groups than had been necessary ten years earlier.[17] But in some respects this worked in their favor, giving liberals new challenges to invigorate their base and keep their issues on the agenda. Farm labor unionization and gay rights were, as we shall see, landmark achievements of the 1970s for the liberal base. And the techniques of the UFW mobilization later enabled Latino liberals to gain a significant powerbase in major centers like Los Angeles.[18]

The Battle of the Budget and the Politics of Stalemate

The major battles in California in the early 1970s over welfare spending and taxes represented the maturation of the developing schism between majorities in each party over the future ideological direction of state politics. They also reflected the inevitable tensions that a decade of policies to expand both economic rights and individual rights, predicated upon the same ideological premise, had created. When Governor Reagan described his crusade to rein in welfare spending in a speech in Los Angeles on 3 March 1971, he touched off a contest between the heirs to Pat Brown and Reagan's own antigovernment forces over the legacy of the social democratic experiment in California politics. The aid to dependent children caseload, he claimed, had risen 39 percent in 1970 alone, bringing with it a 42 percent increase in the cost of the program. "Even cutting back legitimate government services and postponing important and needed projects," Reagan intoned gravely, "we face the fact that to continue the present welfare and Medi-Cal programs without change will require $220 million more than we have." The long economic boom was coming to an end; property taxes were skyrocketing; yet the number of Californians seemingly entitled to claim from the state seemed without limit. "There is virtually no ceiling on earnings above which you become ineligible for welfare although we have found it usually does not go above $1200 a month. At least one man in California, however, managed to keep his welfare grant plus $16,800 a year in salary."[19] Stories abounded of welfare recipients living extravagantly off the system. An example from the *Sacramento Union* in October 1971 detailed the case of a couple in Indiana who were returning to California because they could claim far more in welfare and have more choice over what they could buy using food stamps than in their adoptive home state.[20]

Reagan's proposals were a state-level version of President Nixon's Family Assistance Plan that was being debated in Washington. The California Department of Benefit Payments, under the direction of Reagan appointee David B. Swoap, would implement a new system of work placements or training for those applying for welfare, and establish a new eligibility procedure to make it harder for those with outside income to claim welfare checks. The proposals also claimed to "strengthen family responsibility" by restoring the requirement that relatives of elderly welfare recipients should contribute to their support. The district attorney's office was empowered to collect maintenance for needy children from absent fathers, allowing California to collect an extra $23 million in support payments in 1974 compared to 1969. This gave Swoap the opportunity to claim in 1974 that his office was "making strong headway" in the drive to increase the amount of support for the needy garnered from relatives of recipients, "in large part due to a general recognition that an irresponsible parent—be he a husband or an unmarried father—is at the root of many of our welfare cases." He argued that California had spent a billion dollars less on welfare in the three years after the 1971 reform than would have been the case without the new rules, and that the AFDC rolls had been cut by 350,000 instead of rising at a rate of 40,000 a month.[21] Thirty-five counties were included in the Work Experience Program, involving an estimated 58,000 welfare recipients classed as "employable," and in financially straitened times even a Democratic Assembly was not minded to stop welfare reform in its tracks.[22]

On the face of it Reagan's second term looked like the symbol of the end of the social democratic tendency in state politics that had expanded the reach of government in the realm of economic security over the previous decade. Yet Reagan's attack on the policies of his predecessor galvanized opposition, and far from signaling the triumph of the right in California in fact suggested more of a stalemate, a realization that the political world of the seventies would reflect the contradictory ideological currents that had come to define state politics since the pivotal election of 1958. For one thing, Reagan's much trumpeted welfare reform demonstrated the continued clout that legislative Democrats held over the legislative process after their intensive education through the 1960s. John Burton and Willie Brown had gained significant power in the Assembly by the end of the sixties, organizing what Burton called the "Mice Milk," power lunches for left-leaning legislators like soon-to-be speaker Bob Moretti, Robert Crown, Alan Sieroty of Beverly Hills, Leo Ryan, and John Vasconcellos. Even Jesse Unruh began courting this self-confident, well-organized group of Democrats as he swung his support away from the conservative pressure groups and interests who seemed to have abandoned him for Reagan. Together, they were masters of the legislative process and repeated saboteurs of the Reagan administration's attempts to end the era of generous social policy in California. In 1970 they had forced Reagan to accept a bill to allow old age assistance recipients to keep their money when their OASI benefits were increased, directing welfare rights groups to picket the governor when he made public appearances. In 1971 they added riders to welfare reform to provide cost of living increases for AFDC recipients and state funds for family planning. "Reagan was always a phoney on welfare reform," John Burton later crowed. "[He] never had any idea about what it was and never really accomplished much." Burton and his fellow majority negotiators agreed to the work program, "but said they had to get transportation [and] have a job that was going to lead to something, they could only do it twenty hours a week." They agreed to the relatives' responsibility law but made the contribution requirement "so high that all of the conservative redneck Democrats who supported Reagan were up screaming and within two years that got repealed and so he was left with all the benefits of the program and none of the so-called savings."[23] In 1976 the state Economic Development Department admitted that the whole work experience side of Reagan's welfare reform had flopped: the number of welfare applicants in work experience counties had increased, and the rate of unemployment in those counties fell by less than in other counties. Only 4,760 of a possible 182,735 eligible people had participated in the work program in its peak year of 1974, and Governor Jerry Brown had quietly scrapped the scheme in June 1975.[24]

The fight against Reagan's changes to the welfare system was not just a product of legislative activity: West Coast welfare rights campaigners also lobbied to stop the administration from slashing access to child support services. Many of the leading figures in the California welfare movement had strong links to liberal politicians: Jacobus tenBroek, as we have seen, advised Phil Burton and members of Governor Brown's welfare committee on the liberalization of the state welfare system in the early 1960s, and was also national chair of the National Federation of the Blind and its state affiliate, the California Council of the Blind; he was the first chair of the California Welfare Rights Organization in 1966. Other key figures like Cesar Chavez, Dolores Huerta, Fred Ross, and Saul Alinsky also bridged the divide between independent welfare activism and engagement with elected officials. The efforts to stop Reagan's rollback of welfare and his slashing of state taxes in the early 1970s demonstrate the continued importance of Democratic liberals in resisting the ideological onslaught of their opponents in state government.[25] When Reagan refused to allow OASI recipients to keep their state old age assistance checks when Congress increased their federal payments in 1970, John Burton liaised with senior rights campaigner Ed Peet to organize a protest during Reagan's visit to the World Trade Club. "Some little old lady with tears in her eyes says, 'Why are you taking away my $7.50?'" recalled Burton. "Well, on television it just looked like the shits. . . . So he signed the bill and we got the money."[26]

Reagan's failed attempt to slash state taxes in 1973 also demonstrates the extent to which it had become difficult to reverse the enormous expansion of state government that had occurred in the previous fifteen years. Reagan's attempt to use a public referendum to force the gradual reduction in the proportion of statewide personal income taken in taxes each year through a constitutional amendment and to require a popular vote before any rise in property taxes was partly a response to his administration having raised taxes as often as it had cut them: $500 million more in 1971 and an extra billion in 1972. In fiscal year 1972–1973 California collected $15.2 billion in state and local taxes, almost double the amount collected in Pat Brown's last year as governor.[27] The complex formula underpinning Proposition 1 that would have imposed huge cuts in the spending power of state government confused voters, whereas the hard-hitting campaign led by Speaker Bob Moretti to highlight all the services that would have been slashed was easy to understand. The proposal failed to pass despite Reagan's attempt to frame his stand on taxes in terms of "basic philosophical issues" that had been derailed by "the distracting, irrelevant and confusing play on human fears and the basic emotions of the people which the spending establishment in government emphasized in its campaign strategy."[28] His own administration's failure to halt the massive increase in the size of the state, even adding new statutes on air and water quality that required new state agencies, made his ideological posturing on tax hard to take seriously. That said, voter concern at skyrocketing property taxes and the economic slowdown was becoming obvious, and Reagan was using his platform as governor to channel that concern into a potential launch pad for national office. "Conservative Republicans are disturbed by Ford's efforts at 'consensus' government and accommodations toward the left," argued Reagan's PR team as he prepared to leave office in late 1974. "Conservative Democrats continue to be alienated by the minority-urban liberal axis which seems to be gaining an ever-tighter control of Party machinery. Both groups of conservatives clearly see RR as a symbol of hope." The fact that his last couple of years in Sacramento had clearly been geared toward a future career on the national stage—one report by his advisors in February 1974 argued that "the Governor must look to the public as if he still cares about California"—demonstrates that Reagan's supporters thought that an antitax, antiwelfare program was the way to cement his political future.[29]

Making a "Minority-Urban Liberal Axis"

If the picture of legislative politics in California in the early 1970s was principally one of stalemate, what was happening to the Democratic left in electoral and local politics in these years? There are numerous studies that locate between about 1968 and 1972 a sudden and electorally disastrous concern on the part of national Democratic strategists with the youth vote and with minority interests that divorced the party from its blue collar base and rendered it a captive of culturally progressive but ultimately unpopular pressure groups.[30] In California this process was neither sudden nor as easy to categorize as these accounts suggest. The fluid, volunteer-driven nature of party politics in the Golden State rendered it receptive to new interest groups and the club movement had demonstrated how enthusiastic political neophytes could change the outlook and electoral prospects of a party in the course of just a few years, long before the McGovern-Fraser Commission pushed through changes at the national level.[31] So it was no surprise that the author in 1971 of *Changing Sources of Power*, the Democrats' alternative to Kevin Phillips's *The Emerging Republican Majority*, was Frederick G. Dutton, Pat Brown's right-hand man.[32] Nor was it surprising that Frontlash, an organization founded in 1968 to help encourage young voter registration and "to create effective alternatives to the confrontation politics of the New Left" by renewing "ties between the student community and those lower middle class and working class sectors in the population," established a permanent and well-organized staff and volunteer membership in California, one of six states to do so ahead of the 1970 midterm elections. Frontlash was in many respects a similar operation to CDC, the latter having faded from prominence by the end of the 1960s, as in addition to organizing registration and get-out-the vote activities it sought to "develop an understanding among students about national issues," those that had "great impact in the rest of society: inflation, unemployment, taxes, crime and violence, etc."[33] While it is true that Dutton's vision of a "Silent Generation" of liberal youths no more captured political reality in California than anywhere else, as George McGovern went down to landslide defeat in the 1972 presidential election, it is also true that a politics of cultural liberalism was gaining ever greater control over the electoral citadels of the Democratic Party in California's coastal cities in these years, with significant consequences for the future dynamics of state politics. Frontlash registered almost 100,000 people in working class and minority precincts in California in the 1970 campaign, and was widely credited with the five upset victories in the Assembly and two in the state senate that handed control of the state legislature back to the Democrats.[34]

The 1970 elections had also demonstrated the fluid nature of political affiliation in suburban areas. African American Democrat Wilson Riles unseated Max Rafferty as superintendent of education in 1970, and Riles carried San Mateo and most large counties to defeat Rafferty statewide by half a million votes. The Republicans that year also lost George Murphy's Senate seat by half a million votes, lost control of both houses of the state legislature, and saw Ronald Reagan's margin of victory cut drastically compared to that of four years earlier.[35] Much of that movement away from the right came in Bay Area counties like San Mateo. Even when his House district was shifted southward in 1972 by Phil Burton's reapportionment team to hand the most Democratic parts of the county near San Francisco to Burton man Leo Ryan, maverick liberal Republican congressman Pete McCloskey's new district, based around Stanford and the wealthy suburbs of Santa Clara county north of San Jose, was shifting leftward, giving a near victory to George McGovern in the 1972 presidential election. "This is one of the areas where the pull of the ecology movement has been strongest," noted Barone, Ujifusa, and Matthews. In the "hilly, affluent areas, and in the valley lands below, you cannot avoid seeing how fast the available land is being occupied. . . . It is the kind of place where one constantly sees 'Save the Bay' stickers," a protest against the perceived grasping pro-business policies of Reaganite Republicans.[36] It was also a district of predominantly young professionals concerned at the ever more outlandish outbursts of state GOP leaders. McCloskey came out, so to speak, in favor of gay rights early and publicly in the 1970s on the basis that "government should not intrude on the private behavior of individuals," and his stance never hurt him in the polls.[37]

The case studies that follow explain how long-term changes in the ideological outlook of Democratic politicians in the Bay Area and Los Angeles made the state party the driving force behind a politics of cultural diversity and interest group pluralism that had come to form the heart of Democratic politics nationally by the start of the twenty-first century.

The Respectable Face of Berkeley Liberalism: Ron Dellums Goes to Congress

When African American city councilman Ron Dellums decided in late 1969 that he would follow in the footsteps of Bob Scheer and challenge Jeffery Cohelan in the primary election in the Seventh Congressional District, he framed his attack on Cohelan's record in a way that placed the turmoil of California politics at the turn of the seventies in the context of a much longer tradition of political reinvention. Cohelan, he claimed, was "unresponsive to the needs of the community, to the issues of the Vietnam war, poverty and discrimination.... he has forgotten his roots."[38] It was this question of political roots, of the notion that Cohelan's whole claim to legitimacy sprang from the seismic shift in local politics in the 1950s, that allowed Dellums to circumvent criticism that he was merely a radical gadfly and instead to claim that he was fighting for the soul of a radicalized Democratic Party that Cohelan had forsaken. Dellums quickly gained the support not only of labor and civil rights activists like Cesar Chavez and Coretta Scott King but also of local elected Democrats who had come of age politically in the heady years of the 1950s, such as state senator Nick Petris of Alameda. Petris saw Dellums's candidacy as the obvious outgrowth of volunteer involvement in Democratic politics in California, whereby strongly politicized citizens could use the party as a vehicle for their ideological agenda. Dellums, Petris claimed, was worthy of support because he was "dedicated to achieving social progress through the electoral process rather than seeking it through violence."[39]

In many ways the 1970 campaign in Berkeley and Oakland was a product of its time, as the issues of African American radicalism, the Black Panther Party, the Vietnam War, and the legacy of the Great Society and the upheavals of the 1960s took center stage. Certainly the mainstream press was keen initially to dismiss Dellums as a poster boy for Black Power and militant racial separatism, features of the East Bay political landscape because Oakland was home to the Panthers and because leftist Panther sympathizers like Dellums had added a radical element to Berkeley City Council in 1967.[40] Readers of the *Berkeley Daily Gazette* in January 1970 found an account of Dellums's appearance at a symposium of elected African American officials in Oakland under the headline "Black Panthers Are Scapegoats of the 60s, Dellums Declares."[41] The race gained attention across the nation once it became clear that Dellums was on course to win, but most of the media coverage was unremittingly negative, furnishing readers with barely veiled racist accounts of arrayed masses of African American voters preparing to storm the citadels of Congress.[42] Dellums's primary campaign rhetoric certainly conformed in many respects to the stereotype of the angry radical impatient with the pace of reform in the 1960s. "The military-industrial complex maintains its position of power by perpetuating and exploiting racism for its own ends," claimed a Dellums campaign leaflet. "Unless we decide that human rights and human dignity outweigh property rights, historians may well be writing great novels about the rise and fall of America."[43]

The campaigns of 1970 in Berkeley saw the continuation of a process of affiliation between leftist activism and electoral politics in key districts in California that demonstrated the continued importance of ideology in shaping the dynamics of election campaigns. For one thing, Dellums's campaign was unashamedly of the left: he proposed a national health system, state-sponsored job creation, universal childcare provision, a 50 percent increase in Social Security payments, and opposition to the Vietnam War. "Ron understands the problems affecting us all—unemployment and inflation, discrimination against minorities and women, poorly-financed schools, deteriorating housing, exorbitant property taxes, an abused environment—and at their roots, an absurd war no one wants." His was an ideological position that linked the social democratic agenda of the 1950s on the West Coast with the antiproperty tax, antidiscrimination, pro-environment politics that had sprung from the sixties and remained popular across the Bay Area and across party lines. His campaign also stressed affinity with established Democratic leftist, antiwar politicians George Brown and Phil Burton. Two campaign flyers compared Cohelan's "expedient liberalism" with the worldviews of Brown and Burton, who were described as "courageous" for their refusal to support the Vietnam War and the repression of domestic dissent.[44] This link to established political figures was an attempt to cast Dellums as part of a long term development of progressive politics in California, and not just as a product of East Bay 1970s radicalism.

The primary campaign against Cohelan also reaffirmed the move of radical activists into mainstream party politics that Michael Harrington had proclaimed some three years earlier. "A United States Congressman from Berkeley," argued radical activist Dan Siegel, "while obviously unable to change the direction of the federal government substantially, can serve as a national spokesman for his community and for the movement throughout the nation, thus communicating the Berkeley experience everywhere. At the same time, he can act as a focal point for opposition to reactionary forces within his home district." Siegel was not sympathetic to the Democratic Party as an institution, which he felt was "reactionary and controlled by business interests," but it represented a useful vehicle for bringing together a coalition of interests that could elect a black radical to Congress. Black activists, in particular, were wary of minor party campaigns run by "the typical, ineffective activists of white idealists, with no great stakes in the outcome except moral purity."[45] To supporters of Dellums like Siegel, election campaigns were tools for bringing together a volunteer political base, a policy program, and an articulate candidate who could represent the left in office. This was an identical plan to that of CDC in its early days; only the actors and names had changed. It is true that politicians like Dellums were elected as individuals who pursued political support through links to nonparty grassroots organizations, such as Berkeley Citizens Action.[46] It is important, however, to examine Californian electoral politics through an ideological, as well as organizational, prism: while the state had always had weak party organizations whose importance ebbed and flowed according to circumstance, the development of an identifiable and evolving left-wing presence in electoral politics after World War II contributed to the careers of men like Dellums and Burton, who helped to shift the cultural zeitgeist of party politics in significant ways.

Importantly, once Dellums won the primary and headed into the general election in 1970, he caught the attention of numerous Democratic politicians outside California who wanted to harness his campaign to a broader effort to reform and radicalize mainstream politics. Oklahoma senator Fred Harris, who would enter the Democratic presidential primaries in 1972 and 1976 as a populist figure, became a major patron for Dellums in Washington during the fall of 1970. He welcomed Dellums and key members of his staff to the nation's capital in August, and a fundraising cocktail party exposed the young radical to big names in national Democratic politics, including George McGovern, Alan Cranston, and Coretta Scott King. Harris also helped secure funds for Dellums from the Democratic House Campaign Committee and from labor's Committee on Political Education (COPE).[47] Once Phil Burton had introduced Dellums to Harris, Harris's legislative assistant worked hard to make contacts for Dellums and to raise funds, writing his boss in late July that he felt "that this is one of the best contacts we have made. Ron is sharp and has a lot to offer by way of his contributions in Congress and to communities in general. I think this contact will prove very beneficial in the long run."[48] In October, Harris flew to California and held press conferences with Dellums and assemblyman Willie Brown of San Francisco, hopeful that his support for them would translate into reciprocal approval of his future presidential aspirations. In addition, the nurturing of African American candidates who had embraced the Democratic Party and eschewed the radical fringe provided Democratic strategists with a way of responding to very real racial tensions as they attempted to demonstrate that mainstream politics could represent a broad cross-section of society. "Virtually every national Democratic leader has voiced support for Ron Dellums," Harris stated on his return to Washington from the West Coast, "precisely because he has spoken out strongly against violence and for progress."[49]

Dellums's victory in November placed him at the center of the effort of the left-wing of the party to challenge the established power brokers in Congress and at the state level and reorient political debate around a more clearly defined ideological cleavage. Other Democratic candidates nationwide wanted Dellums to speak up for them, and by the mid-seventies presidential aspirants had to pay attention to California's delegation, now the largest in the nation and seen as a barometer of grassroots opinion on political issues. The *Pasadena Star-News* noted in 1975 that Fred Harris spent more time on the West Coast than anywhere else during his final stab at high office, addressing CDC and gaining political endorsements across the state: "It is not that he is all things to all people," the paper noted drily, "but he might be all things to these people."[50] Men like Dellums, who by 1973 had gained a seat on the House Armed Services Committee and was at the forefront, alongside numerous other House Democrats from California, of a drive to overturn the seniority system and push the House contingent out of the clutches of the party's Southern wing, demonstrated the growing importance of a volunteer tradition in Golden State politics that was having an effect on the national stage by the 1970s. "The overall goal," stated Los Angeles congressman Tom Rees, "is to establish Congress as a more positive function in our government." Even though "the plotters might lose, there exist some congressmen who actually would like to shake up this institution and pull it, yelling and protesting, into twentieth-century America."[51] Rees represented Jimmy Roosevelt's former district in Beverly Hills and the Westside, an area that differed enormously from Dellums's district in socioeconomic and racial terms but was similar in terms of its activist heritage.

Shaping the 1972 Election, California Style

The impact of California activism on national politics transcended the presidential campaigns of long-forgotten bit players like Harris: the 1972 McGovern effort had a similar relationship to Golden State politics as Adlai Stevenson's had in the 1950s. As in 1956, local organizers in California urged the 1972 hopeful to spell out a clearly articulated program in order to gain the attention of a new generation of young Californians searching for a route into active politics. In Bakersfield, local strategist Phil Baldwin informed McGovern in August 1971 that he was "sure that we can get hundreds of college and high school students out in May and June if you succeed in winning in Wisconsin or Nebraska or Oregon." A McGovern interview in *Playboy* was a big coup in the eyes of Californians like Baldwin, as it could form "one of the most effective means of winning the support of the young for this campaign. We need the young voters and we need the doorbell ringers!" Without a vibrant, established party organization, Central Valley cities like Bakersfield were clean slates in which an idealistic candidate like McGovern could thrive provided he established himself as a genuine leftist on the issues. Baldwin worried that McGovern's campaign literature was too anodyne and insufficiently policy-driven for a West Coast audience. "There should be a flyer that lists the *concrete* proposals of the Senator on: Civil Rights, Housing, Jobs, Migrant Agricultural Labor and Farm Worker Unions, the Draft, etc." Existing literature, Baldwin argued, was "disappointing, primarily because it lacks concrete proposals for change." Particularly important in the Central Valley was Chavez's UFW organization, which could provide additional ballast for the campaign but which had to be courted through specific policy commitments.[52] But the volunteer army that was coming together in late 1971 around McGovern also demanded a campaign that engaged with ideology in an obvious way, and became restless when the national organization was perceived as insensitive to grassroots interests.[53] Although the CDC had lost much of its earlier influence, there remained numerous local clubs that wielded considerable power over liberal politicians at least, if not over the electoral success of left-of-center candidates on the national stage. The Twenty-Sixth Congressional District in West Los Angeles, long home to a vibrant CDC club scene, in 1972 had no fewer than sixteen clubs, ranging from stalwarts such as the West Beverly Democratic Club and the Beverly Hills Democratic Club to newer additions the Women's Democratic Club of Beverly Hills and the FDR Young Democrats.[54] The vast majority of respondents to a questionnaire sent out to McGovern volunteers in California shortly before the election, asking them to document their experiences of the campaign for future reference, were in their twenties, and most responses highlighted the excitement of being part of a grassroots movement and their commitment to a political cause that had mobilized them. "Philosophically," one Mill Valley twenty-six-year-old wrote, "my participation renewed my hopes that the democratic process could be a viable expression of political concern."[55]

The importance of the middle class volunteer movement and the decline of organized labor as a force in the 1972 Democratic campaign both highlighted the fact that national politics was following a path blazed on the West Coast. California politics had long been media-driven, open to volunteer armies swayed by promises more than group loyalty, and subject to bitter factional difficulties that undermined what feeble party organization existed. The ambiguous role of labor in all this also signposted stormy times ahead for the liberal project as the last vestiges of the New Deal coalition fell apart. In the Bay Area, labor remained a powerful influence, providing strong support for the Burton brothers and their allies in San Francisco and for George Miller and Pete Stark, new liberal congressmen in the East Bay.[56] And statewide, the AFL-CIO exerted pressure on Democrats in the legislature grateful for funds and support at a challenging time for politicians of all stripes, as the anxious electorate became increasingly capricious and difficult to predict in election cycles in the 1970s. California labor rejoiced when Jerry Brown replaced Reagan in the governor's mansion in January 1975, soon observing that more "legislation of lasting significance to California workers was enacted during the 1975 session than at any time in the history of the state." This legislation included extension at last of collective bargaining rights to farm workers and public school employees, inclusion of farm workers in the state's unemployment insurance system, and raising of unemployment benefits.[57]

Yet labor's less than fulsome endorsement of McGovern in 1972 represented a rejection of the identity politics that dominated his campaign and had particular resonance in California, long home to a mix of traditional New Deal liberal politics and leftist radicalism.[58] Labor's rejection of McGovern suggested that the uneasy coalition of liberal interests that had transformed California politics in the 1950s and 1960s would not survive the 1970s, as the middle class left that had made California Democratic politics so distinctive seemed finally to have pushed the New Deal out of the picture entirely. "In the middle class, even many McGovern liberals were startled by the income-redistribution proposals," commented a piece in *Fortune* magazine in September 1972. "Suburbanites who take what are regarded as liberal attitudes on civil rights or disarmament are not necessarily interested in paying higher taxes to increase incomes for welfare recipients. Many middle class liberals, in fact, are among those screaming loudest against the taxes they now have to pay."[59] The *Wall Street Journal* noted in September that McGovern's biggest source of funds was "a new constituency of wealthy first-time contributors, some of them still in their twenties and thirties—an odd assortment that includes sons of millionaires, antiwar businessmen, civil rights activists and environmentalists."[60] In California this constituency was not new, and had been influencing liberal politics since at least World War II, but in 1972 the Golden State had come into line with national events, and at a time of growing economic crisis it was unclear how far the suburban liberals would retain the link to social inclusion that had given the Democratic Party such wide appeal in that window of opportunity in the early 1960s.

Still, many California activists were aware of the tensions developing in the liberal coalition, and did their best to resolve them. Frontlash established a sophisticated organization in San Francisco ahead of the McGovern campaign, bringing together local legislators, labor leaders, and youth organizers in a concerted effort to register poor and working class residents and persuade them to vote Democratic. California was well represented at a 1971 Frontlash conference in Washington, D.C., at which the keynote speakers were AFL-CIO COPE director Alexander Barkan and veteran gay civil rights leader Bayard Rustin, representing the twin agendas of the progressive movement in the second half of the twentieth century. Barkan praised the "civil rights, youth, labor coalition" for significantly clipping Nixon's coat tails in 1968 and 1970; Rustin commented that building "a coalition does not mean that we have to agree with each other on everything, and support all of each others' positions: it means working in our own interests, but working together to achieve the goals on which we can agree."[61] In San Francisco the effort was particularly noticeable. San Francisco Frontlash director Mike Grimes claimed to have registered over 21,000 people in the city. A coordinated effort by Frontlash, the San Francisco Federation of Teachers, and the City-wide Youth Council had registered over a thousand students at City College and another 1,400 at eight city high schools, using 300 volunteer deputy registrars.[62] Statewide, twenty operations added 63,000 young and low-income voters to the rolls between January and April 1972, and in Fresno Frontlash gained the assistance of a local radio station to stage a rock concert and add another 2,000 voters to the rolls in an afternoon.[63] The leaders of this registration drive were convinced their efforts would shake up the political landscape and bridge the divide between labor and cultural issues. "A new electoral constituency has been created in America," claimed a Frontlash memo in 1971. "Eleven and a half million young people between the ages of 18–21 are now eligible to vote. Over one million live in California. If young people vote in large numbers, and vote cohesively as a block, then some major changes could be forthcoming in American political life."[64]

This prediction turned out to be wildly optimistic. A 1971 poll published in *Life* found that 59 percent of Americans aged fifteen to twenty-one considered themselves "conservative or middle-of-the-road," 23 percent termed themselves "liberal," and a mere 5 percent used "radical." The *Life* article concluded: "People who expect a cataclysmic rejection of traditions, mores and institutions are in for a shock: the young wouldn't overturn society if they could. Most of them are much too satisfied with it as it is."[65] The landslide defeat of George McGovern in November 1972 seemed to underline the impotence of the left in American public life beyond a select coterie of minority interest groups. Nixon gained a majority over McGovern in California of over a million votes. Democrats could take some comfort in the fact that Nixon's 57 percent share of the vote was lower than in all but six small states plus the District of Columbia. Furthermore, Nixon had no coattails at all in California: Republicans had to content themselves with three newly created congressional districts, but the Democrats also gained three new seats and Phil Burton ensured everyone else was protected in their redrawn districts. Reagan would continue to face a Democratic legislature in 1973.[66] If we look at politics on the ground in liberal fiefdoms like San Francisco in the early 1970s, we find that efforts to come to terms with a range of interest groups from labor to gay rights groups were bearing fruit despite the setbacks Democrats were suffering on the national stage. The dramatic changes in San Francisco politics in the 1970s set the stage for the triumph of cultural liberalism over New Deal liberalism in the late twentieth-century Democratic Party, with all the attendant opportunities and pitfalls such a transformation presented.

"Left Coast City": Making Sense of San Francisco Politics in the Seventies

"Almost all the names have changed on the surface of the San Francisco political scene in the last generation," noted Russ Cone in the *San Francisco Examiner* in January 1977, "and the voting power now gushes from several new wells of ethnic, economic and community interests. . . . Big labor and big business now share political clout with vote-rich racial minorities, gays, organized senior citizens and city employees."[67] The task for the liberal wing of the city's political establishment, led by Phil Burton and Willie Brown, was to juggle the different demands of the various interests to stitch together a workable power base and to bridge the divide between economic and civil rights questions. Despite the fact that in terms of wider political clout the City by the Bay was rapidly losing out to Los Angeles in these years, it has received considerable scholarly attention, mainly because of the flamboyance and media-consciousness of its politicians and its importance as a microcosm of the social movements that have come to form the bedrock of the rights revolution of recent times.[68] Yet few studies place the city's politics in the 1970s into a wider state tradition of both economic and individual rights politics, and few emphasize the vital importance of the link between rights activism and mainstream electoral politics, often focusing instead on the tensions between elected politicians, established activists, and a new generation of political figures, such as Harvey Milk, impatient with the pace of change.[69] It is important to note the extent to which the rights discourse of San Francisco politics remained wedded to questions of economic rights in these years, even as the focus of city politics was shifting toward the inclusion of an ever growing number of interest groups and rival clubs and organizations that often drowned out the overarching progressive message. Both political allies of Phil Burton and journalists often noted the fact that the idea of a "Burton machine" in San Francisco was in fact simply a voluntary marriage of enough interests to create a powerful political force. "The reality is that labor consistently goes to the mat for [the Burton brothers] because Phil Burton has, for over a decade, been labor's most consistent and effective voice in the House of Representatives," wrote a journalist in 1982. "Similarly, the Burtons' support from the gay community has been won, not dictated."[70] The appeal of the Burton machine forces us to take seriously the legacy of liberal mainstream coalition-building in the 1960s and 1970s.

Politicians like the Burtons and Willie Brown joined activists like Del

Martin in articulating a language of rights that framed individual freedoms in economic, as well as cultural, terms. As early as 1968 San Francisco party politicians were openly courting the gay vote, but in a way that emphasized their place in a broader struggle for social inclusion. At a SIR candidates' night in October of that year, Brown announced that he would author a bill "which will give the homosexuals an equal opportunity to earn a living in employment," using the notion of economic rights as a "foot in the door" to encourage "further and more meaningful legislation."[71] Phil Burton used his increasingly powerful position in Congress—he became chair of the liberal Democratic Study Group in 1971—to attack the Nixon administration for its discriminatory provision of public services, including the denial of funds to the Los Angeles Gay Community Services Center. "The granting of HEW funds," he wrote Health, Education, and Welfare Secretary and fellow San Franciscan Caspar Weinberger in 1973, "should be based solely on need, and ability to respond to the problems of the community, and it seems to me that the programs of the [Center], especially through their drug and alcohol abuse programs, are addressing just such human needs."[72]

This political strategy dovetailed with the developing liberal agenda of feminist and gay campaigners in San Francisco. Rick Stokes and David Clayton, major figures in SIR and CRH in the early 1970s and part of the city's emerging gay political elite, deprecated the radical posturing of much of the gay liberation movement, but Clayton noted that he favored "a great deal more socialization than we have now. A basic industry that exploits our natural resources should not be allowed to do so for profit. Just being born in this country should entitle everyone to certain basic services. Everyone should be adequately nourished, have good medical care and inexpensive legal services."[73] Del Martin worked hard as representative of the Northern California chapter of NOW to lobby the state assembly in 1970 for an amendment to the California Fair Employment Practices Act to include the category of sex, framing her argument as a defense of the rights of women to economic security: "Contrary to popular belief, those who find themselves in the position of having to accept welfare are *not* doing so by choice, but are forced to because of arbitrary, unfair, and traditional discrimination against women in the job market. . . . The only 'protection' [women] seek is equal opportunity for gainful employment."[74] City politicians keen to use an avowed liberal program to challenge more conservative rivals in San Francisco's factionalized political world tapped into a discourse of social inclusion that bound them to activists like Clayton and Martin. Both

John Burton in his bid for the House and gubernatorial hopeful and city state senator George Moscone approached the crucial 1974 elections with the national issue of universal access to health care as their primary focus. Moscone campaign newsletters asserted that millions "today live with the fear of impending medical catastrophe or with the daily worry of continued medical expenses not covered by health insurance;" he had voted "to help improve the economic circumstances of the underprivileged," and had "fought hard to protect everyone's civil rights . . . introduced and fought hard for strong consumer protection . . . pushed to give women full legal and human rights, and provide a more equitable tax system." Burton linked the human rights struggle to the program of organized labor in the city, writing the secretary-treasurer of the San Francisco Labor Council that "we share a common cause for the development of an equitable national health insurance program. High quality medical care should be available to every American in need." To Willie Brown, keen to promote the Burton group in his own bid for power in the bitter contest for the speakership that year, claimed that "the main beneficiaries of [John Burton's] greatest legislative accomplishments have been the powerless and the dispossessed," aided by Burton's desire to "force government to respond to human needs."[75] Though it is true that this progressive coalition was not always successful—Moscone failed to win the party's gubernatorial nomination—and it is easy to dismiss the easy rhetorical flourishes of politicians, the fact that the language of economic rights provided the bridge between civil rights advocacy and electoral politics demonstrates the lasting legacy of left liberalism in shaping the distinctive contours of San Francisco political life in the 1970s.

What made this political culture significant far beyond San Francisco itself was the opportunity its left politicians provided for rights advocates to enter the legislative process and move from advocacy to policy formation, a key feature of California liberal politics since the late 1950s and one that had a major role to play in the passage of a statewide bill decriminalizing same-sex relations. During the six year battle to pass Willie Brown's bill, its supporters in Sacramento became increasingly attuned to the possibilities offered by grassroots activists to help shape legislative politics, a lesson that had been learned in struggles to enact and preserve enhanced welfare policies. John Burton had noticed George Raya after this young gay activist from Sacramento had campaigned to pass an antidiscrimination ordinance in Berkeley, following on from his formative education in the Sacramento Democratic Central Committee and chair of the Student Senate of Sacramento State University. Burton placed him on his staff on the Assembly Rules Committee, where he gained a rapid education in legislative procedure, before moving to San Francisco in 1973 to immerse himself in the burgeoning gay Democratic club movement there. In December 1974 he returned to Sacramento, and through his Burton contacts was taken under Willie Brown's wing to help work to get the sex bill through a still hesitant state legislature. Brown and Raya "prepared a list of known supporters and opponents. Working from that list, George visited the offices of uncommitted Assemblypersons, giving them a copy of the bill to read, explaining the bill to them, soliciting their support, and updating the tally sheet with their response. While George lobbied 37 Assembly offices, Willie worked the floor of the Assembly, gaining additional commitments."[76] Once they got the assembly votes, Brown and senate leader Moscone conspired in a bizarre caper to get the bill through the senate, sending Lt. Governor Mervyn Dymally out of state and getting senators to believe the bill would tie and not be able to pass, and thus persuading several to vote for it, before secretly flying Dymally back to Sacramento at the eleventh hour.[77] Brown tapped into a committed cadre of activists in Democratic clubs and lobbying groups such as the Friends Committee on Legislation to bring together legislative savvy and grassroots commitment to get socially inclusive bills into law. He then used this victory to press for further change that went beyond a mere revision of the penal code: bills to ban employment discrimination for gay men and women and initiatives to protect same-sex couples "in the area of tax rates, credit, housing, custody of children and in every other area of human interaction" placed individual rights at the center of legislative debate in a wide variety of ways.[78]

San Francisco formed the base for liberal political leadership in California because it was the site of a mushrooming of new club activity in the 1970s that continued the state tradition of using political affiliation as a social networking tool. "In my view," argued Bill Eger, director of the Fifth District CDC in San Francisco as he tried to keep the ramshackle club movement together in 1974, "political parties MUST function as the organization people use to gain control of their government FOR A CAUSE and not merely as an instrument to guarantee the continued employment of those presently in power. . . . I propose a party structure with its basic unit at a neighborhood level and its power invested in endorsement of candidates for office."[79] Although at a statewide level such a structure was becoming hard to achieve after the political upheavals of the previous decade, in San Francisco clubs like the Alice B. Toklas Democratic Club and the Susan B. Anthony Democratic Club did serve as significant centers of political activity during the seventies. By 1978 the Toklas club was able to raise over $10,000 for its political fund from a single banquet and a charity auction, and shoveled over $3,000 to a city slate of endorsed candidates, also providing over 300 voter registrars, doorbell ringers, and leaflet droppers. "Our main goal," wrote Toklas Chair Frank Fitch to the membership, "has been to work within the Democratic Party with special emphasis on monitoring and lobbying for justice, equality and personal freedom for all people."[80] Clubs like Alice Toklas demanded a commitment to social justice from candidates for office, as well as a specific endorsement of gay rights. It had "taken a major responsibility to educate gay people about Democratic politics and politicians about gay people," wrote Harvey Milk right-hand man and prominent activist Dick Pabitch in December 1977. But clubs had also espoused a program to involve "lesbians and gay men in the political process, to advance the rights of gay people, women, workers, and minorities; to protect the environment, and to strive for economic and social justice."[81] It was this link between economic and civil rights that had first bridged the divide between straight and queer politics in San Francisco in the 1960s, and which continued to shape liberal political activism.[82]

There was a price to be paid for the explosion in political activity in the Bay Area in the early 1970s. Rival groups and interests vying for political patronage inevitably encouraged the proliferation of competing voices and programs that undermined the notion of a united progressive coalition. Divisive, for instance, was gay activists' dominant concern with male sexuality, which by 1970 prompted CRH founder member and Daughter of Bilitis activist Del Martin to announce her disillusionment with the gay rights movement in the wake of that year's North American Conference of Homophile Organizations, a gathering that had, in Martin's words, "displayed vividly our divisions rather than our unity." The idea of a united family of gay organizations was, she argued, a sham: "Families usually include women, and they usually include youth—both of whom are integral parts of the homophile community, both of whom were ignored in the grand gesture of unity that closed the festivities. . . . Goodbye to the male chauvinists of the homophile movement who are so wrapped up in the 'cause' they espouse that they have lost sight of the people for whom the cause came into being."[83] This idea of homophile activism, at least in its early stages, as a middle class interest group uncommitted to broader movements of class, race, and gender dovetails with the argument that pressure for broader social acceptance eventually became pressure for freedom as consumers in a burgeoning world of bars and shops tailored to a gay market.[84] Indeed, Martin highlighted the fact that the battle for same-sex sexuality so easily slid into a defense of commercialized male sexual practices.[85] Following the abortive campaign of New York congresswoman Shirley Chisholm for the Democratic presidential nomination in 1972, Martin ruefully contended that gay rights had become "a 'males only' club concerned primarily with defending the toilet habits of those men who make themselves vulnerable to police entrapment" which had played down "the very real discrimination experienced by both female and male in jobs, education, government etc."[86]

The emergence of gay liberation in the wake of the Stonewall riots of 1969 further distanced the politics of sexual identity from the assimilationist rhetoric of mainstream politicians like Willie Brown. Identity politics in the early 1970s had little concrete to say about socioeconomic structures as radical activists struggled to make their voices heard amid a cacophony of rival groups and interests. In 1970, at the crest of a wave of gay liberation activity often associated with the tail-end of new left politics, a Berkeley homophile group was one of many gay rights groups that published SDS member Carl Wittman's article arguing that gay liberationists had not "yet figured out what kind of political/economic system is good for us as gays. Neither capitalist nor socialist countries have treated us as anything other than non grata so far."[87] A leaflet advertising a rally in San Francisco in June 1970 stated that gay liberation "does not care whether this society is capitalist or socialist or aboriginal—as long as men can love men, and women can love women, as openly, as sexually, and as proudly, as men and women can love each other."[88]

In a sense, the performative aspect of California liberal politics, in which people became attracted to politics as a social activity, encouraged activists to emphasize adherence to a radical style as much as to an actual policy program. One long-time gay rights campaigner in the wake of Stonewall found himself "defending the strategic value of law reform against frequent Gay Liberation views that reform is unlikely, worthless, and reactionary."[89] One lesbian activist arrived at "a confrontational meeting of Gay Liberation Front and the Women's Liberation" in 1971 to find GLF radicals defending "the male chauvinist, anti-homosexual bias" of Black Panthers because they were "oppressed, so they have the right to be as they are." Barbara Stephens declared herself appalled and "very skeptical on the future of the Gay Liberation Front.

There are too many divergences politically, and too much naivety about totalitarian organizations. . . . The New Left, frankly, is fucked up; their positions are scarcely different from the Minute Men or the Birch Society when they advocate racial separation, abolition of gun control laws, male chauvinism, sexual fascism, and champion Sirhan Sirhan as their great leader."[90] Stephens concluded her report to Del Martin and Phyllis Lyon with an attempt to drag the debate over sexual freedom back into an engagement with mainstream politics, stating that "regardless of whether we like or dislike the Democratic Party, we should actively support such good cats as Willie Brown, and John Miller of Berkeley."[91]

From the perspective of liberal politicians experimenting with a reconfiguration of the relationship between the individual and society it was inevitable that discussions of social marginalization in the 1950s and beyond would allow a widening of the left-of-center political lexicon that could be responsive to homophile activism. One of Harvey Milk's earliest successes as a leading gay activist in the Castro in 1973 was to help the Teamsters extend a boycott of Coors beer into gay bars, linking gay rights to economic issues and in a sense bringing San Francisco politics back to the image of labor's "Every Other House" broadcast in 1958 that had portrayed union members as part of a broader social fabric in their fight against right-to-work.[92] Yet the very success of gay and feminist activists in opening up avenues for entry to electoral politics in San Francisco encouraged factions and animosities to spring up, as in the bitter fight to succeed Milk on the Board of Supervisors after his tragic assassination. Del Martin, already smarting from the victory of Harry Brit over Milk aide Anne Kronenberg, hoped to see a new challenger in 1979, claiming that Britt's "emphasis on gay, gay, gay is not in context with the whole, and he is creating an anti-gay backlash. . . . Harvey understood that gays can't and didn't elect him, that you need to pull people together into coalitions."[93] Amid these divisions over identity and faction, it was sometimes difficult to tease out an overarching political ideology that could sustain activists in the face of big battles ahead in the Reagan era over corporate development and government cutbacks on the West Coast.[94]

Liberal Los Angeles Comes of Age

If San Francisco was the spiritual home of California liberalism in the 1970s, Los Angeles provided the population and a growing Democratic base to translate ideas into hard votes at the state and federal levels. The changing demographic landscape of the City of Angels had enabled a coalition of liberal Westsiders, Latinos, and African Americans to wrest the mayor's office from Sam Yorty in 1973, and the club movement in West Los Angeles had by the 1970s spawned a cohort of dynamic leaders, including Henry Waxman and Howard Berman, who would make a huge impact on legislative politics in both Sacramento and Washington. In addition, Beverly Hills and Hollywood had the cash and the commitment to liberal causes to make the region's power felt further north. Up until the late 1960s, Southern California had been viewed from the north as the brash country cousin, often conservative and uncouth, whose loud voice and claim on patronage for reasons of voting clout were outweighed by unreliability on the core issues and a tendency to display too openly the deep divisions in society on questions of race and class. By the 1970s, much had changed. If indeed these years were, in Willie Brown's words, "a giddy time for California Democrats," a time when they were "the glamor unit of national Democratic politics," Southern California residents were well-represented in their ranks, including Hollywood stars like Warren Beatty, Shirley MacLaine, and Jack Nicholson, as were the ranks of Westside club leaders who formed a crucial part of the rainbow coalition that had elected Tom Bradley mayor and begun the long process of making Los Angeles the focal point of a liberal Democratic majority in state politics.[95] Raphael Sonenshein's analysis of four key council districts that elected Bradley demonstrates that the wealthy whites in West Los Angeles who had formed the backbone of CDC organizing since the 1950s were the core white support for Bradley, and that a huge black vote and a growing poor Latino vote for reform had tipped the scales to make CDC liberalism a majority in city politics for the first time.[96]

In addition to the demographic changes that were rapidly eroding the powerbase of the city's white, protestant elite by the 1970s, the big shift in Los Angeles politics was the gradual spread of liberal activist success out of the Westside and into key gay, African American, and Latino districts across the city. This patchwork quilt of liberal electoral bases was by no means as clearly defined as in a compact city like San Francisco, but it did serve to extend the organizational knowhow of Westside clubs to new areas of the city, and to divorce many blue collar, ethnic minority districts from established channels of patronage. In 1969, gay activists won their first major electoral victory in Los Angeles with the defeat of incumbent city councilor Paul Lampart by a pro-gay rights candidate, Robert Stevenson. Los Angeles-based gay rights organization ONE zeroed in on the election as a test of the gay vote in a district that included Silver Lake and Echo Park, east of Hollywood, home to a growing gay population drawn to its increasingly diverse range of gay-friendly businesses. The involvement of ONE, and a high-profile article on the race in the *Advocate*, shone a media spotlight on the contest, and Stevenson's victory prompted ONE to claim that "this election was the first in American political history in which a formidable public official was defeated and that a homophile organization had taken a leading role in the campaign."[97] Similarly, Tom Bradley in the Tenth Council District—a mixture of white liberal neighborhoods in Jimmy Roosevelt's congressional district and upwardly mobile African Americans in areas like Baldwin Hills—had put together a coalition of Jewish CDC liberals and African Americans during the 1960s to challenge the Unruh machine in city politics and join the city council as a springboard to his drive to become mayor.[98] Their allies in the Bay Area, including the Burton brothers, redrew congressional and legislative district lines in Los Angeles in the early 1970s to allow people like Henry Waxman to join them in Congress and extend the reach of their left-liberal base to Southern California. "Though Waxman has been accused of building his own little political machine on the west side of Los Angeles," reported political scientists sizing up the newcomer in 1975, "it is certainly not a machine in the old sense, but rather a group of young politicos who can raise dollars and volunteers for each other. Thus in 1972, Waxman's friend Howard Berman was elected to the Assembly from a Hollywood Hills district that had never elected a Democrat before; the Waxman 'machine' had seen the lifestyle change there (from elderly WASP to hip young swingers) and ran their campaign accordingly."[99] Waxman, Berman, and Bradley had all been CDCers, but the difference in the early 1970s was their ability to move from grassroots advocacy to political power.[100]

By the mid-1970s, men and women who believed in the promotion of individual civil and economic rights through state action controlled Democratic Party politics in California. Their efforts to pass liberal legislation, to increase the electoral power of Democrats, and to give Californian liberalism a louder voice on the national stage served as a powerful counterweight to an assertive and self-confident right-wing that has formed such a dominant theme in recent historiography. Its long history of grassroots activism that lay outside the traditional New Deal political order made California ripe to take advantage of the plethora of emerging interest groups seeking to shape post-1960s politics, a politics deeply rooted in suburban and urban quality of life concerns that had formed the lifeblood of Democratic club activity in the Golden State for more than twenty years. As the coalitions of the New Deal era fragmented during the 1970s, California became not the outlier in American politics but the trailblazer for the economic and cultural wars of the late twentieth-century United States.

Epilogue: Liberal Politics in California in an "Era of Limits"

"In the age of anti-politics," said CBS Evening News anchor Walter Cronkite in a March 1976 interview with the governor of California, "Jerry Brown is the consummate anti-politician. He's impossible to classify—a mixture of liberalism, conservatism, populism, existentialism, Zen Buddhism, Puritanism."[1] Brown's policy legacy added to this image of the contradictory politician working in an era of contradictions and mixed messages. The late 1970s witnessed a blizzard of legislative activity in the state legislature, prompting the AFL-CIO to proclaim that more "legislation of lasting significance to California workers was enacted during the 1975 session than at any time in the history of the state."[2] Yet a developing public storm over high taxes, combined with an increasingly self-confident social conservative wing of the state GOP, suggested that Brown was right to refer to the years of his administration as part of an "era of limits" that would significantly circumscribe the expansion of the boundaries of California liberalism. Indeed, though Brown himself owed his election in 1974 to a coalition of traditional liberal forces in state politics, as lines at gas stations lengthened and simmering discontent over high taxes and prices became increasingly hard to ignore, he quickly sought to tap into this heightened public awareness of quality of life issues. "Life is tough, life is a struggle," he told Cronkite, in a somewhat downbeat, solemn tone that presaged Jimmy Carter's politically unfortunate comment to the American people later in the decade that dark times lay ahead, "and it's going to get tougher because we occupy a very special place in the world and the other countries are going to demand a greater share and that means our share is going to decline."[3] A study of two ballot initiatives of 1978, one that saw a victory for antitax conservatives and the other a startling defeat for the religious right, places this period of California history into a longer trajectory of the development of quality of life politics that bridged party affiliation and linked economic rights to individual civil rights. Neither right nor left could claim the final triumph in these battles, but the fortunes of the movements for and against Propositions 6 and 13 shed light on the long-term significance of the grassroots political currents that have been the central theme of this book.

Jerry Brown and the Politics of Managing Expectations

Perhaps the greatest frustration for left-leaning Democrats committed to the maintenance and extension of the welfare state liberal compact established during the Pat Brown years was that despite the difficult prevailing economic winds in the mid-1970s, they still held a considerable amount of political clout in Sacramento and in party circles in these years. To clinch the Democratic nomination for governor, Jerry Brown had to do a good deal of reaching out to labor and activist liberals in order to prevail over State Senator George Moscone, Assembly Speaker Bob Moretti, and Congressman Jerome Waldie, all on the labor-left side of the party. Brown's campaign for the nomination demonstrated the extent to which Democratic politics had become totally dominated by those whose ideological outlook was to the left of mainstream America, regardless of the factional position of individuals. His campaign literature focused on his support for Eugene McCarthy and the peace movement in 1968, and his answers to an ADA questionnaire on key issues attempted to place him firmly in the Burton-Willie Brown wing of the party. "I have always believed it is the responsibility of government to guarantee adequate health care to all citizens," he wrote, "regardless of economic status. Likewise, any civilized society must provide for those who cannot care for themselves—especially the children of those unable to provide for their families."[4] The *California Journal* remarked in February 1974 that darlings of the left like George Moscone had fared poorly in the Democratic race (Moscone had dropped out in January) because "he was unable to identify himself as the only fully credentialed liberal in the pack. He finished second to Brown in a preference poll taken last year by the Southern California Americans for Democratic Action. . . . Brown contends that he, not Waldie, is the most liberal candidate in the race, although he prefers to say that he has the most intense commitment to change."[5] He appealed especially to left CDCers in rapidly growing southern California, mindful of the fact that all his rivals, including more conservative San Francisco mayor Joseph Alioto, were from the Bay Area; Brown's convincing primary victory and narrow general election victory were both thanks to the voting clout of Los Angeles and its environs. "Just as Reagan had been voted in, over Jerry Brown's father, by a sweep in right-trending votes from southern California," declared a trio of political observers of the California election that year, "so Jerry Brown was voted in by a tide of left-trending votes in southern California."[6] Though distant from the Bay Area liberal mafia who tied their flag firmly to the mast of social democracy during the campaign, Brown secured labor support in the wake of his primary win after pledging "to sponsor and to sign liberal legislation benefiting working people and to appoint liberals to key state agencies."[7]

Once in office, Brown's first year witnessed the passage of some landmark bills to extend the reach of Democratic liberalism after the difficult eight years of Reagan. Public school employees got collective bargaining rights; farm workers gained unemployment insurance coverage; the maximum weekly insurance benefits were raised by $14, and the taxable wage base rate was increased from $4,200 to $7,000; employees' tips were protected by law from being skimmed off by employers. The jewel in the crown was the extension of collective bargaining rights to farm workers, a legislative feat only Hawaii had managed before 1975, and an achievement that had huge consequences for hundreds of thousands of rural laborers previously on the margins of economic citizenship.[8] The Agricultural Labor Relations Board finally brought farm labor under the protective umbrella of the New Deal arbitration system, with the attendant rewards and problems. As in the case of the NLRB, what in the late 1970s under Brown was a pro-labor board committed to rebalancing the economic relationship between grower and laborer became under later Republican governors a defender of the interests of farm owners.[9] Assembly Speaker Leo McCarthy remembered the early Brown years as a useful time for Democratic liberals: "Although [Brown] was a lone blithe spirit, [Laughter] he would work reasonably well with Democrats in the legislature, and he signed not all but most of our bills, particularly the ones that meant the most to the Democratic majorities in the state senate and the assembly at the time. So frankly, the years '75, '76, '77, '78 were, aside from the failure on property taxes, really pretty productive years, from a Democrat's point of view. We were able to enact laws that made a statement about what was important to us, and we were able to shape budgets for the most part that carried our priorities."[10] The California Assembly was a hotbed of faction and intrigue in these years, but despite the fact that there was no love lost between McCarthy and impatient liberals like Willie Brown, who vied for power through the 1970s, they were never divided on policy or overall political vision.[11]

Increasingly, however, California Democrats were caught between the twin tides of rising popular expectations about what government could do and of the inexorably rising cost of fulfilling them. Brown, the former seminarian always comfortable with frugality and ascetic values, grew concerned at the spendthrift ways of the legislature, especially as he already in 1976 had his eyes on the White House. When the Assembly voted unanimously in May 1976 to pass on a 6.4 percent cost of living adjustment to welfare recipients, Brown threatened a veto if his administration was not allowed to scale back the increase and pocket some of the funds for administrative purposes.[12] Even without the developing crisis over skyrocketing property taxes, Jerry Brown faced repeated run-ins with legislative Democrats over the cost of state government, compounded by his aloof, whimsical governing style at odds with the arcane, detail-oriented outlook of legislators. "The governor is the worst administrator ever to come down the pike," bemoaned Assembly Rules Committee Chairman Louis Papan (D-Daly City) in March 1978. A late 1977 combined gathering of a by now enfeebled ADA-CDC gave Brown a "C-minus," according to the *San Francisco Examiner*, which summarized the meeting's view as being "that Brown is bad, but Carter is worse."[13] As the tax rebellion gained momentum in 1978, Brown tried to straddle the issue, initially opposing Proposition 13 but assailing "a new class" of state bureaucrats as a self-perpetuating elite out of step with the straitened economic climate. The governor, "denying that he was acting like a recycled Ronald Reagan, renewed his call . . . for a limit on state and local spending, saying the bureaucracy must be shackled."[14] He not only jumped on the bandwagon of Proposition 13 once it has passed, but also championed the increasingly popular cause of a constitutional convention to amend the constitution to require balanced budgets, positioning himself as "both a populist crusader and a moral critic of politics-as-usual."[15] Observers could be forgiven for thinking that Brown's self-proclaimed status as master of ceremonies of an "era of limits" marked the end of the line for his father's conception of "government with a heart" that had driven Democratic politics and activism in the 1950s, 1960s, and early 1970s.

Propositions 6, 13, and the Rhetoric of Rights

Although Proposition 13 effectively crippled the tax raising powers of local government and put an end to the optimism that had surrounded California statecraft since the 1950s, it was in some senses a product of the failure of liberals to grapple with the problem of taxes as much as the success of the right in making government the problem in public debate. Brown's administration had been carefully building up a budget surplus while not giving any of it back to taxpayers, a decision that allowed popular resentment over taxes to build. One *LA Times* columnist argued that Brown was "more interested in enhancing his 'pro-business' image than in providing home owners and renters with tax relief or reform . . . Moreover, his four years of antigovernment rhetoric contributed to the disaffection with government that carried [Prop. 13] to victory and catapulted Howard Jarvis into the national limelight."[16]

The tax crusade had been building for a decade before Proposition 13, and legislators had had numerous opportunities to do something about it. Even Reagan had been unable to pass much in the way of tax relief, and his ill-fated Proposition 1 in 1973 crashed ignominiously to defeat after Democrats cleverly portrayed it as harmful to a broad constituency. Instead, state taxes per capita had risen 144 percent between 1966 and 1976, and Californians paid an average per capita of $964 to state coffers that year, more than in any other state except New York and Alaska.[17] The property tax, levied to fund county and local government, had become a particular point of contention. As property values rocketed in the 1970s, so did the county taxes levied on them, to the point where families of modest means who had bought their homes when prices were far lower were facing annual bills of thousands of dollars. Finally, in early 1978 the legislature was panicked by the campaign for tax reform into passing a bill to reduce property tax rates in inverse proportion to the increase in assessed valuations in order to stabilize the amount homeowners paid, but it was too late.[18] Howard Jarvis, curmudgeonly property speculator and bitter opponent of high taxes, was able to capitalize on the failure of elected politicians to address the growing tax crisis and easily got Proposition 13 on the ballot and then passed with two-thirds of the popular vote. At a stroke, 4.2 million Californians voted themselves a 57 percent cut in property taxes and, more significantly, a cap on future tax rates to 1 percent of the 1975–1976 assessed property valuation, with a requirement of a two-thirds majority to vote any future tax increase. Almost overnight the era of Pat Brown's massive expansion of the responsibilities of state government was brought to an end: Speaker McCarthy predicted the firing of 75,000 state employees, and San Francisco mayor George Moscone had to contend with a halved transit budget and massive cuts across the full range of services. "Tonight was a victory against money, the politicians, the government," barked

Jarvis after the resounding victory. "Government simply must be limited. Excessive taxation leads to either bankruptcy or dictatorship."[19]

This antigovernment, antitax rhetoric fitted neatly into a broader assault on liberalism that seemed to define the political zeitgeist of the late 1970s. Tax revolts were sweeping through state legislatures across the nation, and Republican politicians in particular were using the tax issue as a way of framing a bigger ideological message. "The taxpayer mutiny now rising across America is most of all a revolt against the nation's welfare mess," claimed U.S. representative Charles Thone (R-Neb.).[20] The *Congressional Quarterly*, always sensitive to the latest trends on Capitol Hill, ran a large article in its weekly report in August 1978 on conservatives in Congress, noting that in the 95th Congress "conservatives have developed a surprisingly quick allegiance to the principle of massive tax cuts, used Senate rules to block major legislation in an unprecedented way, traveled to Ohio to discuss unemployment with union officials, and become increasingly outspoken in their hostility to the leadership of the American business community." New York representative Jack Kemp and Delaware senator William Roth put forward their Kemp-Roth tax bill that year, a measure that would slash federal taxes by some 30 percent in three years in the hope that increased private sector spending would boost government revenues enough to bring the budget into balance. "Kemp-Roth has given Republicans a new argument, and a new style, and it's delightful," commented Indiana Republican senator Richard Lugar.[21] California had led the way with Proposition 13, as it had with Reagan's ill-fated Proposition 1 in 1973, emboldening fiscal conservatives nationwide to claim that popular opinion had called a halt to the liberal state that had shaped the post-World War II political landscape.

In many ways, however, the debate over tax reflected a quality of life discourse that defied easy ideological categorization, and demonstrated in California the extent to which issues of lifestyle and standard of living had become markers of political identity in the late twentieth century. Both liberals and conservatives increasingly saw taxation as a thorny issue that had to be tackled, but they differed as to the value of the state once the unfairness of the tax burden had been addressed. The right saw tax as in itself discriminatory and arbitrary; liberals worried that any tax relief should not come at the expense of programs that protected vulnerable citizens. Senator Edmund Muskie of Maine valiantly tried to appropriate the language of limited taxation for a new liberalism, arguing that the public knew that "government has a job to do, and they want it done well—with as little waste as possible, and with the maximum result." George McGovern agreed that government needed to be held accountable for the extent to which it provided value for money, but that "the fault for the heavy burden of unfair taxes rests not on liberal programs, but on needless war, a reckless arms race and an unjust tax system designed and continued by selfish special interests."[22] Welfare rights campaigners were forced to recognize the changed zeitgeist as the NWRO fizzled out in the mid-1970s: "The welfare reform issue was dying out," recalled Arkansas welfare rights leader Gloria Wilson. "It didn't have enough in it for most people. There were too many other issues, like tax reform, which Welfare Rights just didn't take in."[23]

In California, the argument that the burden of taxation was an issue that could not be avoided forever had been a staple of leftist candidates for a decade: Ron Dellums had attacked unfair property taxes in his early campaigns, and Assembly Democrats repeatedly attempted to rethink how taxation functioned, but never quite managed to work out a solution in time to head off the tax rebellion. Assemblyman John Foran (D-San Francisco) attempted in the mid-1970s to revise the state constitution to tax commercial and industrial property at a higher rate than residential property, but the two-thirds majority required in the Senate was too great. "It looked like the legislature was simply ignoring the plight of homeowners," recalled Speaker Leo McCarthy ruefully, "because no matter how many times we said it, we could never communicate that we'd really tried to tax homeowners at a lower rate. The very people now contributing to Proposition 13 had killed that effort. We tried to make all the arguments in early 1978, that Proposition 13 would be a major shift of authority from local government to the state, and that it would produce fiscal instability among many local governments. After Vietnam, Watergate, and our failure to provide homeowner tax relief, we were not trusted."[24] In McCarthy's view, Proposition 13 was not the victory of an unshackled right wing in California, but the failure of liberals to get in first with something better that relieved the burden of taxes on homeowners without completely stripping government of all power to raise taxes and to provide essential public services. He also contended that men like Howard Jarvis, who had stamped on increased commercial tax rates as harmful to their interests, had managed to capture the populist tone of the antitax debate while actually directing the benefits of lower taxes to the wealthy.

If we place the battle over Proposition 13 in the context of the fight that same year against Proposition 6, an initiative that would, if passed, have forced the state to fire all teachers who were gay or who promoted homosexuality, we see that in fact political struggles over economic rights and individual rights used the same rhetorical tools and often the same activist forces. To put it another way, although passage of Proposition 13 was a defeat for liberal forces and the failure of Proposition 6 a victory, the campaigns against 13 and 6 used the same political forces and the same set of ideas, placing civil rights in the context of an activist state that required fiscal freedom of maneuver in order to function. That gay rights activists, in particular, used social democratic language to frame their appeals for social equality reflected the fact that queer politics, as we have seen, appropriated the language of economic rights to gain a voice in mainstream politics. Their attempt to maintain this linkage through involvement in the fight against Proposition 13 shows how important economic issues remained as a point of reference for California liberalism. At the same time, the fact that a large majority of Californians bought Jarvis's argument—that government had become a swollen, interfering Leviathan that needed to be slain—suggested it would be hard to preserve individual rights and social equality as two sides of the same coin at the end of the century.

Key gay rights campaigners, including Harvey Milk, Harry Britt, Bill Kraus, and others saw Proposition 13 as a way of widening their base in a way that the campaign against Proposition 6 alone could not. "The campaign against Proposition 13," wrote Britt a few years later, "was our best chance yet to show other political constituencies in this town that we have something to contribute."[25] Gay Democratic clubs used the taxation issue to throw into relief questions of social justice that could be extended into the arena of sexual freedom. Even after Proposition 13's passage, gay activists used the fallout from the tax rebellion to fight those they felt were not leading from the front on issues of importance to the liberal left. Gay campaigners joined Assembly Speaker Leo McCarthy at a meeting of the Democratic State Central Committee in January 1979 in an attack on Governor Brown for his enthusiastic embrace of Proposition 13 once it had passed. McCarthy condemned Brown for cutting social programs in the wake of Proposition 13. After Brown's retort that the Democrats should "abandon the rhetoric of the 60s in the light of the realities of the 80s," Britt raised the symbol of the recently assassinated Harvey Milk as "a visionary who was well aware of the harsh realities but refused to allow them to hurt his vision." Milk, he argued, had fought Proposition 13 "with all his energy and would not have wanted us to cater to the mentality that produced it."[26] The Harvey Milk Club tapped into the network of Burton-led left forces to widen its remit and expand its influence in the wake of Propositions 6 and 13. The club "has become a leading force in San Francisco politics without compromising the vision of gay liberation and social justice that Harvey sketched for us," proclaimed the club newsletter in June 1982. "Like no other segment of the progressive coalition, Harvey Milk Gay is there with the troops in every battle called to further the agenda of the left—the Barbara Boxer campaign being only the most recent example."[27] The Human Rights Campaign Fund (HRCF), a major gay rights political action committee, channeled funds to candidates committed not only to civil rights for gay men and women but also to issues of economic justice. The HRCF was able to claim in 1982 that its candidates had prevailed in over 80 percent of cases, and that more than $600,000 had been spent to support representatives who, in addition to supporting gay rights, had been cosponsors of fair employment and fair housing legislation.[28] California gay Democratic Clubs formed an important part of the Ted Kennedy presidential campaign of 1979–1980, a campaign that combined appeals to economic liberalism and civil rights, and were keen to keep these twin agendas in the public arena during the Reagan years.[29]

Congressional district victories in 1982 occurred all over the state: Democrats supported by HRCF won in districts as diverse as the First Congressional District, running down the coast from the Oregon border, and the Thirtieth District in East Los Angeles, where the group had given Democrat Marty Martinez $5,000, access to advertisement space in the gay press, and Harvey Milk Club volunteers to distribute slate cards.[30] When Phil Burton faced his toughest election race in years in 1982 against liberal Republican Milton Marks, he enthusiastically agreed to take part in a debate with Marks in front of gay rights organizations. When Marks failed to show Burton released a statement regretting that Marks had not seen fit "to explain his positions in favor of the MX missile and the B-1 bomber and the Reagan tax program or to tell the gay community why he has accepted the support of long-time John Briggs ally H. L. Richardson or that of Interior Secretary James Watt and a number of giant oil and timber companies with a history of despoiling the environment."[31] Burton knew he could benefit politically if he tied the question of gay rights to the questions of economic and social justice that had defined his political career.

Yet Proposition 13 had passed, and Ronald Reagan carried California and the nation in a landslide victory over Jimmy Carter in 1980, giving considerable weight to Jerry Brown's admonition that the "realities of the 80s" would overpower the legislative muscle of the liberal coalition in the years ahead.

Successive state governments managed to paper over the cracks in service provision encouraged by the restrictive tax system bequeathed by Proposition 13, but those cracks gradually widened into unbridgeable chasms. "Middle-class Californians have long griped about paying more taxes than they might pay elsewhere, but for decades this state could boast that it gave them quite a bit in return," argued *LA Times* journalist Evan Halper in March 2009. "Now that contract is in doubt." The problem was not just taxes: a huge rise in the state's demand for prisons to hold an ever-increasing proportion of the population, and the burgeoning costs of Medi-Cal, the state's public health care provider, added crippling burdens to the budget. However, the need for a two-thirds majority in the legislature to fund tax increases and a general reluctance to deal with the political consequences of searching for innovative ways of increasing revenue were taking their toll. In 1975, about 17 percent of the state budget went to higher education; in 2009, under 11 percent was earmarked for that purpose, as costly new burdens crowded the budget with no new taxes to compensate. "Twenty years ago, you could go to Texas, where they had very low taxes, and you would see the difference between there and California," argued Joel Kotkin of Chapman University. "Today, you go to Texas, the roads are no worse, the public schools are not great but better than or equal to ours, and their universities are good."[32] California's rights culture remains as vibrant as ever, but the ability of liberal activists to match their rhetorical power with access to tax dollars for public programs declined in the waning years of the twentieth century, even before the economic collapse of 2008.

Nevertheless, the legacy of the massive changes in California's—and the nation's—political culture since the 1950s continues to resonate. The Golden State came to understand and engage with liberalism in an organized, election-winning way relatively late, at a time when questions of economic prosperity, technological advance, environmental protection, racial and sexual equality, and social diversity were already complicating the political program sketched out during the New Deal. There were no party machines or political bosses to deliver victories for liberalism, and no consistent section of society, such as labor, willing by default to tie its flag to the mast of a party unalterably committed to economic and social justice. Instead, liberal activists in the 1950s framed issues such as Cold War foreign policy, racial justice, fears of nuclear holocaust, among others, as discussion points in political meetings that operated as a form of social networking for people searching for belonging in neighborhoods in which few had been resident for long. Club members then got lucky in finding common cause with organized labor over the question of right-to-work in an already strongly Democratic year. Yet even the labor issue was related to questions of prosperity and the rights of union members to share in the fruits of economic growth and welfare capitalism, issues that united different sections of California society. Both club and labor politics also intersected with complex racial and class dynamics in cities like Los Angeles, and struggles for racial justice in housing and jobs set the stage for the explosion of the rights revolution during and after the 1960s. California did not fit into the standard narrative of a New Deal order betrayed by the upheavals of the New Politics battles of the 1960s and 1970s: Democratic liberalism in the Golden State was forged in the crucible of attempts to force electoral politics to represent the diverse mosaic of society well before the McGovern Commission placed such questions on the national agenda in 1972.[33]

In effect, California was ahead of its time in predicting trends that would come to define more obviously the political climate elsewhere in the nation by the late twentieth century. By the twenty-first century California was the national lynchpin of Democratic votes and of Democratic policy concerns in areas of individual rights and economic justice. It demonstrated how a cross-class alliance could bring together questions of economic and civil rights to provide a motor for a wide range of legislative action in the realms of infrastructure development, welfare state building, education, and civil rights, making it an exemplar of the social compact between capital and social policy that defined many industrialized democracies in the post-World War II era. Politicians and state employees reshaped the California welfare system, established fair employment and antidiscrimination ordinances, expanded the state higher education infrastructure, and built roads, water projects, and other public works. Though this frenzy of legislative activity was relatively short-lived, it had its roots in a strain of progressive politics that took shape in the 1940s and 1950s out of the remnants of both the popular front and the Warren governorship, and its legacy outlived the Pat Brown era as a monument to the ambition of government reform in the early 1960s. Many industrialized democracies between 1945 and 1970 greatly enlarged their social safety net and expended public funds on major infrastructure projects, guided by ideological and programmatic concerns, and my effort to place California into this interpretive framework helps to complicate the picture of the United States as somehow outside or separate from this wider international dynamic.

California also illustrated how the success of rights liberalism in placing questions of social justice on the table roused considerable opposition that would come to define the battle lines between left and right in the United States on questions of race, sexuality, and quality of life issues. The growth of a revitalized right wing in California in the 1960s and 1970s, far from suggesting the inherent fragility of liberalism, was in many senses testimony to the ability of liberal politics to bring about considerable social change in a relatively short space of time, change so dramatic that it sparked visceral opposition from many residents alarmed at the rapid pace of events in these years. Historians have focused often on the deep racial and social fissures in California society that make it difficult to speak of politics in simple left-right terms, as an array of racially diverse and gendered interest groups battled for legitimacy in an era of massive demographic and economic change.[34] Yet if we examine state policymaking on questions of fair employment, economic justice, sexual equality, and public spending between the early 1950s and 1970s, we find that the socioeconomic landscape of California changed dramatically in these decades, prompting a politics of backlash that placed at its core the notion that the West Coast of the early twentieth century had been lost in a tidal wave of social rights.

Underlying the political turmoil that defined these decades between 1945 and 1980 was the fact that California was wealthy, prompting Pat Brown's statement in 1958 that California had a duty to provide public services to its citizens because it could afford it. Twenty years later, skyrocketing local taxation and a weakening economy prompted politicians in both parties to call for an end to big government and the public recognition of a new "era of limits" that would drop the curtain on the dizzying decades of rapid expansion of civil and economic rights. Although many of the civil rights advances brought about by the rise to power of liberal politicians in the 1950s and 1960s remain at least partly in place, the extent to which the question of economic justice, that for a time underpinned those civil rights, can be rejuvenated in an era of limits seems an open question.

NOTES

Introduction: Placing California in Post-World War II American Politics

1. Cricket Levering memo to club legislative chairs, 49th Assembly district, 29 April 1959, Steven Zetterberg MSS, California State Archives, Box 2, CDC 1959–60 file.

2. See Clemens Haeusler, "The Transatlantic Exchanges Between American Liberals, British Labourites, and German Social Democrats from the Mid-1950s to the Mid-1970s," Ph.D. dissertation, University of Cambridge, 2010.

3. See Everett Carll Ladd and Charles D. Hadley, *Transformations of the American Party System: Political Coalitions from the New Deal to the 1970s* (New York, 1975), 93–111.

4. See Jennifer A. Delton, *Making Minnesota Liberal: Civil Rights and the Transformation of the Democratic Party* (Minneapolis, 2002). Important California Democrats of the last forty years include Phil and John Burton, Pat Brown, Tony Coelho, Leon Panetta, Dianne Feinstein, Barbara Boxer, Henry Waxman, and Nancy Pelosi.

5. California does not fit neatly into David Plotke's "building a Democratic order" thesis that focuses on the 1930s and 1940s: Plotke, *Building a Democratic Political Order: Reshaping American Liberalism in the 1930s and 1940s* (Cambridge, 1996).

6. For discussions of gay rights politics, see John D'Emilio, "Gay Politics, Gay Community: San Francisco's Experience," *Socialist Review* 55 (1981): 77–104, and his *Sexual Politics, Sexual Communities: The Making of a Homosexual Minority in the United States, 1940–1970* (Chicago, 1983); Susan Stryker and Jim Van Buskirk, *Gay by the Bay: A History of Queer Culture in the San Francisco Bay Area* (San Francisco, 1996); Nan Alamilla Boyd, *Wide Open Town: A History of Queer San Francisco to 1965* (Berkeley, 2003); Martin Meeker, *Contacts Desired: Gay and Lesbian Communications and Community, 1940s–1970s* (Chicago, 2005). For good discussions of welfare rights politics, see Premilla Nadasen, *Welfare Warriors: The Welfare Rights Movement in the United States* (New York, 2005); Felicia Kornbluh, *The Battle for Welfare Rights: Politics and Poverty in Modern America* (Philadelphia, 2007). My work brings together these histories by looking at ways in which welfare rights and civil rights intersected in electoral and legislative politics.

7. See Lisa McGirr, *Suburban Warriors: The Origins of the New American Right* (Princeton: 2001); Kurt Schuparra, *Triumph of the Right: The Rise of the California Conservative Movement, 1945–1966* (New York, 1998); Bruce J. Schulman and Julian Zelizer,

eds., *Rightward Bound: Making America Conservative in the 1970s* (Cambridge, Mass., 2008).

8. McGirr, *Suburban Warriors*, 271. An interesting treatment of the ambiguities of suburban politics is Matthew Lassiter, *The Silent Majority: Suburban Politics in the Sunbelt South* (Princeton, 2006). See also Kevin M. Kruse and Thomas J. Sugrue, eds., *The New Suburban History* (Chicago, 2006).

9. See Elizabeth Tandy Shermer, "Origins of the Conservative Ascendancy: Barry Goldwater's Early Senate Career and the De-Legitimization of Organized Labor," *Journal of American History* 95, 3 (December 2008): 678–709; Thomas W. Evans, *The Education of Ronald Reagan: The General Electric Years and the Untold Story of His Conversion to Conservatism* (New York, 2006); Elizabeth Tandy Shermer, "Counter-Organizing the Sunbelt: Right-to-Work Campaigns and Anti-Union Conservatism, 1943–1958," *Pacific Historical Review* 78 (February 2009): 81–119.

10. See Risa L. Goluboff, *The Lost Promise of Civil Rights* (Cambridge, Mass., 2007); Robert Rodgers Korstad, *Civil Rights Unionism: Tobacco Workers and the Struggle for Democracy in the Mid-Twentieth-Century South* (Chapel Hill, 2007); Thomas J. Sugrue, *Sweet Land of Liberty: The Forgotten Struggle for Civil Rights in the North* (New York, 2009).

11. Donald T. Critchlow, *Phyllis Schlafly and Grassroots Conservatism: A Woman's Crusade* (Princeton, 2005), 7.

Chapter 1. Politics and Party in California at Mid-Century

1. See U.S. Department of Commerce, *Statistical Abstracts of the United States*, 78th annual ed. (Washington, 1957), 30, table 27.

2. John Aubrey Douglass, "Earl Warren's New Deal: Economic Transition, Public Planning, and Higher Education in California," *Journal of Policy History* 12, 4 (2000): 473ff.

3. See Daniel Hurewitz, *Bohemian Los Angeles and the Making of Modern Politics* (Berkeley, 2007); Robert O. Self, *American Babylon: Race and the Struggle for Postwar Oakland* (Princeton: 2003); Fraser M. Ottanelli, *The Communist Party of the United States from the Depression to World War Two* (New Brunswick, 1991), 118–19; Harvey Klehr, *The Heyday of American Communism: The Depression Decade* (New York, 1984), esp. 173–76.

4. Douglass, "Earl Warren's New Deal," 473.

5. Political scientists such as David Mayhew and James Q. Wilson have described this phenomenon, leading Mayhew to go so far as to assert that there is "no point dwelling" on California's political system insofar as it is "the last place anybody would look to find traditional party organizations." See David R. Mayhew, *Placing Parties in American Politics: Organization, Electoral Settings, and Government Activity in the Twentieth Century* (Princeton: 1986), 185; also James Q. Wilson, *The Amateur Democrat: Club Politics in Three Cities* (Chicago, 1966): 96–109; John R. Owens, Edmond Constantini, and Louis F. Weschler, *California Politics and Parties* (Toronto, 1970).

6. See Hurewitz, *Bohemian Los Angeles*; Self, *American Babylon*.

7. See Ellen Reese, *Backlash Against Welfare Mothers: Past and Present* (Berkeley, 2005), chap. 6, esp. 87.

8. See Currin V. Shields, "A Note on Party Organization: The Democrats in California," *Western Political Quarterly* 7, 4 (December 1954): 673–83.

9. Anthony S. Chen, "'The Hitlerian Rule of Quotas': Racial Conservatism and the Politics of Fair Employment Legislation in New York State, 1941–1945," *Journal of American History* 92, 4 (March 2006): 1238–64. Although Chen situates his argument in the context of the opposition to FEPC in wartime New York, setting the scene for later anti-affirmative action campaigns, Gary Gerstle, in his commentary on Chen's work, makes the key point that "the opposition to civil rights failed to defeat" the state's FEPC law. Gerstle, "The Crucial Decade: The 1940s and Beyond," *Journal of American History* 92, 4 (March 2006): 1292–99, esp. 1297. The very different political situation in California meant there was no serious debate over fair employment legislation until the late 1950s.

10. Harry W. Flannery, "I Blame Cross-Filing: California Has Enough Confusion Without Republicans Running as Democrats and Vice Versa," *Commonweal*, 30 June 1950, James Roosevelt MSS, FDR Library, Box 209, Commonwealth Club file.

11. Roosevelt flyer, "This Is the 26th District—The 'Leftovers' the Republicans Didn't Want!" James Roosevelt MSS, Box 329, 1959 elections file.

12. Whitaker and Baxter editorial box score, 1958 Senatorial election, Whitaker and Baxter MSS, California State Archive, Box 49, file 11. Whitaker and Baxter was a major public relations firm employed by many Republican candidates to manage campaign publicity.

13. Patrick McDonough to George Outland, 22 July 1947, McDonough MSS, Box 1, outgoing letters 1946–47 file.

14. Roosevelt speech to Associated District Newspapers, 9 January 1950, Roosevelt MSS, Box 240, "Freedom to Suppress" speech file.

15. Advertisement, "My Senate Campaign, by Helen Gahagan Douglas," Helen Douglas MSS, Carl Albert Center, University of Oklahoma, Box 172, folder 5.

16. See "Kuchel Democratic Drive Stirs Conflicting Claims," *LA Times*, 28 May 1954, and Yorty's advertisement, "An Open Letter to Tommy [Kuchel]," *LA Times*, 4 June 1954, in Whitaker and Baxter MSS, Box 29, candidates for other offices file.

17. William Murray Hill to Stevenson for President HQ, 8 September 1952, Adlai Stevenson MSS, Princeton University, Box 235, folder 10.

18. "Republicans Given Warning by Levering," *LA Times*, 2 June 1954.

19. Prologue to Earl Warren, *The Memoirs of Earl Warren* (Garden City, 1977), xi.

20. Oral history interview with A. Alan Post by Donald B. Seney, California State Archives Oral History Program, 2002, 231–32.

21. Warren, *The Memoirs of Earl Warren*, 31. See also G. Edward White, *Earl Warren: A Public Life* (New York, 1982): chaps. 1, 2.

22. White, *Earl Warren*, chap. 2.

23. Douglass, "Earl Warren's New Deal," 478.

24. Ibid., 499.

25. Warren, *The Memoirs of Earl Warren*, 187–88. For detailed analysis of the successful AMA campaigns against federal health insurance see Alan Derickson, *Health Security for All: Dreams of Universal Health Care in America* (Baltimore, 2005); Colin Gordon, *Dead on Arrival: The Politics of Health Care in Twentieth-Century America* (Princeton, 2003); Jonathan Bell, *The Liberal State on Trial: The Cold War and American Politics in the Truman Years* (New York, 2004).

26. "Warren, the Myth and the Record," *New Republic*, 23 June 1952, 11–13.

27. Boulware, "Proposed Program of Industrial and Community Relations," 1 August 1945, quoted in Kimberly Phillips-Fein, "American Counterrevolutionary: Lemuel Ricketts Boulware and General Electric, 1950–1960," in Nelson Lichtenstein, ed., *American Capitalism: Social Thought and Political Economy in the Twentieth Century* (Philadelphia, 2006), 254. See also Elizabeth Fones-Wolf, *Selling Free Enterprise: The Business Assault on Labor and Liberalism, 1945–60* (Urbana, 1994).

28. Helen Douglas, "The House Jack Can't Build," speech before the National Association of Housing Officials, Santa Barbara, 18 September 1947, Harold Ickes MSS, Box 55, Helen Douglas file.

29. Richard Donovan, "The Great Los Angeles Public Housing Mystery," *The Reporter*, 4 March 1952, Stevenson MSS, Box 230, folder 5.

30. Robert E. G. Harris to David Bell, 21 August 1952, Stevenson MSS, Box 230, folder 5.

31. See Richard Nixon to Joseph Martin, Richard Nixon MSS, Richard Nixon Library, Yorba Linda, PPS1.21.

32. Leaflet, "What Does Nixon Stand For?" William Knowland MSS, Bancroft Library, UC Berkeley, Box 87, campaign material file 2.

33. Nixon campaign form letter, 21 October 1946, Nixon Library (RNyl), PPS1.206a.

34. Covina Republican Club statement of endorsement of Nixon, 1946, undated, RNyl, PPS1.219.

35. "Communist Infiltration in the United States, Its Nature, and How to Combat It," U.S. Chamber of Commerce, 1946, James Roosevelt MSS, Box 188, communist infiltration file.

36. See Bell, *The Liberal State on Trial*; Alan Derickson, "The House of Falk: The Paranoid Style in American Health Politics," *American Journal of Public Health* 87, 11 (1997): 1836–43; Meg Jacobs, "'How About Some Meat?' The Office of Price Administration, Consumption Politics, and State-Building from the Bottom Up, 1941–1946," *Journal of American History* 84, 3 (December 1997): 910–41.

37. For a stimulating discussion of state-level anti-communist activity, see M. J. Heale, *McCarthy's Americans: Red Scare Politics in State and Nation, 1935–1965* (Athens, 1998).

38. Helen Douglas to Harold Ickes, 31 October 1946, Ickes MSS, Library of Congress, Box 55, Helen Gahagan Douglas file.

39. Carmen Warschaw, "A Southern California Perspective on Democratic Party Politics," Bancroft Regional Oral History Project (1983), 120ff.

40. The Democratic National Committee refused to give Condon funding in 1954. See Stephen Mitchell to California National Committeeman Paul Ziffren, 2 April 1954; attack on Mitchell by Ernest Sells in a letter to Adlai Stevenson, 6 April 1954, Adlai Stevenson MSS, Box 69, folder 3.

41. Jane Dick, Stevenson campaign coordinator, memo, 25 January 1956, Stevenson MSS, Box 303, file 6.

42. Betty Dockham to Jane Dick re Stevenson campaign, 4 April 1956, Stevenson MSS, Box 303, file 7.

43. Gifford Phillips, "The Problem: Organized Confusion," *Frontier*, October 1955.

44. Currin V. Shields, "A Note on Party Organization," 674.

45. Stanley Crook to James Loeb, 31 July 1950, ADA MSS, microfilm, Cambridge University Library, reel 57, no. 5.

46. Roger Kent, "Building the Democratic party in California, 1954–1966," Bancroft Regional Oral History Office (1981): 19.

47. Hurewitz, *Bohemian Los Angeles*, 218ff for the argument that radical leftist politics provided much of the dynamism behind the struggle for racial equality in the city in this period.

48. USW resolution in *San Francisco News*, nd, 1947; "Left-Wing Group Keeps Control of State CIO," *SF News*, 27 November 1947, ADA MSS, reel 31, no. 38.

49. CIO press release, 5 March 1948, ADA MSS, reel 31, no. 38. The debilitating impact of the anticommunist politics of the postwar period on unions is analyzed in an extensive secondary literature, including Nelson Lichtenstein, *Walter Reuther: The Most Dangerous Man in Detroit* (Urbana, 1995); Lichtenstein, *State of the Union: A Century of American Labor* (Princeton, 2002); Robert W. Cherny, William Issel, Kieran Walsh Taylor, ed., *American Labor and the Cold War: Grassroots Politics and Postwar Political Culture* (New Brunswick, 2004); Kevin Boyle, *The UAW and the Heyday of American Liberalism* (Ithaca, 1995).

50. For membership details, see Philip Taft, *Labor Politics American Style: The California State Federation of Labor* (Cambridge, Mass., 1968).

51. Address by Joseph Keenan to the pre-primary convention, CLLPE, 17 April 1950, California Labor League for Political Education/COPE MSS, California State University Labor Archives and Research Center, San Francisco, Box 7, folder 4. For the impact of anticommunism on Fair Deal politics see Bell, *The Liberal State on Trial*, chap. 6; Bell, "Conceptualising Southern Liberalism: Ideology and the 1950 Pepper-Smathers Election in Florida," *Journal of American Studies* 37, 1 (March 2003): 17–45.

52. Douglas address to California League for Political Education, 17 April 1950, CLLPE/COPE MSS, Box 4, folder 7, 96–97. For a good discussion of the politics of the Democratic-labor alliance, see David Plotke, *Building a Democratic Political Order: Reshaping American Liberalism in the 1930s and 1940s* (Cambridge, 1996). For the classic account of the decline of labor's political muscle in the 1940s as it came to terms with the

power of management in the postwar years, see Nelson Lichtenstein, "From Corporatism to Collective Bargaining: Organized Labor and the Eclipse of Social Democracy in the Postwar Era," in Steve Fraser and Gary Gerstle, eds., *The Rise and Fall of the New Deal Order, 1930–1980* (Princeton, 1989), 122–52.

53. 17 April 1950 proceedings of the CLLPE, 63–65.

54. See Ethan Rarick, *California Rising: The Life and Times of Pat Brown* (Berkeley, 2005), 60–65.

55. Hope Mendoza Schechter, "Activist in the Labor Movement, the Democratic Party, and the Mexican American Community," interview by Malca Schall, 1977–1978, Women in Politics Oral History Project, Bancroft Library, University of California, Berkeley, 42–46.

56. See proceeding of the 1952 preprimary convention of the CLLPE, 7 April 1952, 65–76, these 11 pages of the transcript report a debate over whether to endorse liberal Republican Milton Marks for State Assembly as well as his Democratic opponent, an act that would require a change to the endorsement rules. In the end, only the Democrat was endorsed, though numerous incumbent Republicans still gained AFL endorsement in 1952.

57. Ibid., 105, 114–16.

58. Quoted in Paul S. Taylor, "California Farm Labor: A Review," *Agricultural History*, 42, 1 (January 1968): 49–54.

59. See Don Mitchell, *The Lie of the Land: Migrant Workers and the California Landscape* (Minneapolis, 1996), 59; Ernesto Galarza, *Farm Workers and Agribusiness in California, 1947–1960* (Notre Dame, 1977), 35.

60. Mitchell, *The Lie of the Land*, 45.

61. See Cletus E. Daniel, "Radicals on the Farm in California," *Agricultural History* 49, 4 (October 1975): 629–46.

62. Galarza, *Farm Workers and Agribusiness in California*, 27, 35.

63. See J. Craig Jenkins, *The Politics of Insurgency: The Farm Worker Movement in the 1960s* (New York, 1985), chap. 4.

64. Galarza, *Farm Workers and Agribusiness*, 79.

65. Jenkins, *The Politics of Insurgency*, 99–100.

66. Ibid., 109; Galarza, *Farm Workers and Agribusiness*, 162. In 1951 the Teamsters pulled out of supporting a strike in the Imperial Valley because of their desire to head off an anti-secondary boycott bill in the State Legislature.

Chapter 2. Building the Democratic Party in the 1940s

1. See *Statistics of the Presidential and Congressional Election of 7 November 1944* (Washington, 1945); 1946 statistical analysis by Murray Chotiner and Associates, Knowland MSS, Box 86, folder 1.

2. For the Alameda case, see Francis Dunn, Assemblyman, 13th District, to Patrick McDonough, congressional candidate, 7th District in Alameda, 8 October 1945, McDonough MSS, Bancroft Library, Box 1, Democratic Party County Central Committees file.

3. McDonough to Edward Heller, 20 January 1947, McDonough MSS, Box 1, outgoing letters 1946–1947 file.

4. See minutes of the ICCASP campaign committee, Hollywood branch, 30 January 1946, James Roosevelt MSS, Box 192, ICCASP C file; Malcolm Hash, Roosevelt's secretary, to Lela Bullock, 4 April 1946 on Patterson endorsement, ibid., B file.

5. Roosevelt to Howard McGrath, 29 October 1947, Roosevelt MSS, Box 196, McGrath file.

6. Statement of policy of the California Democratic Party, 1947, Roosevelt MSS, Box 189, Democratic State Central Committee file.

7. McDonough to Mrs. F. Hayball, 29 July 1947, McDonough MSS, Box 1, outgoing letters 1946–47 file.

8. McDonough to Outland, copied to James Roosevelt and Democratic grandees Bill Malone, Ed Heller, John McEnery, 22 July 1947, McDonough MSS.

9. McDonough to Roosevelt, copied to Bill Malone and John McEnery, 20 February 1947, McDonough MSS.

10. Outland to McDonough, 2, 29 July 1947, McDonough MSS.

11. See Wallace, "Why I Choose to Run," *New Republic*, 5 January 1948, 5–10. For in-depth discussions of the political turmoil on the left as a consequence of the Wallace candidacy, see Mary Sperling McAuliffe, *Crisis on the Left: Cold War Politics and American Liberals* (Amherst, 1978); Steven Gillon, *Politics and Vision: The ADA and American Liberalism* (New York, 1987); John Culver and John Hyde, *American Dreamer: The Life and Times of Henry A. Wallace* (New York, 2000); Graham White, *Henry A. Wallace: His Search for a New World Order* (Chapel Hill, 1995).

12. Roma Burnett Bishop to Roosevelt, 3 July 1947, McDonough MSS, Roma Burnett Bishop file.

13. McDonough to Gail Sullivan, Democratic Party headquarters, Washington, 8 January 1948, McDonough MSS, outgoing letters 1948 file.

14. McDonough to J. Howard McGrath, 28 June 1948; McDonough to Roosevelt, 16 April 1948, McDonough MSS, ibid.

15. McDonough to I. Riggs, 1 March 1948; McDonough to Kenny, 23 March 1948, McDonough MSS, ibid.

16. "Roosevelt Blasts at 3rd Party: Son of Late President Scores Left-Wing Extremists Before Tacoma Audience," *Tacoma Sunday Ledger News Tribune*, 14 March 1948, Roosevelt MSS, Box 214, speech material, third party file.

17. McDonough to Robert Zarick of the Sacramento Democratic Party, 15 December 1948, McDonough MSS, outgoing letters 1948 file.

18. Resolution of Burbank Democratic Club, 29 March 1946, Ickes MSS, Box 83, Russia 1946–51 file.

19. Walter Packard to James Loeb, Chairman of the Union for Democratic Action, 8 March 1945, ADA MSS, reel 57, section 5.

20. See Plotke, *Building a Democratic Political Order*.

21. Nelson H. Cruickshank to C. J. Haggerty, 10 July 1946, ADA MSS, reel 57, section 5.

22. Art Arthur to editor of the *New Republic*, 12 June 1946; Loeb to Arthur, 19 June 1946, ADA MSS, ibid.

23. Nathalie Panek to Bob Greenock, 28 June 1946, ADA MSS, ibid.

24. Harry Girvetz to Nathalie Panek, 28 September 1946, ADA MSS, ibid. For a discussion of the difficulties of building a postwar liberal movement, see Richard Pells, *The Liberal Mind in a Conservative Age: American Intellectuals in the 1940s and 1950s* (New York, 1985).

25. See Gillon, *Politics and Vision*, chap. 1.

26. ADA statement of principles, 15, ADA MSS, reel 57, section 5.

27. Jeri Despol to Nathalie Panek, 11 July 1947, ADA MSS, reel 57, section 7.

28. Despol to James Loeb, 16 October 1947, ibid.

29. See ibid.; also see flyer for Ziffren's pool party at his Coldwater Canyon home, 13 July 1952, ADA MSS, ibid.

30. See Harry Girvetz to James Loeb, 8 November 1947; Girvetz to Polly Hamilton, 14 March 1951, ADA MSS, reel 57, section 11.

31. Wilson, *The Amateur Democrat*, 258. See also Judy Kutulas, *The American Civil Liberties Union and the Making of Modern Liberalism, 1930–1960* (Chapel Hill, 2006), in which she argues that ACLU affiliates in states like California experienced a renaissance in the early 1950s. The point remains undeveloped, however, as the bulk of the book concerns the New Deal and World War II period.

32. Self, *American Babylon*, chap. 2; Charlotta Bass, acceptance speech to National Committee of the Progressive Party at Chicago, 30 March 1952, Bass MSS, Southern California Library for Social Studies and Research, Los Angeles. Bass stated that she was "more concerned with what is happening to my people in my country than in pouring out money to rebuild a decadent Europe for a new war."

33. John F. P. Tucker, Assistant Executive Secretary of ADA to Stanley Crook of the Berkeley chapter, 31 August 1950, ADA MSS, reel 57, section 5.

34. James Murray of SF ADA to Harry Girvetz, 20 June 1951; Stanley Crook to James Loeb, 22 June 1951; Harry Girvetz to John Tucker, 20 July 1951, ADA MSS, reel 59, section 10.

35. Harry Girvetz to John Tucker, 17 October 1951; Abe Held to Reginald Zalles, 8 April 1952, ADA MSS, reel 58, section 7.

36. Harry K. Girvetz, *From Wealth to Welfare: The Evolution of Liberalism* (Stanford, 1950); Richard Titmuss, *Problems of Social Policy* (London, 1950). Further international examples of a political rethinking of left-of-center political philosophy to suit the postwar age include Harold Laski, *The American Democracy: A Commentary and an Interpretation* (London, 1949), which uses the United States as a framework for conceptualizing a socialist worldview, and C. A. R. Crosland, *The Future of Socialism* (London, 1956). The last two authors are interesting in that both, although stormy in their relationship with the leadership, were active in the Labour Party, and

so their intellectual enterprises had practical political roots. See Michael Newman, *Harold Laski: A Political Biography* (London, 1993); Jeremy Nuttall, *Psychological Socialism: The Labour Party and Qualities of Mind and Character, 1931 to the Present* (Manchester, 2006).

37. John Dewey, *Human Nature and Conduct* (New York, 1930), quoted in Girvetz, *From Wealth to Welfare*, 140.

38. Crosland, *The Future of Socialism*; François Mitterrand, *Ma part de vérité: de la rupture ā l'unité* (Paris, 1969); ibid., *Politique* (Paris, 1977); Charles Hernu, *Priorité à gauche* (Paris, 1969).

39. Harry Girvetz to David Williams, 5 May 1953, ADA MSS, 59, section 11.

40. Ibid. Others also contributed to the final speech notes for Humphrey, including Arthur Schlesinger, Jr. The final piece was not as radical as Girvetz's original version.

41. Carlos Bulosan, "James Roosevelt for Governor," Roosevelt MSS, Box 255, California Election laws file.

42. See Bell, *The Liberal State on Trial*, chap. 6, for the way Democrats and liberal activists retreated from a concern with social and economic rights in the early Cold War, and specifically in 1950.

43. James Roosevelt, announcement speech, 15 November 1949, Roosevelt MSS, Box 239, announcement speech file.

44. James Roosevelt, "The Welfare State," speech at B'Nai B'rith, Chicago, 29 November 1949, Roosevelt MSS, Box 239, welfare state speech file.

45. J. Roosevelt speech at the Commonwealth Club, San Francisco, Roosevelt MSS, Box 239, Commonwealth Club file.

46. See Roosevelt's official launch speech after his primary victory in summer 1950 in which he accused Warren of being "a cool and calculating Republican who has switched his political mask so often that it is now showing. . . . Warren's Republican stripe was broad and pronounced from 1932 to 1942." Roosevelt MSS, Box 241, kick-off speech 30 August 1950 file.

47. Survey of political attitudes in California, July 1949, conducted by Executive Research, Inc., Roosevelt MSS, Box 252, political attitude surveys 1949 file.

48. A survey of political attitudes, California, by George S. Seros, July 1950, Roosevelt MSS, Box 252, political surveys 1950 file.

49. See Louise Darby of the League of Democratic Women in San Diego to Roosevelt, 31 October 1949, in which she warns him to keep his distance from the Douglas campaign lest he offend other elements of the party that might otherwise back him, and also J. R. Files to Edwin Doverpeck of the South-east Inner-city Democratic Coalition, 23 June 1949, arguing that "each may inherit the weakness of candidates for other positions without inheriting their strength." Both letters in Roosevelt MSS, Box 188, DAG-DAW file. See also Carey McWilliams, "And Now Jimmy Roosevelt," *The Nation*, 4 June 1949, for a discussion of the divisions within the party over the Roosevelt and Douglas candidacies. For a discussion of Warren's reaction to Douglas's endorsement of Roosevelt, see Helen Gahagan Douglas, *A Full Life* (New York, 1982), 325–26; Greg Mitchell, *Tricky*

Dick and the Pink Lady: Richard Nixon vs. Helen Gahagan Douglas—Sexual Politics and the Red Scare, 1950 (New York, 1998), 235–36.

50. See Mitchell, *Tricky Dick and the Pink Lady*, 18–29; Ingrid Winther Scobie, *Center Stage: Helen Gahagan Douglas: A Life* (New York, 1992); Douglas, *A Full Life*.

51. See Mitchell, *Tricky Dick and the Pink Lady*; Scobie, *Center Stage*; Bell, *The Liberal State on Trial*, chap. 6. The literature on Nixon and his political ascendancy is vast, and the following represent a tiny sample: Stephen Ambrose, *Nixon: The Education of a Politician, 1913–1962* (New York, 1987); Tom Wicker, *One of Us: Richard Nixon and the American Dream* (New York, 1991); Joan Hoff, *Nixon Reconsidered* (New York, 1995); Anthony Summers, *The Arrogance of Power: The Secret World of Richard Nixon* (London, 2000); Iwan Morgan, *Nixon* (London, 2002); Irwin Gellman, *The Contender: Richard Nixon: The Congress Years, 1946–1952* (New York, 1999).

52. Nixon Modesto speech, 24 March 1950, Nixon MSS, RNyl,PPS208 (1950), 6; Nixon statement to candidates' meetings, April–June 1950, RNyl, PPS208 (1950), 8; Nixon radio script, November 1950, RNyl PPS208 (1950), 44.

53. Newsletter, "Helen Gahagan Douglas Campaigns in 'Copter," 8 May 1950, Helen Douglas MSS, Box 172, folder 5.

54. Jean Begeman, "Million Dollar Senators," *New Republic*, 9 April 1951.

55. Murray Chotiner, "Fundamentals of Campaign Organization," 1950s, Phil Burton MSS, Box 16, 1950s file. Mitchell agrees that Douglas badly miscalculated in trying to argue that Nixon had not supported the Truman administration Cold War foreign policy (*Tricky Dick and the Pink Lady*, 182).

56. Douglas broadcast over ABC California, KECA and KFWB Los Angeles, 6 September 1950, RNyl, PPS3/41.

57. Chotiner gleefully reminisced about the pink sheet and explained its origins in his "Fundamentals of Campaign Organization." Lonigan material in RNyl, PPS3/14–17; PPS3/24–25. Many anecdotes of Nixon's dirty tactics are provided in Mitchell, *Tricky Dick and the Pink Lady*, and Scobie, *Center Stage*.

58. See Bell, *The Liberal State on Trial*, chap. 6, which discusses Senate races in Florida and Ohio as well as California in this regard.

59. Nixon speech, "Criticism of Socialism as Modern Day Slavery," 1950, RNyl, PPS208 (1950), 74.

60. Helen Douglas, "Party, Platform, and Performance," Douglas MSS, Box 172, folder 6.

61. Helen Douglas radio broadcast, "This I Believe," 14 May 1950, Douglas MSS, Box 171, folder 3.

62. Willie Brown, "First Among Equals: California Legislative Leadership, 1964–1992," Regional Oral History Office, Bancroft Library, UC Berkeley, 1999, 33–34.

63. Glenn M. Anderson, Chair Democratic State Central Committee, Analysis of California election returns, November 1950, Clinton P. Anderson MSS, Library of Congress, Box 1052, California file.

64. See *Los Angeles Sentinel*, 5 October 1950, for the editorial backing Nixon. The

Sentinel had form for hedging its bets about Helen Douglas, backing Republican opponent Fred Roberts in 1946 because he was African American. See *Los Angeles Sentinel*, 31 October 1946 for editor Leon Washington's argument that race trumped ideology in that contest. The other major African American daily, headed by popular front leftist Charlotta Bass, vigorously supported Douglas throughout her career.

65. Manchester Boddy, "The Struggle for Security Dominates All Forms of Life," *LA Daily News*, 7 April 1950. Boddy, owner of this newspaper, was chosen by Democrats opposed to Douglas as primary challenger when Sheridan Downey dropped out.

66. L. S. Peterman of Long Beach to James Roosevelt, Eleanor Roosevelt, and Helen Douglas, 13 November 1950, James Roosevelt MSS, Box 230, opposing JR file.

Chapter 3. The Stevenson Effect

1. Quoted in James Q. Wilson, *The Amateur Democrat: Club Politics in Three Cities* (Chicago, 1966), 113–14.

2. Stewart L. Udall, "Why Adlai Stevenson Haunts the Democrats," *New Republic*, 19 May 1958.

3. Jean Ibert to Knowland, 12 November 1951; Bill Conlin to Knowland and Nixon, 10 November 1951, Knowland MSS, Box 93, file 4. There is lots of far right material in this file on the forthcoming 1952 elections.

4. See Gayle Montgomery and James Johnson, *One Step from the White House: The Rise and Fall of Senator William F. Knowland* (Berkeley, 1998); Ethan Rarick, *California Rising: The Life and Times of Pat Brown* (Berkeley, 2005), 87–89.

5. Knowland 1952 campaign manual, Knowland MSS, Box 92, campaign endorsements 1952 file.

6. News release on Democrats for Knowland, 20 May 1952, Knowland MSS, Box 92, miscellaneous 1952 campaign file.

7. State of California Statement of Vote, Consolidated Direct and Presidential Primary Election, 3 June 1952.

8. Werdel quoted in the National Economic Council Inc.'s "Economic Council Letter," 15 April 1951, Robert Taft MSS, Library of Congress, Box 969, foreign policy B file 1 of 2.

9. "So, the Fair Deal Lost," pamphlet by National Precinct Workers, Inc. Accompanying letter from Frank Michey to Knowland, 24 May 1951, Knowland MSS, Box 91, file 4. See Kimberly Phillips Fein, "American Counterrevolutionary: Lemuel Ricketts Boulware and General Electric, 1950–1960," in Nelson Lichtenstein, ed., *American Capitalism: Social Thought and Political Economy in the Twentieth Century* (Philadelphia, 2006), 249–70 for a discussion of this phenomenon on a broader national canvas.

10. State of California Statement of Vote, 4 November 1952, Knowland MSS, Box 66, elections file (1). The Democrats had sponsored a proposition to repeal cross-filing altogether, and the GOP had put on the ballot a rival proposition to allow party affiliation to be listed, hoping both would fail. The plan backfired.

11. Statement of the California Labor League for Political Education on the Presi-

dential Election," in Proceedings of the Pre-General Election Convention of the California Labor League for Political Education, The Armory, Santa Barbara, 27 August 1952, 8–11.

12. McSorley address to the pre-primary convention, CLLPE, 19ff.

13. Hope Mendoza Schechter, oral history, Women in Politics Oral History Project, Bancroft Library, 47.

14. Roger Kent oral history, Bancroft Library, 290.

15. Arthur Schlesinger, "History of the Week," *New York Post*, 27 January 1952.

16. "Some Major Accomplishments of Governor Adlai E. Stevenson's Administration," James Roosevelt MSS, Box 213, Adlai Stevenson file.

17. Stevenson's veto message quoted in Porter McKeever, *Adlai Stevenson: His Life and Legacy* (New York, 1989), 161.

18. John Kenneth Galbraith, *A Life in Our Times: Memoirs* (Boston, 1981), 292, 295.

19. Adam Clayton Powell interview, "What the American Negro Wants," *U.S. News and World Report*, 5 September 1952, 52–59, John F. Kennedy MSS, JFK Library, Boston, Box 110, Af Am file.

20. Charlotta Bass acceptance speech to national committee of Progressive Party, Chicago, 30 March 1952, Bass MSS, Box 1.

21. Douglas Flamming, "Becoming Democrats: Liberal Politics and the African American Community in Los Angeles, 1930–1965," in Lawrence B. De Graaf, Kevin Mulroy, and Quintard Taylor, ed., *Seeking El Dorado: African Americans in California* (Los Angeles, 2001), 279–308.

22. Thurman Arnold and James Rowe to James Loeb, 2 October 1950, ADA MSS, reel 57, section 5.

23. "Adlai E. Stevenson," *New Republic*, 18 February 1952, 9–14; "Adlai Stevenson on the Edge," *New Republic*, 21 July 1952.

24. Porter McKeever telegram to Brooks Berlin in San Francisco, 6 October 1952, Stevenson MSS, Box 245, folder 2.

25. Stanley Bergerman memo, 15 September 1952, Stevenson MSS, Box 245, folder 2.

26. Allen Rivkin to Bob Hind, 29 September 1952, Stevenson MSS, Box 245. folder 2.

27. George Ball introduction to rebroadcast of a Stevenson speech, 16 September 1952, Stevenson MSS, Box 235, folder 10.

28. Summaries of political situation in San Francisco, Oakland, Los Angeles, Richmond, Stevenson MSS, Box 230, file 5. See Robert O. Self, *American Babylon: Race and the Struggle for Postwar Oakland* (Princeton, 2003); Josh Sides, *LA City Limits: African American Los Angeles from the Great Depression to the Present* (Berkeley, 2003). For an excellent study of the dynamics of Californian economic development in this period, see Roger Lotchin, *Fortress California, 1910–1961: From Warfare to Welfare* (New York, 1992).

29. Historian Howard Brick has termed this transatlantic discussion over the future of the global political economy a "postcapitalist vision," consisting of "a range of ideas

that provided some perspective on, and prognosis of, the development of modern society, a view that assumed the obsolescence of the concept of 'capitalism' or forecast the transmutation of capitalist reality into a new social economy (beyond the strict centrality of free markets and capital accumulation) or even into a 'posteconomic' society." See Brick, *Transcending Capitalism: Visions of a New Social Thought in Modern American Thought* (Ithaca, 2006), 5.

30. J. R. Feyrel, "Thoughts on the Welfare State," *New Republic*, 28 January 1952, 11–13.

31. See Jennifer Klein, *For All These Rights: Business, Labor, and the Shaping of America's Public-Private Welfare State* (Princeton, 2003); Jennifer Mittelstadt, *From Welfare to Workfare: The Unintended Consequences of Liberal Reform, 1945–65* (Chapel Hill, 2005); Alice O'Connor, *Poverty Knowledge: Social Science, Social Policy, and the Poor in Twentieth-Century U.S. History* (Princeton, 2001); Alan Derickson, *Health Security for All: Dreams of Universal Health Care in Twentieth-Century America* (Baltimore, 2005); Colin Gordon, *Dead on Arrival: The Politics of Health Care in Twentieth-Century America* (Princeton, 2003); Michael K. Brown, *Race, Money, and the American Welfare State* (Ithaca, 1999).

32. Crosland notes on cities and areas, in his notes on U.S. trip, 1954, Crosland MSS, London School of Economics, 8/1, 47.

33. See Jonathan Bell, "Social Politics in a Transoceanic World in the Early Cold War Years," *Historical Journal*, 53, 2 (April 2010): 401–21.

34. Anthony Crosland, *The Future of Socialism* (London, 1956). For a stimulating analysis of the ways in which Labour attempted to meet the political challenges of an era encapsulated by Prime Minister Harold Macmillan as one where Britons had "never had it so good," see Lawrence Black, *Old Labour, New Britain? The Political Culture of the Left in "Affluent" Britain, 1951–1964* (Baskingstoke, 2002).

35. Crosland notes on U.S. trip, Crosland MSS, 8/1, pp. 12, 32.

36. Ibid., 2, 3, 7, 8.

37. Ibid., 46–47.

38. Michael Young to Crosland, nd, Crosland MSS, 13/8, 5; Richard Crossman to Crosland, 23 October 1956, Crosland MSS, 13/10.

39. Kevin Mattson, *When America Was Great: The Fighting Faith of Postwar Liberalism* (New York, 2004); Brick, *Transcending Capitalism*; Kathleen G. Donohue, *Freedom from Want: American Liberalism and the Idea of the Consumer* (Baltimore, 2003), conclusion.

40. Editorial, *New Republic*, 11 August 1952.

41. Leo Doyle to George Ball, assistant to Stevenson, 14 August 1952, Stevenson MSS, Box 235, folder 10.

42. Ben Heineman to "Dutch" Smith, 27 August 1952, Stevenson MSS, Box 235, folder 10. Bill Malone was a major figure in the San Francisco Democratic Party.

43. Willie Brown, "First Among Equals: California Legislative Leadership, 1964–1992," Bancroft Library, Berkeley, 33.

44. Prof. Wayne Shumaker to Stevenson, 6 November 1952, Stevenson MSS, Box 115, folder 5.

45. Eleanor St. Germain to Stevenson, 5 November 1952, ibid.

46. John J. Saeman to Stevenson, 25 November 1952, ibid.

47. Verne Scoggins, "It Happened in California," 1 September 1953, Byron Rumford MSS, Bancroft Library, Box 10, miscellaneous file 2.

48. "Segregation: Professional Ethics of the Berkeley Realty Board," a report by Berkeley Law Students Democratic Club, Cohelan MSS, Box 5, file 24.

49. Willie Brown oral history, 65, 67.

50. Summary of major issues and background in San Francisco, 3 September 1952, and updates, Stevenson MSS, Box 230, file 5.

51. Jefferson Beaver, President, Urban League, to members, 15 November 1957, C. L. Dellums MSS, Bancroft Library, Box 25, Urban League file.

52. California Committee on FEP brief, "In a Nutshell: The Proposed Fair Employment Practices Law, AB 971," Dellums MSS, Box 8, Calif. FEP 1955 file.

53. "Evaluation of State FEPC: Experiences and Forecasts," American Council on Race Relations release no. 43, 24 March 1949, Dellums MSS, Box 8, FEPC 1946–49 file. The other states were New York, New Jersey, Connecticut, Massachusetts, and New Mexico. The law had gone down to legislative defeat or was passing through the legislatures in fifteen others.

54. See Self, *American Babylon*, 48ff.

55. "FEPC talk may halt forces of reaction," *LA Daily News*, 24 March 1953, Dellums MSS, Box 8, California Committee for FEP 1953 file.

56. Tarea Hall Pittmen to sponsors of California Committee for FEP, 31 March 1953, Dellums MSS, ibid.

57. Val Washington of Republican National Committee to Dellums, 20 April 1953; various letters from Dellums to Warren, 17 Feb through 5 March 1953; Dellums to McIntyre Faries, 17 March 1953, Dellums MSS, Box 8, ibid.

58. See Senator Tom Kuchel to Dellums, 26 March 1953; William Knowland to Dellums, 28 March 1953; Memorandum listing membership of the Committee on Governmental Efficiency and Economy, Dellums MSS, ibid. For an analysis of the way conservative control over legislative committees killed economic and social reform, see Ellen Reese, *Backlash Aagainst Welfare Mothers: Past and Present* (Berkeley, 2005), 87–97.

59. Dellums to Val Washington, Republican National Committee, 10 April 1953, Dellums MSS, Box 8, FEP 1953 file.

60. Paul L. Poirot, "Property Rights and Human Rights: Are They Divisible?" *California Real Estate Magazine*, September 1953, 11–26, Byron Rumford MSS, Bancroft Library, Box 1, file 1. Poirot was a member of the Foundation for Economic Education, a pro-business public relations firm.

61. See Wendy L. Wall, *Inventing the "American Way": The Politics of Consensus from the New Deal to the Civil Rights Movement* (New York, 2008); Elizabeth Fones-Wolf, *Selling Free Enterprise: The Business Assault on Labor and Liberalism* (Urbana, 1994).

62. See Rumford release of FEPC debate, 18 May 1955, Rumford MSS, Box 3, file 7.

63. "Democracy means FAIR employment practices," *CIO Economic Outlook*, October 1951, Rumford MSS, Box 3, file 3. For in-depth analysis of the impact of Cold War ideology on civil rights, see Mary Dudziak, *Cold War Civil Rights: Race and the Image of American Democracy* (Princeton, 2000); Thomas Borstelmann, *The Cold War and the Color Line: American Race Relations in the Global Arena* (Cambridge, Mass., 2001).

64. FEP Comnmittee Fact Sheet #1, 21 January 1952, America Plus, Dellums MSS, Box 25, America Plus file.

65. See Lisa McGirr, *Suburban Warriors: The Origins of the New American Right* (Princeton, 2001); Kurt Schuparra, *Triumph of the Right: The Rise of the California Conservative Movement, 1945–1966* (Armonk, 1998).

66. As John D'Emilio has observed, a number of features of the Mattachine Society founded by these individuals over the course of 1951 "reflected the leftist orientation of its founders," including its secretive, hierarchical structure and the desire of the membership to provide "a systemic analysis for social problems" that would furnish a "theoretical understanding of the homosexual's inferior status." See D'Emilio, *Sexual Politics, Sexual Communities: The Making of a Homosexual Minority in the United States, 1940–1970*, 2nd ed. (Chicago, 1998), 63–64; Daniel Hurewitz, *Bohemian Los Angeles and the Making of Modern Politics* (Berkeley, 2007), chap. 6.

67. "The Mattachine Society Today: An Information Digest, 1954, Don Lucas MSS, GLBT Historical Society, San Francisco, Box 3, folder 1.

68. For a discussion of the antigay hysteria that formed part of the anticommunist craze of the early 1950s see David K. Johnson, *The Lavender Scare: The Cold War Persecution of Gays and Lesbians in the Federal Government* (Chicago, 2004).

69. Christopher Isherwood, *My Guru and His Disciple* (Minneapolis, 2001), 4.

70. Marilyn Rieger to Paul Coates, 13 March 1953, Lucas MSS, Box 1, folder 3.

71. Rowland in minutes of California State Constitutional Convention of Mattachine, 11–12 April 1953, Los Angeles, Lucas MSS, Box 2, folder 20; "Evolution, Not Revolution," Call to 1954 Mattachine convention, San Francisco, Lucas MSS, Box 3, folder 1. The political timidity of the homophile movement of the 1950s is a recurrent theme of the historiography. See D'Emilio, *Sexual Politics, Sexual Communities*, chap. 5, "Retreat to Respectability."

72. Rowland speech in minutes of meeting of 11–12 April 1953, Lucas MSS, Box 2, folder 20; *Mattachine Review* promotional material, Lucas MSS, Box 5, folder 20.

73. Mattachine Society: Missions and Purposes," Lucas MSS, Box 1, folder 4.

74. Report of Chair of Legislative Committee, 1954 convention, 15–16 May 1954, Lucas MSS, Box 3, folder 1. Capital letters are original.

75. Mattachine request to political candidates and questionnaire, nd, Lucas MSS, Box 1, folder 1.

76. Paul Coates column, 12 December 1953, Lucas MSS, Box 1, folder 3.

Chapter 4. A Democratic Order

1. David Plotke, *Building a Democratic Political Order: Reshaping American Liberal-*

ism in the 1930s and 1940s (Cambridge, 1996); Alan Brinkley, *The End of Reform: New Deal Liberalism in Recession and War* (New York, 1995).

2. Pat Brown address before Western States Conference, 8 October 1951, Pat Brown MSS, Box 22, aims of the Democratic Party file. For discussions of the way in which Democratic liberalism was shaping American politics in this period, see Tim Thurber, *The Politics of Equality: Hubert H. Humphrey and the African American Freedom Struggle* (New York, 1999); Jennifer Delton, *Making Minnesota Liberal: Civil Rights and the Transformation of the Democratic Party* (Minneapolis, 2002).

3. *State of California Statement of Vote*, 4 November 1952, Knowland MSS, Box 66; *State of California Statement of Vote, Consolidated Direct and Presidential Primary Election*, 3 June 1952, Knowland MSS, Box 92, Campaign endorsements 1952 file. 1,529,710 voted in the Republican Senate primary (all but 188,540 voted for Knowland); 1,740,843 in the Democratic primary (966,881 voted for Knowland), in a state with a population of 12 million. In 1952 approximately 3,312,000 voters were registered as Democrats and 2,197,000 as Republicans: see Shields, "A Note on Party Organization: The Democrats in California," *Western Political Quarterly* 7, 4 (Deecember 1954): 673

4. Brown speech draft for Asilomar meeting, 31 January 1953, Brown MSS, Box 22, Democratic meeting at Asilomar file, emphasis original.

5. Final report of the Workshop Conference at Asilomar, February 1953, Cranston MSS, Box 11, Asilomar file.

6. Willie Brown oral history, 39.

7. Roger Kent oral history, 35. Wealthy liberal activism in Marin was indeed an impressive force, as the county became increasingly liberal and Democratic as the century went on, even though its socioeconomic composition changed little.

8. Stephen Zetterberg oral interview, State Government Oral History Program, California State Archives, Sacramento, 75.

9. Carmen Warschaw oral interview, "A Southern Californian Perspective on Democratic Party Politics," Bancroft oral history project, 120, 147.

10. James Q. Wilson, *The Amateur Democrat: Club Politics in Three Cities* (Chicago, 1966), 16.

11. Final report of the workshop conference at Asilomar, 30 January–1 February 1953, Zetterberg MSS, California State Archives, Box 1, Democratic by-laws 1953 file.

12. Joseph P. Harris, Professor of Political Science, UC Berkeley, to Alan Cranston, 17 February 1954, Cranston MSS, Box 10, H correspondence file. There was a considerable amount of academic discussion of using other industrialized democracies as case studies of how to advance social democracy in the United States at a time of increasing political conservatism and an uncertain mandate for political liberalism in the wake of the New and Fair Deals. See Shields, "A Note on Party Organization," 673; Report of the American Political Science Committee on Political Parties, "Towards a More Responsible Two-Party System," *American Political Science Review* Supplement 44 (1950); Leslie Lipson, "The Two-Party System in British Politics," *American Political Science Review* 47 (1951): 337–58; Leslie Lipson, *The Politics of Equality: New Zealand's Adventures in*

Democracy (Chicago, 1948). Robert Lynd's review of Lipson's book in the *New Republic* argued that like "a child in a tantrum, we need help from the outside to get down off our high horse. . . . New Zealand is attempting a richer mixture: the synthesis of democratic politics with a socialized economy, the combination of liberty and equality." See *New Republic*, 23 August 1948, 25.

13. Dewey Anderson to Alan Cranston, 4 February 1954, Cranston MSS, Box 10, Anderson file.

14. Miriam Deinard Colf and Rudolph Pacht, "The New California Democratic Party: The Place of the California Democratic Council in the Democratic Party of California," 1955, Cranston MSS, Box 11, CDC History material file.

15. CDC Issues Committee report, March 1959, California Democratic Council MSS, Southern California Library for Social Studies and Research, Los Angeles, Box 5, file 15.

16. Cranston to CDC Board of Directors, Fresno, 6 December 1957, Cranston MSS, Box 11, CDC speeches file. See also Bell, *The Liberal State on Trial*, for the impact of the Cold War on liberal politics.

17. Holifield speech to Democratic Luncheon Club, Los Angeles, 29 September 1955, "Democratic Diagnosis: A Constructive Program for Unified Political Action"; Cranston to Holifield, 6 October 1955, Cranston MSS, Box 11, Cranston/Holifield 1955 file.

18. Kent to O'Brien, 30 July 1957, Cranston MSS, Box 10, Central Committee file; Tom Carvey to Cranston, 24 July 1961, Cranston MSS, Box 13, Carvey memo file.

19. Carmen Warschaw oral interview, 147, 151.

20. Cranston speech to CDC Board of Directors, 6 December 1957; Cranston acceptance of CDC nomination for U.S. Senate, 22 February 1964, Cranston MSS, Box 11, CDC speeches file. Registration figures are contained in Hal Dunleavy and Associates Report "Who Will Win in California: A Forecast of Statewide Races," 1958, Phillip Burton MSS, Bancroft Library, Box 1, 1958 statistics file.

21. Alameda County Democratic Council Revised By-Laws, C. L. Dellums MSS, Box 25, Alameda County Democratic Council file.

22. Zetterberg to Hubert Will, 20 August 1952, Zetterberg MSS, Box 1, Democratic Luncheon Club 1952 file.

23. Pat McDonough to Tom Scully, 27 September 1949, McDonough MSS, Box 1, outgoing letters 1949 file. See also McDonough to Will Rogers, Jr., 14 November 1949, in ibid., saying Scully, a Democratic committeeman from LA, never replied to his letter reporting on McDonough's attempts to set up the organization.

24. Roger Kent oral interview, 101.

25. Ibid., 29–30, 43.

26. Kent speech at meeting of Twenty-First Assembly District Democratic League, 14 June 1956, Kent MSS, Box 3, press releases file 1.

27. Draft of constitution of Claremont Democratic Club, Zetterberg MSS, Box 1, Democratic by-laws 1953 file.

28. President of West Beverly Club, *West Beverly Bray* newsletter, June 1958, CDC

MSS, Southern California Library for Social Studies and Research, Los Angeles, Box 25, file 12.

29. John Lear form letter, December 1959, CDC MSS, Box 25, file 9.

30. *West Beverly Bray*, November 1958, CDC MSS, Box 25, file 12. The West Beverly Club lay in the Twenty-sixth Congressional District held by FDR's liberal son James Roosevelt from 1954 to 1965. Of course once the Democrats gained control of the legislature in 1958 they controlled the redistricting process in 1962, resulting in the Democrats winning nine of Los Angeles County's fifteen seats in Congress. See *Congressional Directory*, 89th Congress (Washington, D.C., 1966).

31. Michael Barone and Grant Ujifusa, *The Almanac of American Politics 1996* (Washington, D.C., 1995), 156–71; Raphael J. Sonenshein, *Politics in Black and White: Race and Power in Los Angeles* (Princeton, 1993).

32. See Minutes of West Beverly Board meetings, 1956 onward, CDC MSS, Box 25, file 7.

33. *West Beverly Bray*, March 1959, 2, CDC MSS, Box 25, file 12.

34. California Federation of Young Democrats newsletter, "Why Join a Political Party?" CDC MSS, Box 26, file 7.

35. *West Beverly Bray*, February 1959, CDC MSS, Box 25, file 12; Memorandum, Marshall Windmiller to Marvin Schachter, Twenty-Sixth Congressional District Democratic Party, 30 August 1960, CDC MSS, Box 27, file 8.

36. *West Beverly Bray*, February 1963, 2; March 1964, CDC MSS, Box 25, file 13.

37. For studies of the right-wing equivalent of grassroots organizations that encouraged people to become "joiners" on the basis of political enthusiasm, see Lisa McGirr, *Suburban Warriors: The Origins of the New American Right* (Princeton, 2001); Kurt Schuparra, *Triumph of the Right: The Rise of the California Conservative Movement, 1945–1966* (Armonk, 1998).

38. Sheldon Pollack to Marvin Rosenberg, 18 July 1956; Pollack to ADA organizing committee, 12 June 1957; Pollack to Rosenberg, 28 February 1958, ADA MSS, reel 57, no. 5.

39. Paul Seabury to Sam Beer, national chairman of ADA, nd, late 1950s, ADA MSS, ibid.

40. Sheldon Pollack to Paul Seabury, 18 December 1959, ADA MSS, ibid.; Pollack to Violet Gunther, 6 March 1961, ADA MSS, reel 58, no. 5.

41. Nathalie Panek to David Williams, ADA director of education, 20 May 1954, ADA MSS, reel 58, no. 7.

42. Northern California Stevenson-Kefauver release, 15 October 1956, Democratic Party MSS, Bancroft Library, Berkeley, Box 1, Dollars for Democrats file.

43. Martin Huff, Treasurer, Northern Division of Dollars for Democrats, to Paul Butler and Roger Kent, 10 September 1957, Democratic Party MSS, Box 1, Dollars for Democrats file.

44. Joseph Wyatt memo to CDC members, 15 August 1958, Democratic Party MSS, Box 1, Dollars for Democrats file.

45. Steve Zetterberg oral interview extract, Zetterberg MSS, Box 1, oral history file.

46. Roger Kent oral interview, 43, 102–3.

47. Clinton McKinnon, Chair Dime a Day for Democracy, to James Roosevelt, 3 July 1953, Roosevelt MSS, Box 189, Democratic State Central Committee file.

48. See Warschaw oral interview, 236.

49. Anthony Beilenson, oral history interview, California State Archives, 110–111.

50. Research report, "The Stevenson Campaign in California," Edward L. Greenfield and Company, Stevenson MSS, Box 299, folder 5.

51. Warschaw oral interview, 51, 173.

52. Orrin Cassmore letter to unidentified recipient, 6 November 1963, Burton MSS, Box 2, February 1964 election file—correspondence. There is an excellent narrative biography of Burton: John Jacobs, *A Rage for Justice: The Passion and Politics of Phillip Burton* (Berkeley, 1995).

53. Burton to Gifford Phillips, publisher of *Frontier* magazine, nd 1954, Burton MSS, Box 1, 1954 campaign file.

54. "Burton's Program" campaign leaflet, 1954, in ibid. See Tim Tilton, *The Political Theory of Swedish Social Democracy Through the Welfare State to Socialism* (Oxford, 1990) for a discussion of the ideological premises of social democracy.

55. California CIO report on 1954 elections, September 1955, Burton MSS, Box 1, 1954 campaign file. After Berry's victory the Democratic County Committee were at liberty to appoint a Democrat in his place to contest the November general election, and they chose liberal party regular John O'Connell, who duly won the election, although O'Connell would join Burton on the radical wing of the party once safely ensconced in office.

56. Young Democrat electoral analysis, 1956; State of California Statement of Vote, 1956, Twentieth Assembly District, Burton MSS, Box 1, 1956 campaign folder. Burton won 17,807 votes to Maloney's 17,148. It was the last time a Republican came anywhere close to victory in the Twentieth District and its successors in the legislature.

57. "'I'll Never Retire from Politics': *Maloney v. Burton*—An Intense Local Fight," *San Francisco News*, 31 October 1956, 1. See proceedings of the 1956 Pre-General Election Convention of the California Labor League for Political Education (LLPE) (AFL) and press release of William Kilpatrick, San Francisco County Democratic Central Committee, 5 October 1956, Burton MSS, Box 1, 1956 campaign file, for evidence of opposition to Burton.

58. An example of a study that argues for the importance of political ideas in establishing European left-of-center parties in power is Martin Francis, *Ideas and Policies Under Labour, 1945–1951, Building a New Britain* (Manchester, 1997).

59. Burton form letter to registered Democrats, 1962 campaign, Burton MSS, Box 1, 1962 Twentieth Assembly District file.

60. "Memorandum on the Negro Vote in California," 1956, Cranston MSS, Box 13, Democratic State Central Committee file.

61. Burton to Pat Brown, 27 February 1958, Burton MSS, Box 17, 1958 other campaigns file; see material in Burton MSS, Box 18, 1963 press releases file.

62. "Phillip Burton: Statesman of Welfare": A tribute delivered by Professor Jacobus tenBroek, 30 October 1963, Welfare Achievements Luncheon, Jewish Community Center, San Francisco, Burton MSS, Box 18, 1963 press releases file.

63. Vote tallies in Burton MSS, Box 1, 1960 statistics file; *New York Times*, 23 February 1964 on Burton's election to Congress in a special election, "his mind full of strong liberal views and far-reaching social welfare programs."

Chapter 5. Turning Point: California Politics in the 1950s

1. See Totton J. Anderson, "The 1958 Election in California," *Western Political Quarterly* 12, 1, Pt 2 (March 1959): 276–300; Ethan Rarick, *California Rising: The Life and Times of Pat Brown* (Berkeley, 2005); Gayle Montgomery and James Johnson, *One Step from the White House: The Rise and Fall of Senator William F. Knowland* (Berkeley, 1998); Totton Anderson, "Extremism in California Politics: The Brown-Knowland and Brown-Nixon Campaigns Compared," *Western Political Quarterly* 16, 2 (June 1963): 371–72.

2. "California Democratic Council: The First Eight Years," 24, Zetterberg MSS, Box 1, CDC file.

3. Willie Brown oral interview, 36. See also Jacobs, *A Rage for Justice*.

4. Jerd F. Sullivan to W. K. Serumgard, 6 May 1954, Whitaker and Baxter MSS, California State Archives, Box 25, local supporters file.

5. Roger Kent, oral interview, 68–69.

6. *Delano Record*, 13 May 1954, Whitaker and Baxter MSS, Box 29, campaign tour file.

7. Ethan Rarick, *California Rising*, 76.

8. "Knight Says He'll Sweep Primary," *San Francisco Chronicle*, 25 May 1954, Whitaker and Baxter MSS, Box 29, campaign tour file.

9. Gerald Ray to Leone Baxter, 25 March 1954, Whitaker and Baxter (W&B) MSS, Box 25, general correspondence and dates file.

10. William McMullen to W&B, 28 May 1954, in ibid.

11. Ray to Baxter, 25 March 1954, in ibid.

12. Gregory Harrison to Stephen Mitchell, 4 June 1954; "Repudiate 'Smear' of Graves, Knight Asked," *LA Times*, 4 June 1954, W&B MSS, Box 25, Democratic committee against radical party leadership press file.

13. "FDR Jr Hits at Jimmy for Family Break," *California Eagle*, 1 June 1954. The *Eagle* was supporting an African American against Roosevelt in the primary for the Twenty-Sixth Congressional District. See also Stephen Mitchell to Paul Ziffren, California National Committeeman, 2 April 1954, Stevenson MSS, Box 69, folder 3. "Knight Addresses Adventist Meet," *San Francisco Call-Bulletin*, 3 June 1954, W&B MSS, Box 29, campaign tour file.

14. "The Record of Richard Graves," W&B MSS, Box 25, general correspondence and dates file.

15. Proceedings of the CLLPE Pre-Primary Convention, 12 April 1954, 37–38, 48–49, California LLPE-COPE MSS, Box 7, folder 8.

16. "Knight and FEP," *Daily People's World*, 28 April 1954, W&B MSS, Box 29, "colored groups" file.

17. See Proceedings of CLLPE Pre-Primary Convention, 127, 145–62, 174–83.

18. Proceedings of the Pre-General Election Convention of the CLLPE, 26 August 1954, Santa Barbara, CLLPE-COPE MSS, Box 7, folder 9.

19. Ernesto Galarza, *Farm Workers and Agribusiness in California, 1947–1960* (Notre Dame, 1977), 81.

20. Ibid., 258–60.

21. Ibid., 285.

22. The principal frame of reference for historian J. Craig Jenkins is the need to theorize the obstacles to and catalysts for successful mobilization of farm laborers from the bottom up. See Jenkins, "The Transformation of a Constituency into a Movement: Farmworker Organizing in California," in Jo Freeman, ed., *Social Movements of the Sixties and Seventies* (New York, 1983), 52–70; Jenkins, *The Politics of Insurgency: The Farm Worker Movement in the 1960s* (New York, 1985).

23. See Randy Shaw, *Beyond the Fields: Cesar Chavez, the UFW, and the Struggle for Justice in the Twenty-First Century* (Berkeley, 2008), 16–17; Jacques E. Levy, *Cesar Chavez: Autobiography of La Causa* (New York, 1975), 97–102.

24. Unattributed summary report on Santa Clara County, 18 November 1961, California Democratic Party MSS, Box 8, Santa Clara file.

25. "Republicans given warning by Levering," *Los Angeles Times*, 2 June 1954.

26. Richard Graves to Dr. Howard C. Naffziger, 29 April 1954, W&B MSS, Box 25, general correspondence and dates file. Naffziger had sent the Graves letter to Whitaker and Baxter to warn them that Graves was attempting to move into their territory.

27. 1954 California Democratic Party platform, James Roosevelt MSS, Box 300, 1954 platform file.

28. See W&B MSS, Box 29, Election returns, general file.

29. See William Knowland MSS, Box 66, elections file 1.

30. List of Democratic headquarters in Twenty-Sixth District; Twenty-Sixth Congressional District Democratic Council letter to campaign staff, 23 September 1954, Roosevelt MSS, Box 300, 1954 campaign file.

31. Roosevelt announcement of candidacy, Roosevelt MSS, Box 300, 1954 campaign file.

32. Democratic press release, 30 November 1955, Stevenson MSS, Box 248, folder 6.

33. Glen Slaughter to Joe Keenan, Secretary of the International Brotherhood of Electrical Workers, 26 October 1955, Stevenson MSS, Box 248, folder 6.

34. Porter McKeever, *Adlai Stevenson: His Life and Legacy* (New York, 1989), 357–58.

35. Press release by Harry Lerner and Associates, San Francisco PR firm, 10 November 1955; Stevenson for President campaign budget, 17 November 1955, Stevenson MSS, Box 248, file 6.

36. "The Consumer in the Modern Market-Place," CDC issues brochure, February 1960, California Democratic Party MSS, Box 1, consumers file.

37. "Consumer Beware!" leaflet, California Democratic Party MSS, Box 1, consumers file; "California: A Survey," *The Banker*, November 1968, 992–95. This British journal noted the importance of California to the world economy, stating that "California's statistics are more akin to a country than a state" (992).

38. See Lizabeth Cohen, *A Consumer's Republic: The Politics of Mass Consumption in Postwar America* (New York, 2004); Meg Jacobs, *Pocketbook Politics: Economic Citizenship in Twentieth-Century America* (Princeton, 2004); Elizabeth Fones-Wolf, *Selling Free Enterprise: The Business Assault on Labor and Liberalism, 1945–1960* (Urbana, 1994); Thomas W. Evans, *The Education of Ronald Reagan: The General Electric Years and the Untold Story of His Conversion to Conservatism* (New York, 2006); Elizabeth Tandy Shermer, "Counter-organizing the Sunbelt: Right-to-Work Campaigns and Anti-Union Conservatism, 1943–1958," *Pacific Historical Review* (February 2009).

39. "The Stevenson Campaign in California—A Research Report from Edward L. Greenfield and Company," Stevenson MSS, Box 299, folder 5 and Box 249, folder 1.

40. San Francisco party reply to Stevenson campaign questionnaire, Stevenson MSS, Box 248, folder 7. Emphasis original.

41. Gerald O'Gara to Ken Hechler of Stevenson campaign staff, 26 April 1956, Stevenson MSS, Box 248, file 7.

42. L. Howard Bennett to James A. Finnegan, 27 July 1956, Stevenson MSS, Box 248, file 1.

43. Harry Harris to Edward Greenfield, 6 March 1956, Stevenson MSS, Box 268, file 4; Walter Reuther press conference, 26 April 1956, Stevenson MSS, Box 268, file 9.

44. Stevenson campaign research report, Stevenson MSS, Box 299, folder 5.

45. Letter from unnamed Stevenson informant to Stevenson, 17 January 1956, Stevenson MSS, Box 303, file 6.

46. Stevenson campaign research report, Edward L. Greenfield and Company, Stevenson MSS, Box 299, folder 5.

47. See McKeever, *Adlai Stevenson*, 366; Gerald O'Hara to Ken Hechler, 26 April 1956, Stevenson MSS, Box 248, file 7.

48. Jane Dick to Barry Bingham and Archibald Alexander, nd, re California, Stevenson MSS, Box 248, file 7.

49. Jane Dick to Wilson Wyatt, 18 April 1956, Stevenson MSS, Box 303, file 7.

50. See statement of vote of California primary, 5 June 1956, Stevenson MSS, Box 280, file 8; Fred Dutton to James Finnegan, 7 June 1956, Stevenson MSS, Box 249, file 1. For a discussion of the setting up of a Stevenson drive in African American neighborhoods see Bill Joyce to Jane Dick, 26 October 1956, Stevenson MSS, Box 304, file 2.

51. Roger Kent to Bill Blair and Adlai Stevenson, 26 June 1956, Stevenson MSS, Box 249, file 1.

52. Sam Yorty press conference, 31 July 1961, CDC MSS, Box 8, file 12.

53. Yorty quoted in Kent oral interview, 125.

54. Warschaw oral interview, 176.

55. Delegate Ralph E. Palmer (Chemical Workers Local No. 1, Long Beach) to LLPE preprimary endorsement convention, San Francisco, 6 April 1956, LLPE/COPE MSS, Box 7, file 10.

56. Address by William J. McSorley, Assistant National Director, Committee on Political Education, to LLPE convention, 14 September 1956, 9ff; Richard Richards address to same, 29ff; LLPE/COPE MSS, Box 7, file 11.

57. State of California statement of vote, 5 June 1956, Stevenson MSS, Box 280, file 8.

58. Kent oral interview, 136.

59. George McGovern press release, 17 January 1956, "Cost of Living Investigation Is Proposed: Your Congressman's Notebook," McGovern MSS, Princeton University, Box 657, file 1. McGovern had won his House seat in a staunchly Republican farm state in 1954.

60. Chase Woodhouse to William Benton, 30 September 1957, Benton MSS, University of Chicago, special collections, Box 282, folder 5.

Chapter 6. The Liberal Moment

1. Iwan Morgan, *Eisenhower Versus the Spenders: The Eisenhower Administration, the Democrats and the Budget, 1953–60* (London, 1990), 125.

2. Kevin Phillips, *The Emerging Republican Majority* (New Rochelle, 1969).

3. Still the most lively treatment of this topic remains Alan Matusow, *The Unraveling of America: A History of Liberalism in the 1960s* (New York, 1984).

4. In the words of historian Kurt Schuparra, Knowland's campaign "gave many conservatives their initial sense of unity and mission, thus providing the spark for ensuing political activism and electoral successes." See Schuparra, *Triumph of the Right: The Rise of the California Conservative Movement, 1945–1966* (Armonk, 1998), 28; Lisa McGirr, *Suburban Warriors: The Origins of the New American Right* (Princeton, 2001); Thomas W. Evans, *The Education of Ronald Reagan: The General Electric Years and the Untold Story of His Conversion to Conservatism* (New York, 2006).

5. Elizabeth Fones-Wolf, *Selling Free Enterprise: The Business Assault on Labor and Liberalism, 1945–60* (Urbana, 1994), chap. 9.

6. This is the view of Gayle B. Montgomery and James W. Johnson in their suggestively titled *One Step from the White House: The Rise and Fall of Senator William F. Knowland* (Berkeley, 1998).

7. See Scuparra, *Triumph of the Right*, 27–28.

8. Whitaker and Baxter statement for Knight in response to Knowland's announcement that he sought the governorship, 1 October 1957, W&B MSS, Box 50, file 51.

9. "This is what I believe" reproduced in Whitaker and Baxter manual for campaign workers, W&B MSS, Box 49, file 27.

10. Lemuel Boulware to Raymond Moley, 9 April 1957 and 18 February 1958, Raymond Moley MSS, Box 6, Boulware file.

11. Constitution and by-laws, National Right to Work Committee, revised and amended 21 June 1958, NRTWC MSS, Hoover Institution, Stanford University, Box 1.

12. Reed Larson, "How Right to Work Was Adopted in Kansas," January 1959, NRTWC MSS, Box 2.

13. L. R. Hart to T. R. Dwyer, 16 September 1957, Knowland MSS, Box 105, political campaign 1958, Oct 1957 file.

14. KQED program, "Profile Bay Area," 20 November 1957, hosted by Roger Boas with guests Sydney Kosser, political editor, *The News*, and William Flynn, Bureau editor, *Newsweek*, W&B MSS, Box 50, file 49.

15. See Elizabeth Tandy Shermer, "Counter-Organizing the Sunbelt: Right to Work Campaigns and Anti-Union Conservatism, 1943–1958," *Pacific Historical Review* 78, 1 (February 2009): 81–119; Kimberly Phillips-Fein, "American Counter-revolutionary: Lemuel Ricketts Boulware and General Electric, 1950–1960," in Nelson Lichtenstein, ed., *American Capitalism: Social Thought and Political Economy in the Twentieth Century* (Philadelphia, 2006), 249–70; Evans, *The Education of Ronald Reagan*, chap. 6.

16. Knowland speech to the student body and faculty of San Bernardino Valley College, 29 September 1958, Knowland MSS, Box 103, press releases and speeches file.

17. Knowland rally at Santa Monica, 9 October 1958; Knowland address to Republican Assembly at Stockton, 4 October 1958, Knowland MSS, Box 102, Santa Monica rally file.

18. Knowland speech at luncheon at Concord, 3 October 1958, Knowland MSS, Box 103, press releases and speeches file.

19. "Double Right-to-Work Victory in California," *Right to Work National Newsletter*, October-November 1957, NRTWC MSS, Box 4.

20. "Facts About the Bay Area," Bay Area Council, 14 October 1957, Knowland MSS, Box 106, labor file.

21. Whitaker and Baxter to Roger Lapham, 1 April 1958, W&B MSS, Box 49, file 53.

22. Bill McClure of W&B to Dick Watkins of the Cupertino Courier, 11 April 1958; Knight speech "California Leading National Recovery," W&B MSS, Box 49, file 4; Knight speech to Republican Volunteer Organizations of Alameda County, 12 May 1958, W&B MSS, Box 49, file 9.

23. *Sacramento Bee*, 20 November 1957, W&B MSS, Box 49, file 11.

24. "Politics in California IV: Mr. Knowland's Opponent," *New Republic*, 30 June 1958, 11–15.

25. Quoted in TRB column, *New Republic*, 27 October 1958, 2. See also Thomas W. Evans, *The Education of Ronald Reagan*, 91–96.

26. Californians for Yes on 18 leaflet, Knowland MSS, Box 107, unions, right to work file 1 of 4.

27. Knowland speech, undated, Knowland MSS, Box 107, unions, right to work file 1 of 4.

28. "Meet the Man Who Wants to Rule America," Knowland MSS, Box 107, right to work file 2 of 4; *New Republic*, 22 September 1958, 2.

29. "*New York Times* Links Knowland and Wife to 'Fascistic, Anti-Semitic Forces,'" California State Federation of Labor newsletter, 19 September 1958, Knowland MSS, Box 108, political 1958 file; Helen Knowland, "At Stake in California: Why Knowland Backs Right-to-Work," *Human Events*, 29 September 1958, Knowland MSS, Box 115, prop 18 file.

30. Helen Knowland to Jim___, 14 October 1958, Knowland MSS, Box 114, Mrs. Knowland file. See also Helen Knowland to Paul Manolis, 3 July 1958, in which she discusses the distribution of campaign literature.

31. Goldwater address "What Has Happened to the Republican Party in Michigan?" at United Republican dinner in Detroit, 20 January 1958, Knowland MSS, Box 113, union literature file.

32. Moley, "Crisis in California," *Newsweek*, 21 July 1958, Knowland MSS, Box 112, labor, Michigan file.

33. Elizabeth Tandy Shermer, "Origins of the Conservative Ascendancy: Barry Goldwater's Early Senate Career and the De-Legitimization of Organized Labor," *Journal of American History* (December 2008): 678–709. What worked in Arizona had a more difficult time in California when we consider that even after decades of mainly Republican administrations state taxes in California were nearly twice as high as in Arizona and the size of government programs to cope with a vastly higher population was much greater. Regulation of business freedom dated back to the clampdown on railroads in the 1910s and the progressive legacy in state politics, though now weak in the state GOP, still made California much less likely than "Sunbelt" states to buy the antilabor, pro-business agenda of the Republican right in its entirety. See comparison of state taxes, fiscal year 1957, in Knowland MSS, Box 112, labor, Michigan file.

34. Lemuel Boulware to Raymond Moley, 20 April 1960, Moley MSS, Box 6, Boulware file.

35. Pat Brown to Raymond Moley, 23 June 1958; Brown to Moley, 30 July 1958, Raymond Moley MSS, Box 6, Pat Brown file.

36. GOP memo, "Pertinent Points, California Political Scene," Knowland MSS, Box 101, election statistics file.

37. "Politics in California III: The Republican Moment of Truth," *New Republic*, 23 June 1958, 11–13.

38. Knowland speech at the Commonwealth Club, San Francisco, 24 October 1958, Knowland MSS, Box 102, Commonwealth Club file.

39. Ethan Rarick, *California Rising: The Life and Times of Pat Brown* (Berkeley, 2005), chaps. 1–3.

40. "Politics in California IV: Mr. Knowland's opponent," *New Republic*, 30 June 1958, 11–15. See Rarick, *California Rising*, 104.

41. Kent oral interview, 291, 145.

42. For the vote on Senate endorsement see Proceedings of the 1958 preprimary

convention of CLLPE, San Francisco, 14 April 1958, 41, and pregeneral election convention, 27 August 1958, 148; James McDevitt speech in preprimary convention proceedings, 32–34.

43. TV script, "Every Other House," KRON-TV and KQED, broadcast 31 August and 1 September 1958, David Selvin MSS, Labor Archives and Research Center, San Francisco State University, Box 27, file 10.

44. David Selvin to George Johns, nd, Selvin MSS, Box 27, file 11.

45. Labor Committee against Proposition 18 radio spot, Selvin MSS, Box 27, file 10.

46. "18 good reasons for voting NO," Selvin MSS, Box 28, file 2.

47. R. W. Johnson, Western Manager, Public Relations, General Electric, statement 22 September 1958, Selvin MSS, Box 27, file 11.

48. "Let's Get Our Campaign Rolling—in High Gear!" open letter, Selvin MSS, Box 27, file 10.

49. San Francisco Labor Council press release, 25 August 1958, Selvin MSS, Box 27, file 13; Prop 18 precinct worker handbook, Selvin MSS, Box 28, file 2.

50. "Who Will Win In California: A Forecast of Statewide Races," Hal Dunleavy and Associates, 1958, Phil Burton MSS, Box 1, 1958 statistics file.

51. Burton press release, 19 May 1958; Burton form letter 1958, Burton MSS, Box 16, 1958 reelection effort file. Burton had won his district by a few hundred votes in 1956; he carried it by more than 3–1 in 1958.

52. Brown speech, 2 September 1958, KTTV station, Knowland MSS, Box 101, Brown radio-TV file. Meg Jacobs examines the relationship between the state and consumerism in her excellent book *Pocketbook Politics: Economic Citizenship in Twentieth-Century America* (Princeton, 2004). Her study argues that the strong relationship between government and the marketplace peters out after World War II, whereas I argue that in California the idea of economic citizenship as part of a governmental regulatory agenda really takes off in these years.

53. Brown speech, 2 September 1958, KTTV, Knowland MSS, Box 101, Brown radio-TV file.

54. Brown speech at Fairmont Hotel, 15 October 1958, Knowland MSS, Box 101, Brown press releases and speeches file.

55. "Politics in California IV: Mr. Knowland's Opponent," *New Republic*, 30 June 1958, 12.

56. "Politics in California III: The Republican Moment of Truth," *New Republic*, 23 June 1958, 13.

57. "The State's Responsibility for Urgent Problems of Urban Expansion and Improvement in California," 7 February 1958, Brown MSS, Box 6, cities and metropolitan problems file.

58. See, for example, Henry Brandon, "A Conversation with Walter Reuther: How Do We Live with Business?" *New Republic*, 21 July 1958, 13–18; "Leon Keyserling on Economic Expansion," *New Republic*, 17 November 1958, 16–17; Arthur Schlesinger Jr., "The Future of Liberalism: The Challenge of Abundance," *The Reporter*, 3 May 1956.

Some of these debates are also analyzed in Kevin Mattson, *When America Was Great: The Fighting Faith of Postwar Liberalism* (London, 2004). An analysis that remains fresh and important is Richard Pells, *The Liberal Mind in a Conservative Age: American Intellectuals in the 1940s and 1950s* (New York, 1985).

59. Schlesinger, "The Future of Liberalism," Brown MSS, Box 7, liberalism/conservatism file.

60. Nathan statement in Brown MSS, Box 6, employment/unemployment file 2.

61. Hubert Humphrey address at the Jefferson-Jackson Day Dinner, San Francisco, 21 September 1957, Brown MSS, Box 7, political speeches and statements file.

62. Steven Zetterberg, "Medical Care and California Issues 1958," 5 February 1958, Brown MSS, Box 7, medical care file.

63. See Zetterberg oral interview, 110–12.

64. Brown speech, "Government with a Heart," Brown MSS, Box 46, government with a heart file.

65. Brown speech at Oakland, 29 October 1958, Brown MSS, Box 46, Oakland speech file.

66. Brown speech, "The Progressive Spirit," Brown MSS, Box 55, progressive spirit file.

67. Quoted in "Politics in California IV: Mr. Knowland's Opponent," *New Republic*, 30 June 1958, 11–15.

68. Brown statement on civil rights, Brown MSS, Box 6, civil rights file.

69. Brown speech to CDC Convention, Fresno, 10 January 1958, Brown MSS, Box 49, CDC file.

70. Wendy Wall, *Inventing the "American Way": The Politics of Consensus from the New Deal to the Civil Rights Movement* (New York, 2008); Fones-Wolf, *Selling Free Enterprise*; McGirr, *Suburban Warriors*.

71. Knowland speech on civil rights, Knowland MSS, Box 101, civil rights file. The definitive appraisal of the relationship between economic power and racial discrimination in an urban context remains Thomas Sugrue, *The Origins of the Urban Crisis: Race and Inequality in Postwar Detroit* (Princeton, 1996).

72. Vernon H. Gaston to Jesse Unruh, 29 July 1958, Brown MSS, Box 38, Republican Committee file.

73. Frank G. Nolan form letter to doctors, 28 July 1958, Brown MSS, Box 38, doctors' committee file; Brown statement to California Medical Association, 8 February 1958, Brown MSS, Box 6, medical care file.

74. Dewey Anderson, "Voting in California: Tabulations and Comments on Registration, Senatorial and Gubernatorial Elections, 1932–1956 with Application to the 1958 Elections," 32, Brown MSS, Box 38, research committee file.

75. Roger Kent to John F. Kennedy, 15 May 1958, Brown MSS, Box 45, Roger Kent file.

76. Brown Fresno visit agenda, 11–12 February 1958, Brown MSS, Box 49, CDC file.

77. "A Political Convention in Britain: Issues, Not Ballyhoo, Hold Stage. Labor Party

Meeting Is Unlike Political Jamborees Held in US—Policies Are Put Above Personalities," *New York Times*, 1 October 1958, 16.

78. Report of the Resolutions Committee of CDC, 1958 convention, CDC MSS, Box 31, file 2.

79. *West Beverly Bray*, March 1958; *West Beverly Bray*, June 1958, CDC MSS, Box 25, file 12.

80. Ed Lybeck to James Roosevelt, 22 July 1958, Roosevelt MSS, Box 302, California political 1958 file.

81. Democratic Party Issues conference, 3 August 1958, CDC MSS, Box 31, file 2.

82. See, for example, research paper for CFYD "The Foreign Policy Proposals of Acheson, Kennan, and Bowles," March 1959, CDC MSS, Box 18, file 5.

83. Report of Democratic Conference on Issues, CFYD, Monterey, 7–8 September 1957, Burton MSS, Box 16, 1950s file.

84. "McCarthy Rips Demo. Unit as 'Hot-Rod Set,'" *San Francisco Call-Bulletin*, 19 February 1958.

85. Mary Ellen Cone to James Roosevelt, 1 August 1958; Roosevelt to Cone, 23 August 1958, Roosevelt MSS, Box 302, California political 1958 file.

86. Arthur Schlesinger, "Death Wish of the Democrats," *New Republic*, 15 September 1958, 7–8.

87. Paul Shaw quoted in "Eggheads and Bosses: Replies to Arthur Schlesinger Jr.," *New Republic*, 29 September 1958, 7–8.

88. Robert Ash and J. L. Childers to all affiliated unions, 24 January 1958, C. L. Dellums MSS, Box 22, Alameda County Council on Political Education 1958 file.

89. "New Faces," *New Republic*, 6 October 1958, 14–16; Jeffery Cohelan to David Thelen, 25 March 1959, Cohelan MSS, Carl Albert Center, University of Oklahoma, Box 5, file 3.

90. Twenty-Second District Democrat campaign brochure, Selvin MSS, Box 24, file 4.

91. San Francisco Labor Council COPE release, 15 September 1958, Selvin MSS, Box 27, file 13; "Justice/Equity," leaflet by LA CIO Council, Selvin MSS, Box 27, file 8.

92. Burton press release, Burton MSS, Box 16, 1958 reelection effort file.

93. Willie Brown oral interview, 112–13.

94. Hal Dunleavy and Associates mail poll, 15–22 August and 29 September to 6 October 1958, Selvin MSS, Box 28, file 1. See also McGirr, *Suburban Warriors* for a discussion of the background to right-wing politics in Orange County, and compare it to Robert O. Self, *American Babylon: Race and the Struggle for Postwar Oakland* (Princeton, 2003).

95. Dollars for Democrats drive, Northern California, 12 November 1958, returns by county; Memorandum from Fay Porter to Dollars for Democrats coordinators, 3 November 1958, re receipts and reports, California Democratic Party MSS, Box 1, D-Day 1958 file.

96. Summary of primary vote in Twenty-Sixth Congressional District; Lewis J. Miller to members of Sixty-First Assembly District Club, 9 June 1958; Crispus Wright

election flyer; Jimmy Roosevelt/Assemblyman Lester McMillan election flyer, Roosevelt MSS, Box 303, California political 1958 file 2.

97. George O'Brien of Electrical Workers to Roosevelt, 22 July 1958, Roosevelt MSS, Box 303, California political 1958 file 2.

98. See Totton J. Anderson, "The 1958 Election in California," *The Western Political Quarterly*, 12:1 part 2, March 1959, 276–300; Results summarized in "California Democratic Council: The First Eight Years," Zetterberg MSS, Box 1, CDC file.

99. Anderson, "The 1958 Election in California," 300.

100. Byron Rumford press release on FEPC, 12 February 1959, Rumford MSS, Box 3, FEPC file. For a snapshot of the durability of the Democratic gains, particularly after redistricting in 1962, see Congressional Directory, 89th Congress, January 1966, 12–22.

101. James Roosevelt statement, 23 May 1958, Roosevelt MSS, Box 303, California political 1958 file 2.

Chapter 7. Democratic Politics and the Brown Administration

1. *Sacramento Story*, AFL-CIO brochure, 1959, Selvin MSS, Box 27, file 6.

2. See Ethan Rarick, *California Rising: The Life and Times of Pat Brown* (Berkeley, 2005) chaps. 6, 7; John Jacobs, *A Rage for Justice: The Passion and Politics of Phillip Burton* (Berkeley, 1998) chaps. 4, 5.

3. Two very accomplished examples are Jennifer Mittelstadt, *From Welfare to Workfare: The Unintended Consequences of Liberal Reform, 1945–1965* (Chapel Hill, 2005) and Jennifer Klein, *For All These Rights: Business, Labor, and the Shaping of America's Public-Private Welfare State* (Princeton, 2003).

4. James Rorty, "FEPC in the States: A Progress Report," *Antioch Review*, Fall 1958, Rumford MSS, Box 3, file 1. For a useful discussion of the broader implications of FEPC in international political terms, see Mary Dudziak, *Cold War Civil Rights: Race and the Image of American Democracy* (Princeton, 2000).

5. Byron Rumford press release, 12 February 1959, Rumford MSS, Box 3, file 2.

6. Rumford press release, 19 February 1959, Rumford MSS, Box 3, file 2; clipping on FEPC passage in Assembly, 19 February 1959, Phil Burton MSS, Box 17, 1959 publicity file.

7. Cohelan statement to the House Judiciary Sub-committee in support of FEPC, 30 April 1959, Cohelan MSS, Box 3, file 5.

8. "$1.25 Minimum Pay Asked," *San Francisco News*, 5 February 1959; George Brown, "Human Rights," CDC Issues paper, February 1960, Democratic Party MSS, Box 1, civil rights 1957-present file.

9. Memo from Fred Gunsky, Education Officer, FEPC, to commissioners and staff, 10 April 1961, C. L. Dellums MSS, Box 8, FEP incoming 1961–62 file.

10. See clipping on passage of FEPC, nd, Burton MSS, Box 17, 1959 publicity file; "Minimum Wage: Half-Loaf," *Labor Review*, 8 April 1959, Burton MSS, Box 16, California Assembly file.

11. Statement of Edward Howden, Executive Officer, FEPC, before Subcommittee on Employment and Manpower, U.S. Senate Committee on Labor and Public Welfare, 29 July 1963, Brown MSS, Box 641, FEPC file.

12. California FEPC report on 1961 civil rights legislative priorities for 7 July and 4 August 1960 conferences, Brown MSS, Box 71, civil rights general file.

13. See Ernesto Galarza, *Farm Workers and Agribusiness in California, 1947–1960* (Notre Dame, 1977), 261–63.

14. See *Congressional Quarterly Almanac*, 1965, 132–33.

15. *Congressional Quarterly Almanac*, 1964, 118.

16. Elizabeth Tandy Shermer, "Creating the Sunbelt: The Economic and Political Transformation of Phoenix, Arizona," Ph.D. dissertation, University of California Santa Barbara, 2009, esp. chap. 8; Elizabeth Fones-Wolf, *Selling Free Enterprise: The Business Assault on Labor and Liberalism, 1945–60* (Urbana, 1994), chap. 9.

17. Carmen Warschaw, oral interview, 432.

18. Steven Zetterberg oral interview, 112, 121, 133.

19. Introduction to "Health Care for California: Report of the Governor's Committee on Medical Aid and Health," December 1960, Zetterberg oral interview, Appendix A.

20. Dr. E. Richard Weinerman, "Trends in Medical Care in California: Implications for Medical Education," presented before Committee on Medical Care Teaching, Association of Teachers of Preventive Medicine, Annual Meeting of American Public Health Association, San Francisco, 31 October 1960, Steve Zetterberg MSS, Box 1, CDC medical articles etc., file.

21. Tom Carvey to Betty Quenon, 24 July 1961, CDC MSS, Box 12, Tom Carvey 1961–62 file.

22. Zetterberg to W. L. Parker, Zetterberg MSS, Box 1, CDC medical articles etc. file.

23. Zetterberg oral interview, 175–204.

24. Draft of CDC medical policy statement, Zetterberg MSS, Box 1, CDC medical articles etc. file.

25. See Colin Gordon, *Dead on Arrival: The Politics of Health Care in Twentieth-Century America* (Princeton, 2003); Alan Derickson, *Health Security for All: Dreams of Universal Health Care in America* (Baltimore, 2005); Jacob Hacker, *The Divided Welfare State: Debate over Public and Private Social Benefits in the United States* (Cambridge, 2002).

26. See material in Burton MSS, Box 15, summary social welfare 1957–63 file; "Governor Signs Pension Bill to Aid Non-Citizens," *Eastside Journal*, 27 July 1961, Burton MSS, Box 8, 1950s clippings file.

27. Napoleon Tercero, Jr., to Brown, received 29 November 1962, Brown MSS, Box 582, political governor December file.

28. Paul Ward to Hale Champion, 29 April 1963, Brown MSS, Box 641, labor through April file.

29. Rarick, *California Rising*, 226; see chap. 10, for the full account of Brown's water project.

30. *Ramparts*, October 1966, 23. Labor and the California Grange opposed the bond

issue to pay for the expansion of the CVP because agribusiness was lobbying successfully to exempt itself from federal excess land law restrictions in order to gain free access to the extra water supply. See Lawrence B. Lee, "California Water Politics: Opposition to the CVP, 1944–1980," *Agricultural History* 54, 3 (July 1980): 402–23.

31. A good alternative case study of this dilemma is the debate between pro-growth and quality of life liberals in San Francisco from the 1970s onward. See Richard DeLeon, *Left Coast City: Progressive Politics in San Francisco, 1975–1991*(Lawrence, 1992).

32. Violet Gunther, National Director of ADA, to Gordon Robinson, nd, *ADA World*, quoted in *Los Angeles Times*, 8 September 1961, ADA MSS, reel 58, no. 5.

33. Sheldon Pollack to Violet Gunther, 6 March 1961; Pollack to Samuel Beer, 25 July 1961, ADA MSS, reel 58, no. 5.

34. "ADA Lists State as 1961 Target: Bay Area First, Los Angeles Will Follow Under Program," *Los Angeles Times*, 8 September 1961, ADA MSS, reel 58, no. 5.

35. Alan Ware, *The Breakdown of Democratic Party Organization, 1940–1980* (Oxford, 1985). Ware's work uses several case studies from different parts of the United States, but includes much material on the party in Berkeley and the East Bay. See also Doug Rossinow's excellent *Visions of Progress: The Left-Liberal Tradition in America* (Philadelphia, 2008), which argues that much common ground shared by different left-wing groups was sacrificed in the cultural battles over the Cold War and civil rights in the 1960s.

36. Lisa McGirr, *Suburban Warriors: The Origins of the New American Right* (Princeton, 2001); Matthew Dallek, *The Right Moment: Ronald Reagan's First Victory and the Decisive Turning Point in American Politics* (New York, 2004); Rick Perlstein, *Before the Storm: Barry Goldwater and the Unmaking of the American Consensus* (New York, 2001); Rick Perlstein, *Nixonland: The Rise of a President and the Fracturing of America* (New York, 2008).

37. Confidential memo, "A Note on the Politics of Reacting to the Reactionaries," 7 November 1961, Kent MSS, Box 1, speeches and prepared remarks file 1 of 4. Emphasis original.

38. Roger Kent, "The Liberal Position," nd, Kent MSS, Box 1, speeches and prepared remarks file 1 of 4.

39. For an analysis of the intellectual architecture of social democracy see Tim Tilton, *The Political Theory of Swedish Social Democracy: Through the Welfare State to Socialism* (Oxford, 1990); Michael Newman, *Socialism: A Very Short Introduction* (Oxford, 2005), chap. 2.

40. Kent radio speech, nd, Kent MSS, Box 1, speeches and prepared remarks file.

41. "Nixon and Brown? Setting an Example?" *Texan Observer*, October 1962, Brown MSS, Box 580, Democratic Campaign October 25–29 file. For Proposition 24 and its political background, see Kurt Schuparra, *Triumph of the Right: The Rise of the California Conservative Movement, 1945–1966* (Armonk, 1998), 70–71.

42. Schuparra, *Triumph of the Right*, chap. 4.

43. Tom Carvey to Brown, 21 September 1962, Brown MSS, Box 582, CDC Aug-Dec file.

44. Brown press release, 29 August 1962, and Democratic platform of 1962, Brown MSS, Box 585, political press releases file.

45. Brown address to the biennial convention of the California Federation of Labor, Long Beach, 20 August 1962, Brown MSS, Box 585, political press releases file.

46. Brown press release, 11 September 1962, Brown MSS, Box 585, ibid.

47. Flyer and Kyle Palmer sheet in Brown MSS, Box 582, CDC file.

48. Roger Kent oral history, 196–204.

49. Shermer, "Creating the Sunbelt," chap. 8, 46–47: Shermer notes that California Chambers of Commerce after the 1962 election were disappointed by the GOP's failure to control the political agenda and looked enviously to neighboring Arizona for lessons.

50. Otis Chandler to Pat Brown, 29 November 1962, Brown MSS, Box 582, political governor December file. Brown replied on 26 December 1962 that "I regard the result of the election as a mandate from *all* of the people, not from special interest groups, and I fully intend to carry out that mandate with the support of the *Times* and other fair-minded members of the press."

51. Dr. S. W. Brossman to Brown, 31 May 1962, Brown MSS, Box 586, Orange County file.

52. *Orange County Register* editor C. C. Wilkinson was a major figure on the right in Southern California, and he wrote to Brown on 23 April 1962 to solicit his views on these topics for his readers, clearly as a prelude to the launch of a far-right challenge to Brown in the gubernatorial election: see Brown MSS, Box 586, ibid, and McGirr, *Suburban Warriors*, 154; Schuparra, *Triumph of the Right*, chap. 3.

53. William F. Stanton campaign leaflet, 1962, Cohelan MSS, Box 5, file 31.

54. Nancy Swadesh summary report on Santa Clara County, 18 November 1961, Democratic Party MSS, Box 8, unlabeled file 5 of 11.

55. Santa Clara Democratic Party release, 21 September 1962, Brown MSS, Box 585, political press releases Aug-Dec file.

56. See *Congressional Directory*, 89th Congress, 14–15. Don Edwards won the Ninth District in the House, comprising part of San Jose and part of southern Alameda County, and became a liberal stalwart in Washington for the next thirty years.

57. Text of statement of Thomas Pitts of the CFL to Democratic Platform Committee, 25 July 1962, Kent MSS, Box 1, California Labor Federation file.

58. Beilenson oral interview, 115–26.

59. Willie Brown oral interview, 79–93; "Brown Cops CDC Endorsement," *Sun-Reporter*, 5 May 1962, Phil Burton MSS, Box 1, 1962 other SF campaigns file.

60. For details of the politics of Berkeley see William Rorabaugh, *Berkeley At War: The 1960s* (New York, 1989), 53–54; Ware, *The Breakdown of Democratic Party Organization, 1940–1980*, 55–56. Sarria quote from a campaign postcard, Sarria MSS, GLBT Historical Society, San Francisco, Box 28, file 6. See also Nan Alamilla Boyd, *Wide Open Town: A History of Queer San Francisco to 1965* (Berkeley, 2003), 59–60; 210–12.

61. Robert F. Wilcox, "Filling the Leadership Gap," *CDC Bulletin*, August 1962, Democratic Party MSS, Box 1, CDC file.

62. Tom Carvey, "Governor Brown, Nixon, and the CDC," CDC campaign bulletin, 6 August 1962, Democratic Party MSS, Box 1, CDC file.

63. G. M. Snyder to Pat Brown, 19 August 1962, Brown MSS, Box 582, CDC Aug-Dec file.

64. Richard F. Curt to Brown, 17 October 1962, Brown MSS, Box 582, Democratic State Organization political file.

65. Zetterberg to Richards, 27 July 1962, Brown MSS, Box 582, CDC June-July file.

66. Frank Fraggiosa to Brown, 28 December 1962, Box 581, political contributions 20 Nov.-Dec. file.

67. Report of the Southern California Get-Out-the-Vote Committee of the California Democratic Council, 27 January 1963, Zetterberg MSS, Box 2, CDC 1963 file.

68. See *Congressional Directory*, 88th Congress, 1st Session; California Statement of Vote, November 1962.

69. Press release re appointment of Carmen Warschaw and Robert Kingsley as cochairs of Women's Activities in southern California, 25 April 1962, Brown MSS, Box 585, political press releases Jan.–July file. Warschaw was an Unruh loyalist who was distrustful of CDC, but both she and Unruh were committed to the same agenda as CDC Democrats in the 1960s even if their personalities and methods differed.

70. Californians for Liberal Representation leaflet, 1962, Burton MSS, Box 1, 1962 other campaigns file.

Chapter 8. Welfare Reform and the Idea of the Family

1. Wilbur Cohen, "A New Look at Welfare," speech at Eastern Massachusetts chapter, National Association of Social Workers, Boston, 16 November 1961, Burton MSS, Box 18, Assembly, medical care file.

2. For a discussion of the federal background, see Julian Zelizer, *Taxing America: Wilbur D. Mills, Congress, and the State, 1945–1975* (Cambridge, 2000); Alan Matusow, *The Unraveling of America: A History of Liberalism in the 1960s* (New York, 1984). A very good recent analysis of the ability of state bureaucracies to perpetuate themselves is Gareth Davies, *See Government Grow: Education Politics from Johnson to Reagan* (Lawrence, 2007). A full description of Phil Burton and his role in passing AB 59 can be found in John Jacobs, *A Rage for Justice: The Passion and Politics of Phillip Burton* (Berkeley, 1995); Jonathan Bell, "Social Democracy and the Rise of the Democratic Party in California, 1950–1964," *Historical Journal* 49, 2 (June 2006): 497–524.

3. Harry Girvetz to Alexander Pope, 20 April 1960, Brown MSS, Box 71, social welfare, general file.

4. Helen Nelson, governor's office, to Alexander Pope, 18 July 1960, Box 73, consumers file. The relationship between the state and the idea of the consumer is a burgeoning field of historical enquiry, but tends to focus on consumerism as a substitute for social welfare rather than a part of it, particularly in the postwar years when antistatism was resurgent. See Meg Jacobs, *Pocketbook Politics: Economic Citizenship in Twentieth-Century America* (Princeton, 2004), which argues that the state enforcement of a fair

relationship between producer and consumer dwindled after the war. See also Lizabeth Cohen, *A Consumer's Republic: The Politics of Mass Consumption in Postwar America* (New York, 2004); Kathleen Donohue, *Freedom from Want: American Liberalism and the Idea of the Consumer* (Baltimore, 2005).

5. See Bell, "Social Democracy and the Rise of the Democratic Party in California," 517–18.

6. Jacobus tenBroek and Floyd W. Matson, *Hope Deferred: Public Welfare and the Blind* (Berkeley, 1959), 1, 2, 25, 127–29, 137.

7. Girvetz to Alexander Pope, 20 April 1960, Brown MSS, Box 71, social welfare, general file.

8. Wedemeyer to Pat Brown, 7 July 1961, Brown MSS, Box 74, social welfare file.

9. Governor's Welfare Commission interim committee report, 8 December 1960, Burton MSS, Box 18, Governor's Welfare Committee file.

10. See Brown, *Race, Money, and the American Welfare State*; Michael Katz, *The Price of Citizenship: Redefining America's Welfare State* (New York, 2002); Jacob Hacker, *The Divided Welfare State: The Battle over Public and Private Social Benefits in the United States* (Cambridge, 2002); S. Jay Kleinberg, "Widows' Welfare in the Great Depression," in *The Roosevelt Years: New Perspectives on American History, 1933–1945*, ed. Robert Garson and Stuart Kidd (Edinburgh, 1999); Robert Lieberman, *Shifting the Color Line: Race and the American Welfare State* (Cambridge, Mass., 1998); Ira Katznelson, *When Affirmative Action Was White: An Untold Story of Racial Inequality in Twentieth-Century America* (New York, 2005).

11. Jacobus tenBroek, "The Law of Crimes and the Law of Welfare," address to California State Welfare Workers Organization, 7 February 1961, CDC MSS, Box 31, file 5.

12. Ralph Goff to Tammie Stephens, 30 August 1963; Goff to Esther Smith, 28 August 1963, Brown MSS, Box 616, Aid to Needy Children July-December file.

13. Statement of Mrs. Maryland Gray, Hearings of the California Assembly Committee on Social Welfare, 12–13 December 1966, San Francisco, California State Archives file LP105:14.

14. William MacDougall, "Public Welfare in the Sixties: A County Long-Range Look," 16 November 1961, Burton MSS, Box 18, ibid.

15. Jacobus tenBroek, "Phillip Burton: Statesman of Welfare," 30 October 1963, Welfare Achievements Luncheon, San Francisco, Burton MSS, Box 18, 1963 press releases file.

16. Burton quoted in Richard Reinhardt, "The Cockatoo Squawks," *San Francisco Magazine*, January 1964.

17. See Jacobs, *A Rage for Justice*, 89–90, and chap. 5.

18. Kent oral interview, 21, 28.

19. Assembly Bill 59 summary, Jack Casey MSS, California State Archives, LP161:123.

20. Memorandum, Tom Moore, Legislative Coordinator, California Department of Social Welfare, to Cal Locker, Health and Welfare Agency, 26 February 1963, Brown MSS, Box 642, health and welfare file 2.

21. Assembly Bill 266, Aid to Disabled, incorporated into AB 59, Burton MSS, Box 15, AB 266 file.

22. AB 59 summary, 21.

23. See Burton press releases on Assembly bills in Burton MSS, Box 16, California Assembly bills file.

24. AB 59 summary, 5.

25. "Burton Smiles at Welfare Critics," *San Francisco News*, 23 May 1963. For an in-depth discussion of Burton's efforts to enact major changes in California welfare laws, see Jacobs, *A Rage for Justice*, chap. 5.

26. *Cal-Tax News*, October 1963; Kern County Board of Supervisors, resolution on AB 59, 7 January 1964, Burton MSS, Box 18, AB59 opposition file.

27. Jacobs, *A Rage for Justice*, 102–10.

28. AB 59 summary details the various stages of the bill's legislative passage on pages 23–27.

29. Ibid., 23.

30. Director's newsletter, California Department of Social Welfare, Dec 63-Jan 64, Casey MSS, LP161:123.

31. H.R. and Mary Drummond to Pat Brown, 28 January 1963, Casey MSS, LP 161:123.

32. Resolution of Kern County Board of Supervisors, 7 January 1964, Casey MSS, LP161:123.

33. Memo from Georgina Stewart to Jack Casey re Welfare's role in relation to the Economic Opportunities Act, 2 September 1964, Casey MSS, LP161:124.

34. Martin Rein, "The Strange Case of Public Dependency," *Trans-Action*, March–April 1965, 16–23 in California Social Welfare Committee MSS, California State Archives, Sacramento, LP104:32.

35. Rein acknowledged his "debt to the seminal works of Richard Titmuss" on the first page of his article. See also Richard M. Titmuss, *The Philosophy of Welfare: Selected Writings of Richard M. Titmuss*, ed. Brian Abel-Smith and Kay Titmuss (London, 1987); D. A. Reisman, *Richard Titmuss: Welfare and Society* (London, 1977). The classic American exposition of this thesis is Frances Fox Piven and Richard Cloward, *Regulating the Poor: The Functions of Public Welfare* (London, 1972).

36. "Social Services for Public Welfare Recipients" agenda, 30–31 July 1965, Jack Casey MSS, California State Archives, LP161.126.

37. See John Burton oral history interview, 1986–87, by Julie Shearer, Regional Oral History Office, Bancroft Library, BANC 90/81c, 37–40: Burton argues Reagan often only managed paper victories in practice, and that legislative stalemate was normal during his governorship. See also Matthew Dallek, *The Right Moment: Ronald Reagan's First Victory and the Decisive Turning Point in American Politics* (New York, 2004), passim.

38. See John D'Emilio, "Gay Politics, Gay Community: San Francisco's Experience," *Socialist Review* 55 (1981): 77–104, and his *Sexual Politics, Sexual Communities: The Making of a Homosexual Minority in the United States, 1940–1970* (Chicago, 1983); Su-

san Stryker and Jim Van Buskirk, *Gay by the Bay: A History of Queer Culture in the San Francisco Bay Area* (San Francisco, 1996); Nan Alamilla Boyd, *Wide Open Town: A History of Queer San Francisco to 1965* (Berkeley, 2003); Martin Meeker, *Contacts Desired: Gay and Lesbian Communications and Community, 1940s–1970s* (Chicago, 2005). There are many other studies, many focused on particular case studies. An example of an urban study is Marc Stein, *City of Sisterly and Brotherly Loves: Lesbian and Gay Philadelphia, 1945–1972* (Chicago, 2000); a rural milieu is depicted in John Howard, *Men like That: A Southern Queer History* (Chicago, 1999).

39. On the latter point, an excellent treatment remains Randy Shilts, *The Mayor of Castro Street: The Life and Times of Harvey Milk* (New York, 1982).

40. D'Emilio rightly notes in his landmark survey of San Francisco gay political development that sexual "orientation created a kind of unity, but other aspects of identity brought to the surface conflicting needs and interests," "Gay Politics, Gay Community," 94. Randy Shilts is less reserved, noting that many gay activists in Democratic clubs in the 1970s that were direct descendents of SIR and CRH were unwilling to campaign hard for openly gay men and women to run for elected office "as long as there was an adequate supply of liberal friends willing to attend their cocktail parties, make annual appearances at Toklas [Club] dinners and assure members that there were heterosexuals who thought gays were just fine after all," *The Mayor of Castro Street*, 150.

41. Another example was the CRH, and often the same key individuals took central membership positions in several different groups that aimed to recruit support for the homophile cause from different sources. There is a flourishing literature on homophile activism in this period, key works being Martin Meeker, *Contacts Desired: Gay and Lesbian Communications and Community,1940s–1970s* (Chicago, 2005); Boyd, *Wide-Open Town*; John D'Emilio, *Sexual Politics, Sexual Communities: The Making of a Homosexual Minority in the United States, 1940–1970*, 2nd ed. (Chicago, 1998). An interesting new theoretical perspective on how gay activism uses public protests to advance its political agenda is Amin Ghaziani, *The Dividends of Dissent: How Conflict and Culture Work in Lesbian and Gay Marches on Washington* (Chicago, 2008).

42. Quoted in Meeker, *Contacts Desired*, 154; see chap. 4, for a full analysis of the media "discovery" of queer subcultures in the 1960s.

43. This was never a simple division, and would inspire vigorous debate in both movements in later years, but it was a political strategy in the 1960s: see Ghaziani, *The Dividends of Dissent*, 19; Premilla Nadasen, *Welfare Warriors: The Welfare Rights Movement in the United States* (New York, 2005).

44. Minutes of the meeting of SIR committee, 14 December 1964, Lucas MSS, Box 11, folder 2.

45. Report to the President and Board of SIR, nd, Lucas MSS, Box 11, folder 2.

46. For neat summaries of these events, including in addition the repeal of the state's vagrancy law, the State Supreme Court decision that decoupled the licensing of bars from the sexual orientation of the clientele, the aftermath of the police raid on the Tay-Bush Inn, and well-known drag queen Jose Sarria's run for Supervisor in 1961, see Boyd,

Wide Open Town, 204–18; Christopher Agee, "Gayola: Police Professionalization and the Politics of San Francisco's Gay Bars, 1950–1968," *Journal of the History of Sexuality* 15, 3 (September 2006): 462–89.

47. SIR form letter from President William Beardemphl and Secretary Mark Forrester, nd, Phyllis Lyon and Del Martin MSS, Box 19, file 7.

48. Introduction to the Statement of Purpose of SIR, 1965, Don Lucas MSS, Box 11, folder 2.

49. Consultation on the Church and the Homosexual, Report from Group 1, summary by Del Martin, 30 May-2 June 1964, Lyon/Martin MSS, Box 17, file 14. For discussions of the relationship between Christianity and civil rights, see David L. Chappell, *Stone of Hope: Prophetic Religion and the Death of Jim Crow* (Chapel Hill, 2003); Mark Newman, *Divine Agitators: The Delta Ministry and Civil Rights in Mississippi* (Athens, 2003); Newman, *Getting Right with God: Southern Baptists and Desegregation, 1945–1995* (Tuscaloosa, 2001).

50. Report to the President and Board of SIR, Don Lucas, Lucas MSS, Box 11, file 2. The classic study of Mattachine and the problems it faced in its search for respectability in the 1950s remains D'Emilio, *Sexual Politics, Sexual Communities*, early chapters.

51. Program for the DOB 4th annual convention, San Francisco, 20 August 1966, Lyon/Martin MSS, Box 20, file 21.

52. SIR leaflet, "Tuesday 3 November 1964: Vote Today," Lucas MSS, Box 11, folder 3.

53. A. Cecil Williams, "On Getting and Using Power," *Vector*, January 1965, 4.

54. *Vector*, January 1965, 12.

55. *Vector*, September 1965.

56. SIR memo to members re meeting with Moscone and Hedricks, 1966, Lyon/Martin MSS, Box 19, file 7.

57. Burton made reference to his longstanding alliance with Martin and Lyon since the early 1960s in his 1982 campaign literature, when he was forced to run an aggressive campaign for the first time in years against Republican Milton Marks after letting his constituency work languish—see Burton for Congress Committee handout, 1982, Burton MSS, Box 4, gay/lesbian file 2. The boast is supported by Del Martin herself, quoted in Burton's literature that year as saying "I'll never forget Phil Burton being at gay organizations twenty years ago—when no other public official would have dreamed of coming around." See Jacobs, *A Rage for Justice*, 462.

58. Paper "Directions for SIR in 1965," Lucas MSS, Box 11, file 2.

59. Mark Forrester of SIR to gay rights activists, nd, Lyon/Martin MSS, Box 19, file 7.

60. For the national story see Michael K. Brown, *Race and the American Welfare State* (Ithaca, 1999); Gareth Davies, *From Opportunity to Entitlement: The Transformation and Decline of Great Society Liberalism* (Lawrence, 1996); Robert Lieberman, *Shifting the Color Line: Race and the American Welfare State* (Cambridge, 1998). For material on San Francisco, the Don Lucas papers at the GLBT Historical Society in San Francisco provided much useful material.

61. See Calvin Brook Colt, chair, Steering Committee of the Central City Citizens'

Council, to Edward Anderson, chair, Mission Community Action Board, 18 March 1966, Don Lucas MSS, Box 15, folder 2.

62. See CCCC membership list, Lucas MSS, Box 15, folder 3.

63. Edward Hansen, Fred Bird, Mark Forrester, and Victor De Marais, "The White Ghetto: Youth and Young Adults in the Tenderloin Area of Downtown San Francisco," Lucas MSS, Box 15, folder 5. Forrester was president of SIR, and Ed Hansen was involved in the Glide Memorial Church, a prominent center of homophile activism. The CRH also contributed material to the drafting of the report: see Lucas MSS, Box 15, folder 7. See also "Proposal for Confronting the Tenderloin Problem: A Proposal submitted to the EOC by Mattachine Society Inc." Lucas MSS, Box 15, folder 1.

64. Calvin Brook Colt of CCCC to Edward Anderson, 18 March 1966; Colt to members of EOC, 29 April 1966, Lucas MSS, Box 15, folder 2; for implementation of Central City project, see Lucas MSS, Box 11, folder 11; Box 13, folders 13, 14, 15.

65. Hansen, Bird, Forrester, and De Marais, "The White Ghetto," 12–13.

66. Nancy May, SIR Political Committee report, *Vector*, December 1965, 9.

67. See Felicia Kornbluh, *The Battle for Welfare Rights: Politics and Poverty in Modern America* (Philadelphia, 2007), chap.7.

68. Central City target area statistical profile, Lucas MSS, Box 15, folder 1.

69. Colt to EOC, 29 April 1966, Lucas MSS, Box 15, folder 2.

70. Colt to Anderson, Chair, Mission Community Action Board, 18 March 1966, Lucas MSS, Box 15, file 2.

71. Hansen, Bird, Forrester, and De Marais, "The White Ghetto."

Chapter 9. Culture Wars, Politics, and Power

1. Lisa McGirr, *Suburban Warriors: The Origins of the New American Right* (Princeton, 2001); Matthew Dallek, *The Right Moment: Ronald Reagan's First Victory and the Decisive Turning Point in American Politics* (New York, 2004); Rick Perlstein, *Before the Storm: Barry Goldwater and the Unmaking of the American Consensus* (New York, 2001); Kurt Schuparra, *Triumph of the Right: The California Conservative Movement, 1945–1966* (Armonk, 1998).

2. See Michael Flamm, *Law and Order: Street Crime, Civil Unrest, and the Crisis of Liberalism in the 1960s* (New York, 2005).

3. See Ronald Radosh, *Divided They Fell: The Demise of the Democratic Party, 1964–1996* (New York, 1996); Perlstein, *Before the Storm*; Rick Perlstein, *Nixonland: The Rise of a President and the Fracturing of America* (New York, 2008).

4. Bruce Miroff, *The Liberals' Moment: The McGovern Insurgency and the Identity Crisis of the Democratic Party* (Lawrence, 2007). A stimulating debate on this book, which hinges on the question of whether the weaknesses of the McGovern campaign were unavoidable given the fact that his campaign was a product of minority groups, can be found in Kenneth S. Baer, "Glory Days: A Review of Bruce Miroff's *The Liberals' Moment*," *Forum* 5, 4 (2008), Article 9, and there is also a response from Miroff.

5. Real estate listing, Byron Rumford MSS, Box 7, prop 14 correspondence file 1 of 2.

6. *Carta*, editorial, 1 August 1964, Rumford MSS, Box 1, folder 9.

7. Thomas Sugrue, *The Origins of the Urban Crisis: Race and Inequality in Postwar Detroit* (Princeton, 1996). See also Robert O. Self, *American Babylon: Race and the Struggle for Postwar Oakland* (Princeton, 2003), esp. chap. 4.

8. "Where Shall We Live?" Report of the Commission on Race and Housing, Conclusions from a three-year study of racial discrimination in housing (Berkeley, 1958), 1: 43, Rumford MSS, Box 1, folder 1.

9. Bayard Rustin, "From Protest to Politics: The Future of the Civil Rights Movement," *Commentary*, February 1964, 25–31. For a good analysis of this theme in national civil rights politics, see Dona Cooper Hamilton and Charles V. Hamilton, "The Dual Agenda of Civil Rights Organizations Since the New Deal: Social Welfare Policies and Civil Rights," *Political Science Quarterly* 107, 3 (Autumn 1992): 435–52.

10. See statement by Alan Cranston to the Western Democratic Conference, 15 February 1957, Cranston MSS, Box 11, CDC speeches file: "I come to you directly from the South—Texas, Mississippi, Alabama, and Georgia. I went to feel the winds of freedom blowing there—and the counterminds of fear and suppression. And I want to put Western thinking to a Southern test."

11. Assembly Bill 1240 (Rumford Act), Rumford MSS, Box 1, folder 3.

12. See details of legislative sponsors of civil rights bills in California in Rumford MSS, Box 1, folder 1; details of Senate chairmanships in Rumford MSS, Box 1, folder 2. In a series of cases the U.S. Supreme Court would mandate the redrawing of state legislative boundaries to reflect population density.

13. "Freedom Ride Urged to Aid Rumford Bill," *Berkeley Daily Gazette*, 30 May 1963, Rumford MSS, Box 1, folder 2.

14. Daniel Klein broadcast over KCBS radio, San Francisco, 13 July 1964, Rumford MSS, Box 1, folder 9.

15. Phil Garrison editorial, *Antelope Valley Ledger-Gazette*, 23 December 1963; L. H. Wilson to CREA members, 31 December 1963, Rumford MSS, Box 1, folder 7.

16. Radio script "Battle of the Ballots," Rumford MSS, Box 7, Prop 14 file 2 of 3.

17. Schuparra, *Triumph of the Right*, 105–8.

18. Letter from CRA officers to *Los Angeles Times* headed "CRA Officers Take Issue with Chief's Words on Proposition 14, Rumford MSS, Box 6, AB1240 file 1 of 3; Anderson quoted in "It's Different in California, Where Prejudices Are Imported," *Sunday State Bulletin and Advertiser*, 4 October 1964, A5, Rumford MSS, Box 7, Prop 14 correspondence file 2 of 2. Despite CRA moderates' claims that Frizzelle's views "would convert 'Jim Crow' into our national purpose," they could not regain control of the CRA committee. See McGirr, *Suburban Warriors*, chap. 3, for an account of the right's takeover of CRA in the early 1960s and its use as a vehicle for Goldwater's 1964 campaign and in favor of Prop 14.

19. "Californians Against Proposition 14" mailer, 1964, Rumford MSS, Box 7, Prop 14 file 2 of 3.

20. Schuparra, *Triumph of the Right*, 105–6.

21. "Scope of Move Against Fair Housing Is Vast," *Sacramento Bee*, 11 April 1964, Democratic Party MSS, Box 8, Californians for Fair Housing 1964 file.

22. "Hawaii's Hall Raps Racist Realty Group," *The Dispatcher*, 27 November 1964, Rumford MSS, Box 2, file 3.

23. "Racialism in California," *New York Times*, 22 September 1964.

24. Jesse Unruh, "Civil Rights and Civil Wrongs," speech to Associated Students of UCLA, Westwood, 8 January 1964, Rumford MSS, Box 4, file 3.

25. Rumford, "The Fair Housing Act," Rumford MSS, Box 1, file 5.

26. "Minority Groups and Intergroup Relations in the San Francisco Bay Area," September 1962, Rumford MSS, Box 4, files 1 and 2.

27. FEPC statement concerning fair housing, 20 June 1966, Rumford MSS, Box 6, AB1240 file 3 of 3.

28. "Housing Initiative Vote Is Blow to Rights Advocates," *Sacramento Bee*, 10 November 1964.

29. "Brown Says He Accepts Will of People on 14," *Sacramento Bee*, 10 November 1964. Brown's view may have been influenced by reading the views of correspondents writing that anti-fair housing voters wanted the right "to determine whether or not they want to live next to a Negro, with a low moral standard, a large percentage of their children illegitimate and who constitute a very large percentage of our criminal element." This same correspondent claimed that he had "no prejudice against Negroes." See James Gammon to Jesse Unruh, 27 February 1963, Brown MSS, Box 640, housing discrimination file.

30. Roger Kent oral interview, 296, 298.

31. Carmen Warschaw oral interview, 246.

32. Ibid., 247. Pat Brown persuaded Mosk to withdraw from the race, possibly using allegations of marital infidelity to help make up his mind. Brown later appointed him to the State Supreme Court. See Ethan Rarick, *California Rising: The Life and Times of Pat Brown* (Berkeley, 2003), 280.

33. Alan Cranston acceptance speech at CDC convention, Long Beach, 22 February 1964, Cranston MSS, Box 11, CDC speeches file.

34. Cranston release re his speech at Mexican American Political Association State Convention, Biltmore Hotel, 9 November 1963, Cranston MSS, Box 503, AC issues 1964 file.

35. Cranston speech at National Press Club, Washington DC, 22 April 1964, Cranston MSS, Box 503, AC issues 1964 file.

36. Kent oral interview, 16–17. On Unruh see Bill Boyarsky, *Big Daddy: Jesse Unruh and the Art of Power Politics* (Berkeley, 2008); Jackson K. Putnam, *Jess: The Political Career of Jesse Marvin Unruh* (Lanham, 2005); John Jacobs, *A Rage for Justice: The Passion and Politics of Phillip Burton* (Berkeley, 1995), chap. 5; Rarick, *California Rising*, 278–81.

37. CDC vote in "Alan Cranston: The Cause of Peace," *CDC Bulletin*, May 1964, Cranston MSS, Box 503, CDC '64 Long Beach file; district breakdown in Convention voting tally, Cranston MSS, Box 503, CDC convention file.

38. Rarick, *California Rising*, 282–83, 189–204.

39. Pierre Salinger of U.S. Senator press release, 12 May 1964, California Democratic Party MSS, Box 4, 1964 campaigns file.

40. *Liberal Democrat*, June 1964, 1.

41. California Labor Council on Political Education 1964 primary election guide, Cranston MSS, Box 503, ibid. For a discussion of organized labor's engagement with party politics in this period, see Nelson Lichtenstein, *Walter Reuther: The Most Dangerous Man in Detroit* (Urbana, 1995); Kevin Boyle, *The UAW and the Heyday of American Liberalism, 1945–1968* (Ithaca, 1995); Taylor Dark, *The Unions and the Democrats: An Enduring Alliance* (Ithaca, 1999).

42. Cranston address to African American political leaders at the Furniture Mart, Los Angeles, 5 May 1964, Cranston MSS, Box 503, AC on issues 1964 file.

43. Rally for Cranston and James Roosevelt, Hamilton High School, 26 May 1964, Cranston MSS, ibid.

44. Cranston press release of speech at San Bernardino, 28 May 1964; press release of speech at Baptist Ministers' Council, Los Angeles, 12 May 1964, Cranston MSS, Box 503, ibid.

45. California official statement of vote, 2 June 1964, Cranston MSS, Box 503, official statement of vote file.

46. Cathie Brown to Cranston, 3 June 1964, and others like it, Cranston MSS, Box 503, correspondence file.

47. Kent oral interview, 234.

48. "Burton's Record Fits Him for Job," *Union Service Reporter*, January 1964, Burton MSS, Box 2, PB remembrance 1964 file.

49. "An open letter to Phil Burton," *The Mallet*, 14 December 1963; "Burton 'Image' Assailed," *San Francisco Chronicle*, 6 February 1964.

50. See William Rorabaugh, *Berkeley at War: The 1960s* (New York, 1989); Rarick, *California Rising*, chap. 14.

51. See Gerald Horne, *Fire This Time: The Watts Uprising and the 1960s* (Charlottesville, 1995); Michael W. Flamm, *Law and Order: Street Crime, Civil Unrest, and the Crisis of Liberalism in the 1960s* (New York, 2005).

52. *Congressional Directory*, 89th Congress, 2nd session, 1966, 21. See Mike Davis, "The Next Little Dollar: The Private Governments of San Diego," in Mike Davis, Kelly Mayhew, and Jim Miller, *Under the Perfect Sun: The San Diego Tourists Never See* (New York, 2003), 82.

53. "CDC's New Chief to War on Unruh," *Los Angeles Herald-Examiner*, 22 March 1965, A3.

54. Philip Soto to Si Casady, 23 March 1965, CDC MSS, Box 12, file 5.

55. Pat Brown to Casady, 16 September 1965, CDC MSS, Box 12, file 4.

56. Lou Shaw, "The Last Hurrah," CDC MSS, Box 12, file 4.

57. "Explanation of Charges Relating to the Competency of Simon Casady as President of the California Democratic Council," 24 October 1965, CDC MSS, Box 12, file 4.

58. "Cranston Working to Oust Casady," *San Diego Union*, 22 January 1966.

59. "Answer to the Charges Against Simon Casady," CDC MSS, Box 12, file 4.

60. See CDC endorsed candidates list, 2–3 April 1966, Democratic Party MSS, Box 2, candidates, primary 1966 file. CDC endorsed Cohelan's challenger Bob Scheer, plus Congressmen Robert Leggett, Phil Burton, Don Edwards, B. F. Sisk, James Corman, Tom Rees, George Brown, Ed Roybal, Richard Hanna, and Lionel Van Deerlin.

61. Jeffery Cohelan to Olin Teague, 27 May 1966, Cohelan MSS, Box 6, file 23.

62. Good studies of the politics of Berkeley and the East Bay include Rorabaugh, *Berkeley at War*, esp. chap. 3; Robert Cohen and Robert Zelnick, eds., *The Free Speech Movement: Reflections on Berkeley in the 1960s* (Berkeley, 2002).

63. See Marshall Windmiller, "Vietnam and the Berkeley Congressman," broadcast on KPFA Berkeley, 7 April 1966, Cohelan MSS, Box 6, file 23; Rorabaugh, *Berkeley at War*, 99–103.

64. Robert Pickus, "Peace Politics, the New Left and the Pity of It All," essay in Cohelan MSS, Box 6, file 25.

65. Rorabaugh, *Berkeley at War*, 101.

66. "Inside Report: A New Left Near Win," *Washington Post*, 29 June 1966.

67. "Inside Report: Leftist Wrecking Crew," *Washington Post*, 7 February 1966.

68. "Scheer Takes a Stand," campaign leaflet, Cohelan MSS, Box 6, file 27.

69. Scheer campaign material, Cohelan MSS, Box 6, file 23.

70. Buddy Stein and David Wellman, "The Scheer Campaign," *Studies on the Left*, Jan/Feb 1967, Social Protest MSS, UC Berkeley, microfilm reel 73.

71. Carolyn Craven, Buddy Stein, Dave Wellman, "Notes from the Underground: A Critique of the Scheer program," nd, Social Protest MSS, reel 72.

72. Scheer for Congress letter, Social Protest MSS, reel 72.

73. See Maurice Isserman, *The Other American: The Life of Michael Harrington* (New York, 2000).

74. Michael Harrington, "Why I Am a Democratic Socialist," Harvard-Radcliffe YPSL, April 1967, Social Protest MSS, reel 72.

75. See Cranston MSS, Box 516, Cranston on the issues file.

76. Cranston speech at AFL-CIO state convention, 24 September 1968, Cranston MSS, Box 517, AFL-CIO convention file.

77. Memo from David Thompson to Sandy Wiener re the black community—a strategy, Cranston MSS, Box 515, black community organization file.

78. Alameda county analysis, Cranston MSS, Box 519, post-election analysis file.

79. An *LA Times* poll in October noted that "Cranston continues to receive very heavy support from the ethnic minorities. He does well among Catholic voters and particularly well among Negroes and Jews. . . . Rafferty continues to do better among Caucasians and Protestants than he does among voters as a whole; and there is a continuing

tendency for his support to increase as the age and income level of the respondents rise." See *LA Times*, 7 October 1968.

80. See Brennan, *Turning Right in the Sixties*, for a good discussion of the 1960s as a decade in which clearer ideological identities were established in party politics.

81. Perlstein, *Nixonland*.

82. See Kimberly Phillips-Fein, *Invisible Hands: The Rise of the Right from the New Deal to Reagan* (New York, 2009). There have been some recent studies of liberal politics, notably Miroff, *The Liberals' Moment*, but many studies have now given up on the left as a viable topic.

83. Bud Curtis analysis of 1968 campaign, Cranston MSS, Box 519, post-election analysis file.

84. Charles Warren to Jeffery Cohelan, 6 July 1966, Cohelan MSS, Box 6, file 20.

85. Warschaw oral interview, 307; emphasis original.

86. Kent oral interview, 260.

87. Ibid., 298.

88. "Golden State's Financial Crisis," newsletter from Research Center, Republican State Central Committee, 20 March 1964, Democratic Party MSS, Box 4, 1964 campaigns file.

89. Robert Sutton, VP CBS Radio and General Manager KNX radio, broadcast 20 August 1965, Roosevelt MSS, Box 328, 1965–66 district office file.

90. A full treatment of this theme is provided in Flamm, *Law and Order*, esp. chap. 6.

91. Memo to J. Roosevelt attached to transcript of Sutton broadcast of 20 August 1965, Roosevelt MSS, Box 328, 1965–66 district office file.

92. See Thomas W. Evans, *The Education of Ronald Reagan: The General Electric Years and the Untold Story of His Conversion to Conservatism* (New York, 2006), 164–81.

93. Robert Coate, press release, 5 January 1966, Democratic Party MSS, Box 4, press releases office and mimeos file.

94. Roger Kent press release, 13 May 1965, Kent MSS, Box 3, press releases file 2.

95. Evans, *The Education of Ronald Reagan*, 170–76.

96. Kent oral interview, 289.

97. Dallek, *The Right Moment*; Sean Wilentz, *The Age of Reagan: A History, 1974–2008* (New York, 2008); Perlstein, *Nixonland*.

Chapter 10. The Legacy of the Democratic Party Renaissance

1. Michael Barone, Grant Ujufusa, Douglas Matthews, *The Almanac of American Politics 1976: The Senators, the Representatives, the Governors—Their Records, States, and Districts* (New York, 1975), 45.

2. See Michael Klarman, *From Jim Crow to Civil Rights: The Supreme Court and the Struggle for Racial Equality* (New York, 2004); Laura Kalman, *Legal Realism at Yale, 1927–1960* (Chapel Hill, 1986); William Leuchtenburg, *The Supreme Court Reborn: The Constitutional Revolution in the Age of Roosevelt* (New York, 1995); Gareth Davies, *See*

Government Grow: Education Politics from Johnson to Reagan (Lawrence, 2007); "American Historical Review Forum: The Debate over the Constitutional Revolution of 1937," *American Historical Review* 110, 4 (October 2005): 1046–115; William J. Novak, "The Myth of the 'Weak' American State," *American Historical Review* 113, 3 (June 2008): 752–72.

3. "Trailblazing Bench: California High Court Often Points the Way for Judges Elsewhere," *Wall Street Journal*, 20 July 1972, 1.

4. Bernard Schwartz, *Some Makers of American Law* (Calcutta, 1985), 115–16.

5. See *Annual Survey of American Law 1966* (New York, 1967), 447. The case, Mulkey v. Reitman, was one of a number of cases contested in the wake of Proposition 14. See *Mulkey v. Reitman*, 64 Cal. 2d. 529, 413 P. 2d. 825, 50 Cal. Rptr. 881 (1966); *Hill v. Miller*, 413 P. 2d. 852, 50 Cal. Rptr. 908 (1966), vacated, 64 Cal. 2d. 757, 415 P. 2d. 33, 51 Cal. Rptr. 689 (1966); *Thomas v. Goulis*, 64 Cal. 2d. 884, 413 P. 2d. 854, 50 Cal. Rptr. 910 (1966).

6. *Reitman v. Mulkey*, 387 US 369, 18 L. Ed. 2d. 830, 87 S. Ct. 1627, *US Supreme Court Reports*, 18 L Ed. 2d, 836.

7. Ibid., 840. *Shelley v. Kraemer* was a landmark federal case in which restrictive covenants had been declared unconstitutional.

8. *Reitman v. Mulkey*, 842, 845.

9. For a discussion of this point focusing on federal education policy, see Davies, *See Government Grow.*

10. See J. Craig Jenkins, *The Politics of Insurgency: The Farm Worker Movement in the 1960s* (New York, 1985); Jacques E. Levy, *Cesar Chavez: Autobiography of La Causa* (New York, 1975); Randy Shaw, *Beyond the Fields: Cesar Chavez, the UFW and the Struggle for Justice in the Twenty-First Century* (Berkeley, 2008).

11. Shaw, *Beyond the Fields*, 3.

12. See Levy, *Cesar Chavez*, 218.

13. Chavez statement to House Committee on Labor, 15 August 1968, Burton MSS, Box 6, farm labor file.

14. "Burton Bill Would Curtail Sale of Non-Union Grapes," *San Mateo Union Gazette*, 3 July 1970.

15. NWRO press release, 27 June 1969, and other materials in Burton MSS, Box 7, national AFDC freeze file.

16. County-by-county analysis of Cranston campaign, Cranston MSS, Box 519, post-election analysis file.

17. See material in Burton MSS, Box 2, 1972 Phil Burton material file.

18. See Shaw, *Beyond the Fields*, chap. 7.

19. Ronald Reagan speech at Town Hall, Los Angeles, 3 March 1971, McCloskey MSS, Box 133, welfare file.

20. "Former Residents Return to Golden State of Welfare," *Sacramento Union*, 10 October 1971.

21. "California's Experience with Welfare Reform," report by David B. Swoap, De-

cember 1974, California Department of Benefit Payments, Deaver and Hannaford MSS, Box 65, California's experience with welfare file.

22. See eight-year record of Reagan administration, Deaver and Hannaford MSS, Box 65, summary of actions and programs of Governor Ronald Reagan's administration file.

23. John Burton oral history, 12–13, 18, 28, 38.

24. "Reagan's Welfare Plan Didn't Work," *San Francisco Chronicle*, 13 April 1976.

25. Felicia Kornbluh, *The Battle for Welfare Rights: Politics and Poverty in Modern America* (Philadelphia, 2007), 32–33, 27–33.

26. Burton oral history, 18.

27. Tom Goff, "Legacy for State: Footprints, But No Permanent Monuments or Scars," *Los Angeles Times*, 29 September 1974, Deaver and Hannaford MSS, Box 56, Reports California 1973 file.

28. Reagan form letter, 16 November 1973, Deaver and Hannford MSS, Box 17, political 1973 file.

29. "Ronald Reagan: Building a National Organization," 4 November 1974; Untitled briefing document, 25 February 1974, Deaver and Hannaford MSS, Box 1, Ronald Reagan general file, budgets and programs 1974–77.

30. See Byron Shafer, *Quiet Revolution: The Struggle for the Democratic Party and the Shaping of Post-Reform Politics* (Washington, 1983); Steven Gillon, *The Democrats' Dilemma: Walter F. Mondale and the Liberal Legacy* (New York, 1992); Bruce Schulman, *The Seventies: The Great Shift in American Culture, Society, and Politics* (Cambridge, Mass., 2002), 35–42. A more sympathetic treatment of the cultural turn in Democratic strategy is Bruce Miroff, *The Liberals' Moment: The McGovern Insurgency and the Identity Crisis of the Democratic* Party (Lawrence, 2007). On Nixon's attempt to build a new majority on the Republican side see Robert Mason, *Richard Nixon and the Quest for a New Majority* (Chapel Hill, 2004).

31. See Shafer, *Quiet Revolution*, 278–84. Shafer notes that volunteer parties with weak organized structures like the Democrats in California were sympathetic to reform and reinvention because there were few powerful vested interests who would be threatened by change: "these parties were frequently *led* by individuals who had been drawn into politics by considerations of citizen duty or by an explicit interest in reform" (284).

32. See Mason, *Richard Nixon and the Quest for a New Majority*, 140–42.

33. Frontlash 1970 press release, "Students Carry on Major Voter Registration Drives," Frontlash MSS, Box 1, folder 1.

34. Carl Gershman, "Youth Power at the Polls," *New Leader*, 19 April 1971, 15.

35. See correspondence in McCloskey MSS, Box 79, Wilson Riles file; voting statistics in Box 134, California briefing folder.

36. Barone, Ujifusa, Matthews, *Almanac of American Politics 1976*, 74.

37. McCloskey to Ralph Alvarado, 15 June 1978, McCloskey MSS, Box 275, gay rights file. McCloskey supported New Age (the New Alliance for Gay Equality), a California pressure group led by LA activist Troy Perry and supported by a host of high profile liberal politicians, few of them Republicans.

38. "Dellums: Cohelan the target," *Berkeley Daily Gazette*, 24 December 1969, Cohelan MSS, Box 6, file 41.

39. "Dellums, Healy Camps Both Predict Victory," *Berkeley Daily Gazette*, nd, Cohelan MSS, Box 6, file 41.

40. See Alan Ware, *The Breakdown of Democratic Party Organization, 1940–1980* (Oxford, 1985), 94–96.

41. *Berkeley Daily Gazette*, 20 January 1970.

42. Examples include "Black Panther Sympathiser Favored for Congress Seat," *Tulsa Tribune*, 16 October 1970, Fred Harris MSS, Carl Albert Center, University of Oklahoma, Box 215, file 26; "A Congressman for Panthers," *Richmond News Leader*, 16 November 1970, Harris MSS, Box 206, file 3.

43. Leaflet, "Ron Dellums Says: First Take Care of Business at Home," Social Protest MSS, reel 72.

44. Leaflets "Ron Dellums Stands on Issues That Unite Us . . . "; "Cambodia: The Price of Expedient Liberalism"; "Jeffery Cohelan and the Price of Timid Liberalism," Social Protest MSS, reel 72.

45. Leaflet, "YES!," February 1970, Social Protest MSS, reel 72.

46. Ware, *The Breakdown of Democratic Party Organization*, 137–40.

47. See Clifford Alexander to Fred Harris, 8 September 1970; Dellums to Harris, 7 August 1970, Harris MSS, Box 176, file 13; Harris to Dellums, 25 August 1970, Harris MSS, Box 206, file 3; newpaper clipping, nd, "Democrats and the Candidate from Oakland," Harris MSS, Box 215, file 26.

48. Memo, Frank Cowan to Harris, 30 July 1970, Harris MSS, Box 215, file 26. See also Richard Lowitt, *Fred Harris: His Journey from Liberalism to Populism* (Lanham, 2002), 141–43.

49. Harris schedule for weekend of 3–5 October 1970; Harris statement against Agnew, 10 October 1970, Harris MSS, Box 215, file 26.

50. See letter from Richard McLaughlin, Democratic candidate in Youngstown, Ohio, to Harris, 22 February 1972, Harris MSS, Box 270, folder 30; "Fred Harris: Presidential Candidate," *Pasadena Star-News*, 12 May 1975, Harris MSS, Box 290, folder 5.

51. Tom Rees press release, 25 November 1968, Carl Albert MSS, Albert Center, University of Oklahoma, Box 46, file 5.

52. Phil Baldwin to George McGovern, 10 August 1971, McGovern MSS, Box 587, California BA-BL 1971 file.

53. See Miroff, *The Liberals' Moment*, 161–62.

54. List of CDC clubs, McGovern MSS, Box 637, California, supporters lists file.

55. Michael Leon Marowitz response to questionnaire, McGovern MSS, Box 637, California grassroots questionnaires file.

56. See Burton labor material in Selvin MSS, Box 24, file 6.

57. See AFL-CIO News, "California AFL-CIO Issues '75 Report on Legislature," Selvin MSS, Box 24, file 5.

58. See "AFL-CIO vs. McGovern," *Honolulu Advertiser*, 21 July 1972: "[George] Meany seems intent on showing the Democrats that they need him more than he needs them, even if Richard Nixon is the price to be paid for the lesson."

59. "The McGovern Wave Is No Passing Ripple," *Fortune*, September 1972.

60. "McGovern Moneymen a Lot of Skinny Cats and Some Fat Kittens," *Wall Street Journal*, 1 September 1972.

61. Frontlash press release, "Major Coalition Leaders Address Youth Gathering," nd, Frontlash MSS, Box 1, file 2.

62. Mike Grimes to George Johns, 21 September 1971, Frontlash MSS, Box 1, file 2.

63. Frontlash Organizing News, July 1972, Frontlash MSS, Box 1, file 3.

64. Organizing notes for California drives, 15 April 1971, Frontlash MSS, Box 1, file 13.

65. *Life* poll quoted in Carl Gershman, "Youth Power at the Polls," *New Leader*, 19 April 1971.

66. Nixon received 4,544,134 votes to McGovern's 3,431,824 in California. Yet only in Massachusetts and D.C., where McGovern won, and in Minnesota, Oregon, Rhode Island, South Dakota, and Wisconsin was McGovern's share of the vote higher than in California. See *Congressional Quarterly Weekly Report*, 11 November 1972, 2950, 2956.

67. "Where the City's Power Is," *San Francisco Examiner*, 22 January 1977.

68. See John D'Emilio, "Gay Politics, Gay Community: San Francisco's Experience," *Socialist Review* 55 (1981): 77–104; John Jacobs, *A Rage for Justice: The Passion and Politics of Phillip Burton* (Berkeley, 1995); Richard Edward DeLeon, *Left Coast City: Progressive Politics in San Francisco, 1975–1991* (Lawrence, 1992); Randy Shilts, *The Mayor of Castro Street: The Life and Times of Harvey Milk* (New York, 1982). Of three papers at a roundtable "Rethinking the Queer 1970s" at the AHA meeting in San Diego in January 2010, two were focused on San Francisco political activism; see AHA annual meeting program, 95.

69. Randy Shilts, for instance, argued that many gay activists in Democratic clubs in the 1970s, direct descendents of SIR and CRH, were unwilling to campaign hard for openly gay men and women to run for elected office "as long as there was an adequate supply of liberal friends willing to attend their cocktail parties, make annual appearances at Toklas [Club] dinners and assure members that there were heterosexuals who thought gays were just fine after all." See Shilts, *The Mayor of Castro Street*, 150.

70. "The Burton Machine Myth," *San Francisco Examiner*, 13 March 1982; see also George Moscone to Burton, 13 June 1972, Burton MSS, Box 2, 1972 Phil Burton material file: "I wonder when anyone will realize that Burton 'machinery' is just hard work and service to the constituency."

71. "Candidates Seek Homosexuals' Vote," *Vector*, October 1968, 11. See Brown's account of his courting of the gay vote in 1968 in Willie Brown, *Basic Brown: My Life and Our Times* (New York, 2008), 100–102.

72. Burton to Weinberger, 26 September 1973, Burton MSS, Box 9, Gay/lesbian community pre-1980 file.

73. See *Vector*, December 1971, 5.

74. Martin letter to the California Assembly Committee on Labor Relations, 12 March 1970, Martin/Lyon MSS, Box 55, folder 9.

75. Moscone newsletter "Campaign Comments," Social Protest MSS, reel 72; "Moscone Newsmaker," July 1973, California COPE MSS, Box 22, folder 17; John Burton to John F. Crowley, 12 March 1974 and Willie Brown form letter on behalf of John Burton, 1974, Selvin MSS, Box 24, file 6.

76. "'Unnatural' Sex Bill Passes!" *Vector*, April 1975, 24–25.

77. Brown, *Basic Brown*, 105–7.

78. *Vector*, April 1975, 25.

79. "A Proposal for Restructuring the California Democratic Party," Bill Eger memo to SF Democrats, 11 February 1974; see also Bill Eger memo, nd, 1974, Martin/Lyon MSS, Box 151, file 3.

80. Frank Fitch et al. to Toklas Club membership, 22 December 1978, Martin/Lyon MSS, Box 151, file 4.

81. Dick Pabitch to Toklas members, 19 December 1977, Martin/Lyon MSS, Box 151, file 4; advertisement for Harvey Milk Gay Democratic Club, Social Protest MSS, reel 28.

82. For a fuller statement of this argument see Jonathan Bell, "'To Strive for Economic and Social Justice': Welfare, Sexuality, and Liberal Politics in San Francisco in the 1960s," *Journal of Policy History* 22, 2 (2010): 193–222.

83. Del Martin, "If That's All There Is," 5 September 1970, Lyon/Martin MSS, Box 35, file 12.

84. Jeffrey Escoffier, *American Homo: Community and Perversity* (Berkeley, University of California Press, 1998), esp. chap. 2.

85. Del Martin, "If That's All There Is," 5 September 1970, Lyon/Martin MSS, Box 35, file 12.

86. Martin handwritten notes, Martin/Lyon MSS, Box 149, file 7.

87. Committee of Concern for Homosexuals, Berkeley, Carl Wittman, "Refugees from Amerika: A Gay Manifesto," Fall 1970, Social Protest Collection (microfilm), Bancroft Library, Berkeley, reel 28.

88. Gay liberation leaflet, 27 June 1970, Social Protest MSS, reel 28.

89. Jim Kepner, "Angles on the March," *The Advocate*, March 1970, 2.

90. Barbara Stephens to Phyllis Lyon and Del Martin, 1971, Lyon/Martin MSS, Box 21, file 6. See also David Eisenbach, *Gay Power: An American Revolution* (New York, 2006); for a contemporary account of gay liberation, see Donn Teal, *The Gay Militants* (New York, 1971).

91. Stephens to Lyon and Martin, Lyon/Martin MSS, Box 21, file 6.

92. See Shilts, *The Mayor of Castro Street*, 83–84.

93. Martin, handwritten notes, Martin/Lyon MSS, Box 149, file 6.

94. A good analysis of the dilemmas facing civil rights and anticorporate progressives in San Francisco is DeLeon, *Left Coast City*, esp. chap. 2.

95. Brown, *Basic Brown*, 136.

96. See Raphael Sonenshein, *Politics in Black and White: Race and Power in Los Angeles* (Princeton, 1993), table 7.5, 109.

97. "ONE Sparks an Election," nd, Social Protest MSS, reel 27; see also *California Scene*, January 1970, 2.

98. Sonenshein, *Politics in Black and White*, chap. 4.

99. Barone, Ujifusa, Matthews, *Almanac of American Politics 1976*, 93–94.

100. Bradley stated that the "coalition effort began as a result of my involvement in CDC. Out of that experience, I gained a group of friends throughout the city." Quoted in Sonenshein, *Politics in Black and White*, 61.

Epilogue: Liberal Politics in California in an "Era of Limits"

1. Walter Cronkite interview with Brown, 31 March 1976, Selvin MSS, Box 24, file 5.

2. "California AFL-CIO Issues '75 Report on Legislature," Selvin MSS, Box 24, file 5.

3. Cronkite interview in ibid. In a televised speech to the nation on 24 October 1978, Carter described the battle against inflation as one that would involve "hard choices" at a "time of national austerity." See Edward D. Berkowitz, *Something Happened: A Political and Cultural Overview of the Seventies* (New York, 2006), 124–25. Other useful studies of this period include Peter Carroll, *It Seemed like Nothing Happened* (New York, 1982); Bruce J. Schulman, *The Seventies: The Great Shift in American Culture, Society, and Politics* (New York, 2001). A new revisionist study that takes left liberalism seriously as a political force in the late 1970s is Timothy Stanley, *Kennedy vs. Carter: The 1980 Battle for the Democratic Party's Soul* (Lawrence, 2010).

4. See "News from Californians for Brown," November–December 1973; "Brown on the Issues: Answers to ADA questionnaire," 11 April 1974, Social Protest MSS, reel 74.

5. "Front-Runner Jerry Brown—Republican Enemy Number One," *California Journal*, February 1974.

6. Michael Barone, Grant Ujifusa, and Douglas Matthews, *Almanac of American Politics 1976* (Washington, 1976), 48. Brown won the Democratic primary. with 38 percent to Alioto 19 percent, Moretti 17 percent, Waldie 8 percent, and the rest for minor candidates. In the general election Brown edged moderate Republican Houston Flournoy by 3,131,648 to 2,952,954.

7. Willie Brown form letter for Moretti, nd, Social Protest MSS, reel 74; "California AFL-CIO Sets Up Labor Committee for Brown," *California AFL-CIO News*, 11 October 1974, Selvin MSS, Box 24, file 5.

8. "AFL-CIO Issues '75 Report on Legislature," Selvin MSS, Box 24, file 5.

9. See Leo McCarthy oral history, California State Archives, 101–2.

10. Leo McCarthy oral history, 134.

11. See Willie Brown, *Basic Brown: My Life and Our Times* (New York, 2008), chap. 15.

12. "Brown Hit on Aid to Needy," *San Francisco Chronicle*, 11 June 1976.

13. "Liberals' Report Card: Brown, C-minus," *San Francisco Examiner*, 5 December 1977.

14. "Brown Claims Bureaucracy Is Becoming 'A New Class,'" *San Jose Mercury*, 12 August 1978.

15. Iwan Morgan, "Unconventional Politics: The Campaign for a Balanced-Budget Amendment Constitutional Convention in the 1970s," *Journal of American Studies* 32, 3 (1998): 421–45, 430.

16. Derek Shearer, "Can He Take Credit After Contributing to Crisis?" *Los Angeles Times*, 27 June 1978.

17. Figures quoted in *Time*, 19 June 1978, 15.

18. "Passed Reluctantly by Angry Senate," *San Jose Mercury*, 3 March 1978.

19. "Sound and Fury over Taxes: Howard Jarvis and the Voters Send a Message: 'We're Mad as Hell,'" *Time*, 19 June 1978, 14, 13.

20. See "Proposition 13 Fallout: Congress Weighs the Message," *Congressional Quarterly*, 8 July 1978, 1725.

21. "The Right in Congress: Seeking a Strategy," *Congressional Quarterly*, 5 August 1978, 2022–28. For an in-depth study of the political shift toward tax cuts at the expense of a commitment to budgetary prudence, see Iwan Morgan, *The Age of Deficits: Presidents and Unbalanced Budgets from Jimmy Carter to George W. Bush* (Lawrence, 2009).

22. *Congressional Quarterly*, 8 July 1978, 1725.

23. Quoted in Madeleine Adamson and Seth Borgos, *This Mighty Dream: Social Protest Movements in the United States* (Boston, 1985), 119.

24. Leo McCarthy oral history, 105–6.

25. Harry Britt, "My Loss, the Movement's Gain," *Bay Area Reporter*, 29 April 1982. Accounts of Proposition 6 do not always give much of an account of Proposition 13, even though they were bedfellows in liberal demonology at the time. Randy Shilts does not mention it; see Shilts, *The Mayor of Castro Street: The Life and Times of Harvey Milk* (New York, 1982).

26. "McCarthy Comes Out for Gay Rights," *Gay Vote: News from the Harvey Milk Democratic Club*, January 1979, Burton MSS, Box 9, gay/lesbian community pre–1980 file.

27. *Gay Vote*, June 1982, page 2, Burton MSS, Box 4, 1981–82 PB campaign (gay/lesbian) file. Barbara Boxer had won the hard-fought Democratic primary in the Sixth Congressional District, comprising part of San Francisco and Marin County, after John Burton announced his retirement from Congress.

28. HRCF press release, 12 November 1982, Burton MSS, Box 4, 1981–82 PB campaign (gay/lesbian) file.

29. See Stanley, *Kennedy vs. Carter*, 105–7.

30. See HRCF list of election results, 2 November 1982, Burton MSS, ibid.

31. Burton press release, 10 October 1982, Burton MSS, ibid.

32. Evan Halper, "State's Middle Class Getting Less for Its Tax Dollars," *Los Angeles Times*, 1 March 2009.

33. A number of national-level studies date the decline in Democratic Party fortunes to the rise of interest group pluralism in the party in the 1970s. See Kenneth S. Baer, *Reinventing Democrats: The Politics of Liberalism from Reagan to Clinton* (Lawrence,

2000); Ronald Radosh, *Divided They Fell: The Demise of the Democratic Party, 1964–1996* (New York, 1996); Steven Gillon, *The Democrats' Dilemma: Walter F. Mondale and the Liberal Legacy* (New York, 1992).

34. See Scott Kurashige, *The Shifting Grounds of Race: Black and Japanese Americans in the Making of Multiethnic Los Angeles* (Princeton, 2008); Robert O. Self, *American Babylon: Race and the Struggle for Postwar Oakland* (Princeton, 2003); Raphael Sonenshein, *Politics in Black and White: Race and Power in Los Angeles* (Princeton, 1993).

INDEX

ACKNOWLEDGMENTS

I have benefited from the professional and personal help of a wealth of individuals and organizations in completing this book. I am forever indebted to the assistance and guidance of archivists in repositories across the United States (and not just in California, where I had imagined I would be spending all my time when I started the project). In particular, I would like to thank David Kessler and the team at the Bancroft Library at the University of California at Berkeley; the staff at the California State Archives, Sacramento; Carolyn Hanneman and Erin Sloan at the Carl Albert Center, University of Oklahoma; Bob Clark at the FDR Library; Rebekah Kim at the GLBT Historical Society in San Francisco; Catherine Powell at the Labor Archives and Research Center at San Francisco State University; the staff at the Southern California Library for Social Studies and Research in Los Angeles, at the Seeley G. Mudd Library at Princeton University, and at the Hoover Institution at Stanford University; and the archivists at the archives of the London School of Economics and Cambridge University Library.

My research would not have been possible without the financial assistance of research councils, research institutions, and organizations on both sides of the Atlantic. The Arts and Humanities Research Council awarded me a grant to allow me to concentrate fully on writing the manuscript. I received financial assistance for conducting research and attending conferences from the British Academy. I was also awarded research grants from the Carl Albert Center and from the FDR Library. I also benefited from generous support from my own institution, the University of Reading, including travel expenses from my department and buy-out from teaching provided by the Faculty of Arts and Humanities. I am grateful to them all for keeping me solvent over the years it has taken me to complete this project.

Although the ideas and arguments in this book are my own, they would have been considerably less developed and rather less convincingly expressed without the aid of scholars and friends who went way beyond the call of duty in responding to my frequent cries for help. John Thompson, already no stranger to my convoluted prose and half-developed thought patterns, read the entire manuscript and helped me sharpen my ideas, a task he undertook with good humor and characteristic rigor. Doug Rossinow, appointed initially as an anonymous reviewer for the press, revealed his identity and generously shared ideas and read reworked chapters for me; his keen eye for the big picture and infectious enthusiasm kept me motivated in the later stages of bringing the project to completion. Nelson Lichtenstein, Robert Mason, and Iwan Morgan read individual chapters and helped me make them better. Nelson also invited me to speak at his Labor History seminar at UCSB in 2007, an experience I found both useful and invigorating. Gareth Davies encouraged me to think about the legal aspects of political change, and gave me research material he had dug up that proved very useful. I am grateful to colleagues who invited me to speak at seminars or to join conference panels where I could talk about my work, or who showed interest in my ideas in chats and discussions over recent years, including Josh Zeitz, Tony Badger, Liz Cohen, Don Critchlow, Robert Mason, Iwan Morgan, Ellie Shermer, Richard Lowitt, Axel Schäfer, Matt Worley, Bruce Schulman, Tim Stanley, Tom Packer, Bill Rorabaugh, Eileen Boris, Lindy Graham, Alice O'Connor, Richard Bosworth, Ethan Blue, Michael Ondaatje, and Martin Meeker.

Bob Lockhart at the University of Pennsylvania Press showed interest in my work from an early stage, and his commitment to adding my project to such a distinguished series is something for which I am very grateful. I also thank the series editors, Glenda Gilmore, Michael Kazin, and Tom Sugrue, for their enthusiasm for my work, and all the staff at the press who have worked to turn a rough manuscript into a finished product.

I could not have completed the book without the hospitality and friendship of so many who put up with my constant demands for a bed for the night, a drinking partner, someone to talk political history with, or general emotional sustenance while I worked. Friends in the United States who provided help, accommodation, and a vital link to the outside world when I was away from home include Andrew Keating, David Weinreich, Doug Ostertag, Anne Routon, Andrew Carter, David Murphy, Nathan Weintraub, John Maull, Monika Collins, Chris VanderStouwe, Brock Thompson, and Aaron Baker. I have benefited from a supportive group of colleagues at the University of Reading, as well as by wonderful friends in the academic community in the UK, especially Emily West, Adam Smith, Kendrick Oliver, Dan Scroop, Bruce Baker, Matt Worley. Andrew Nash has been a loving companion as well as a flawless proofreader and agony aunt throughout the making of this book, for which I will always be grateful.

Finally, Julia Young and Ray Swartz gave me a roof over my head in their home in San Francisco for weeks on end, showing me more love and friendship than I had a right to expect, and the book literally could not have been possible without their hospitality: for that reason, I dedicate the book to them.